The Lively Experiment

The Lively Experiment

Religious Toleration in America from Roger Williams to the Present

Chris Beneke and Christopher S. Grenda

Foreword by Jon Butler

ROWMAN & LITTLEFIELD
Lanham • Boulder • New York • London

Published by Rowman & Littlefield
A wholly owned subsidiary of The Rowman & Littlefield Publishing Group, Inc.
4501 Forbes Boulevard, Suite 200, Lanham, Maryland 20706
www.rowman.com

Unit A, Whitacre Mews, 26-34 Stannary Street, London SE11 4AB

British Library Cataloguing in Publication Information Available

Library of Congress Cataloging-in-Publication Data

The lively experiment : religious toleration in America from Roger Williams to the present / edited by Chris Beneke and Christopher S. Grenda.
pages cm
Includes index.
ISBN 978-1-4422-4872-4 (cloth : alk. paper) — ISBN 978-1-4422-4873-1 (electronic)
1. United States—Religion—History. 2. Religious tolerance—United States—History. 3. Religions—Relations. I. Beneke, Chris (Christopher J.), editor.
BL2525.L585 2015
201'.50973—dc23
2014045492

∞™ The paper used in this publication meets the minimum requirements of American National Standard for Information Sciences Permanence of Paper for Printed Library Materials, ANSI/NISO Z39.48-1992.

Printed in the United States of America

Contents

Foreword

Religious toleration. Such a simple thought. Then again, maybe not. Judging by the hackles, protests, harassment, persecution, and killings that religion has produced in the United States for more than three hundred years, any notion about the simplicity of religious toleration, whether in the seventeenth century or the twenty-first, is a figment of our imaginations.

Yet emphasizing doubts about the obvious good of religious toleration seems particularly ironic for the United States. After all, religious toleration is the bedrock sentiment that supports the First Amendment to the U.S. Federal Constitution, whose first sixteen words brought forth notions more radical than mere toleration: "Congress shall make no law respecting an establishment of religion, or prohibiting the free exercise thereof." If toleration means at least putting up with many or all religions, the First Amendment, ratified in 1791, went further: It denied Congress the power to create a government establishment of "religion," which men and women of the time well understood to mean a phenomenon far larger than merely "church" or "denomination." It also upheld the "free exercise" of any kind of religion, without even one qualification, such as limiting free exercise to Christianity, or maybe even just Protestantism or Catholicism.

But why did religious toleration bring forth such heated argument in the past, and why are these arguments still with us? The questions are far harder to answer than we might imagine, in good part because they stumble on persistent and powerful myths about both religion and toleration in the present as well as in the past.

One of the most debilitating myths about religion and toleration in modern times, especially in Europe and America, is that religion no longer counts. Sociologists, historians, and political scientists call this the "secularization thesis." Convictions about advancing secularity emerged in the late nineteenth century and derived principally from two sources. One was the turn of major intellectual figures away from religion. Max Weber famously described the modern world as "disenchanted." He meant that modern society could no longer support beliefs in miracles, saints, visions, and other religious phenomena as it became more bureaucratized, corporate, institutional, and anonymous. Sigmund Freud regarded religion as an artifact of the past that would and should be replaced by modern sciences, whose investigations of human biology and psychology could reach far deeper understandings of humanity than religion had ever offered.

The decreasing hold of traditional organized religion on would-be believers, especially in cities, added to the perception of growing secularization in modern society. Twentieth-century Europe was especially well known for its general indifference to religious services and rites; attendance and participation declined sharply during that century. Americans did not abandon organized religion as precipitously as did Europeans, but, to the orthodox, the culture now seemed worryingly impervious to religious principles and intuitions. Late nineteenth- and early twentieth-century U.S. religious leaders complained without end about indifference to religion in America's cities. Hollywood movies, Broadway plays, reading habits, radio, and television reinforced the glamor of sex, money, and power, not faith.

Yet modern secularization has hardly been complete and did not dampen religious hatred, prejudice, and violence. Few cultures were more notorious for their secularity than Berlin of the 1920s, epitomized in Kurt Weill's *Threepenny Opera*. Yet the Nazi Holocaust of the 1930s and 1940s not only exterminated six million Jews in the next two decades but also did so on religious and racial grounds actively and passively supported by many of Germany's Christian churches and clergy. American anti-Semitism did not prohibit Jewish worship, but into the 1950s it circumscribed Jewish participation in American private and public life, restricting Jews from hotels and enrollment at private colleges and obstructing the sale of property to Jews, all buttressed by widespread employment discrimination. And not until 1960 could the United States elect a Catholic president (and then only by a narrow margin). Our own times are aflame with faith, from Iowa evangelicals' sullen rejection of Mitt Romney in the state's 2008 presidential primary to the violent clashes between Jews and Arabs in Gaza; a host of wars and civil wars in Afghanistan, Iraq, and Libya; the several Egyptian revolutions; and rising anti-Semitism and anti-Islam sentiment in seemingly secular Europe.

Myths about the past abound as well. Perhaps the most common is a fairly widespread view that toleration emerged with the eighteenth-century Enlightenment as a commonsense reaction to previous centuries of religious violence. But religious toleration trode a bumpy path, no less in the eighteenth century than before or since. That is the point of many of *The Lively Experiment*'s contributions. Indeed, the route to religious toleration has been more than merely bumpy. When push comes to proverbial shove, many Americans, like others in so many nations, not only have found specific expectations of toleration difficult but also have found them seriously objectionable, perhaps even to the point of questioning the principle itself.

But why is religious toleration so problematic? Part of the problem rests with toleration itself. Humans in every known culture have long found it difficult to abide threatening, alien ideas and behavior. We quarrel over money, power, politics, love, and land. We kill to have our way, individually and collectively. Toleration shows weakness. But more than weakness, it sanctions defeat. Someone else gets what we want. It means surrender to the illegitimate as the false triumphs over right and truth is dishonored (or "disrespected," to use our twenty-first-century vocabulary).

The result is a sentiment Mark Twain satirized in a vignette never published in his lifetime but probably written during the 1898 Spanish-American War: "The War Prayer." Twain observed that while worshipers sanctimoniously prayed for the protection of their own soldiers in wartime, they really desired their enemies' excruciating annihilation. If it weren't simply improper and embarrassing, they really would pray, "O Lord our God, help us tear their soldiers to bloody shreds with our shells; help us to cover their smiling fields with the pale forms of their patriot dead; help us to drown the thunder of the guns with the shrieks of their wounded, writhing in pain." Toleration? Not in this setting.

If toleration in many forms can be difficult and even impossible, religious toleration may stand at the apex of that difficulty. One reason centers on the sheer centrality that cultures, societies, nations, and individuals have long attached to religion and still do in modern times. Religion might be important simply as inherited or adopted faith and the truth that such faith represents. But whether voiced or assumed, in modern times and past centuries, religion is often taken even by secularists to represent what the twentieth-century Protestant theologian Paul Tillich termed the "ground of being itself." Tillich had complex, sophisticated theological notions in mind when he used that phrase. But his phrase can also rightly be taken simply: for believers, religion has been and is the groundwork of everything, of one's very existence. Religion conveys the heart of a person and the whole of a society, culture, or nation. Religion is therefore not trifling, and tolerating "other" religions, false by definition, might be not only difficult but also anathema. Thus, religious toleration is far more consequential than tolerating many political opinions and activities or allowing freedom of expression in literature and art.

Of course, narrower reasons have made religious toleration difficult and still do. Many rest on the broad conviction that since "other" religions are false, allowing their expression constitutes blasphemy, an insult to the sacred and a sacrilege of the holy. Such views can be as potent when they are held implicitly or unthinkingly as they are when articulated explicitly. Yet, no matter how they appear, their consequences can be disastrous. They fueled religious disputes in the pre-Christian Roman Empire, Christian attacks on "pagans," the Crusades, Protestant-Catholic hatred, Massachusetts Puritan execution of Quakers, whippings of Virginia Baptist ministers on the eve of the American Revolution, the 1834 burning of Boston's Catholic Ursuline convent, and the assassination of the Mormon prophet Joseph Smith in 1844, among so many other incidents. Rejecting the employment of Catholics, Jews, Mormons, Muslims, Hindus, Scientologists, Buddhists, and followers of Santería, or making snarky asides about such individuals' character or citing zoning regulations to prohibit buildings to be used for worship by disliked groups, all represent underlying rejections of both the legitimacy of these religions as well as the principle of tolerating all or any of them.

The Lively Experiment offers fascinating contributions on the surprising paths religious toleration in America actually has followed. They fascinate because they reveal how the seemingly simple, straightforward notion of religious toleration has never been simple, with the obvious implication that this is as likely to be true in the future as it has been in the past. Take the notion of the origins of religious toleration in America. We learn here that Rhode Island was not unique; yet it was critically important. We learn how different religious traditions played sometimes surprising roles in the origins of a broad religious toleration in America. We learn that religious toleration wasn't just set down in one nearly magical moment, such as the passage of the First Amendment, but that it has had a long, tough road through American history, right up to the present.

This volume's authors tell us how complicated religious toleration is in practice and how such a grand notion gets messy when applied. Should, for example, religious toleration trump all other values in American constitutional practice, politics, and culture? Are there limits to religious toleration, just as there are—or, as some jurists argue, there should be—to "free speech"? If so, is the dividing line just where we decide it should be in each instance, or should we develop widely approved principles to tell us where that line should be? What happens when religious commitment or behavior seems a threat to individuals and society alike? When this happens, does the question hinge on the religion or the behavior?

Perhaps one immediate and obvious benefit of *The Lively Experiment* is that its chapters remind us that no one should have been surprised by the most recent controversy about religious toleration expressed in the U.S. Supreme Court's so-called Hobby Lobby decision of 2014. In *Burwell v. Hobby Lobby*, a 5–4 Supreme Court majority exempted for-profit corporations from providing some contraceptives for female employees through the Affordable Care Act on grounds of both the free-exercise provision of the First Amendment and the Religious Freedom Restoration Act, where closely held corporations expressed religious disagreements with the contraceptive requirements. Justices in the minority dissented vigorously, and the decision provoked national, and often angry, discussion about the just limits of religious toleration in the United States.

In *The Lively Experiment*, readers will learn that *any* decision in *Burwell v. Hobby Lobby* should have been expected to raise controversy. *The Lively Experiment* opens out the amazingly different ways in which controversies about the meaning of religious toleration have been with us for centuries and are likely to be never ending, just as it demonstrates how intelligent, learned discussion clarifies the complex meanings of religious toleration and the implications of their practice for individuals and the nation alike.

Jon Butler
Minneapolis, Minnesota

Acknowledgments

The editors are deeply grateful to the Rhode Island Council for the Humanities, the George Washington Institute for Religious Freedom, and, above all, the Newport Historical Society and its executive director, Ruth Taylor, for their generous support of this volume and the Spectacle of Toleration conference that inspired it. They also wish to thank the members of the conference steering committee—Daniel Cowdin (Salve Regina University), Linford D. Fisher (Brown University), C. Morgan Grefe (Rhode Island Historical Society), James M. Ludes (Pell Center, Salve Regina University), Timothy B. Neary (Salve Regina University), Margot Nishimura (John Carter Brown Library, Brown University), and Ken Yellis (Spectacle of Toleration Project Coordinator)—for their work in bringing scholars from around the world to Newport, Rhode Island, to discuss religious toleration and mark the 350th anniversary of Rhode Island's 1663 charter.

Introduction

Chris Beneke and Christopher S. Grenda

For generations, Americans have told inspiring stories about their history of toleration and religious diversity, reassuring themselves with the conviction that this was a country where dissenters might find refuge from persecutors. These were often misleading tales, stocked with pleasant illusions and suspiciously right-thinking characters, disclosing more about the historians and their audiences than they did about the past they purported to depict. [1]

Yet some of those older accounts contained fragments of a larger truth. Parts of early colonial North America actually did provide sanctuary for religious minorities who had been oppressed in their former lands. Among them was the small, seaboard colony of Rhode Island. In fact, the first more or less true story about American religious toleration may have been told in 1663 when Rhode Island's leading citizens petitioned the king for a charter. The document alleged that the monarchy had approved their emigration to North America. Finding that the Puritans of Massachusetts Bay could not abide disagreement, the intrepid nonconformists made a perilous southward journey into Narragansett country. There they established a prosperous and increasingly populous community called Rhode Island and Providence Plantations. The charter also noted that the petitioners were undertaking a wholly new kind of enterprise and declared that they intended to "hold forth a lively experiment," testing the proposition that a people could remain good civil subjects while permitting "a full liberty in religious concernments."

To be sure, this sympathetic telling of Rhode Island's origins was embellished. Yet it didn't stray all that far from the evidence. Rhode Island was an asylum for nonconformists, persecuted religious minorities, and colonial malcontents of all sorts. By the middle of the seventeenth century, critics deemed it a religious cesspool where the refuse of every denominational tradition collected—such as the Rhode Island minister and statesman Roger

Williams. To Williams and his fellow citizens, of course, Rhode Island was something else: an ark for dissenters, offering safe passage through a vast and devouring ocean of religious persecution.

In many ways, the story told in the 1663 charter was Williams's. Though we don't know what he looked like, or much about his personal affairs, it's possible to trace the general contours of his life. Following an education overseen by England's powerful and disputatious jurist, Sir Edward Coke, Williams gravitated toward the more radical elements within contemporary Protestantism, joining the great Puritan migration to New England in 1630. Still pushing the theological envelope, he proceeded to exasperate Massachusetts Bay authorities for several years (by condemning their remaining ties to the Church of England, their mingling of church and state power, and their unjust claim to Native American lands) before they finally determined to lock this headstrong dissident away. Tipped off, Williams fled his home in Salem amid the driving snow and bitter cold of a New England blizzard. After a brief sojourn with the Wampanoag Indians, he established a settlement in Narragansett country that he and a group of fellow travelers named Providence. More dissenters, including the perpetually maligned Quakers and Anne Hutchison's exiled "antinomians," followed close behind. Over the ensuing decades, Williams would serve as a colonial agent to England and president of Providence Plantations, among other weighty responsibilities.

In certain respects, Williams was an unlikely candidate to lead anything, let alone a colony. Though charismatic and beloved by a host of friends, he was unfailingly dogmatic and argumentative. Yet lead he did. "Never," Edmund Morgan once wrote, "was a man of action more an intellectual."[2] And seldom has a more compassionate and charming person been more quarrelsome. But if Williams found most everyone else deficient in their faith, he rarely faltered in defending their freedom to exercise their creeds, including those he presumed fated for damnation (a rather large fraction of the population).

For Williams, liberty of conscience depended on church and state carrying out distinct responsibilities. He thought churches should maintain order in spiritual matters while the state did so in worldly affairs. The idea, now referred to generically as "separation of church and state," represented a radical new justification for religious liberty. Williams made his most rigorous case for the principle in four hundred scripturally soaked pages that he titled *The Bloudy Tenent of Persecution for Cause of Conscience*. That dense tome appeared in 1644 while Williams was in London securing Rhode Island's first charter. Chapter 1 opens symptomatically: "Because *Christ* commandeth that the *Tares* and *Wheat* (which some understand are those that walke in the *Truth*, and those that walke in *Lies*) should be *let alone* in the *World*, and not *plucked* up untill the *Harvest*, which is the end of the *World*, *Matth*. 13. 30. 38. &c."[3] The sum of this passage—and much of the book—

was that earthly authorities were incapable of distinguishing the truly converted and saved (the wheat) from the deluded and damned (the tares, or
weeds). Until God sorted saints and sinners at the end of time, human laws
should not interfere with the pursuit of eternal truths. Individuals should be
free to pray, worship, argue, and proselytize as they see fit.

Williams's argument was as inclusive as any theory of toleration before
it. To appreciate how radical it was, consider that the leading English advocates for religious toleration at the time were willing to extend some rights of
belief and worship to Protestants who maintained slightly different conceptions of church polity or the terms of salvation, certainly not the multitudes of
those called "pagans" and "infidels." By contrast, Williams would have admitted Protestants of all varieties as well as Jews, Muslims, Catholics, and
Native Americans to the proverbial ship of state.[4] Williams didn't want them
in his church, of course, but he was willing to have them as fellow members
of his civil society, even in charge of its political institutions.[5]

In his own day, Williams was renowned, celebrated, and vilified, as are
all innovators in church and state. This is well established. Less clear is
Williams's subsequent influence. Great reformers often veer toward the enigmatic, and thenceforth to irrelevance. And Williams was as enigmatic as they
come. Yet his principles didn't remain pious abstractions. They were woven
into Rhode Island's institutions and practices. From the beginning, religious
minorities from less accommodating regions came to the shores of Narragansett Bay and stayed. The popular nineteenth-century historian George Bancroft remarked of Williams's Rhode Island that it contained "the strangest
and most incongruous elements; anabaptists and antinomians; fanatics, as its
enemies asserted, and infidels; so that if a man had lost his religious opinions, he might have been sure to find them again in some village of Rhode-
Island."[6] In the latter decades of the seventeenth and early decades of the
eighteenth century, Rhode Island was home to a fractious democratic community of ill-used Quakers, Diaspora Jews, and a bevy of other beleaguered
groups, mostly Protestant and frequently unconventional. There were few
places like it.

By the time the 1663 charter was drafted, Williams and his Rhode Island
neighbors had already been embarked on this remarkable voyage for more
than two decades. The charter conferred royal sanction on the enterprise,
ensuring its long-term viability. Though it accords with some critical modern
presumptions about society and politics, that document also confronts today's reader with the utter strangeness of seventeenth-century thinking. The
text is bejeweled with the intricate qualifications that make contemporary
sentiments so mysterious and so unsatisfactory to twenty-first-century eyes.
It presumes neither a multicultural nor a secular perspective. Those expecting
to encounter a straightforward endorsement of equality will be disheartened
by the charter's condescending injunctions to convert "poor ignorant Indian

natives." Meanwhile, the secular-minded will take little inspiration from the suggestion that the charter was to abet those with "sober, serious, and religious intentions" so they could strengthen themselves "in the holy Christian faith and worship."

Thus, despite its resonance with modern views on rights of conscience, the charter was emphatically a creature of its time. So was Williams. The great dissident's writing was occasionally resurrected in later decades—but only occasionally. Among those who summoned Williams's thinking on church-state relations was the influential Connecticut minister Isaac Backus, a Revolutionary-era advocate of church-state separation. Like Williams, he was a convert to the Baptist faith and to the un-compromisable sanctity of conscience. Reflecting on Williams's achievements in 1778, Backus reckoned that Williams had "founded the first civil government, that ever established equal religious liberty, since the rise of Antichrist [the Roman Catholic church]."[7] This invocation of Williams was the exception. Most of the major Revolutionary heralds of religious liberty, including James Madison and Thomas Jefferson, were unriveted by Rhode Island's founder and his achievements. As Denise Spellberg notes in chapter 5, Jefferson possessed "the largest private library in the United States" and "never owned a single volume by Roger Williams."[8] Yet neither the American Revolution nor figures like Madison and Jefferson have been the sole touchstones for freedom of conscience in American history. And by pointing to Williams, Backus gestured to this other, equally fecund tradition.

Because of Williams and the charter he helped secure, Rhode Island served as prologue to salient features of the modern world, not least its rowdy pluralism and raucous outpourings of opinion. The resulting conflicts between differently believing groups on the one hand and between civil authorities and determined religious minorities on the other proved as durable as the ideas that inspired them. A corollary of Williams's defense of conscience was the conviction that individuals should enjoy the freedom to exercise their faith, including the right to evangelize, criticize, and condemn vigorously. Williams also recognized that the imperatives of conscience and the obligations imposed by civil law might sometimes clash, and that misguided souls would always contend that they could not properly exercise their faith *and* obey the law, be true to their consciences *and* rise to the colony's defense. To Williams, these presumptions reflected an imperfect understanding of liberty. Being forced to support someone else's church or submitting to a religious test for office constituted an unjust burden on conscience; paying to support the civil functions of the commonweal or bearing arms when the colony was under attack did not.

To illustrate the challenges confronting states guaranteeing religious exercise, Williams proposed—in a famous 1655 letter to the town of Providence—that his fellow citizens imagine a ship at sea with Williams as commander. Even in such hazardous circumstances, Williams thought he would have no business shackling the consciences of Protestants, Catholics, Jews, or Muslims. None would be "forced to come to the ship's prayers of worship, nor compelled from their own particular prayers or worship." And yet it was the commander's duty to ensure that "justice, peace, and sobriety" were maintained. All must contribute to the ship's costs, as well as its defense; all must "obey the common laws" that contributed to "their common peace or preservation."[9] Though perhaps more inclined to indulge irascible critics and rude dissenters than are modern advocates of religious tolerance, Williams was loath to entertain the exemptions from generally applicable laws that Congress and higher courts have permitted in recent decades.

On this occasion and others, Williams was acutely concerned with the proper bounds of religious exercise, the civil implications of religiously inspired actions and words. When Thomas Jefferson advanced a frequently cited interpretation of the First Amendment in an 1802 letter to the Danbury Baptists, he inadvertently recalled Williams's conviction that church and state were best confined to distinct realms of life. Jefferson wrote that religion was a private affair and that the amendment's religious clauses had erected "a wall of separation between Church & State." He also claimed that civil governments had jurisdiction over actions, just not opinions (on another occasion he wrote that his neighbors' opinions were entirely immaterial; they neither picked his pocket nor broke his leg). These were fairly radical statements for the time. They were also well suited to an American *philosophe* whose mature beliefs settled into a mild, contemplative deism and remained there. But for revivalists and evangelicals, the socially aberrant and religiously obstreperous, and those whose religion depended on brash, public witnessing of their opinions, something more was needed. And for them, Williams's faith-friendly vision has represented the more compelling and more useful one.[10]

Despite their differences, Williams and Jefferson both favored robust legal protections for conscience. Both were also willing to accommodate a broad spectrum of believers and nonbelievers. In this sense, "toleration" is too restrictive a term for the liberal system of church-state relations they advocated. Williams and Jefferson embraced an approach more precisely designated "religious liberty," which goes beyond the mere exemption of dissenting beliefs from a state establishment of religion (the system that prevailed in Europe and much of colonial America) to religious equality before the law. But toleration is probably the best term—at least the most comprehensive and identifiable term—for the larger constellation of social attitudes (religious tolerance), institutional arrangements (church disestablishment), and legal guarantees (constitutionally protected rights) that have created varying degrees of space for religious belief and its exercise throughout colonial and U.S. history.

The chapters in this volume all deal in some form or another with the complications and contradictions surrounding toleration in this broader sense. Their story is not one of straightforward progress from oppressive colonial beginnings to a liberated present. Among the more interesting elements of the story are the paradoxes of inclusion and exclusion that Williams himself embodied. Many of the contributions demonstrate how Americans managed to build walls between themselves and differently believing others, even as they set aside old divisions and prejudices. There are stories here about interdenominational cooperation and intradenominational conflict, about Catholic parents' struggles to secure their own religious liberty by fighting for control over their children's religious upbringing, and about liberal Protestant efforts to restrict illiberal radio broadcasts.

As much as anything, then, this is a book about the numberless expressions of religion in American history, no small number of which proved abhorrent to those compelled to endure them. The right to proselytize, criticize, and exercise one's faith in public are essential and generally overlooked features of the liberty that Williams advocated. In the twenty-first century as in the seventeenth, what people do with their religious liberty can seem downright appalling to others. Its exercise discomfits, unsettles, vexes, and offends. Disputes over the Muslim call to prayer (often issued via loudspeakers five times a day) or the Jewish eruv (a line stretched around communities that allows Orthodox believers to move about on the Sabbath without violating it) represent the latest examples of religious exercise that exceed the community's capacity to fully assimilate all of its manifestations and the enduring legacy of experimentation that continues to enliven American public life.

WHAT CAME BEFORE, AND WHAT FOLLOWS

Rhode Island's was not the only seventeenth-century experiment that tested the efficacy of a society premised on religious liberty. As Evan Haefeli points out in chapter 1, similar trials were undertaken across the Atlantic World and beyond. The charters of Maryland, Pennsylvania, and the Carolinas all contained provisions for conscience. The English accommodated a number of other contemporary experiments in religious toleration in places as distant from one another as Barbados, Dunkirk, and Algiers. This, Haefeli explains, often had less to do with a principled embrace of religious tolerance than a pragmatic concession to complicated local and imperial dynamics. William Penn's efforts to conduct a "holy experiment" in Pennsylvania, explains Andrew R. Murphy in chapter 2, grew from the same stormy political and social circumstances that inspired Williams's journey. And like Williams, Penn had to revise his approach to church and state as he confronted the practical challenges of governing a democratic citizenry embold-ened both by deep religious conviction and by the relative absence of legal restraints. Williams and Penn understood that they walked a thin line be-tween religious liberty and political chaos, and they adjusted accordingly.

Though few experiments were as religiously inclusive as Rhode Island's or Pennsylvania's, there was an emerging seventeenth-century agreement on the political value of toleration, as well as its intrinsic justice. It may seem odd that the British monarch, the official head of the Church of England (whose direct rule New England's Pilgrims and Puritans had both fled), would approve the charter proposed by religious outcasts who settled in and around Providence. But the politics of toleration have always possessed their share of opaque motives and logical paradoxes. As Scott Sowerby shows in chapter 3, this was particularly true of late seventeenth-century England, where Charles II's reputed Catholic leanings and strong antipathy to the Whig majority made him an improbable ally of Protestant nonconformists (dissenters from the Church of England). These were the theological descen-dants of the revolutionaries who had overthrown the monarchy and beheaded his father in 1649. Strange circumstances indeed.

Of course, Rhode Island did not merely "allow" dissent but offered some-thing more akin to religious liberty. Williams rejected church establishments along with limits on religious speech, publication, or law-abiding worship practices. More than that, he endorsed rough-and-tumble religious disputes and showed little concern for social niceties. In chapter 4, Teresa M. Bejan reminds us how contentious Williams was and how he advocated forms of public life that could accommodate such contentiousness. Considering Williams's verbal thrashing of Quakers—one of the small and unorthodox but legally entitled groups in Rhode Island—Denise Spellberg wonders in chapter 5 how Williams might have treated a Muslim minority under the same circumstances. It's a mostly hypothetical question. Williams surely had acquaintance with Muslims elsewhere, as well as their own church-state arrangements. Yet there were no known Muslims in the colony. Still, the exceptionally uncivil and universal toleration that Williams espoused makes this an interesting question and prompts yet another: Must a tolerant society also be a polite one?

Then, as now, there are serious challenges confronting any society that permits religious truths to compete openly and vociferously. Social tension and hurt feelings are likely consequences in liberal, democratic societies. More dire consequences confronted early modern regimes and slave soci-eties. Predictably, perhaps, some of the harshest constraints on colonial and early national proselytizing were enacted against those who attempted to make converts on slave plantations. As Christopher C. Jones documents in chapter 6, rival clerics, suspicious planters, and local government leaders resisted Methodist evangelizing among Africans on both sides of the postrevolutionary Atlantic. More than just the loss of adherents, they feared social disorder and mass disobedience, probably for good reason. The great eighteenth-century revivals, known as the First Great Awakening, sparked social ruptures even in colonial communities that were predominantly free and evenly propertied. If the evangelical conviction that all people were equal before God took hold in a slave society, there was no telling what might happen.

It has long been understood that evangelicals were among those making the most vigorous case for toleration in the eighteenth and early nineteenth centuries. Along the way, they forged an accidental alliance with elite rationalists (believers who gave priority to the efficacy of reason over the authority of scripture and tradition). Rationalists shared few theological tenets with evangelicals, but like them sought protection for minority religious opinions. Behind this combined effort, the principle of religious toleration gained solid cultural traction. As Keith Pacholl shows in chapter 7, the rising medium of periodicals (the eighteenth-century equivalent of magazines) played a pivotal role in advancing the rationalist case for rights of conscience in colonial and early national America. Contributors to these sophisticated elite publications advanced the proposition that religion—just about any religion, but especially its rationalist varieties—fostered virtue. This inclusive vision of what counted as religion and the generous accounting of the good that it did remained a crucial justification for rights of conscience through the twentieth century, as did the notion that Protestants differ on few genuine matters of substance. In doing so, periodical writers and publishers undermined the clergy's monopoly on the public discussion of religion. Imbuing toleration with a powerful new civic justification, Pacholl argues, they nudged the wider culture toward less sectarian and more ecumenical understandings of true religion.

The American Revolution made Roger Williams a prophet of church-state relations. The U.S. Constitution (1787–1788) outlawed religious tests and the First Amendment (1789–1791) forbade Congress from creating a national establishment or restricting the free exercise of religion. Most states enacted similar provisions. These, together with new laws permitting all religious organizations to incorporate under general and relatively easy conditions, spurred church and synagogue building during the first decades of the nineteenth century. Religious observance and church membership surged.

It's likely that Williams would have gazed approvingly on all this. Yet many elite contemporaries expressed unease about the brusque proselytizing and vigorous religious disputes that he found so congenial and that suffused American culture by the early nineteenth century. Leading Revolutionary-era figures, notably Benjamin Franklin and George Washington, were more inclined to have religious differences addressed amicably and without noticeable departures from social propriety. Prominent early national Roman Catholics, as Nicholas Pellegrino shows in chapter 8, also became advocates of religious civility as they discovered its utility in fending off Protestant attacks on their church's history and theology. In the republic's first decades, their struggle was not just for equal rights with Protestants but also for a sympathetic view of their church's history.

Whether they were civil about it or not, nineteenth-century Americans proceeded to integrate the principle of religious liberty into their institutions, social practices, and understanding of what the nation represented. The federal government actually had little to do with all of this—at least directly. It lacked the powers to materially infringe religious liberty, except in the case of Native Americans, Mormons, and other outsider groups who were forced beyond state boundaries into U.S. territories. Nonetheless, the religious clauses of the First Amendment became a model for state governments and local religious institutions. And so did the republican political ideas that Susanna Linsley (chapter 9) discovers within early national churches, where clergy and laypeople had to adapt to the tidal force of contemporary republicanism. The Revolution solidified an already hardening notion that the norms of republican government (characterized by elected leaders and majority-determined laws) should suffuse all aspects of life, including church life. As Linsley explains, managing differences within republican-oriented church institutions was one of the great challenges confronting early national religious groups. Emboldened and empowered dissent was an acute problem within religious institutions, as well as outside them.

In a sense, all of nineteenth-century America became Rhode Island. The decades preceding the Civil War were an age, in Terryl Givens's words, of "proliferating heterodoxies."[11] Visions abounded and prophecies of the most unusual kind burst forth. Unorthodox religious migrants of every description continued to find a home here. Americans switched faiths with regularity as theological debates, both good-natured and rancorous, swayed believers back and forth on turbulent religious seas. Meanwhile, the climate for nonbelievers remained about as inhospitable as it was in early Rhode Island. Skeptics and atheists were generally not welcome (though a few, such as the irreverent Massachusetts freethinker Abner Kneeland, actually gained some positive notoriety). Long-standing blasphemy laws that forbade the open denigration of Christianity and religious tests that forbade nonbelievers from serving as court witnesses or assuming state office cast a pall over irreverent and skeptical expression.

The nation's professions of religious toleration were sorely tested during the three decades preceding the Civil War as millions of poor Irish and German Roman Catholic migrants arrived on American shores. When a significant proportion of these arrivals began sending their children to public schools and church leaders began demanding shares of state funding for their own Catholic institutions, they challenged Protestant claims that the schools were offering "nonsectarian" religious instruction. Protestants (many curiously unaware of how they violated the very principles they espoused) contended that individual denominations should keep their noses out of state business, and that they intended to neither discriminate against Catholics nor impose Protestantism on them, but merely to offer students access to scripture "without note or comment." As Steven Green argues in chapter 10, the emerging Protestant argument for separation of church and state was not wholly disingenuous, nor was it confined to educational controversies. Protestant advocacy of nonsectarian religious education was in fact a symptom of a broader and generally inadvertent movement toward a more secular law and culture, though few realized it at the time.

Protestant and Catholic tensions simmered into the twentieth century. In many ways, as Jacob Betz discusses in chapter 11, the problems revolved around Protestant control of public institutions and Catholic efforts to sustain a distinctive religious identity amid Protestant cultural dominance. By the 1890s, Catholics made up more than a sixth of the U.S. population and a much higher proportion of urban dwellers.[12] And it was in the large cities where much of the friction occurred, as Protestants and Catholics contended for local resources and state recognition. Betz explores the case of New York's proposed Freedom of Worship Bill, which would have prohibited Protestant evangelizing of incarcerated Catholic children. The resulting debate raised deeper philosophical questions about toleration and the proper handling of religious differences by a rights-protecting, faith-friendly state: Who, for example, has the primary responsibility for a child's religion—the state, the parents, or the child herself? There was no easy resolution here.

Despite residual animosity between their faiths and the resurgence of anti-Catholicism and anti-Semitism in some parts of the country, many Protestants (a diverse lot themselves) and Catholics began inching closer together at the turn of the twentieth century. Liberal Jews, Catholics, and Protestants exchanged affirmations of respect and praised the nation's inclusionary traditions.[13] Dreams of still more expansive forms of interreligious communion accompanied the 1893 World's Parliament of Religions, which brought adherents of dozens of different faiths (including Hindus, Buddhists, and Muslims) to that year's Columbian Exposition in Chicago. However, American ecumenism generally extended no further than the Abrahamic circle of Protestants, Catholics, and Jews.[14]

Those three groups fit into what early twentieth-century Americans began calling the "Judeo-Christian" tradition. By the 1920s, liberal-leaning members of these faiths were stressing their shared theological principles and democratic values. This inclusive outlook rested on the notion that doctrinal differences should be subordinated to a religion's social utility. But as David Mislin shows in chapter 12, ecumenical affirmations among these groups antagonized conservative members within each. And thus interfaith understanding between some Protestants, Catholics, and Jews was matched by mounting internal discord. These evolving lines of division illustrate the sometimes paradoxical nature of religious toleration, through which new forms of inclusion and exclusion are perpetually generated.

The expansion of the U.S. government, especially its military, between World War I and II (c. 1914–1945) made toleration a federal problem and a national concern. That was particularly true when it came to the seemingly trivial matter of engraving dog tags. To maximize the information contained on these metal identifying discs that hung from soldiers' necks, mid-twentieth-century American military authorities used single-letter abbreviations to specify a religious identity: P for Protestant, C for Catholic, and H for Jewish (or Hebrew). Of course, that failed to capture the full spectrum of American religious diversity. As Ronit Stahl explains in chapter 13, the Protestant P came to serve as a catch-all category that encompassed everyone who wasn't Catholic or Jewish (including Buddhists, Eastern Orthodox Christians, and Muslims). The system also lumped evangelical and mainline Protestants with Mormons, Adventists, and Christian Scientists, despite major theological gulfs between them. In 1955, the military finally permitted soldiers to spell out their full religious affiliation, whatever it might be. By that point, two things were clear: (1) the federal government now had the power to materially impact religiously inspired exercise; and (2) its officers would struggle to comprehend, let alone manage, the vibrant heterogeneity of American religious life.

While early twentieth-century America drew millions of migrants, particularly from Roman Catholic and Eastern Orthodox regions, much of America's religious innovation and many of its new forms of religious diversity still arose within the Protestant majority. Among the upstart groups that pressed against the boundaries of acceptable religious practice was the New England Pentecostal group known as the First Fruit Harvesters, whose plight Evelyn Sterne recounts in chapter 14. In certain ways, the Harvesters exemplify the travails of an illiberal minority within a liberalizing culture. Led by a spiritual traveler named Joel Adams Wright, the Harvesters sought to recreate the purity of the early Christian Church by cutting denominational ties, following strict standards of behavior, and pursuing "gifts of the Spirit." They quickly fanned out across New England, speaking in tongues and bringing their good news to potential converts. Like so many other newly budding faiths, the Harvesters made enemies as they made converts. One community unprepared for these holy rollers was Jefferson, New Hampshire, where opponents dynamited the Harvesters' chapel and ran them out of town.

The Jehovah's Witnesses were yet another outgrowth of the innovative, millennium-focused Protestant culture that characterized large swaths of late nineteenth-century America—and yet another example of how fragile the practical and constitutional protections for religious dissent could be. Witnesses elevated one part of the Christian trinity (Jehovah) at the expense of its other parts (Christ and the Holy Ghost), refused to drink alcohol or smoke cigarettes, and lambasted Catholics. Expecting an imminent end to the world, Witnesses evangelized provocatively across twentieth-century American neighborhoods. More ominously for their social and political prospects, they refused to serve in the military, salute the American flag, or recite the Pledge of Allegiance. Unwelcome in peace, these views seemed intolerable in war. During the Second World War, as Shawn Francis Peters demonstrates in chapter 15, mobs attacked Witnesses, and their children were expelled from schools. An unsympathetic Supreme Court initially sanctioned the latter and, by doing so, may have unofficially legitimized the former. Witnesses mounted a spirited legal campaign, and they ultimately succeeded in getting the court to reverse itself, thereby securing their rights to abstain from saluting or pledging allegiance. In the process, Peters argues, they also laid the legal groundwork for the rights revolution that transformed American jurisprudence in the 1950s and 1960s.

The Witnesses paid a steep price for their refusal to accommodate themselves to the norms of American culture and politics. Other twentieth-century religious minorities proved more inclined to assimilate and therefore became less susceptible to religious intolerance. Among them were the Mormons, or Latter-day Saints (LDS). Nineteenth-century Mormons endured harassment and violence resembling that inflicted on Jehovah's Witnesses a century later. But during the middle decades of the twentieth century, as Cristine Hutchison-Jones explains in chapter 16, Mormons came to seem a lot like non-Mormon Americans. The assimilative process began in earnest after the LDS abandoned the practice of "celestial marriage," or polygamy, in 1890. This momentous shift was triggered in part by the 1878 Supreme Court case *Reynolds v. United States*, in which Chief Justice Morrison Waite invoked Thomas Jefferson's "wall of separation" metaphor to argue that although the federal government had no cognizance over beliefs, it could restrict actions issuing from them. Therefore, Waite contended, Mormon polygamy wasn't protected by the Constitution.[15]

Compelled to renounce polygamy, the Mormons made a fast march into the American mainstream, a move heralded by the popular ascension of the Mormon Tabernacle Choir, which became an object of national adoration in the 1950s. By that point, Hollywood had already reconfigured Brigham Young as an all-American hero—and advocate of religious toleration—in the big-budget film *Brigham Young: Frontiersman* (1940). National political power followed in short order. Mormons served at the highest levels of the Eisenhower administration and the Mormon governor of Michigan, George Romney, was a leading contender for the presidency in 1968. It was a remarkable turnaround for one of the nation's long-reviled outsider groups, a church and a people that the governor of Missouri urged his constituents to expel or "exterminate" in 1838 and whose first elected senator, Reed Smoot, was initially blocked from office because of concerns about his faith (1904–1907).

Much of the energy behind political and religious inclusion in the 1950s and 1960s—for civil rights and religious tolerance, among other causes—drew from the ecumenical Protestant churches (Methodists, Episcopalians, Presbyterians, etc.) who defined the American mainstream.[16] Yet these groups exhibited their own forms of intolerance and exclusion. During the 1960s, a coalition of left-leaning religious groups, descendants of the Protestants who had forged Tri-Faith America, used decidedly illiberal methods to combat conservative religious radio. In chapter 17, Paul Matzko discusses how the liberal National Council of Churches (NCC) bullied a number of conservative broadcasters by means of the Federal Communications Commission's newly instituted "Fairness Doctrine." The NCC considered conservative evangelical support for racial segregation, along with their accusations of communist and anti-Christian motives among liberal Protestant churches, beyond the pale of legitimate public expression. By requiring that conservative stations insert countervailing liberal voices into their programming, they made it impossible for many of these evangelicals to continue broadcasting, thereby shutting down a vibrant (albeit reactionary) form of religious and political expression. In these and other ways, the politics of twentieth-century toleration remained as complicated and counterintuitive as they had in the seventeenth.

A stiffer challenge to modern America's conception of itself as a haven for religious dissidents arose with the rapid spread of new groups with charismatic leaders, some of whom breached basic social norms by restricting members' interactions with fellow citizens. Scholars developed an entire sociological category, New Religious Movements (NRMs), to describe the Children of God, the Unification Church, Hare Krishna, and Scientology. The more common designation was "cults." The sudden emergence of such highly committed groups during the 1960s and 1970s, as James Bennett discusses in chapter 18, triggered fears of a "cult crisis." Several grassroots organizations sprang up to counter the perceived threat. The impetus came from parents who were dismayed that their children had neglected family, education, and career to join NRMs. The anticult movement claimed that these groups were not religions and therefore had no claim to religious tolerance or the constitutional protection of free exercise. They drew from social science, law, and politics to make the case that the cults relied on physical and psychological coercion (especially brainwashing) to recruit and retain members, rather than the more conventional forms of evangelization and conversion. Though the modern anticult movement achieved only limited success before fizzling out in the mid-1990s, it shed light on the way

Americans construct the boundaries of acceptable religion and reconcile unconventional exercises of faith with democratic citizenship.

The trouble Americans had in categorizing and containing NRMs was a premonition of the multicultural direction that late twentieth-century religious life would take. Rising immigration from Asia brought millions of Muslims, Hindus, Buddhists, and Sikhs into American cities and towns. This development had the effect of both raising the profile of Asian religions in American culture and stretching the ordinary meaning of "religion" and religious exercise.[17] For example, the Islamic requirement that women wear head and facial coverings in public places, even for official photographs such as driver's licenses and passports, exceeded traditional understandings of what religious observance entailed and thereby the scope of constitutional protections needed to guarantee it.

Some Native Americans pressed at those same boundaries by ingesting the sacramental hallucinogenic known as peyote. The Supreme Court ruled in the 1990 case of *Employment Division v. Smith* that two Native American employees who had been denied unemployment benefits because they had been fired for peyote use did not have their constitutional rights violated. In response, Congress passed an act that addressed one of the very challenges Roger Williams had confronted three centuries before. The Religious Freedom Restoration Act (RFRA) stipulated that purportedly neutral laws "may burden religious exercise as surely as laws intended to interfere with religious exercise" and that "governments should not substantially burden religious exercise without compelling justification."[18] A 1997 Supreme Court ruling precluded application of RFRA to state and local governments, leaving the line between inviolable civil responsibilities and inviolable religious commitments as ill defined and hotly contested as it had been in Williams's day.

The tensions between civil responsibilities and deep religious commitments persist into the twenty-first century. When Goshen College, a small Mennonite institution in Indiana, refused to play the national anthem before sporting events in 2010, it ignited a firestorm in the conservative media. Like the Jehovah's Witnesses, Anabaptists (who include Mennonites and other like-minded groups) regard the invocation of providential favor on American endeavors, especially in war, as idolatrous, a confusion of patriotic purposes with God's. As Kip Wedel explains in chapter 19, Anabaptist estrangement from American civic rituals isn't new. Mennonites and other conscientious objectors were harassed during the colonial wars and during the American Revolution. The massive national mobilization required in World War I, World War II, and the Vietnam War brought still more tribulation upon them. The framers of early American constitutions had wrestled with the question of whether to exempt such dissenters from wartime obligations and came to no definitive conclusion. So the question festered.

Of course, Roger Williams understood that conscience and civic commitments were bound to clash, as they did in the Goshen College case. And as devoted as he was to guaranteeing the former, Williams refused to compromise the latter. In some ways, modern America is more indulgent of conscientious objection than was Williams's Rhode Island. But you would not know that from the reaction that the college's policy triggered. Conservative detractors responded that the nation's "civil religion," as it is sometimes termed, is an indispensable part of American civic identity. Perhaps critics would have appreciated the sentiments expressed in the 1663 Rhode Island Charter "that true piety rightly grounded upon gospel principles . . . will lay in the hearts of men the strongest obligations to true loyalty." In the end, Goshen met civil religionists halfway by substituting the singing of the less bellicose "America the Beautiful" for "The Star-Spangled Banner."

In these and many other ways, the politics of religious toleration remain as thorny as they were in the seventeenth century. The contributors to this volume have commenced the first full experiment in writing its ever-enlarging story. It will assuredly not be the last.

THE LARGER MEANING OF RELIGIOUS TOLERATION

American religious toleration has never been independent of larger forces in American life: the democratizing influence of newspapers and magazines in the eighteenth century, the secularizing effects of industrialization in the nineteenth, and the homogenizing impact of mass communications in the twentieth. Toleration has also been inseparable from broader social configurations, especially the power and privilege attached to race, class, and gender. Native Americans were considered objects of proselytization from the beginning of European settlement, their faiths subjected to continual onslaughts of evangelization, criticism, and misrepresentation. Into the twentieth century, blasphemy prosecutions tended to fall upon those of low social standing, while African American and white female preachers were sometimes harassed because of their race or gender, or both.

One of the many things revealed in the following chapters is how religious rights and civil rights, race privilege, and religious tolerance have been entangled in more ways than historians have previously understood. As Shawn Peters explains, the Supreme Court's decisions regarding the Jehovah's Witnesses helped pave the way for the civil rights movement. At roughly the same time, the indisputable whiteness of most Mormons was easing their transition into the American religious mainstream. As religious tolerance begat more racial tolerance in the case of the Witnesses, racial privilege begat more religious tolerance in the case of the Mormons. And when, as Paul Matzko recounts, evangelical Protestants employed the Fairness Doctrine against pro-segregation evangelicals, it knotted race and religion in yet another way.

The manifest complexities of religious toleration have prompted cynics to suggest that little has changed for religious minorities, that the United States is no better at accommodating differently believing people today than it was 350 years ago. This is surely a misleading way of looking at things. Our standards for measuring religious liberty and religious tolerance are much more rigorous than they were in the seventeenth century. In recent years, we have discovered religious intolerance in places that few bothered to look in the past—in intangible social slights (e.g., failing to serve religiously appropriate foods at public events) and subtle forms of discrimination (e.g., the invocation of "God" in the Pledge of Allegiance) that went largely unnoticed for most of human history.

And though there is often still social stigma attached to nonbelief and religious skepticism (something Williams might have endorsed), those of no faith have long been accorded the same legal privileges as those who have it. Meanwhile, the United States accommodates forms of religious exercise that earlier generations simply would not have countenanced, such as Sikh turban-wearing in the U.S. armed forces and officially sanctioned Hindu prayer in the U.S. Senate.[19] Thus, while the story of religious toleration in the United States is hardly a straightforward tale of expanding liberties, it is no myth.

Roger Williams and the 1663 charter that he helped forge sanctioned a radical and mostly untried approach to an urgent modern problem: How can we create a well-functioning and democratic society made up of groups that believe and worship in very different ways? This question plagued many early modern states and has since bedeviled countless more. By approving the charter, Charles II acceded to Williams's novel proposition that a community could flourish without an established church and with expansive provisions for rights of conscience. There was nothing inevitable about what ensued. This was, after all, an "experiment." Many more followed. *The Lively Experiment* represents an effort to reckon with this long, contentious, and enduringly boisterous tradition.

NOTES

1. Debunking those fictions has become a popular pastime among twenty-first-century journalists and scholars. The two most notable examples are David Sehat, *The Myth of American Religious Freedom* (Oxford: Oxford University Press, 2010), and Kenneth C. Davis, "America's True History of Religious Tolerance," *Smithsonian* magazine, October 2010, available online at http://www.smithsonianmag.com/history/americas-true-history-of-religious-tolerance-61312684/?no-ist. The study of religious intolerance in America is experiencing a broader prosperity. See, for example, John Corrigan and Lynn S. Neal, *Religious Intolerance in America: A Documentary History* (Chapel Hill: University of North Carolina Press, 2010);

Peter Gottschalk, *American Heretics: Catholics, Jews, Muslims and the History of Intolerance* (New York: Palgrave Macmillan, 2013); and Martha C. Nussbaum, *The New Religious Intolerance: Overcoming the Politics of Fear in an Anxious Age* (Cambridge, MA: Belknap Press of Harvard University Press, 2012).

2. Edmund S. Morgan, *Roger Williams: The Church and the State* (New York: W. W. Norton, 2007 [orig. 1967]), 4.

3. Roger Williams, *The Bloudy Tenent of Persecution for Cause of Conscience*, ed. Samuel L. Caldwell, 1st ser., vol. 3 (Providence, RI: Narragansett Club, 1867), 29.

4. It warrants notice that neither the 1663 Rhode Island Charter nor the postindependence constitutions explicitly protected the consciences of the enslaved. Their general legal subordination was so encompassing that an express grant of religious rights might have presented an unmanageable paradox even for someone as unfriendly to slavery as Williams. The omission is nonetheless emblematic of larger patterns.

5. Williams, *The Bloudy Tenent*, 399.

6. George Bancroft, *A History of the United States* (Boston, 1834), 1:461.

7. Isaac Backus, *Government and Liberty Described; and Ecclesiastical Tyranny Exposed* (Boston, 1778), 9.

8. See Denise Spellberg, "Muslims, Toleration, and Civil Rights, from Roger Williams to Thomas Jefferson" (chapter 5 in this volume).

9. Roger Williams to the Town of Providence, January 1655. Available online at http://press-pubs.uchicago.edu/founders/documents/amendI_religions6.html.

10. For more on this strain of Williams's thought, see Timothy L. Hall, *Separating Church and State: Roger Williams on Church and State* (Urbana: University of Illinois Press, 1998).

11. Terryl L. Givens, *The Viper on the Hearth: Mormons, Myths, and the Construction of Heresy*, rev. ed. (New York: Oxford University Press, 2013), 68.

12. James O'Toole, *The Faithful: A History of Catholics in America* (Cambridge, MA: Harvard University Press, 2009), 100–101.

13. For more on this phenomenon, see William R. Hutchison, *Religious Pluralism in America: The Contentious History of a Founding Ideal* (New Haven, CT: Yale University Press, 2003), 111ff.

14. See Kevin M. Schultz, *Tri-Faith America: How Catholics and Jews Held Postwar America to Its Protestant Promise* (New York: Oxford University Press, 2011).

15. Twentieth-century Supreme Court decisions were more circumspect about the religious actions that the federal government could regulate, but the separation metaphor stuck.

16. See David A. Hollinger, *After Cloven Tongues of Fire: Protestant Liberalism in Modern American History* (Princeton, NJ: Princeton University Press, 2013).

17. On the twisting currents of twentieth-century religious jurisprudence, see Sarah Barringer Gordon, *The Spirit of the Law: Religious Voices and the Constitution in Modern America* (Cambridge, MA: Belknap Press of Harvard University Press, 2010); on the impact of Asian religions in the United States, see Diane Eck, *A New Religious America: How a "Christian Country" Has Now Become the World's Most Religiously Diverse Nation* (San Francisco: Harper, 2001); on the implications of the early twentieth-century's expanded meaning of "religion," see Tisa Wenger, *We Have a Religion: The 1920s Pueblo Indian Dance Controversy and American Religious Freedom* (Chapel Hill: University of North Carolina Press, 2009); and on the conflicts resulting from new religious sounds in America's cities, see Isaac Weiner, *Religion Out Loud: Religious Sound, Public Space, and American Pluralism* (New York: New York University Press, 2014).

18. Religious Freedom Restoration Act, accessed at http://www.law.cornell.edu/uscode/text/42/2000bb.

19. Both of these examples are cited in Nussbaum, *The New Religious Intolerance*, 7–8.

Part I

Roger Williams and the Seventeenth Century's Lively Experiments

Chapter One

How Special Was Rhode Island?

The Global Context of the 1663 Charter

Evan Haefeli

In an unusual departure from conventional forms, the men of Rhode Island and Providence Plantations inserted a narrative into their 1663 charter describing their colony's origins and special religious mission, thereby establishing an interpretive framework that continues to influence historical accounts of the colony. The charter recounts how the first colonists, "pursuing with loyal minds their serious intentions of godly edifying themselves in the holy Christian faith as they were persuaded, together with the conversion of the Indian natives, did . . . transport themselves into America" (by which was meant Massachusetts Bay Colony). Starting at Providence with Roger Williams, his family, and a few friends in 1636, the colony now comprised a handful of towns, each founded by a different group of (mostly) radical English Protestants. Despite their different origins, they shared a common aversion to the Congregational Church establishment of Massachusetts. The charter portrays the move to Rhode Island as the realization of their religious hopes for America. They left Massachusetts, "not being able to bear . . . their different apprehensions in religious concernments . . . and transplanted themselves into the midst of the most potent Indian people of that country, where (by the good Providence of God, from whom the plantations have taken their name), they have not only been preserved to admiration, but have prospered [through] plantations, ship building, supply of pipe-staves, and commerce with his Majesty's southern plantations." Here, in short, is the now-classic story of Rhode Island as a religious refuge, where religious liberty allowed colonists to thrive economically as well as religiously.[1]

Over time, Americans have accepted this story of religious refuge as a distinguishing national characteristic. And Rhode Island—with Rhode Island's founder, Roger Williams—has retained pride of place within it.[2] Yet is Rhode Island really typically American? To be sure, there were distinctively American aspects to Rhode Island's origins: the Narragansetts, an indigenous group powerful enough to shelter Williams and other Protestant radicals; its emergence from the neighboring colony of Massachusetts, whose narrow orthodoxy, impossible to establish in England, drove the radicals into exile; and, of course, the area's fertile and healthy climate, which allowed the early colonists to not just survive but also thrive, building a society worthy of a royal charter by 1663. As a refuge from New England as much as old England, however, Rhode Island stood apart from its neighbors, not least in its dependence on English influence.

On closer inspection, the Rhode Island story looks less like a distinctly American story than a variant of a distinctive history of religious tolerance playing out across the English world. The 1663 charter is an important reminder of the extent to which Rhode Island's "lively experiment" depended on this broader English context. After all, not every New England colony was lucky enough to have its autonomy preserved by a royal charter. New Haven, another small New England colony founded in 1637, was absorbed by Connecticut in 1664, while by the 1690s Massachusetts had swallowed up first Maine, then Plymouth, and even, for a time, New Hampshire. The fates of these colonies remind us that the lively experiment could not have succeeded in the American environment without help from overseas. England kept Rhode Island free. Rather than a beacon anticipating the United States, it was an extension of English authority, one of a growing number of colonial enterprises for which England's new king in 1660 permitted religious tolerance of some sort.

Keeping in view the wider contemporary English context of 1663 makes it clear that religious tolerance set Rhode Island apart from New England but not from the broader English world. For different reasons and in different ways, toleration was deployed with increasing frequency by English authorities during the so-called Restoration period of English history (1660–1688); the Stuart monarchy returned to the throne in the person of King Charles II, who had spent years in exile after a revolutionary regime executed his father and abolished "the kingly office" in 1649.[3] The restored monarch and his councilors had to bring under control a religiously diverse and combustible set of territories stretching from India to the Americas while fending off the conspiracies of disgruntled revolutionaries and strengthening royal authority in the face of an assertive Parliament. Charles had a variety of reasons to endorse Rhode Island's "lively experiment" in 1663, especially if it ensured the loyalty and obedience of the colony at a time when he could take neither of these factors for granted anywhere in his realms.[4]

I

Set within the broader context of the seventeenth-century English Empire, Rhode Island's bold claims about religious liberty seem less extraordinary than the traditional focus on New England alone would suggest.[5] Even compared to other parts of the future United States, Rhode Island's example of religious liberty was not unique. Marylanders have been arguing since the 1780s that their colony made a decisive contribution to American religious liberty.[6] Founded by Catholics a few years before Roger Williams fled Massachusetts, Maryland also rejected the established Church of England. Moreover, it also served as a haven from an intolerant American neighbor, providing refuge to Puritans from Virginia (only later did it acquire a reputation as a refuge for Catholics as well). Finally, like Rhode Island, Maryland depended on English support. When the Catholic Lord Baltimore pointed out in 1653 that the "refuge" his colony offered was "for such as shall continue faithfull to" the new republican regime in England, he was defending his rights to Maryland by emphasizing his loyalty to the revolutionary commonwealth.[7]

Nonetheless, there were significant differences in the religious liberty available in Rhode Island and Maryland. The 1663 charter brought the diffuse origins of the colony into a system of religious liberty that was clearly Protestant without explicitly favoring any particular church. While Williams had acquired the initial charter for the colony from England's revolutionary government in 1644, John Clarke, a Baptist, did much of the work of drafting and securing the 1663 charter. Clarke, more than Williams, deserves credit for articulating the vision of the colony contained in the charter, proclaiming that "it is much on their hearts to hold forth a lively experiment that a flourishing civil state may best be maintained among his Majesty's subjects with full religious liberty, and that true piety will give the greatest security for sovereignty and true loyalty." Charles, according to the charter, was "willing to preserve to them that liberty in the worship of God which they have sought with so much travail and loyal subjection." Moreover, "because some of them cannot conform to the liturgy, ceremonies, and articles of the Church of England," which had recently been reestablished in May 1662 by the Act of Uniformity, the king granted and declared "that no person within the said colony shall hereafter be any wise molested or called in question for any difference in opinion in matters of religion that does not disturb the civil peace of the colony." To this guarantee of local religious liberty, royal agents added the qualification, "hoping that the same, by reason of distance, may be no breach of the uniformity established in this nation," suggesting that Rhode Island was not quite the model that Clarke hoped it would be.[8]

Maryland's religious liberty, by contrast, was enshrined in the famous "Act concerning Religion." Drafted in England by Lord Baltimore in the wake of the execution of Charles I, it was passed by the Maryland Assembly in April 1649, setting the tone for religious liberty in a colony dominated by a Catholic proprietor and a small Catholic elite. It had much in common with contemporary measures passed or proposed in England. Like them, the act drew the limit of tolerance at Trinitarian Christianity, punishing blasphemy or any denial of the Trinity "with death and confiscation or forfeiture of all his or her lands and goods to the Lord Proprietary and his heires." However, it also contained Catholic-friendly dimensions that were absent in both Britain and Rhode Island. It set heavy fines (five pounds sterling or a public whipping and imprisonment if they did not have the funds) for those who "utter any reproachfull words or Speeches concerning the blessed Virgin Mary the Mother of our Saviour or any Apostles or Evangelists." The protection of Catholic beliefs and priests was strong: Three-time offenders would be banished from the province forever. Lesser fines were to be imposed upon those who failed to observe the Sabbath or who branded others "heretick, Scismatick, Idolator, puritan, Independant, Prespiterian popish priest, Jesuite, Jesuited papist, Lutheran Calvenist, Anabaptist, Brownist, Antinomian, Barrowist, Roundhead, Separatist, or any other name or terme in a reproachfull manner relating to matter of Religion." Again, the Rhode Island charter lacked such sanctions, which explicitly protected Catholics as much as Protestants.[9]

In theory, Catholics, Jews, and even members of the established Church of England could live and worship in Rhode Island under the 1663 charter (although none did until much later). Nonetheless, the colony's religious arrangements favored radical Protestants over others. They formed the bulk of the European inhabitants: Baptists, Quakers, and some idiosyncratic individuals, like Williams and Samuel Gorton, who are perhaps best described as "Seekers." This arrangement was a continuation of the system established under the colony's first patent, granted by the revolutionary Parliament in March 1644. It had said nothing about religion or church order, but that already was a significant departure from previous colonial charters, including those of Massachusetts Bay and Maryland, which invoked the established Church of England. Conferring upon the inhabitants of Providence, Portsmouth, and Newport the corporate power to form a civil government, its sole restriction was that their "Laws, Constitutions, and Punishments . . . be conformable to the Laws of England, so far as the Nature and Constitution of the place will admit."[10]

At the local level, Rhode Island had produced a series of laws and statements on behalf of religious liberty in the 1640s that articulated the radical Protestant priorities of the founders. Where Providence declared itself "a shelter for persons distressed in conscience," the town of Newport's court ordered in 1641 "that none bee accounted a delinquent for Doctrine: Provided, it bee not directly repugnant to ye Government or Lawes established." The colony's 1647 civil code proclaimed that "all men may walk as their consciences perswade them, every one in the name of his God." Although it did not overtly endorse a particular religion, the 1647 code is organized according to biblical, not common law, categories, revealing how deep were the scriptural assumptions that preoccupied the early colonists.[11] By making the individual conscience as well as scripture the ultimate religious authorities in the colony, Rhode Island's religious liberty favored the priorities of radical Protestant religion. However, it also had its limits. The assumption that there was a better form of religion to which the colony's inhabitants should conform, however loosely, is made explicit in the 1663 charter's express hope that the indigenous population would convert to Protestantism (a wish that accorded with Roger Williams's vision of evangelical toleration, which Teresa Bejan discusses in chapter 4).

II

If Rhode Island's lively experiment wasn't a model for the English world, it paralleled wider trends within it during the 1660s. Colonial American historians have assumed that the Restoration Empire sought centralization and "the reimposition of the Church of England as part of the project of ensuring allegiance to the king." The inconvenient fact that neither centralization nor the uniform imposition of the Church of England took place has led scholars to conclude that either there was no coherent policy or, in religious matters especially, it "worked at cross-purposes." British leaders, it is argued, only permitted religious liberty reluctantly and remained committed to the hope of securing colonial loyalty through a shared allegiance to the state church. Indeed, statements to this effect were made regularly by various individuals across the English world.[12] Nonetheless, there is a good deal of evidence that the pivotal figure in shaping colonial religious policy, King Charles II, had a religious and political vision that favored religious diversity over uniformity.

Charles had good reason to doubt that imposing the Church of England on all of his subjects was the best way to attain political obedience and stability. After all, Britain had erupted into revolution largely in reaction to his father's efforts to do just that.[13] The resulting civil war demonstrated that religious allegiance and political loyalty did not always go hand in hand. Many British Protestants turned against the king, while English Catholics proved themselves conspicuously loyal (the loyalty of Irish Catholics was less obvious). This experience encouraged Charles to value political loyalty over religious conformity, and he repeatedly advocated religious toleration for Catholics and Protestant Dissenters. Some have argued that his refusal to marginalize Catholics, as many of his Protestant subjects desired, stemmed from a secret lifelong attachment to Roman Catholicism. After all, since turning sixteen in 1646, he had spent his years of exile living in Roman Catholic countries. His mother had been a French Catholic, his wife was a Portuguese Catholic, and various episodes in his political career were haunted by the suspicion that he might convert, as his brother James, the Duke of York, did in 1669. However, he consistently favored only Catholics who demonstrated political loyalty. Personally, he resisted persistent pressures to convert until his deathbed, when he finally became a Roman Catholic.

For political and personal reasons, then, Charles had an ambivalent relationship to the official church of his realm, and he regularly tried to protect those who could not conform to it. Already in April 1660, a month before Parliament proclaimed him king and invited him to return to England, he sought to reassure the religiously diverse revolutionaries in power by making a conciliatory declaration from his refuge in the Dutch city of Breda. The so-called Declaration of Breda offered Parliament control over much of the political settlement for the restored regime, including the composition of the Church of England. However, it also expected an "act of parliament . . . for the full granting of that indulgence"—that is, "a liberty to tender consciences, and that no man shall be disquieted or called in question for differences of opinion in matter of religion which do not disturb the peace of the kingdom."[14] Expressing Charles's concern that toleration of religious difference be linked to professions of political loyalty, the language of the Declaration of Breda made its way into several colonial charters, including Rhode Island's.[15]

Admittedly, Charles was neither consistent nor principled in his religious policies, intermittently permitting persecution. While Charles never ordered anyone executed strictly for their religious beliefs, over four hundred Quakers and other Protestant Dissenters died in prison during his reign: more than the roughly three hundred Protestants executed by the notorious persecutor Queen Mary in the sixteenth century. In addition, about thirty-five Catholics were executed during the political hysteria of the Popish Plot (1679–1681). Charles's approach to shielding religious dissenters from civil law is seen by historians to have been largely opportunistic. He favored toleration when it allowed him to circumvent the powers of Parliament by exempting individuals from parliamentary religious laws. When he could not circumvent Parliament, he became, as one historian puts it, "indifferent" to toleration. This apparent inconsistency was partly the result of the ways Parliament and the Church of England limited his authority over religious matters. Parliament, not the king, was responsible for the laws that put the nonconformists in prison and the trials that killed Catholics. Of course, the king supported the execution of religious dissidents who he believed to be political subversives, with the suppression of radical Scots covenanters in the 1670s and 1680s being the clearest example. Obedience was his ultimate concern, regardless of religion.[16]

The Restoration Parliament differed from Charles in prioritizing religious conformity over political obedience. The 1662 Act of Uniformity was not the fulfillment of the king's wishes. Charles preferred a more comprehensive and flexible church settlement that would have allowed many Dissenters, especially Presbyterians, to remain within the national church, along with recognition of his prerogative to exempt religious minorities from the full brunt of parliamentary legislation. Accordingly, in December 1662, several months after the Act of Uniformity was passed, he expressed his wish that Parliament would agree that he had the power to protect Protestant Dissenters who could "not conform" to the Church of England "through scruple and misguided conscience" from the full rigor of the act. Likewise, he proclaimed that Catholics who "shall live peaceably, modestly and without scandal" had reason "to hope for a toleration of their profession." Four months later, Parliament and the Church of England forced him to retract these promises. For the rest of his reign, these two institutions strove to clamp down on dissenting religious worship, beginning with the passage of two further laws: the 1664 Conventicle Act, which forbade unofficial meetings for worship, and the 1665 Five Mile Act, which forbade nonconformist ministers from coming near congregations they had served before the Act of Uniformity was passed. Overseas, however, there was little they could do to impede Charles's tolerating inclinations.[17]

The conflict between royal and parliamentary priorities within England provides crucial context for understanding why Charles endorsed Rhode Island's lively experiment. Since the colonies clearly lay within the royal prerogative, he could permit a degree of religious diversity overseas that he could not at home, as long as the colony professed to be loyal. Three months before Rhode Island received its charter, the king had bestowed upon several aristocratic supporters the charter for Carolina, which permitted the lords proprietor to "grant liberty of conscience."[18] Carolina's lively experiment charted a course that was both more conservative and potentially more radical than Rhode Island's. As its language of "indulgences and dispensations" suggests, it was assumed that the Church of England would or could be the established church (which happened in the early eighteenth century). Initially, however, the lords proprietor wanted to appeal to "all interests, especially that of New England, whence the greatest stock of people will in all probability come."[19] In 1670, Carolina's Lords Proprietor were also granted a charter to the Bahamas Islands, which gave them the power "to grant indulgences and dispensations with regard to religious worship," much as they had in Carolina.[20]

The potential of Carolina (and perhaps even the Bahamas) to become a remarkable "lively experiment" can be seen in the Fundamental Constitutions, drafted for the colony in 1669 by Lord Shaftesbury, one of the proprietors and an important member of the early Restoration government, together with his secretary, John Locke. Although they were never fully implemented, the proposed laws say much about what at least some of the proprietors found acceptable. They opened the colony up to "Jews, heathens, and other dissenters from the purity of Christian religion," while expressing the hope that, "by good usage and persuasion," these individuals might "be won over to embrace and unfeignedly receive the truth" of the Church of England. In the meantime, colonists were only required to acknowledge that there was a God who was to be publicly worshipped. With that one proviso, the Fundamental Constitutions allowed for the public exercise of any religion on which "seven or more persons" could agree, with just three restrictions. First, everyone had to belong to a church and every church had to keep a strict record of its membership. Second, no one could "use any reproachful, reviling, or abusive language against any religion of any church or profession," a rule that could be used to restrain aggressive proselytizing (at the time a practice primarily associated with Quakers). Finally, the constitutions allowed for the eventual establishment of the Church of England by the colonial assembly; no other church could ever receive official funds. Although proposing a remarkably wide-ranging tolerance, these requirements also excluded certain people, most obviously those "that doth not acknowledge a God, and that God is publicly and solemnly to be worshiped."[21] In other words, atheists, scoffers, and nonmonotheists.

Elsewhere around the world, Charles II's government was permitting alternative forms of toleration. Different modes of imperial acquisition—and different colonial cultures—produced varying religious arrangements. Jamaica and Dunkirk had been conquered from Spain by the Cromwellian regime; the cities of Tangiers and Bombay were acquired as part of the dowry of Charles's new Portuguese queen; and New York was conquered from the Dutch in 1664. Many of these territories contained Catholics, while Tangiers, Jamaica, and Bombay also contained non-Christians (Jews, Muslims, and others). In each case, the challenge they posed to English Protestant religious diversity was addressed in significantly different ways, none of which coincided either with the Rhode Island model or with Parliament's desire for conformity to the Church of England.

Dunkirk, captured in 1658 after a joint siege with the French, was initially imagined as the most tolerant territory in the English world. The strategic and economic importance of this Low Country port city prompted English planners to think of it as a possible alternative to Amsterdam. One official suggested some extraordinary religious provisions to drive this home: If a Jewish synagogue were tolerated, he claimed not only that Jews would gladly pay "60,000 or 80,000 pound for that freedom," but also that it would encourage all of Amsterdam's Jewish merchants to relocate to Dunkirk. If, in addition to that, the Protestant English rulers granted liberty of conscience to Catholics (the majority population of the city and region) and allowed them to cross over the border to worship in neighboring towns, it would attract many French and Dutch merchants. If French Huguenot and Dutch Reformed churches were established in the town, merchants from those countries would certainly take up residence for business. With this officially permitted religious diversity, Dunkirk could become a "flurrishing commonwealth of it selfe" that within five years would be "nott much inferior to Amsterdam as Amsterdam is nowe."[22]

The dream of an English Amsterdam was never quite realized. Cromwell preferred to turn Dunkirk into a Protestant bastion to bolster the cause of the Huguenots in France as well as the Dutch Republic. The transfer of Dunkirk to the English had been one of the conditions of the Anglo-French alliance against Spain. After King Louis XIV dutifully turned over the keys to the city to the English commander, Sir William Lockhart, Cromwell's council immediately resolved to send Bibles to the soldiers and recruit "an able minister to be sent thither" to introduce Protestantism into the Catholic city.[23] While Lockhart was a devout Reformed Protestant, he was also an astute politician. As Cromwell's ambassador to the French, he insisted that there be concessions made to Catholic worship within Dunkirk. With the French keeping a close eye on how the English governed the city, the diplomatic stakes were too high not to tolerate Catholics. Thus, at a time when the Cromwellian government was suppressing Catholic worship in Ireland, Dunkirk's population of roughly five thousand was allowed to retain its fifty-nine priests and monks and fifty-three nuns. Although Catholic public processions were banned and priests were required to swear an oath of allegiance, there was no disguising the fact that in Dunkirk, alone of all the territories under Cromwellian control, Catholic worship was openly tolerated.[24]

After the Restoration, Charles not only continued the toleration of Catholic worship in Dunkirk but actually encouraged it more than the previous regime. He eased the restrictions on Catholic processions and appointed as governor a Scottish Catholic, Andrew Rutherford, who had served so long in the French army that in his letter of acceptance he begged "pardon for his English, being more accustomed to the French tongue." However, this English experiment in tolerating Catholicism did not last long. Pressed for funds and unwilling to support the aggressive foreign policy that would have been necessary to maintain Dunkirk, Charles's government sold it to the French in November 1662.[25]

The loss of Dunkirk coincided with the beginning of a new set of colonial tolerations of Catholics. Andrew Rutherford's next posting was Tangiers, a former Portuguese colony that had been transferred to the English (along with Bombay) as part of the dowry of the Portuguese princess Catherine of Braganza, who had married Charles II in the spring of 1662. Tangiers was a Portuguese Catholic fortress town surrounded by Muslims, who lived and worked in the city but were not permitted to worship there. The terms of the handover guaranteed Catholics the practice of their religion and the use of the cathedral, while the Jewish community was permitted a synagogue (the first synagogue the English world had seen in centuries). The Church of England became the town's official church: no other forms of Protestantism were permitted. However, Protestants were scarce in the city; even a number of the soldiers were Irish and Catholic. Toleration in Tangiers thus included Catholics and Jews in ways Rhode Island did not, even as it excluded the Protestant Dissenters who benefited most from the "lively experiment." It, too, failed to flourish. Always an embattled outpost, Tangiers was abandoned to the Moroccans in 1684 after great expense, many battles, and the eventual expulsion of the Jews.[26]

Bombay, the other part of the Braganza dowry, began in 1665 as a royal colony like Tangiers before it eventually came under the control of the East India Company in 1668. Consequently, it was founded on a somewhat different footing than the other East India Company outposts, which, as a rule, favored the established church and permitted only some religious liberty.[27] In Bombay as in Tangiers, Charles II condoned a policy of tolerance for local religions, exempting his new subjects from conformity to the Church of England as long as they were politically loyal. He ordered its first governor "to give such encouragement as securely you may to such natives and others as shall submit to live peaceably under Our obedience and in due submission to the government of the island; and you are to suffer them to enjoy the exercise of their religion without the least interruption or discountenance."[28]

Although Bombay and Tangiers were both formerly Portuguese territories, the Catholic presence in Bombay, dense with Jesuits, was stronger. While Tangiers gained a reputation as overly friendly to Catholics, Bombay created common ground between the Protestant English rulers and the Indians through anti-Jesuit sentiment. While Jesuits were permitted in the colony, and Catholics could worship in their churches (as per the transfer agreement), the English found excuses to seize property from the Jesuits and other prominent Portuguese who resented the English takeover, gradually weakening the Catholic community.[29] The English made use of toleration to further undermine Jesuit influence. Already in March 1665 one English officer commented that the "Jesuits are much troubled at our being here," but "the Gentues, Moores, and Banians" were flocking to the colony for "the liberty of conscience." Initially, they were urged "to use their ceremonies in their houses privately."[30] Soon, however, Bombay's governor, wanting "to draw hither as many merchants (Banians as well as Moores and Persians) as possibly I can from" the great trading cities of the west coast of India, requested that Charles "graunt liberty to buyld them pagados and mesquitas to exercise theyr religion publiquely in." With these new religious privileges, he felt "noe doubt then but this weill bee made a very famous and opulent port." He assured the king that taking such actions would "bee no more scandalous unto our Christian religion" than the pope "permitting in Rome the Jews (who crucifyied our Blessed Saviour) to have publique sinagogues," a policy, he noted, that was also adopted by the king of Poland, the Republic of Venice, and the grand duke of Tuscany. Such an official toleration did not become policy in Bombay until much later. Nonetheless, the sacred footprint of non-Christians increased noticeably in the ensuing decades.[31]

Jamaica took a more direct approach to Roman Catholicism: outright suppression. The Cromwellian forces, some of them veterans of the conquest of Ireland, showed no more interest in accommodating what they condemned as "idolatry" than they had in Ireland. Since the resident Spanish Catholic population fled the island—except for a handful who fought a long guerilla war in the hopes of keeping the island Spanish and Catholic—the conquerors had no reason to make any religious concessions and did not. However, as in Ireland, the conquering army tolerated a range of Protestants—Baptists, Presbyterians, Congregationalists, and others—even as it forbade the practice of Roman Catholicism.[32] Initially, the hope was that Jamaica would be populated by good Protestants "who know and fear the Lord" like "those of New England." Accordingly, the English government tried to recruit colonists from there, as well as other Puritans fleeing "the violent prosecution of some ill-affected persons" in Bermuda.[33] In the end, most of the colonists came from the other Caribbean islands, but these included people that Puritans approved of, like the "most sober, godley and discrete person" of Luke Stokes, the governor of Nevis, who led the migration of some 1,600 colonists from his island to Jamaica in 1656.[34]

Given Jamaica's Cromwellian origins, the Restoration government was advised to grant "religious toleration . . . to all who desire it," even as it established the Church of England in the now royal colony.[35] Edward D'Oyley, one of the Cromwellian colonels, confirmed as its first royal governor in February 1661, was ordered to "give the best encouragement to Ministers that Christianity and the Protestant religion, according to the profession of the Church of England, may have due reverence and exercise amongst them."[36] Soon thereafter, Jamaica's Assembly began to create parishes and draw up provisions for an established church. Although not all the island's colonists were expected to conform to the church, it was intended that "they be Protestants." D'Oyley's successor, Thomas, Lord Windsor, made this policy official in his proclamation of October 1662 that all "persons professing the faith of our Lord Jesus Christ, though differing in religious worship, shall enjoy all the liberties and privileges of other inhabitants, provided they observe the civil laws and customs."[37] The arrangement seems to have worked. In 1682 the governor reported that the "Quakers and Independents" (Congregationalists) who were "the chief sects" on the island were "very submissive to the civil government and enjoying toleration." At the same time, he voiced the hope that this need not be a permanent situation, claiming they "may perhaps be won back, by the preaching and virtuous lives of our ministers, to the Church."[38]

Jamaica's religious arrangement reflected the pattern evident in the other Caribbean islands. From its earliest days, the English Caribbean was religiously diverse. Puritans had played a role in the early colonization of virtually every island, but this did not prevent the creation of parishes at an early date. At the same time, the creation of parishes did not guarantee religious uniformity in the Caribbean any more than it did in England. Catholics, mostly Irish, had lived on Barbados and in the Leewards since the 1630s. The Leeward island of Montserrat actually had an Irish majority. However, Catholic worship was never officially permitted. As in Ireland and Britain, Catholics had to make do with, at best, private, clandestine services. Baptists arrived in the 1640s, starting on Barbados and spreading to the Leeward Islands, where the Puritan governor of Nevis "was much perplexed with some annebaptest" in 1655.[39] That same year, Barbados, which had adopted a policy of liberty of conscience in the 1640s, was described by a visitor as "inhabited with all sortes: with English, French, Dutch, Scotes, Irish, Spaniards they being Iues [Jews]."[40] In 1656, Quakers entered the Caribbean. Although few could be found in the Leeward Islands (the son of John Winthrop was one), several hundred Barbadian planters converted, making it a rival to Rhode Island as the center of Quakerism in the Americas.[41]

After the Restoration, much of this religious diversity was constrained by the reestablished Church of England. Already in March 1661, a year before the passage of the Act of Uniformity in England, the Council of Barbados prohibited "unlawful and seditious meetings and conventicles under pretence of religious worship."[42] The new royal governor of Barbados and the Leeward Islands was directed to "take especial care that the Gospel be preached and propagated according to the doctrine of the Church of England, that Divine service be decently and reverently celebrated, and the Sacraments duly administered."[43] In contrast to Rhode Island, the mere fact of religious diversity did not discourage authorities from supporting the established church, which could at times be seen as a bastion of loyalty.

The exception to this general Caribbean pattern was Surinam. Founded by colonists from Barbados in 1651 and claimed by Lord Willoughby of Parham as his own proprietary colony, it benefited from Willoughby's willingness to use toleration to encourage immigration. Although a Presbyterian by inclination, Willoughby never imposed a Presbyterian church on the colony, nor was a parish system set up after the Restoration. Instead, in 1662 the colony's assembly proclaimed "liberty of conscience to all that shall live peaceably under government in the land."[44] The royal patent (dated May 1663) promised "liberty to such as inhabit said province and cannot conform to the Church of England," giving Lord Willoughby and his fellow proprietor Lawrence Hyde the power "to grant such dispensations as they think fit, provided said persons continue in loyalty and obedience to his Majesty."[45] The hand-ful of ministers who benefited from it seem to have all been Congregational-ists, including John Oxenbridge, who went to Surinam after the Act of Uni-formity deprived him of his post in England.[46] More extraordinarily, in 1665, the governor and assembly granted Jews full freedom of worship and status as English subjects. Such a possibility would not exist in the rest of the colonies until the 1740 Naturalization Act. In England it took until 1845.[47]

Unfortunately, a Dutch expedition captured Surinam in 1667, cutting short this "lively experiment" in the Caribbean. The Dutch Republic retained it in the peace negotiations, in exchange for their North American colony of New Netherland, captured by the English in 1664 and transformed into the colony of New York. In New York, yet another mode of toleration was put into place. The resident Dutch Reformed and Lutherans were permitted to worship openly (although the colony deprived the Reformed of the privileged position they had enjoyed under the Dutch). Meanwhile, the Duke's Laws of 1665 set up a system of establishment for the colony's English inhabitants that favored Presbyterians and Anglicans (although there were no more than a handful of Anglicans present) while discouraging strict Congregationalists and Quakers.[48]

III

When placed within the broader context of the Restoration Empire, Rhode Island's religious toleration hardly seems unique, though it still stands out as extraordinary. What distinguished it was its particular version of toleration, one of a variety endorsed by the Restoration monarchy in the 1660s. Like the other arrangements, it was adapted to the particular local circumstances of the colony and did not adhere to a general or universal principle that offered equal opportunities for all. Instead, like the other arrangements, it favored some religious groups over others—in this case, the radical Protestants who made up the majority of its population. It made no particular concessions to Catholics, unlike Maryland. Nor did it make the least concession to any formal religious establishment, in contrast to Carolina, most of the Carib-bean, and New York.

For all the importance of local factors, Rhode Island ultimately depended on the support of King Charles II for its charter. The king had many reasons to accept Rhode Island as a distinctive piece of diversity within the increas-ingly complex mosaic of religious pluralism he presided over. Some may call it pragmatism, the acceptance of a fait accompli. However, the fates of other colonies demonstrate that there was a clear alternative. He could have al-lowed Rhode Island to be absorbed into Connecticut or Massachusetts or imposed the Church of England, as in Jamaica, and put a check on what many regarded as a troublesome nest of sectarians. Fortunately for Rhode Island, Charles accepted the Rhode Islanders' professions of loyalty, perhaps seeing in the colony a useful counterpoint to its less obedient neighbors and their powerful religious establishments. Ultimately, the cumulative effect of this very English legacy of religious and political indulgence, in which Charles's reign was more decisive than any regime or colony before American independence, made American religious pluralism possible.

NOTES

1. W. Noel Sainsbury et al., *Calendar of State Papers: Colonial Series, America and West Indies*, 37 vols. (London: Longman, 1860–), vol. 5, *1661–1668*, 148. Hereafter cited as *CSPC*.
2. For a recent example, see Martha Nussbaum, *Liberty of Conscience: In Defense of America's Tradition of Religious Equality* (New York: Basic Books, 2008).
3. "An Act for the abolishing the kingly office in England and Ireland, and the dominions thereunto belonging, 17 March 1649," in *The Stuart Constitution: Documents and Commentary*, ed. J. P. Kenyon (Cambridge: Cambridge University Press, 1986), 306.
4. On the religious and political challenges facing Charles within the British Isles alone, see Tim Harris, *Restoration: Charles II and His Kingdoms* (London: Penguin, 2005), 1–205.
5. For an overview, see Evan Haefeli, "Toleration and Empire: The Origins of American Religious Diversity," in *British North America in the Seventeenth and Eighteenth Centuries*, ed. Stephen Foster, supp. vol., *Oxford History of the British Empire*, ed. William Roger Louis (Oxford: Oxford University Press, 2013), 103–35.
6. For the beginning of this debate, see Chris Beneke, *Beyond Toleration: The Religious Origins of American Pluralism* (New York: Oxford University Press, 2006), 183–86.
7. Cecil Calvert, *The Lord Baltemores Case, concerning the Province of Maryland* (London, 1653), 15. John D. Krugler has been arguing for years that "Cecil Lord Baltimore . . . was not involved in founding a Catholic refuge as such. . . . Uppermost in his mind was the establishment of a colony that would return some dividend on the family investment." "Lord Baltimore, Roman Catholics, and Toleration: Religious Policy in Maryland during the Early Catholic Years, 1634–1649," *Catholic Historical Review* 65 (1979): 73.
8. *CSPC, 1661–1668*, 148. For the process of securing the charter, see Sydney V. James, *John Clarke and His Legacies: Religion and Law in Colonial Rhode Island, 1638–1750*, ed. Theodore Dwight Bozeman (University Park: Pennsylvania State University Press, 1999), 59–84.
9. William Hand Browne et al., eds., *Archives of Maryland*, 72 vols. (Baltimore: Maryland Historical Society, 1883–1972), 1:244–46.
10. See http://avalon.law.yale.edu/17th_century/ri03.asp; Stephen Wright, *The Early English Baptists, 1603–1649* (Woodbridge, UK: Boydell Press, 2006), 75–142; David Como, "Apocalyptic Caribbean: Sectaries, Soldiers, and Slave in the English Atlantic, c.1639–1660" (paper presented to Columbia Seminar on Religion in America, 17 September 2013).
11. Theodore Dwight Bozeman, "Religious Liberty and the Problem of Order in Early Rhode Island," *New England Quarterly* 45 (1972): 54, 55, 60; G. B. Warden, "The Rhode Island Civil Code of 1647," in *Saints and Revolutionaries: Essays in Early American History*, ed. David D. Hall et al. (New York: W. W. Norton, 1984), 138–51.
12. Carla Gardina Pestana, *The English Atlantic in an Age of Revolution, 1640–1661* (Cambridge, MA: Harvard University Press, 2004), 6–8, 223, 260.
13. While pointing out that religious issues were not the only cause of the revolts in Scotland, Ireland, and England, Tim Harris, in *Rebellion: Britain's First Stuart Kings, 1567–1642* (Oxford: Oxford University Press, 2014), demonstrates that the effort to impose conformity to the Church of England on them (as represented by Archbishop William Laud) was a major factor in destabilizing Britain, as well as the motive for the Puritan emigration to New England.
14. Declaration of Breda, reprinted in Kenyon, *Stuart Constitution*, 331–32.

15. Sydney James, *The Colonial Metamorphoses in Rhode Island: A Study of Institutions in Change*, ed. Sheila L. Skemp and Bruce C. Daniels (Hanover, NH: University Press of New England, 2000), 265n31.

16. Ronald Hutton, *Charles II: King of England, Scotland, and Ireland* (Oxford: Oxford University Press, 1989), 273–74, 292–93, 455–57, quote on 306; Harris, *Restoration*, 196–99, 331–38.

17. Kenyon, *Stuart Constitution*, 380–81; Hutton, *Charles II*, 180–98.

18. *CSPC, 1661–1668*, 126, 270.

19. *CSPC, 1661–1668*, 269.

20. *CSPC, 1675–1676*, 122–23.

21. "Fundamental Constitutions of Carolina, March 1, 1669/70," in *North Carolina Charters and Constitutions*, ed. Mattie Erma Edwards Parker (Raleigh, NC: Carolina Charter Tercentenary Committee, 1963), 181–83; W. L. Saunders, ed., *The Colonial Records of North Carolina*, 26 vols. (Raleigh, NC: Printer to the State, 1886–1890), 1:156, 202–4; L. H. Roper, *Conceiving Carolina: Proprietors, Planters, and Plots, 1662–1729* (New York: Palgrave Macmillan, 2004), 128–31.

22. Quoted in Samuel R. Gardiner, "Cromwell and Mazarin in 1652," *English Historical Review* 11 (1896): 485.

23. Mary Anne Everett Green, ed., *Calendar of State Papers: Domestic Series, 1658–1659* (London: Longmans, 1885), 78. Hereafter cited as *CSPD*.

24. Clyde L. Grose, "England and Dunkirk," *American Historical Review* 39 (1933): 5–17. On Cromwellian policies in Ireland, see Toby Barnard, *Cromwellian Ireland: English Government and Reform in Ireland, 1649–1660* (Oxford: Clarendon Press, 2000), 90–182, and Micheál Ó Siochrú, *God's Executioner: Oliver Cromwell and the Conquest of Ireland* (London: Faber and Faber, 2008), 100, 116–17, 233–34.

25. Rutherford was appointed in June 1661. *CSPD, 1660–1661*, 80, 140, 228; *CSPD, 1661–1662*, 4, 10; Grose, "England and Dunkirk," 16–22; David Parrott, "Rutherford, Andrew, Earl of Teviot (d. 1664)," in *Oxford Dictionary of National Biography* (Oxford: Oxford University Press, 2004); online ed., May 2006, accessed 5 August 2013, http://www.oxforddnb.com/view/article/24360.

26. E. M. G. Routh, *Tangier: England's Lost Atlantic Outpost, 1661–1684* (London: John Murray, 1912), chaps. 13–15.

27. Philip J. Stern, *The Company-State: Corporate Sovereignty & the Early Modern Foundations of the British Empire in India* (Oxford: Oxford University Press, 2011), chap. 5.

28. William Foster, *The English Factories in India*, 13 vols. (Oxford: Clarendon Press, 1906–1927), vol. 1661–1664, 128.

29. Glenn J. Ames, "The Role of Religion in the Transfer and Rise of Bombay, c.1661–1687," *Historical Journal* 46 (2003): 332–38; J. Ovington, *A Voyage to Surat in the Year 1689*, ed. H. G. Rawlinson (London: Oxford University Press, 1929), 148, 156–57.

30. Foster, *The English Factories in India, 1665–1667*, 44–46.

31. Ibid., 51–54.

32. On the conquest, see S. A. G. Taylor, *The Western Design: An Account of Cromwell's Expedition to the Caribbean* (The Hague: Institute of Jamaica and the Jamaica Historical Society, 1965).

33. *CSPC, 1574–1660*, 430, 453.

34. John Thurloe, *A collection of the state papers of John Thurloe*, ed. T. Birch, 7 vols. (n.p., 1742), 3:754. Hereafter cited as *Thurloe*. For the migration of the Nevis colonists, see Taylor, *Western Design*, chap. 11.

35. *CSPC, 1574–1660*, 491.

36. *CSPC, 1661–1668*, 6.

37. *CSPC, 1661–1668*, 38, 42, 96, 111.

38. *CSPC, 1681–1685*, 314.

39. *Thurloe*, 3:754. On the emergence of Baptists in the 1640s, see Como, "Apocalyptic Caribbean."

40. Henry Whistler, "Extracts from Henry Whistler's Journal of the West India Expedition," in *The Narrative of General Venables: With an Appendix of Papers Relating to the Expedition*

to the West Indies and the Conquest of Jamaica, 1654–1655, ed. C. H. Firth (London, 1900), appendix E, p. 14; Larry D. Gragg, *Englishmen Transplanted: The English Colonization of Barbados, 1627–1660* (Oxford: Oxford University Press, 2003), 75–78.

41. Larry D. Gragg, "A Puritan in the West Indies: The Career of Samuel Winthrop," *William and Mary Quarterly*, 3rd ser., 50 (October 1993): 768–86; Gragg, *Englishmen Transplanted*, 68–87; Natalie Zacek, *Settler Society in the English Leeward Islands, 1660–1776* (Cambridge: Cambridge University Press, 2010), chaps. 2 and 3.

42. *CSPC, 1661–1668*, 7, 16.

43. *CSPC, 1661–1668*, 142.

44. Leverton to Morton, 13 May 13 1662, fo. 18, accessed 16 March 2014, http://www.nickleverton.com/Site/Life_and_Death.html.

45. *CSPC, 1661–1668*, 131.

46. See http://www.nickleverton.com/Site/Life_and_Death.html, accessed 16 March 2014; Michael P. Winship, "Oxenbridge, John (1608–1674)," in *Oxford Dictionary of National Biography* (Oxford: Oxford University Press, 2004), accessed 14 April 2014, http://www.oxforddnb.com/view/article/21048.

47. Jacob Selwood, "Present at the Creation: Diaspora, Hybridity and the Place of Jews in the History of English Toleration," in *Religious Tolerance in the Atlantic World: Early Modern and Contemporary Perspectives*, ed. Eliane Glaser (New York: Palgrave MacMillan, 2014), 19–213.

48. On the transition to New York, see Evan Haefeli, *New Netherland and the Dutch Origins of American Religious Liberty* (Philadelphia: University of Pennsylvania Press, 2012).

Chapter Two

"Livelie Experiment" and "Holy Experiment"

Two Trajectories of Religious Liberty

Andrew R. Murphy

Roger Williams had been in America for more than a dozen years before William Penn was even born. Penn's 1682 journey from England to his nascent "holy experiment" in Pennsylvania thus occurred nearly twenty years after Rhode Island secured the royal charter that lauded its own "livelie experiment." Despite this generational difference, the colonies of Pennsylvania and Rhode Island stand side by side in traditional accounts of American religious liberty. It's not hard to understand why. The two settlements share a legacy of vibrant (often contentious) religious diversity, established by men who played important roles in the development of religious liberty in both theory and practice on both sides of the Atlantic. If the legacy of the American Revolution lay in securing a religious settlement that moved the new nation "beyond toleration," this revolutionary achievement is unthinkable without the seventeenth-century colonial foundations of American religious politics laid by figures like Penn and Williams. [1]

Combining biographical reflection on the careers of the two founders with an examination of the early histories of the colonies they helped establish allows us to consider two different colonial traditions that fed the American development of liberty of conscience. Both Pennsylvania and Rhode Island have always been closely associated with their respective founders, who were shaped by and remained intimately connected with events in England. Each founder articulated a powerful theory of religious liberty years before John Locke. Locke's *Letter Concerning Toleration* is generally considered the gold standard for early theories of toleration, an

example of both early modern trends toward religious inclusion and philosophical coherence. Yet, in many ways, Williams and Penn offered theories
of toleration that were more inclusive and capacious than Locke's, and they
did so while engaging in the practical business of governing in ways that
Locke never did (despite his involvement with the Carolina colony).[2]

One consequence of each founder's involvement in the practical matters
of governance was a firsthand experience with the contentiousness that religious diversity injected into colonial politics. Rhode Island and Pennsylvania
each struggled in their early years with establishing and maintaining civil
order in the midst of such diversity. Nor did these struggles take place solely
within their own borders. Governing elites in each colony also had to navigate boundary disputes with American neighbors. Rhode Island's ongoing
conflicts with Massachusetts Bay were a constant source of concern, and
Penn's struggle with Lord Baltimore over the line between their two colonies
would stretch on into the 1760s. Regime changes in England—the Restoration of 1660 in the case of Rhode Island, the Revolution of 1688 for Pennsylvania—further complicated the transatlantic context that shaped the colonies'
prospects for survival and territorial integrity.

But if such broad parallels between the two colonies are worth careful
consideration, their differences are equally instructive. To frame it in the
sharpest terms: in Rhode Island the practice of religious liberty preceded the
theory, while in Pennsylvania theory preceded practice.

Penn and Williams came to their respective colonies in different ways.
Penn was an established theorist of religious toleration and an English Dis-
senter, a proprietor equipped with a royal grant of authority. Williams was a
fugitive and exile. The settlement of Providence and Rhode Island predated
the publication of Williams's most famous writing on religious liberty, *The
Bloudy Tenent of Persecution* (1644). Settlement also predated the 1644
parliamentary patent and the 1663 royal charter, which lent political legitimacy to Williams's colonial endeavor. Conversely, Pennsylvania's charter
initiated an English colonial enterprise more or less from scratch. In fact,
Penn had been active in the English struggle for liberty of conscience for
more than a decade by the time he became a colonial proprietor in 1681.

The time is ripe for a comparative reconsideration of the two founders
and their respective settlements. Williams has recently attracted the attention
of scholars attempting to think through contemporary questions of diversity,
conscience, and social conflict. For example, he plays a central role in Martha Nussbaum's reconstruction of American religious liberty, which locates
Williams at "the beginning of a distinctive tradition of thought about religious fairness that resonates to the present day."[3] Similarly, John Barry has
argued that even though Williams "was not the first to call for religious
freedom . . . he was the first to link that call to individual liberty in a political
sense and to create a government and a society informed by those beliefs."[4]

James Calvin Davis calls Williams "America's earliest pioneer for religious liberty," who "eternally symbolizes the distinctive contribution of religious figures, traditions, and communities to the consideration of freedom of conscience in America."[5] Penn, however, seems at once both more familiar and more remote, a figure far more often talked about than carefully studied, about whom judgments have ranged widely, from Mabel Brailsford's 1930 exultation that Penn was "the greatest Englishman and the greatest European of his time" to Mary Geiter's view of a Jacobite Penn knee-deep in conspiracy.[6] Like Williams, Penn has enjoyed a recent upsurge in scholarly attention, with treatments stressing his role in the development of Quaker political theory, the founding of Pennsylvania as an episode in the history of political thought and practice, and early Pennsylvania's embodiment of "liberal civil religion."[7] Though scholarship on these two has often included a fair amount of hagiography—an overly heroic vision of the individual's life and a rage for labeling one thinker as the "first" or "best" articulator of a widely held ideal—this recent upsurge in attention to both Williams and Penn has generally been a boon to the scholarly community and is fully justified by their involvement in, and influence on, events on both sides of the Atlantic.

What has been missing up to this point is a comparative look at these two important pioneers of religious liberty in their own unique contexts.[8] This chapter represents the beginnings of such an account. In what follows, I emphasize three broad parallels between Williams and Penn, along with several important divergences, to highlight the complex blend of theory and practice that lies at the heart of American religious liberty as it developed out of English disputes and English colonization in North America. As we shall see, what sets Williams and Penn apart from many of their tolerating counterparts was less their theoretical insights than their involvement in the day-to-day complexities of governance, which led them to an understanding of both the difficulty and the importance of adjusting principles to political realities. Their theoretical commitments about conscience, church, and state, together with their experience with the give-and-take of practical politics, led both Penn and Williams to embrace a modus vivendi settlement in which civil behavior, independent of religious belief, formed the essential ingredient of civil life.

WILLIAMS AND PENN, RHODE ISLAND AND PENNSYLVANIA: THREE BROAD PARALLELS

One key parallel between Penn and Williams was how their immersion in the religious and political turmoil of seventeenth-century England led them to intense and personal involvement in American colonization. Each man participated in a series of English debates and conflicts central to modern political thinking about church, state, and toleration. Each sought in America a species of liberty that he considered hopelessly out of reach in England. Penn and Williams each arrived in America in their thirties, seeking to transcend what they saw as the errors of religious establishment in England: its tendency to produce hypocrites, its stoking of religiously inspired civil conflict, and its impositions on individual conscience. Yet each also found religious and civil peace elusive—even in the apparently more promising atmosphere of America.

The religious and political conflicts of England's Restoration period (1660–1688) were crucial to Penn's development and to his aspirations for the colony he founded in 1681. After bursting on the national scene during the late 1660s, playing a key part in the organization of the Society of Friends under the leadership of George Fox during the 1670s and supporting the cause of religious toleration throughout that decade, Penn received a royal charter for his colony in 1681. The proprietor's voluminous promotional literature painted a picture of Pennsylvania as a beacon for persecuted religious minorities of Europe and a place where "sober people of all sorts" would live in harmony with their neighbors regardless of religious difference, in stark contrast with prevailing practice in Europe.[9] Although Friends occupied the most influential positions in society, government, and the economy, a variety of ethnic (German, Dutch, French, Swedish, Scot, and Irish) and religious (Anglican, Presbyterian, Baptist, and Lutheran, to name just a few) groups contributed to a vibrant colonial religious life from the colony's earliest days.[10] Pennsylvania's first decade was not without tensions, but it lacked the periodic waves of persecution and the religious vitriol—often directed at Quakers—that characterized Restoration England.[11]

Despite his high hopes for the American colony, Penn would spend relatively little time there—only about four of his final thirty-six years. Returning to England for what he thought would be a relatively brief visit to prosecute his dispute with Lord Baltimore over their colonies' borders, Penn found himself embroiled in English politics after the accession of his friend the Duke of York to the throne as King James II in 1685. As the "intellectual architect of the king's toleration project and one of its leading exponents," Penn was disgraced after the king's ouster in 1688 and only fully returned to public life in the mid-1690s.[12] Another brief visit to Pennsylvania in 1699 lasted just under two years, and Penn left his colony in 1701, never to return.

Roger Williams likewise pursued religious liberty on both sides of the Atlantic and was a noted public figure in both England and America. For his part, Williams came from an earlier generation of English Puritan dissenters who drove the "Great Migration" to New England. Born in 1603, more than four decades before Penn, he came of age during another era of tension between English kings and Parliaments. Williams left England in 1630, seeking in New England a church free from political interference and purified of human innovations—in other words, a church he no longer considered possible in England. Arriving in Boston in February 1631, Williams was welcomed with open arms; John Winthrop's journal reports the arrival of "Mr. Williams (a godly minister)."[13] But Williams's Separatism represented a sharp departure from the religious sensibilities of many of the Boston elite, and his years in the colony were marked by discord and dissent. He played a leading role in what Glenn LaFantasie calls a "Separatist revival" in Salem, which exacerbated already-existing tensions between that town and the Boston establishment, and the Massachusetts Bay General Court's banishment of him in 1635 marked the end of one of the most divisive episodes in the young colony's history.[14]

Although Williams's expulsion from Boston initiated his lifelong association with Providence and, later, Rhode Island, he was never far from events in England.[15] He returned in 1643 to secure a colonial charter for Rhode Island from Parliament and again in 1652, this time seeking reconfirmation of the charter. Each of these trips enabled Williams to view English religious and political conflict firsthand and cemented his views about the nefarious consequences of coercion in matters of conscience. Williams published his magnum opus, *The Bloudy Tenent of Persecution*, not in New England (where he had very limited access to a printing press) but in London, in the thick of a civil war fired by religious disputes, where Parliament ordered it to be burned.[16]

For both Williams and Penn, colonial endeavors in British North America represented newfound possibilities, the potential to construct societies decidedly different than Old England. Penn's famous invocation of a "holy experiment" for religious liberty contrasted American potential with English reality: "There may be room there, though not here," Penn wrote to James Harrison upon receiving his charter, "for such an holy experiment."[17] During the Pequot War, Williams wrote to John Winthrop, arguing that Massachusetts Bay was not essentially different from Old England, with its national church, and predicted "the end of one vexation . . . [and] the beginning of another, till conscience be permitted (though erroneous) to be free amongst you."[18] The statues of William Penn atop Philadelphia City Hall and Roger Williams overlooking Providence from Prospect Terrace provide visual reminders of the interlinking of a man with a place (more specifically, with an American place).

Yet, despite these similarities, Penn and Williams traveled very different paths in the new world. Williams arrived in Providence a fugitive and an exile; Penn came as a royally designated proprietor. And those differences shaped their experiences as colonial leaders.

Williams's journey through the New England snow and his arrival in Providence as an exiled fugitive during the winter of 1635 is a piece of the founding mythology of American religious liberty. He was never a wealthy man, and his correspondence reveals a man perpetually concerned about the repayment of debts owed him.[19] After helping to settle Providence and the surrounding towns, Williams played a number of pivotal roles over the course of the next forty-odd years: ambassador to the surrounding native tribes, colonial agent in England, chief governing officer, trader, farmer, preacher, colonial agent in England (again), president of Providence Plantations, and mediator of factions. His travels to England related directly to colony business. Fellow colonists requested that Williams safeguard the colony's legal standing, which he did by securing the first charter from Parliament in 1644.

If Williams arrived in his colony as an outcast and exile, Penn arrived in all the pomp attendant on royalty-granted proprietorship. He received his province directly from the Crown; a number of already-existing settlements of English, Dutch, and Swedish inhabitants were incorporated into the new province of Pennsylvania, along with territory ceded by his personal friend the Duke of York (later King James II). Upon his arrival, Penn assembled the inhabitants at the courthouse, examined the credentials and commissions of the magistrates, and set about directing the ongoing physical construction of Philadelphia according to plans he had drafted in England.

From these divergent beginnings, two founders shaped by their respective generations' religious and political conflicts in England would attempt to carve out oases of religious and civil peace in America. Yet if the theory of religious liberty seems relatively straightforward—a series of theological, political, epistemological, and pragmatic arguments—the realities of forming societies that safeguarded individual conscience would prove elusive. Indeed, a second broad parallel follows from the first: both Penn and Williams found creating a civil society of ordered liberty, without an established religion, to be a difficult undertaking. Internal dissension, American neighbors, and English rivals all contributed to the difficulties of securing order.

Early Rhode Island was the scene of fractious political debates about liberty of conscience, as well as more mundane matters. The rejection of the idea that civil authority should enforce moral and spiritual orthodoxy struck at the heart of conventional understandings of the legitimate functions of government and provided the colony's early residents with the enormous challenge of creating civil order amid a vibrant and devoted religious culture.[20] Williams was often dismayed by his fellow Rhode Islanders' unwillingness to submit to civil authority. Demographics heightened the challenge, as a surfeit of young, contentious, religiously heterodox single men migrated to the colony. Religious troublemakers also found their way there. Samuel Gorton, who gathered followers wherever he went (his followers were notorious for their insubordination to magistrates and their resistance to taxes), briefly settled in Providence, and Williams wrote Winthrop that "almost all suck in his poison."[21] More troubling, however, was the Gortonists' effect on the town of Pawtuxet, where a group of anti-Gorton residents subjected themselves to the authority of Massachusetts in an effort to bring a firm hand of civil authority to bear against these religious radicals.

Late in the 1640s Williams wrote to John Winthrop Jr. that "our colony is in civil dissension."[22] Such contention and disorder stretched into the 1650s. The hostility of the Massachusetts Bay settlements proved a constant source of concern and land disputes between towns persisted. Moreover, William Coddington's 1651 commission as governor for life of Aquidneck Island, issued by the Council of State in London, threw the surrounding settlements into turmoil and prompted them to dispatch Roger Williams and John Clarke to England in hopes of confirming the 1644 parliamentary patent. Reports of turmoil and contention led the sympathetic Sir Henry Vane, in early 1654, to lament the presence of "headinesses, tumults, disorders, [and] injustice, the noise whereof echoes into the ears of all, as well friends as enemies, by every return of ships from those parts."[23]

In some respects, at least, Pennsylvania has had a quite different reputation. As opposed to the well-documented (and, by their English and New English critics, well-publicized) anarchic tendencies of Rhode Island, the history of Pennsylvania has long been considered a singular success story in the development of Anglo-American religious liberty. And yet Pennsylvania was not simply an oasis of peace and harmony. From the very beginning, Penn's "Quaker colony" had to contend with a sizable population of non-Quakers, who brought their own ideas about governance to the legislature and who often voted as a bloc in pursuing their own interests. Of those attending the first meeting of the colonial assembly, non-Quakers almost outvoted Friends, and Penn reported in correspondence that the assembly only narrowly failed to elect a non-Quaker as assembly speaker.[24] Widespread disputes over land cast a constant shadow over Penn's first visit to America. The Keithian schism of 1692–1694, which began as an internal Quaker debate about theological principles and grew into a full-fledged attack on the colony's leadership, provided an especially vivid example of how difficult it was to establish civil order while preserving liberty of conscience.[25] Representatives of Pennsylvania's Quaker elite believed that claims to liberty of conscience did not excuse disorderly behavior and stressed the fragility of social order in a young colony. "In the infancy of the settlement of Pennsylvania," Samuel Jennings argued, "the legislators saw cause to make provision by a law, to secure the reputation of the magistrates from the contempt of others."[26] No claim of conscience could justify the sort of seditious behavior that the Keithians had engaged in, Jennings said. George Keith and his followers argued just as passionately that they were being persecuted, not unlike Penn himself had been persecuted in Restoration England or, for that matter, Quakers were persecuted in New England.[27]

Reports of the schism emboldened Penn's critics in England and America, causing the founder to fret, from England, that "the trial of [George Keith] has been industriously spread all about the nation."[28] Quaker political and economic dominance in the young colony reflected the founder's vision but aroused resentment among non-Quakers. This resentment, along with infighting among Pennsylvania Quakers themselves, led to civil strife and tense standoffs in the assembly. After 1701, two entirely separate assemblies met, one in New Castle and the other in Philadelphia, precursors to the later formation of a separate Delaware colony. Pennsylvania's Anglicans successfully petitioned for a church of their own in 1695, criticized Quaker hegemony, and accused Friends of everything from fixing legal proceedings to turning a blind eye to smuggling. Their frequent complaints about their exclusion from power indicate that Pennsylvania's religious diversity did not always operate harmoniously and that concerns about discord were ever present during the colony's early years.

In Pennsylvania as in Rhode Island, then, fears of disorder often grew from religious differences, arising either from competing claims to liberty of conscience or the intergroup frictions that bedeviled all colonies (Quakers and Anglicans in Pennsylvania and the Lower Counties, for example). And where social order could not be taken for granted, calls for religious liberty always stood on shaky ground, no less in the tolerationist circumstances of Pennsylvania or Rhode Island than in the most orthodox New England community.

What makes the careers of Penn and Williams so instructive in this regard is that in the early modern world the problem of order was quite often a problem of religion, and the permanence of religious diversity was in many places only slowly and grudgingly admitted (to say nothing of the rights of conscience). The search for order involved something that we might consider rather minimal by today's standards: what tolerationists like Penn and Williams sought, ultimately, was a modus vivendi—literally, a way of living together, a way of negotiating the inevitable differences that arise between groups short of suppression or bloodshed; a public space in which individuals and groups of differing persuasions could live out their own deepest commitments with some degree of integrity. Of course, this practical achievement was supported by principled arguments about how diversity of belief could coexist with civil cooperation; we shall see below how both Williams and Penn were not merely political actors but political *thinkers* of the first order.[29]

Just as both Williams and Penn were entangled in the *practical dimensions* of religious liberty during the seventeenth century, so did each articulate a powerful *theory* of religious liberty. These theories reflected larger debates in contemporary England and predated—and arguably went beyond—the more famous theory later put forward by John Locke. Although

Locke's *Letter Concerning Toleration* (1689) would become the most widely celebrated exposition of what we now call "liberal" tolerationism, Williams and Penn put forward their theories decades earlier (Williams during the 1640s, Penn during the late 1660s and 1670s). Williams and Penn also offered more ambitious theories that expressed a more robust understanding of the individual conscience and a broader range of protected beliefs and behaviors than Locke's. Penn, for example, refused to impose oaths in Pennsylvania legal proceedings out of respect for those who objected to swearing, and after 1692 Pennsylvania was the only American colony to allow public celebration of the Catholic Mass.[30] For his part, Williams famously claimed in *The Bloudy Tenent* that a "pagan or anti-christian pilot may be as skillful to carry the ship to its desired port, as any Christian mariner or pilot in the world," a clear reference to the validity of a non-Christian head of state.[31] By the standards of the time—even by the standards of the leading tolerationists—these were generous accommodations to conscience.

Williams's articulation of liberty of conscience, as presented in *The Bloudy Tenent*, was animated by a deep concern for the purity of the church and for the sanctity of the individual conscience. He echoed the arguments made by early Baptists in England, drawing a clear distinction between the political and the spiritual realms—the state and the church—and noting that Jesus had famously claimed in John 18:36 that his kingdom was not of this world. The theoretical separation between the spiritual and the carnal undergirded much of the tolerationist literature for the remainder of the seventeenth century.[32] Civil affairs were the proper provenance of the state and necessarily involved the exercise of coercion; in other words, human magistrates had authority over people's bodies, while God governed their souls. As Williams put it, "all civil states . . . [are] essentially civil, and therefore not judges, governors, or defenders of the spiritual of Christian state and worship."[33]

As Williams saw it, meddling in church affairs by civil rulers—for example, permitting governors to enforce religious orthodoxy—sullied the churches. Indeed, Williams traced many of the shortcomings of Christianity in his day to the fatal consequences of its adoption by the Roman Empire, writing on one occasion that "Christianity fell asleep in Constantine's bosom."[34] Later, in his famous "ship of state" letter to the town of Providence, Williams depicted the political community as a ship containing very different types of members, all in need of a firm but fair commander who could oversee the entire endeavor. A vessel putting out to sea, populated by passengers of such a variety of religious persuasions, he wrote, "is a true picture of a common-wealth, or an human combination, or society," and "the commander of this ship ought to command the ship's course . . . and also command that justice, peace and sobriety, be kept and practiced, both among the seamen and all the passengers."[35] Williams had used the same imagery in

The Bloudy Tenent, when he stressed the common interest that "papists, protestants, Jews, or Turks" have in the smooth functioning of their shared community.

Yet this radical commitment to religious toleration had an orthodox theological foundation. Williams drew upon the traditional Christian notion of conscience, admitting that conscience could err, even while holding that individuals should not be persecuted for their erroneous religious views. As he put it in *The Bloudy Tenent*, "to molest any person, Jew or Gentile, for either professing doctrine, or practicing any worship merely religious or spiritual, it is to persecute him, and such a person . . . suffereth persecution for conscience."[36] Since conscience was a faculty of the understanding and not the will, individuals could not be coerced into believing anything of which they were not fully persuaded by their own judgment.

Penn shared many of the commitments that animated Williams's thinking on these matters, and he laid out the basic elements of his theory over the course of the 1670s when he was involved in ongoing, though largely unsuccessful, efforts to secure toleration for English Dissenters.[37] In Penn's view, as in Williams's, persecution was rooted in spiritual pride and a fundamental misunderstanding of the nature of Jesus's ministry. A proper understanding of the nature of Christ's kingdom—namely, that it forsook coercion—and of the nature of the individual conscience would lead in turn to a proper understanding of earthly politics and to firm guarantees of religious liberty. In one of his earliest publications, Penn laid out an understanding of government that would remain central to his thinking for over four decades, calling on magistrates to remember

> that their authority cannot reasonably extend beyond the end for which it was appointed, which being not to enthrone themselves sovereign moderators in causes purely conscientious . . . but only to maintain the impartial execution of justice, in regulating civil matters with most advantage to the tranquility, enrichment and reputation of their territories, they should not bend their forces, nor employ their strength, to gratify the self-seeking spirit of the priests, or any private interest whatsoever.[38]

In *The Great Case of Liberty of Conscience* (1670), Penn offered a more sustained reflection on the nature of government, which he defined as "an external order of justice, or the right and prudent disciplining of any society, by just laws."[39] All of these arguments together formed the basis of Penn's view of England as a *civil commonwealth*. And it was some version of this theory that Penn sought to plant—with all the ambiguity inherent in such an attempt—in America.

Notwithstanding this broad parallel, it is also worth noting an important distinction: Penn's political career involved a movement from theory to practice, whereas Williams developed his theory of religious liberty empirically, out of his experience of persecution in Massachusetts Bay. During his time in Massachusetts, historian Clark Gilpin observes, Williams "gave scant evidence of that large-minded tolerance today popularly associated with his name."[40] Rather, he developed his theory in his public debate with John Cotton in the mid- to late 1640s, a full decade after his expulsion from the Bay colony.[41] Indeed, we have few extant clues about the substance of Williams's views on liberty of conscience during his time in Massachusetts. The contemporaneous evidence is largely written by his enemies, and yet none of them point to Williams as an advocate of such liberty. Instead, they refer to him as a troublesome perfectionist Separatist, willing to disrupt political and social order for the sake of religious purity. This brief account of the genesis of Williams's theory of religious liberty reminds us that early modern toleration came about through the confluence of a great many factors, both theoretical and practical.

By contrast, from the very start of Penn's career as a public figure, he insisted on liberty of conscience. Penn's *Great Case of Liberty of Conscience* contains all the basic building blocks of his later theory. Penn was thus a published theorist of religious liberty long before setting foot in America or even envisioning his colonizing enterprise as a "holy experiment" in liberty of conscience. His careful attention to issues of conscience and liberty in both the West Jersey *Concessions* of 1677 and the drafts of Pennsylvania's founding documents circulated to colleagues during 1681 and 1682 testify to his careful thinking about the colony's potential to embody the kinds of commitments he had articulated in his writings over the past decade. The contentious early months of Penn's residency in Pennsylvania demonstrated the difficulty of putting the theory of religious liberty, so central to his political career in England, into practice in America.

THE "LIVELIE EXPERIMENT," THE "HOLY EXPERIMENT," AND THE ROAD TO RELIGIOUS LIBERTY

One important distinction between the two colonies lies in the nature of their legal foundations: Rhode Island was a chartered colony, whereas Penn's was a proprietary one. Furthermore, the 1663 royal confirmation of Rhode Island and Providence Plantations' existence as a community constituted a sovereign endorsement of an existing settlement that had liberty of conscience at its heart. In other words, the charter strengthened the legal foundation of settlements that had already been in existence for some time. Offering a compressed narrative of New England history, the charter noted that "the inhabitants of Rhode Island had transport[ed] themselves out of this kingdom of England into America, but also . . . did once again leave their desirable stations and habitations, and . . . did transplant themselves into the middest of the Indian natives . . . where, by the good providence of God . . . they have not only been preserved to admiration, but have increased and prospered."[42]

Pointing out that "in their humble address, they have freely declared, that it is much on their hearts . . . to hold forth a lively experiment, that a most flourishing civil state may stand and best be maintained . . . with a full liberty in religious concernments," the king placed his unambiguous imprimatur on this lively experiment. To be sure, the royal approval of Rhode Island's particular organization of church and state was forthcoming not simply because the king saw the wisdom of Rhode Island's arrangement of church and state but also because, "by reason of the remote distances of those places," they will "be no breach of the unity and uniformity of established in this nation." From such a distance Rhode Island's experiment would not interfere with England's establishment (in other words, what they are doing over *there* will not interfere with what we are doing over *here*).

By contrast, the prospective nature of the 1681 Pennsylvania charter stands in sharp relief next to the language of the Rhode Island charter. The Pennsylvania charter was granted to Penn himself as proprietor, pointing out that he had "humbly besought leave of us to transport an ample colony unto a certain country . . . in the parts of America not yet cultivated and planted."[43] By 1681, Penn had already articulated the basic elements of the theory that he would hold for the better part of four decades. It remained only to put the theory into practice, a task facilitated by Penn's extensive networks among dissenting religious groups across Europe and his successful promotional efforts, including the rapid translation of promotional writings into Dutch, German, and French. The charter declared the king's intention to "make, create, and constitute" Penn the proprietor of Pennsylvania and claim the allegiance of Penn and "all other proprietaries, tenants, and inhabitants that are or shall be within the territories and precincts aforesaid." Also included in the charter was the right to "divide the said country and islands into towns . . . and to erect and incorporate" towns, boroughs, and cities. Penn had never set foot in America prior to receiving his charter and in fact took more than a year to prepare for his first journey. He arrived with a plan for government already made (and soon to be amended!), which reflected the overriding importance of the proprietor and reflected Penn's vision of the principles and practices of government.[44]

The examples of Williams and Penn, Rhode Island and Pennsylvania, highlight the fact that toleration is both a theoretical ideal *and* a set of political practices. Furthermore, those practices are constantly contested and evolving, such that one era's toleration shapes the context in which future movements for broader inclusion must begin. Yet those future movements are also unique in their own right, responsive to the dynamics of their own historical particularities. It is unhelpful to say (as one historian has) that Williams's theory "augments and corrects" those of Locke and Jefferson, or that he "worked with a more complex understanding of religious commitment than did either Locke or Jefferson," since what passed for toleration in seventeenth-century New England or the Middle Atlantic colonies was not necessarily relevant to American national politics a century later. Nonetheless, liberty of conscience certainly did constitute an enduring element of social and political life.[45]

Rhode Island and Pennsylvania, then, trace two trajectories of religious liberty in early America: Rhode Island's incremental development, a "lively experiment" that was later ratified by Parliament (1644) and still later by the Crown (1663), and Pennsylvania's carefully orchestrated enterprise, animated by Penn's vision of a "holy experiment" and implemented by a variety of individuals and groups who traveled to America at his urging and sometimes even under his direction. These two very distinct trajectories point us away from straightforward narratives that suggest that religious liberty was an inevitable byproduct of religious diversity or enlightened theorizing. Moreover, a consideration of each in light of the other provides a richer account of the complex development of the theory and the practice of American religious liberty and of its origins in English politics, religion, and philosophy.[46]

NOTES

1. See Chris Beneke, *Beyond Toleration: The Religious Origins of American Pluralism* (New York: Oxford, 2006).

2. John Locke, *Letter Concerning Toleration* (London, 1689).

3. Martha C. Nussbaum, *Liberty of Conscience: In Defense of America's Tradition of Religious Equality* (Cambridge, MA: Harvard University Press, 2008), 58.

4. John M. Barry, *Roger Williams and the Creation of the American Soul: Church, State, and the Birth of Liberty* (New York: Viking, 2012), 6.

5. James Calvin Davis, *On Religious Liberty: Selections from the Works of Roger Williams* (Cambridge, MA, and London: Belknap Press of Harvard University Press, 2008), 1, 3.

6. Mabel Brailsford, *The Making of William Penn* (London and New York: Longmans, Green, 1930), ix; Mary Geiter, "William Penn and Jacobitism: A Smoking Gun?" *Historical Research* 73 (2000): 213–18; Steven C. A. Pincus, *1688: The First Modern Revolution* (New Haven, CT: Yale University Press, 2009).

7. See, for example, Jane E. Calvert, *Quaker Constitutionalism and the Political Thought of John Dickinson* (Cambridge: Cambridge University Press, 2009); Scott Sowerby, *Making Toleration: The Repealers and the Glorious Revolution* (Cambridge, MA: Harvard University Press, 2013); Andrew R. Murphy, "The Emergence of William Penn, 1688–1681," *Journal of Church and State* (forthcoming), and "The Limits and Promise of Political Theorizing: William Penn and the Founding of Pennsylvania," *History of Political Thought* 34 (2013): 639–68; and Christie N. Maloyed, "A Liberal Civil Religion: William Penn's Holy Experiment," *Journal of Church and State* 55 (2013): 669–89.

8. Each of these figures is in need of a good scholarly biography. In the absence of such a volume, for Williams consider Edmund S. Morgan, *Roger Williams: The Church and the State* (New York: Norton, 2007); Ola Elizabeth Winslow, *Master Roger Williams* (New York: Macmillan, 1957); or Barry, *Roger Williams*. On Penn, see Catherine Peare, *William Penn: A Biography* (Philadelphia: J. P. Lippincott, 1957), or Samuel Macpherson Janney, *The Life of William Penn* (Philadelphia: J. P. Lippincott, 1851).

50 *Andrew R. Murphy*

9. The phrase appears in the first of Penn's "Fundamental Constitutions of Pennsylvania" (summer 1681), an unpublished document that represented an early attempt at framing the colony's government. See Jean R. Soderlund, ed., *William Penn and the Founding of Pennsylvania: A Documentary History* (Philadelphia: University of Pennsylvania Press, 1983), 98.

10. See the accounts in Albert Cook Myers, ed., *Narratives of Early Pennsylvania, West New Jersey, and Delaware* (New York: Scribner, 1912).

11. See Adrian Davies, *The Quakers in English Society, 1655–1725* (New York: Oxford University Press, 2000).

12. Scott Sowerby, "Of Different Complexions: Religious Diversity and National Identity in James II's Toleration Campaign," *English Historical Review* 124 (2009): 41. See also Sowerby, "Forgetting the Repealers: Religious Toleration and Historical Amnesia in Later Stuart England," *Past and Present* 215 (2012): 85–123.

13. James Kendall Hosmer, ed., *Winthrop's Journal (History of New England, 1630–1649)* (New York: Scribners), 1:57.

14. See Roger Williams, "The Road to Banishment," in *The Correspondence of Roger Williams*, ed. Glenn W. LaFantasie (Hanover, NH, and London: Brown University Press, 1988), 1:12–23. Hereafter cited as *Correspondence*.

15. Williams recounts this story more than thirty years after the fact in correspondence with Major John Mason, 22 June 1670, in *Correspondence*, 2:609–10.

16. Williams, *The Bloudy Tenent of Persecution* (London, 1644).

17. William Penn to James Harrison, 25 August 1681, in Soderlund, *William Penn and the Founding of Pennsylvania*, 77.

18. "To Governor John Winthrop," 21 July 1637, in *Correspondence*, 1:106.

19. See, for example, *Correspondence*, 1:330.

20. G. B. Warden has described Rhode Island during the 1640s as facing "an acute identity crisis, which in turn entailed a fundamental crisis of authority." See G. B. Warden, "The Rhode Island Civil Code of 1647," in *Saints and Revolutionaries: Essays on Early American History*, ed. David D. Hall, John M. Murrin, and Thad W. Tate (New York: Norton, 1984), 140.

21. Roger Williams to John Winthrop, 8 March 1640/1641, in *Correspondence*, 1:215.

22. Roger Williams to John Winthrop Jr., before 29 January 1648/1649, in *Correspondence*, 1:268.

23. Sir Henry Vane to the Town of Providence, 8 February 1653/1654, in *Correspondence*, 2:389–90. "It was largely through efforts to establish an effective mastery over . . . civil disorder that Rhode Islanders hoped to justify their experiment in religious toleration," writes Theodore Dwight Bozeman, "by providing a . . . demonstration that violent chaos was not the necessary result of a departure from the established model of religious uniformity." See Bozeman, "Religious Liberty and the Problem of Order in Early Rhode Island," *New England Quarterly* 45 (1972): 45, 57.

24. "To Jasper Batt," 5 February 1683, in *The Papers of William Penn*, ed. Richard S. Dunn and Mary Maples Dunn (Philadelphia: University of Pennsylvania Press, 1981–1987), 2:347.

25. I pass over the details of the events of the schism. For a collection of the primary documents, see J. William Frost, ed., *The Keithian Controversy in Early Pennsylvania* (Norwood, PA: Norwood Editions, 1980), and Andrew R. Murphy, "Persecuting Quakers? The Politics of Toleration in Early Pennsylvania," in *The First Prejudice: Religious Tolerance and Religious Intolerance in the Making of America*, ed. Chris Beneke and Christopher S. Grenda (Philadelphia: University of Pennsylvania Press, 2010).

26. Samuel Jennings, *The State of the Case, briefly but impartially given* (London, 1694), 45.

27. See George Keith, *New England's Spirit of Persecution transmitted to Pennsylvania, and the pretended Quaker found persecuting the true Christian-Quaker in the tryal of Peter Boss, George Keith, Thomas Budd, and William Bradford, at the sessions held at Philadelphia the nineth, tenth and twelfth days of December, 1692: giving an account of the most arbitrary procedure of that court* (New York: W. Bradford, 1693).

28. William Penn to Friends in Pennsylvania, 11 December 1693, in Dunn and Dunn, *Papers of William Penn*, 3:383.

29. See Davis, *On Religious Liberty*, 36–38. Elsewhere, Teresa Bejan focuses on Williams's use of "civility" to describe a central tolerationist aspiration; see Bejan, "'The Bond of Civility': Roger Williams on Toleration and Its Limits," *History of European Ideas* 37 (2011): 409–20. Bejan points out that, for Williams, civility represented "a kind of minimal, sufficient condition qualifying one for toleration" (410). See also Bejan's chapter in this volume.

30. See Joseph J. Casino, "Anti-Popery in Colonial Pennsylvania," *Pennsylvania Magazine of History and Biography* 105 (1981): 279–309. Scott Sowerby has written that "with his advocacy of a carefully limited toleration and his endorsement of principles that could be used to exclude Catholics from toleration, John Locke chose not to challenge forces that the repealers met head-on" (*Making Toleration*, 259). Sowerby is referring to supporters of James II's tolerationist program, of whom Penn was one of the best known.

31. Williams, *Bloudy Tenent*, chap. 132.

32. The significance of the English Baptists and their influence on the American tradition via Williams and Isaac Backus forms a major theme of Nicholas P. Miller's *The Religious Roots of the First Amendment: Dissenting Protestants and the Separation of Church and State* (New York: Oxford University Press, 2012).

33. Williams, *Bloudy Tenent*, 3.

34. Williams, *Bloudy Tenent*, 184.

35. Roger Williams to the Town of Providence, c. January 1654/1655, in *Correspondence*, 2:423–24. The ship of state metaphor is not, of course, unique to Williams; it appears in book 6 of Plato's *Republic*.

36. Williams, *Bloudy Tenent*, 41, 63. For the orthodox notion of conscience see Thomas Aquinas, *The Disputed Questions on Truth*, and question 79 of his *Summa Theologica*. For surveys of the complexities of this topic, see J. H. Hyslop, "Conscience," in *The Encyclopedia of Religion and Ethics*, vol. 4, ed. James Hastings (New York: Charles Scribner's Sons, 1908); Douglas Langston, *Conscience and Other Virtues* (University Park: Pennsylvania State University Press, 2001); Timothy C. Potts, "Conscience," in *The Cambridge History of Later Medieval Philosophy*, ed. Norman Kretzmann, Anthony Kenny, and Jan Pinborg (Cambridge: Cambridge University Press, 1982).

37. See my introduction to *The Political Writings of William Penn* (Indianapolis, IN: Liberty Fund, 2002).

38. William Penn, *The Guide Mistaken, and Temporizing Rebuked* (London, 1668), 62–63.

39. William Penn, *The Great Case of Liberty of Conscience* (London, 1670), 23.

40. W. Clark Gilpin, *The Millenarian Piety of Roger Williams* (Chicago: University of Chicago Press, 1979), 16.

41. Williams's theory appears not only in his exchange of letters with Cotton, which were published, but also in the even longer exchange that began with Williams's *The Bloudy Tenent of Persecution* and continued in Cotton's response—*The Bloudy Tenent Washed and Made White in the Blood of the Lamb*—which in turn motivated Williams to respond with *The Bloudy Tenent Yet more Bloudy, by Mr. Cottons attempt to wash it in the blood of the Lambe* (to which, we can all be thankful, Cotton declined to respond).

42. Royal charter of 15 July 1663. Even the parliamentary patent, which preceded the royal one by two decades, made reference to the preexisting nature of the settlements, citing the "well-affected English inhabitants" who "have adventured to make a nearer neighborhood and society with the great body of the Narragansetts," and it expressed Parliament's desire "to encourage the good beginnings of the said planters" (parliamentary charter of 14 March 1643/1644).

43. Charter for the Province of Pennsylvania, 4 March 1681, in Soderlund, *William Penn and the Founding of Pennsylvania*, 41–50.

44. See the preface to William Penn, *The Frame of Government . . . of Pennsylvania* (London, 1682).

45. Davis, *On Religious Liberty*, 41, 45.

46. To be comprehensive, of course, one would also need to link the story of Pennsylvania with its Dutch influences. On this, see Jonathon Scott, *Algernon Sidney and the Restoration Crisis, 1677–1683* (New York: Cambridge University Press, 1991), 134–35.

Chapter Three

Toleration and Tolerance in Early Modern England

Scott Sowerby

The words *toleration* and *tolerance* have often been used interchangeably, but some historians have begun to apply them differently. *Toleration* is now commonly used to refer to legal rules and government policies, while *tolerance* refers to interpersonal attitudes or social practices exercised informally on a day-to-day level.[1] Though not every historian has adopted this shorthand, many employ similar concepts. One historian has distinguished between intellectual histories focused on "questions of religious liberty" and a more anthropological approach that examines "the tolerance of practical rationality" as exercised by peoples of different faiths living closely together. Another scholar, reaching for a similar distinction, contrasted "the evolving idea of tolerance developed by the intellectuals" with "the practical philosophy of tolerance" as expressed by those who "actually experienced religious diversity at firsthand."[2] Although the precise terminology remains unsettled, the driving impulse of historians in recent years has been to draw a distinction between two kinds of *tolerantia*, one embodied in philosophical texts and codes of law and another in social norms and behaviors.

The distinction between these two modes of tolerance has become especially important as the attention of historians has shifted from legal codes to social ones. This change in focus has decisively recast the master narrative of the subject, subverting an older Whiggish narrative of progress in which post-Reformation Europe gradually became more enlightened as religious toleration won out over the forces of intolerance. Histories of tolerance as a social practice have often charted a more cyclical course, emphasizing that both tolerance and intolerance existed side by side in the medieval, early modern, and modern periods.[3] In these new histories, modernity has no special claim on tolerance, in part because of the difficulties involved in measuring the amount of tolerance in any given society. As many scholars have pointed out, there is no such thing as perfect religious toleration; there are only multiple ways of managing religious diversity, each uniquely accommodating to certain activities and inimical to others.[4] The impossibility of perfect toleration can be seen in the classic dilemma of how the tolerant should approach the intolerant. To challenge intolerance is to be intolerant of it, but to tolerate intolerance is to allow it to thrive. Who, then, is more tolerant: the one who confronts intolerance or the one who permits it?

The recent emphasis of historians on social practices rather than legal codes has meant that comparatively few scholars have explored the relationship between the two phenomena, with most preferring to emphasize their separate trajectories. Several historians have noted that the codification of toleration in law was not necessarily preceded by any widespread reduction in intolerant attitudes, given that governments might choose to enact tolerationist legal codes for pragmatic or economic reasons. Conversely, as other historians have noted, informal tolerance could subsist without legal codification, given that local populations regularly resisted intolerant edicts imposed from above.[5] This interpretive tendency has at times had the unfortunate effect of divorcing tolerance and toleration entirely. But the interactions between these twin phenomena are surely worth attending to, especially in societies where the laws relating to religious diversity were undergoing rapid changes.[6]

One such society was England in the period from the accession of King James II in 1685 to the end of the Stuart dynasty in 1714. In 1689, shortly after the revolution that dethroned James and elevated William and Mary, the English Parliament passed a bill, commonly known as the Act of Toleration, that suspended penalties on most Protestant nonconformists. The act was limited in scope, not extending to non-Christians, Roman Catholics, or even non-Trinitarian Protestants such as the Socinians. (Jews were tolerated in England at the time under a separate series of royal orders permitting their worship.)[7] But the act did permit freedom of worship to the four largest Protestant nonconformist groups: the Presbyterians, Congregationalists, Baptists, and Quakers.

In the quarter century before the accession of James II, England had been ruled by James's older brother, Charles II, who, while in many ways personally tolerant, had signed into law a series of parliamentary acts designed to buttress the power of the established church. These included the Corporation Act of 1661, which restricted the ability of nonconformists to hold public office in town governments; the Test Act of 1673, which required all office holders under the Crown to take the Anglican sacrament and renounce the Catholic doctrine of transubstantiation; and the Test Act of 1678, which barred Catholics from serving in Parliament. The Toleration Act of 1689, while offering freedom of worship to most of the Protestant nonconformists, did not repeal or suspend the Test and Corporation Acts; as a result, only Anglicans had full political rights after 1689. The bill commonly known as the "Act of Toleration" did not even include the word *toleration* anywhere in its text. In the weeks before and after its passage, it was sometimes referred to as the "Toleration Act," but it was also sometimes called the "Bill of Indulgence." One diarist, reflecting the confusion, called it "the Bill of Indulgence, Ease, or Toleration." Its official title was "An Act for Exempting their Majesties Protestant Subjects, Dissenting from the Church of England, from the Penalties of Certain Laws."[8] The absence of the word *toleration* from the title was hardly an oversight. As one Whig member of Parliament explained, with reference to the committee of the House of Commons that had drafted the legislation, "the Committee, though it were for an Indulgence, were for no Toleration."[9]

The Act of Toleration was thus an expression of both tolerance and intolerance. Its limits reflected the prejudice of many members of Parliament against Protestant nonconformists, who gained freedom of worship but not political equality. The act evinced an even more robust prejudice against Catholics, who were excluded from its terms entirely. James II had been overthrown in the so-called Glorious Revolution of 1688–1689 in part because he was Catholic, and the revolutionary Parliament proceeded to restrict Catholic possession of arms.[10] The enactment of a limited form of toleration after the revolution was a strategic concession by leading Anglicans, many of whom had come to believe that toleration was politically necessary even if it was not desirable. King James had spent much of his short reign offering toleration to Protestant nonconformists, and he continued to make those offers during his exile in France and Ireland as he amassed an army in an effort to retake his throne.[11] Many nonconformists had joined the king's toleration campaign in 1687 and 1688. In 1689, leading Anglicans feared that the Quakers and Baptists might join with Catholics again and become supporters of the exiled king. As the Whig MP Sir Henry Capel put it in the parliamentary debate over the Toleration Act, "I would not give them [the nonconformists] occasion to throw themselves out of the Protestant interest."[12] The need for a palliative concession to mollify the nonconformists was felt across the political spectrum. Tories joined with Whigs in passing an act that was designed to strengthen the Protestant interest by incorporating the nonconformists within it.

If the Act of Toleration had been passed into law by the Whig Party alone, then it would be easier to see it as the direct outcome of enlightened attitudes. The Whigs, from the origins of their party in the late 1670s, had championed greater liberty for Protestant nonconformists. A bill to relax the laws penalizing nonconformity had nearly passed the Whig-dominated second Exclusion Parliament, though it was lost when Charles II abruptly prorogued the session in 1681.[13] The dissolution of the 1681 Parliament was followed by a period known as the "Tory reaction," which saw the most savage repression of nonconformists in the entire seventeenth century.[14] Tories were still persecuting nonconformists at the accession of James II in 1685 while showing no signs of relinquishing their prejudices, which made their willingness to grant toleration four years later highly remarkable.

The legislative history of the Toleration Act gives some inkling as to why the Tories changed tack. Neither the Whigs nor the Tories had complete dominance of the House of Commons in 1689, as the existence of a shifting group of "court Tories" and Whig churchmen meant that the Whigs could pass most bills related to civil government while the Tories could block most bills related to church government.[15] On March 21, one observer wrote, "The Church of Eng[land] has a Majority in both Houses." A week later, another observer, referring to the recent trials of party strength in the House of Commons, noted that "of late there have been very fair Tryals, and the C[hurch] of E[ngland] men have always had the better [of them]." Edward Harley wrote on March 26, "Toryism is now in the ascendant," adding a few days later, "The Tories in Parliament are still rampant."[16] The party clashes of March 1689 were related in part to the possibility of relaxing the liturgy of the Church of England to enable some of the Presbyterians to rejoin it. They were also related to a proposal by King William—briefly floated and then hastily abandoned in the teeth of parliamentary opposition—that would have permitted Protestant nonconformists to hold public office. The recent parliamentary votes, wrote Lord Yester on March 26, had shown "how strong the Church party is in both [houses of Parliament], and that yett too much remains of theire animositye against the dissenters."[17]

When the Act of Toleration passed the House of Commons a few weeks later on May 17, it was part of a legislative maneuver. The Tories agreed to back toleration while simultaneously foisting any potential liturgical changes onto an elected convocation of clergy of the Church of England, to which Parliament would delegate the authority to determine which church rules should be loosened to accommodate the scruples of some of the nonconformists. It is unclear whether a compromise to advance the toleration bill while delaying church reform was explicitly struck by the Tories with their Whig counterparts, but the sequence of events suggests that this was the case. It was widely anticipated that a convocation of Anglican clergy would refuse to broaden the church, and the proposals for comprehension were duly quashed when the body met in the autumn.[18] The bulk of the Tories, then, should not be seen as eagerly embracing toleration, but rather as being dragged by events into accepting a concession they would have preferred to avoid. They might have blocked the toleration bill, just as they blocked the church reform bill, had England's geopolitical situation been more secure and had James II not been amassing an army with French support across the channel. None of this is to deny that more tolerant attitudes toward Presbyterians and Congregationalists helped to ease the passage of the Act of Toleration, especially among members of the Whig Party who had always been more favorably inclined toward religious dissent. But the more decisive factor, given the controlling influence of the Tories, was the fear of a breach between Anglicans and nonconformists at a time when both groups were needed to defend England from invasion.

The modest Toleration Act of 1689 was designed to prevent more radical change. King James, with his "Declaration for Liberty of Conscience" of 1687, had decreed an unbounded toleration that extended, in theory, to all faiths, both Christian and non-Christian, and that included the right to serve in government office. [19] If the exiled king returned to the throne, his declaration would likely return with him, unless he canceled it, which he had not done even in the autumn of 1688 when threatened with a Dutch invasion and a popular uprising. The English Parliament in 1689 enacted a carefully measured grant of toleration that only suspended the penal laws rather than repealing them permanently and that did not include the right to serve in public office. Although the act was limited, it still ceded enough to the nonconformists to solidify their loyalty to the new regime of William and Mary in the midst of Jacobite counterrevolution. In that sense, it achieved what its makers had intended.

The genesis of the Act of Toleration suggests that toleration and tolerance did not necessarily proceed in lockstep in late Stuart England. Legislated toleration could be derived as much from reasons of state and political expediency as from a principled commitment to religious liberty. The product of toleration, moreover, was not necessarily widespread tolerance. On the contrary, legislated toleration might easily produce a backlash by an aggrieved majority outside Parliament that found its privileges had been eroded by changes in law. This backlash was a prominent feature of English politics in the quarter century after the passage of the Toleration Act.

Many Anglicans feared the effects of religious toleration on England's national church. Toleration was believed to promote not only nonconformity but also irreligion. As the Tory clergyman Humphrey Prideaux wrote in 1692, "The Act of Toleration hath almost undon[e] us, not in increaseing the number of dissenters but of wicked and profane persons; for it is now difficult almost to get any to church, all pleadeing the license [of the act], although they make use of it only for the alehouse." Seven years later, in 1699, Prideaux was still beating the drums of discontent, writing that the Toleration Act would "soon extinguish all religion among us, since it is now claimed by a vast number of people . . . of noe religion at all." He called the act the "mother of confusion" and wrote that it had "made a greater step towards driveing Christianity out of this realme then any that hath been made since it came into it; for it tolerates men that are noe Christians, I mean the Quakers."[20]

Other Tories made similar complaints, and in 1709 they found a champion to rally around. Dr. Henry Sacheverell was a Tory clergyman who published in that year a sermon lambasting the ill effects of toleration and proclaiming that the Church of England was in danger from the combined forces of nonconformists, skeptics, and Catholics. His work was titled *The Perils of False Brethren, Both in Church, and State*. It proved a publishing sensation, selling at least fifty thousand and perhaps as many as one hundred thousand copies. The Whig Party controlled both houses of Parliament at the time and leading Whigs elected to prosecute the doctor for high crimes and misdemeanors. The House of Lords found him guilty by a vote of 69–52, though the punishment they prescribed was quite lenient, with the doctor merely banned from preaching for three years.[21]

More significant than the trial itself was the public reaction to it. The Tories rallied behind Sacheverell. Large crowds of partisans escorted the doctor to and from the courtroom on each of the ten days of the trial. On the evening of the third day, a pro-Sacheverell crowd decided to take action against Protestant nonconformists, who had been castigated in the doctor's sermon for their purported attempts to undermine the doctrines and privileges of the Church of England. Five nonconformist meetinghouses in London had their interior contents stripped and burned in bonfires. Some of the rioters contemplated attacking the Whig-dominated Bank of England, though in the end they did not succeed in pushing that far into the city. A paper distributed among the crowd read, "Down with the Bank of England and the Meeting-Houses; and God damn the Presbyterians and all that support them." The rioters were eventually dispersed by mounted troops, but the public mood remained unsettled as the doctor's fate was being debated in the House of Lords. The guilty verdict was expected, but the light punishment was greeted with joy by Tories across England and Wales. Partisan crowds celebrating the doctor's supposed triumph threatened the homes and churches of nonconformists in several provincial towns, including Sherborne, Wrexham, and Gainsborough. Sacheverell eagerly seized the moment, arranging a public progress through the English Midlands, where he was greeted by thousands of cheering followers. A few months later, when new parliamentary elections were held, the Tories gained control of the House of Commons in a landslide.[22]

The Tories used their new majority to pass an act designed to limit the political power of nonconformists: the Occasional Conformity Act. Their aim was to close a loophole in the Test Act of 1673. Under the terms of that act, those who wished to serve in public office had to obtain a certificate indicating that they had taken the sacrament in the Church of England. Many moderate nonconformists, especially Presbyterians, were willing to take the

Anglican sacrament once, obtain the certificate, and return to their accustomed house of worship thereafter. The new act of 1711 aimed to halt this practice, forbidding office holders from attending a nonconformist assembly after having taken the Anglican sacrament in order to qualify for their post; violators would be fined forty pounds, ejected from office, and barred from any future government service. [23] The act, with its obvious anti-nonconformist animus, was repealed by a subsequent Whig government in 1719.

The Tory backlash against the newfound freedom of nonconformists endured for at least a quarter century. Over time, it diminished. It is difficult to date this shift precisely, but by the 1730s, many Tories seem to have made their peace with the Act of Toleration. In 1736, the Tory MP Sir John St Aubyn described the "laws of toleration" as part of the "constitution" of England: "they protect, as they certainly ought, the established religion of our country, and, at the same time, allow a separate right in religious worship." [24] In 1753, the Tory bishop of Gloucester preached a sermon in which he praised the Act of Toleration as "a wise Provision" that was "just and reasonable." He said that he wished it had been enacted sooner, for then it would have "prevented many Disturbances" (presumably meaning the civil wars of the 1640s). [25]

By the mid-eighteenth century, the Act of Toleration had largely ceased to be controversial. It may have helped that the growth of membership in the four leading nonconformist denominations—the Quakers, Baptists, Congregationalists, and Presbyterians—appears to have slowed over time. Although the number of nonconformists grew moderately from 1689 to the end of the Stuart era in 1714, with an increase of perhaps 25 percent, it is far from clear whether that rate of growth was maintained into the following decades. By the 1720s, the Quakers were closing meetings, and by the 1730s, reports of a decline in dissenting numbers were widespread. [26] It was easier to fear a Quaker takeover in the 1650s and 1660s, when their numbers were increasing rapidly, than it was seventy years later, when their numbers were stable or diminishing. A generational turnover also left its mark on political debates. By 1730, the Toleration Act no longer represented a dramatic change; it had been the status quo for forty years and the radical move would have been to overturn it rather than to retain it. A new generation of Tory Anglicans found new things to fear, switching their attention from the Quakers and Baptists to a different set of bugbears, including Socinians, deists, and freethinkers. The Tories may have come to accept the Quakers in part because they had found something to dislike more.

Catholics, however, remained anathema. The same Tory bishop of Gloucester who praised the Act of Toleration in 1753 said that one of its chief benefits was that it had allowed different sorts of Protestants to unite against a common foe. The true enemy, in his view, was the "Persecuting Spirit of Popery" that was "destructive of all true Religion, and even of our common

Humanity."[27] When Parliament eventually provided some legislative relief for Catholics in 1778, popular outrage led to the Gordon Riots, which brought the deaths of nearly three hundred people in London.[28] The Act of Toleration may have promoted tolerant attitudes toward Quakers and Baptists in England, but it did nothing for Catholics except to ratify their continued exclusion.

The relationship between legal toleration and social tolerance was a vexed one. The English example suggests that growing tolerance for excluded groups, such as that exhibited by the Whigs toward Protestant nonconformists, could help to smooth the way for legislated toleration of those groups, but that it might not be sufficient on its own to overcome the resistance of privileged sections of society. Legislated toleration, however, could lead to a sharp backlash against newly enfranchised groups, though time might serve to soften that hostility. Moreover, the expansion of legal protections to some groups (such as nonconformists) could also be a strategy aimed at maintaining the exclusion of others (such as Catholics).

The history of toleration is full of unexpected conjunctures. Toleration is not necessarily created by tolerance; it can also, in certain situations, be created by intolerance. Offering toleration to some groups can serve as a means of denying it to others. Toleration can result from a bargain struck to purchase the assent of a formerly troublesome group; it is not necessarily the product of widespread charitable sentiments toward that group. At times it may take an external shock, such as an armed invasion or the threat of one, to push together groups that had previously been at loggerheads with each other.

The results of these contingent alliances, however, can be surprisingly enduring. It would have been easy to leave the Quakers out of the Toleration Act in 1689, given that many Anglicans at the time saw the Quakers as barely Christian.[29] But once the Quakers were granted freedom of worship under law, it became difficult to restrict their meetings. Legal traditions have their own influence on society, and path dependency suggests that those groups protected by the status quo will be likely to maintain their protections in the absence of a concerted revolution designed to overthrow existing legal norms. The fear of many Tories immediately after the Glorious Revolution was that toleration, once granted, could not easily be rescinded; this is why some Tories argued in the House of Commons in 1689 for a sunset clause whereby toleration would lapse automatically after seven years unless a positive vote was taken by Parliament to extend it.[30] These fears proved to be prescient. The Act of Toleration was never seriously threatened in subsequent parliaments, and fifty years later, it was hard to find anyone, even in the Tory Party, who would argue that it should not endure forever.

NOTES

1. For somewhat varying definitions of the difference between *toleration* and *tolerance*, see Andrew R. Murphy, "Tolerance, Toleration, and the Liberal Tradition," *Polity* 29 (1997): 595–602; Ned C. Landsman, "Roots, Routes, and Rootedness: Diversity, Migration, and Toleration in Mid-Atlantic Pluralism," *Early American Studies* 2 (2004): 273; Stuart B. Schwartz, *All Can Be Saved: Religious Tolerance and Salvation in the Iberian Atlantic World* (New Haven, CT: Yale University Press, 2008), 6; Christopher Grasso, "The Boundaries of Toleration and Tolerance: Religious Infidelity in the Early American Republic," in *The First Prejudice: Religious Tolerance and Intolerance in Early America*, ed. Chris Beneke and Christopher S. Grenda (Philadelphia: University of Pennsylvania Press, 2011), 287. Benjamin Kaplan reverses the terms, describing *tolerance* as an intellectual concept or governing policy and *toleration* as a social practice of coexistence: see Kaplan, *Divided by Faith: Religious Conflict and the Practice of Toleration in Early Modern Europe* (Cambridge, MA: Belknap Press of Harvard University Press, 2007), 8–11. For an astute overview by an early modern historian who rejects as unhelpful the emerging distinction between *toleration* and *tolerance*, see Evan Haefeli, "Toleration," *Religion Compass* 4 (2010): 253–59.

2. Bob Scribner, "Preconditions of Tolerance and Intolerance in Sixteenth-Century Germany," in *Tolerance and Intolerance in the European Reformation*, ed. Ole Peter Grell and Bob Scribner (Cambridge: Cambridge University Press, 1996), 32–33, 38; C. Scott Dixon, "Introduction: Living with Religious Diversity in Early-Modern Europe," in *Living with Religious Diversity in Early-Modern Europe*, ed. C. Scott Dixon, Dagmar Freist, and Mark Greengrass (Farnham, UK, and Burlington, VT: Ashgate, 2009), 9.

3. Alexandra Walsham, *Charitable Hatred: Tolerance and Intolerance in England, 1500–1700* (Manchester, UK: Manchester University Press, 2006), 5–13, 39, 230–32, 287, 300–301; Kaplan, *Divided by Faith*, 2–8, 352–56; Schwartz, *All Can Be Saved*, 7; Scribner, "Preconditions of Tolerance," 33–34, 43.

4. Michael Walzer, *On Toleration* (New Haven, CT: Yale University Press, 1997), 2–5; John Christian Laursen and Cary J. Nederman, "General Introduction: Political and Historical Myths in the Toleration Literature," in *Beyond the Persecution Society: Religious Toleration before the Enlightenment*, ed. John Christian Laursen and Cary J. Nederman (Philadelphia: University of Pennsylvania Press, 1998), 1, 4, 8; Peter van Rooden, "Jews and Religious Toleration in the Dutch Republic," in *Calvinism and Religious Toleration in the Dutch Golden Age*, ed. R. Po-Chia Hsia and Hank van Nierop (Cambridge: Cambridge University Press, 2002), 147; Evan Haefeli, *New Netherland and the Dutch Origins of American Religious Liberty* (Philadelphia: University of Pennsylvania Press, 2012), 6–9, 12–15, 281.

5. Andrew R. Murphy, *Conscience and Community: Revisiting Toleration and Religious Dissent in Early Modern England and America* (University Park: Pennsylvania State University Press, 2001), xiii; Karen Barkey, *Empire of Difference: The Ottomans in Comparative Perspective* (Cambridge: Cambridge University Press, 2008), 110; Schwartz, *All Can Be Saved*, 5; Scribner, "Preconditions of Tolerance," 32, 35–39, 46–47; Herbert Butterfield, "Toleration in Early Modern Times," *Journal of the History of Ideas* 38 (1977): 573, 584.

6. For an exception to this tendency, see Chris Beneke's work on the relationship between legal toleration and cultural pluralism in eighteenth-century America, in his *Beyond Toleration: The Religious Origins of American Pluralism* (Oxford: Oxford University Press, 2006).

7. On the royal orders tolerating Judaism from 1664 onward, see Todd M. Endelman, *The Jews of Britain, 1656 to 2000* (Berkeley: University of California Press, 2002), 28–29; Lucien Wolf, "The First Stage of Anglo-Jewish Emancipation," in *Essays in Jewish History*, ed. Cecil Roth (London: Jewish Historical Society of England, 1934), 117–43; David S. Katz, "The Jews of England and 1688," in *From Persecution to Toleration: The Glorious Revolution and Religion in England*, ed. Ole Peter Grell, Jonathan I. Israel, and Nicholas Tyacke (Oxford: Clarendon Press, 1991), 217–49.

8. 1 Gul. & M., sess. 1, cap. 18; *The Statutes at Large from the First Year of King James the First to the Tenth Year of the Reign of King William the Third*, new ed. (London, 1770), 424. For "Toleration Act," see Humphrey Humphreys to Thomas Mostyn, 6 June 1689, University of Wales Bangor, Mostyn Additional MSS, no. 9071/11; for "Bill of Indulgence," see

newsletter of 6 April 1689, British Library (hereafter BL), Add. MS 72596, fol. 96v; for the diarist, see Mark Goldie, John Spurr, Tim Harris, Stephen Taylor, Mark Knights, and Jason McElligott, eds., *The Entring Book of Roger Morrice, 1677–1691*, 7 vols. (Woodbridge, UK: Boydell Press in association with the Parliamentary Yearbook Trust, 2007–2009), 5:118. The mixed nomenclature continued into the next decade. A search of *Early English Books Online* for the 1690s turns up eighteen pamphlets referring to the "Act of Toleration," twelve referring to the "Act of Indulgence," and four that used both names for the act.

9. Anchitell Grey, *Debates of the House of Commons, from the Year 1667 to the Year 1694*, 10 vols. (London, 1763), 9:261.

10. 1 Gul. & M., sess. 1, cap. 15; *The Statutes at Large, from the First Year of K. William and Q. Mary, to the Eighth Year of K. William III* (London, 1764), 15–18.

11. James II, *By the King, a Proclamation* (Dublin, 1689; Wing J269), 2; *Historical Manuscripts Commission, Ormonde*, n.s., 8:391–92; Gilbert Burnet, *Bishop Burnet's History of His Own Time*, ed. M. J. Routh, 2nd ed., 6 vols. (Oxford, 1833), 4:21.

12. Grey, *Debates*, 9:261; for contemporary concerns about a potential alliance between the Quakers and the exiled King James, see [Robert Harley] to Sir Edward Harley, 19 April 1689, BL, Add. MS 70014, fol. 219; Isaac Sadly to Joseph Knight, 2 July 1689, Library of the Society of Friends, London, portfolio 15.104.

13. H. Horwitz, "Protestant Reconciliation in the Exclusion Crisis," *Journal of Ecclesiastical History* 14 (1964): 209–14.

14. Grant Tapsell, *The Personal Rule of Charles II, 1681–85* (Woodbridge, UK: Boydell Press, 2007), 64–91.

15. On the composition of the 1689 Parliament, see Basil Duke Henning, ed., *The House of Commons, 1660–1690*, 3 vols. (London: Published for the History of Parliament Trust by Secker and Warburg, 1983), 1:47.

16. [Arthur Maynwaring] to James Harrington, 21 March 1689, BL, Add. MS 36707, fol. 62; James Newton to Arthur Charlett, 28 March 1689, Bodleian Library, MS Ballard 22, fol. 48; *Historical Manuscripts Commission, Portland*, 3:435–36.

17. Lord Yester to Earl of Tweeddale, 26 March 1689, National Library of Scotland, MS 14404, fol. 32; see also Henry Horwitz, *Revolution Politicks: The Career of Daniel Finch, Second Earl of Nottingham, 1647–1730* (Cambridge: Cambridge University Press, 1968), 91; Henry Horwitz, *Parliament, Policy and Politics in the Reign of William III* (Newark: University of Delaware Press, 1977), 22.

18. Horwitz, *Revolution Politicks*, 93; Horwitz, *Parliament, Policy and Politics*, 25–26; G. V. Bennett, "King William III and the Episcopate," in *Essays in Modern English Church History, in Memory of Norman Sykes*, ed. G. V. Bennett and J. D. Walsh (New York: Oxford University Press, 1966), 112–20; John Spurr, "The Church of England, Comprehension and the Toleration Act of 1689," *English Historical Review* 104 (1989): 938–39; Scott Sowerby, *Making Toleration: The Repealers and the Glorious Revolution* (Cambridge, MA: Harvard University Press, 2013), 250–54; Andrew Browning, ed., *Memoirs of Sir John Reresby: The Complete Text and a Selection from His Letters*, rev. Mary K. Geiter and W. A. Speck (London: Offices of the Royal Historical Society, 1991), 572.

19. Sowerby, *Making Toleration*, 171.

20. Edward Maunde Thompson, ed., *Letters of Humphrey Prideaux Sometime Dean of Norwich to John Ellis*, Camden Society, n.s. (Westminster, 1875), 15:154; *Historical Manuscripts Commission, Fifth Report*, 377.

21. Henry Sacheverell, *The Perils of False Brethren, Both in Church, and State* (London, 1709, STC N20069), 3, 9, 13, 19, 30; Geoffrey Holmes, *The Trial of Doctor Sacheverell* (London: Eyre Methuen, 1973), 74–75, 145; Brian Cowan, ed., *The State Trial of Doctor Henry Sacheverell* (Malden, MA: Wiley-Blackwell for the Parliamentary Historical Yearbook Trust, 2012), 1, 39.

22. Holmes, *Sacheverell*, 128, 156–57, 161–74, 234–35, 243–48; Geoffrey Holmes, "The Sacheverell Riots: The Crowd and the Church in Early Eighteenth-Century London," *Past and Present*, no. 72 (August 1976): 62–65. The contents of a sixth nonconformist meetinghouse in London were ripped out but not yet burned by the time the queen's troops arrived to disperse the pro-Sacheverell crowd.

23. 10 Anne, cap. 6; *The Statutes of the Realm Printed by Command of his Majesty King George the Third*, 9 vols. (London, 1810–1822), 9:551–53.

24. *Cobbett's Parliamentary History of England from the Norman Conquest, in 1066, to the Year 1803*, 36 vols. (London, 1806–1820), 9:1162.

25. James Johnson, *A Sermon Preach'd before the Lords Spiritual and Temporal, in the Abby Church, at Westminster* (London, 1753), 14; see also Stephen Taylor, "Sir Robert Walpole, the Church of England, and the Quakers Tithe Bill of 1736," *Historical Journal* 28 (1985): 62; Stephen Taylor, "Plus ça Change . . . ? New Perspectives on the Revolution of 1688," *Historical Journal* 37 (1994): 465; J. C. D. Clark, *English Society, 1660–1832*, 2nd ed. (Cambridge: Cambridge University Press, 2000), 256, 273–74; Pasi Ihalainen, *Protestant Nations Redefined: Changing Perceptions of National Identity in the Rhetoric of the English, Dutch and Swedish Public Churches, 1685–1772* (Leiden: Brill, 2005), 501–3.

26. Holmes, *Sacheverell*, 37; E. D. Bebb, *Nonconformity and Social and Economic Life, 1660–1800* (London: Epworth Press, 1935), 35–41, 45, 174–75; Michael R. Watts, *The Dissenters*, vol. 1, *From the Reformation to the French Revolution* (Oxford: Clarendon Press, 1978), 384–93, 509; John Stephenson Rowntree, *Quakerism, Past and Present: Being an Inquiry into the Causes of Its Decline in Great Britain and Ireland* (London, 1859), 71–82; William C. Braithwaite, *The Second Period of Quakerism* (London: Macmillan, 1919), 458–59; Richard T. Vann and David Eversley, *Friends in Life and Death: The British and Irish Quakers in the Demographic Transition* (Cambridge: Cambridge University Press, 1992), 67–68.

27. Johnson, *Sermon Preach'd*, 14.

28. George F. E. Rudé, "The Gordon Riots: A Study of the Rioters and Their Victims," *Transactions of the Royal Historical Society*, 5th ser., 6 (1956): 99; Nicholas Rogers, "The Gordon Riots Revisited," *Historical Papers/Communications Historiques* 23 (1988): 16–34; John Seed, "'The Fall of Romish Babylon Anticipated': Plebeian Dissenters and Anti-Popery in the Gordon Riots," in *The Gordon Riots: Politics, Culture, and Insurrection in Late Eighteenth-Century Britain*, ed. Ian Haywood and John Seed (Cambridge: Cambridge University Press, 2012), 69–92.

29. For John Evelyn's proposal in autumn 1688 that toleration should be accorded to all nonconformists except for "Socinians, Independents, and Quakers," see letter of John Evelyn, November 1688, BL, Add. MS 78299, fol. 53. When a largely Tory parliament in Westminster passed an act of toleration for Scotland in 1712, the Quakers, along with the Catholics, were not included in its terms. See Alasdair Raffe, *The Culture of Controversy: Religious Arguments in Scotland, 1660–1714* (Woodbridge, UK: Boydell Press, 2012), 30, 89.

30. Grey, *Debates*, 9:260–62.

Chapter Four

"When the Word of the Lord Runs Freely"

Roger Williams and Evangelical Toleration

Teresa M. Bejan

The 1663 charter that confirmed the small, coastal territory purchased by Roger Williams from the Narragansett Indians as "the English Colony of Rhode Island and Providence Plantations" has long been hailed as a high point in the history of religious toleration.[1] The hypothesis to be tested in this "livelie experiment"—that a society might survive, even flourish, while granting its members "full liberty in religious concernments"—at the time represented the cutting edge of tolerationist theory and practice. Citizens of Rhode Island were not simply permitted to dissent from a state-supported church or to hold heterodox opinions in private. Rather, the charter granted colonists an unprecedented "free exercise and enjoyment of all their civil and religious rights" regardless of religion, in a society with no established church at all.[2]

The success of the experiment in "Rogues Island" was far from guaranteed. Neighbors complained that its policy of toleration had made the colony a "receptacle for all sorts of riff-raff," "the sewers (*latrina*) of New England."[3] Yet, despite these uncertain beginnings, generations of scholars have pointed to Rhode Island and its founder, Roger Williams, as pioneers in a distinctively American tradition of liberalism with the principle of toleration at its core.[4] Today, Williams's reputation as the "First Founder" has never been more secure.[5] One recent monograph credits him with nothing less than "the creation of the American soul," while Martha Nussbaum has elevated Williams as an exemplar of "America's tradition of religious equality," a figure whose life and works embody ideas of fairness and respect that "continue to be central to the best work in recent political philosophy in the Western tradition."[6]

While Williams offers the rare example of a political thinker who successfully put his theories into practice, for modern-day revivers he also offers something more: an inclusive, proto-multicultural vision of a tolerating society ahead of its time and far beyond that of other early modern thinkers. John Locke's seminal *Letter Concerning Toleration* (1689) excluded Catholics and atheists from toleration in a way reminiscent of medieval *tolerantia*— a limited policy of permission toward "acknowledged evils" like sewage, prostitutes, and Jews. By contrast, Williams's 1644 manifesto, *The Bloudy Tenent*, declared "a *permission* of the most *Paganish, Jewish, Turkish*, or *Antichristian* [i.e., Catholic] *consciences* and *worships* [for] *all* men in all *Nations* and *Countries*" to be "the will and command of *God*."[7] In this visionary openness to diversity in both religious beliefs and practices, his admirers suggest, Williams's extraordinary friendship with the Narragansett played a formative role.[8]

Yet these celebrations of Williams and Rhode Island as bearers of an early modern toleration in tune with modern cultural pluralism have obscured the *evangelical* core of his toleration arguments and the lively experiment they inspired. The Rhode Island charter commended Williams and other settlers by name for "godly edifying themselves, and one another, in the holy Christian faith and worship, as they were persuaded," while also diligently attending to the "conversion of the poor ignorant Indian natives . . . to the sincere profession and obedience of the same." Twenty years earlier, in *The Bloudy Tenent*, Williams made the evangelical foundations of his toleration explicit: "He that is a *Briar*, that is, a *Jew*, a *Turke*, a *Pagan*, [or] an *Antichristian* today, may be (when the Word of the *Lord* runs freely) a member of *Jesus Christ* to morrow."[9]

These passages in *The Bloudy Tenent* and Rhode Island charter provide paradigmatic statements of what I call *evangelical toleration*.[10] In each, religious liberty is linked directly with evangelism, which provides both a justification *for* and an object *of* toleration. Of course, the phrase *evangelical toleration* may strike many readers as an oxymoron. Today, tolerance is usually associated with equal respect and esteem for others, as well as for their diverse beliefs and ways of life. Evangelism, on this view, appears rather as a source of *intolerance* directly opposed to diversity in its efforts to convert others to one—namely, one's own—faith. Thus, the Massachusetts Bay charter's statement that evangelizing the Indians was the "principall Ende of the Plantacion" has bolstered its modern reputation as the persecuting society par excellence. The Rhode Island charter's similar call for "the conversion of the poor ignorant Natives," however, has been almost entirely ignored.[11]

Recent scholarly accounts have likewise avoided the conceptual complexity and centrality of Williams's robust evangelism to his theory of toleration. They have sought to establish his tolerationist credentials instead on his purported lack of conversionary zeal, especially toward Native Americans. For instance, Nussbaum insists that "despite his fervent Christian beliefs, there is no record that he ever tried to convert any of them."[12] Underlying such claims is an assumption derived from modern sensibilities that Williams's commitment to liberty of conscience can be taken seriously *only* if it was also issued in respect for the contrary religious commitments of others. Had he been an ardent evangelist, this latter-day logic goes, he could not have been "tolerant" at all.

This desire to distance Williams from a proselytizing spirit and missionary expectations more commonly associated with persecution is highly misleading. Worse, it risks occluding some of the most fascinating and useful elements of his vision of toleration for the present day. I argue that the idiosyncratic ideas about evangelism Williams developed in the course of his own evangelical efforts among American "Pagans" and Protestants alike fundamentally shaped his toleration project. The first section below demonstrates that, despite persistent scholarly claims to the contrary, Williams conversed regularly with Native Americans about God, the Word, and damnation. His objections to competing Puritan missionary efforts did not arise from opposition to evangelism among the Americans as such, but rather from a conviction that free conversation and critical exchange were the only effective and legitimate means of propagating the Gospel and "preparing" others' souls for repentance. The recent discovery of a hitherto unknown tract on infant baptism written by Williams late in life suggests that his views on Indian evangelization remained consistent and that he both preached *and* practiced this agonistic form of evangelism to the very end.[13]

The second and third sections demonstrate that this distinctive evangelical approach also had profound ethical and institutional consequences for Williams's views on toleration, both as an individual practice and as a public endeavor. A tolerant society in which "the Word of the Lord runs freely" must allow, even encourage, religious competition and controversy among its members. Institutional protections for religious conscience alone would not suffice. A culture of free and conscientious expression leading in turn to robust and continuous disagreement between individuals about religion would also be required. This nascent connection between religious freedom and free speech implicit in Williams's evangelical toleration scandalized his contemporaries and eventually brought him into conflict with other radical Protestants in New and Old England, including the Quakers, whose similar commitment to evangelical liberty tested the limits of his own toleration.

The evangelical thrust of Williams's life and works, I will argue, is his most significant contribution to a distinctively American tradition of religious liberty. Although he is most often remembered for promoting a "wall of separation" between church and state, it was actually this commitment to evangelical liberty that informed the broader and arguably more influential understanding of "free exercise" enshrined in the Rhode Island charter and forwarded thereafter by other sectarian Protestants in the eighteenth century. The dual commitment to religious freedom and free speech characteristic of America's "First Amendment Faith" is thus less self-evident—and less secular—in its origins than many imagine.[14]

WITNESSING IN THE WILDERNESS

Historians of toleration have long read *The Bloudy Tenent* in isolation as a charming, if overly theological, first draft of Locke's *Letter*.[15] Yet, in order to understand its arguments fully, one must look beyond its reputation as one of the great Western defenses of religious freedom to its more immediate context, including the complicated political circumstances surrounding its publication, as well as Williams's personal experiences of radical diversity in the New World.[16] *The Bloudy Tenent* was only one of many pamphlets Williams published in London while trying to secure a patent for his fledgling colony. The first, *A Key Into the Language of America* (1643), appeared immediately after his arrival and had, on the surface at least, little to do with toleration. Williams's study of Narragansett language and culture offered a conversation manual and phrasebook illustrated by detailed descriptions of American life that captivated English audiences. Parliament was also impressed. Strikingly, in granting Williams his patent, the Committee for Foreign Plantations cited his "great industry and travail in his printed Indian Labours," not his views on the liberty of conscience.[17] *The Bloudy Tenent* was published only after his departure, whereupon the same Parliament ordered it be publicly burned.

Williams's decision to frame the *Key* as a handbook for evangelization may explain its relatively warm reception. The preface proclaimed that "a man may, by this *helpe*, converse with *thousands* of *Natives* all over the *Countrey*."[18] As evidence that "such converse" with the Americans might, in time, lead to the spread of both "*civilitie*" and "*Christianitie*" among them, Williams cited his own role in the conversion of a Pequot warrior named Wequash recently reported in *New England's First Fruits* (1643).[19] He made his own desire to convert the Americans absolutely clear.

The suggestion made by some historians that after an early period of "evangelical optimism" Williams simply "gave up" on his missionary endeavors is based not on the *Key* but on his follow-up work on Indian affairs, *Christenings Make Not Christians* (1645).[20] Although it was written around the same time, Williams delayed *Christenings'* publication (as he did *The*

Bloudy Tenent) until after his departure from England. The delay suggests that Williams anticipated a similarly negative reaction, and it is not difficult to see why.[21] *Christenings* threw cold water on the evangelical enthusiasm stoked by his previous work, explaining that although it had been "easie for my selfe, long ere this, to have brought many thousands of these Natives, yea the whole country, to a far greater Antichristian conversion than ever was yet heard of in *America*," Williams had nevertheless refrained out of principle. "Antichristian" was a popular Protestant epithet for Catholics, as well as any religious displays or ceremonies viewed as "outward," hypocritical, or insincere. In employing it in *Christenings*, Williams meant to suggest that the conversions hitherto undertaken by missionaries in the New World were, in fact, the "subversion of the soules of Millions."[22]

This emphasis on evangelical restraint was not, however, a reversal of Williams's earlier opinions or a rejection of evangelization as such, as it is often presented. Rather, the reservations expressed in *Christenings* reflected his long-standing beliefs about the stringent requirements of a true conversion along with millenarian scruples about apostolic succession.[23] *Christenings* expanded upon Williams's claim in the *Key* that he "could easily have brought the [Americans]" to observe the Sabbath, "but that I was perswaded, and am, that Gods way is first to turne a soule from its Idolls, both of heart, worship, and conversation, before it is capable of worship to the true and living God."[24] Williams was concerned that the missionary programs called for by his fellow Englishmen, like those of the Jesuits in Canada and South America, would neglect this essential first step of *preparation*—that is, the "turning" of the soul from false worship to repentance. As he put it in the *Key*, "The two first Principles and Foundations of true Religion . . . are Repentance from dead workes, and Faith towards God . . . the want of which I conceive, is the bane of million soules in England and all other Nations [brought] to Baptisme and fellowship."[25]

When organized Puritan missionary efforts commenced in Massachusetts shortly after his return, Williams feared they would condemn Indian proselytes to the same fate. John Eliot, minister of the "unseparated" Puritan congregation at Roxbury, which maintained formal ties to the Anglican Church, led these efforts to convert the local native population.[26] Eliot's missionary program began in earnest in 1646 with the preaching of regular sermons to local tribes in his best approximation of Algonquin. The composition of a catechism and a translation of the New Testament into the same soon followed, as did the establishment of fourteen "Praying Towns" in which Indian proselytes could be catechized and "civilized" before baptism and, eventually, form their own congregations.

To Williams, Eliot's method of civilization and Christianization was anathema. Any "conversions" resulting from such a program of doctrinal instruction and civil conformity—not to mention any churches established in the metaphorical "wilderness" before Christ's return—must be "outward," "Antichristian," and inevitably false. Eliot's "Praying Indians" might receive baptism and adopt congregational church government, but without adequate preparation such ordinances would serve as obstacles to their true conversion, which could only take place "by the free proclaiming or preaching of Repentance & forgivenesse of sins" issuing in a "turning of the whole man from the power of *Sathan* unto God."[27]

While Williams cautioned against attributing the work of God's grace to human effort, he still thought that individual Christians had an important role to play in evangelization. His skepticism regarding proselytism undertaken by the ministers of existing (and false) churches did not absolve the true saints from their duty of preparing others' souls by "*calling* of his *people* more and more out of the *Babel of confused Worships, Ministries*, &c. and the finishing of their Testimony against the *Beast*."[28] In stark contrast to Eliot's Indian catechism, evangelism for Williams was a largely *negative* affair consisting of witnessing against the spiritual errors of others.[29] Williams had displayed this evangelical impulse to negative witness immediately upon arriving in New England in 1631, much to his fellow Puritans' chagrin. Nevertheless, the Massachusetts authorities tolerated Williams and his public denunciations of their manifold sins for several years before they banished him—and inadvertently launched him on his unlikely career as a transatlantic champion of toleration.[30]

Williams described himself in these early years as "a faithfull Watchman on the walls to sound the Trumpet" against "publike sins," and he viewed his participation in the myriad religious and political pamphlet wars that raged in England in the 1640s and 1650s as a continuation of this "purgative testimony" in a different medium.[31] In *Christenings*, his audience and main target were the "unconverted and *unchristian Christians*" of England, who had "no more of Christ then [*sic*] the name." They labeled the Americans "heathens," and yet, not "knowing [themselves] what it is to come by true Regeneration within," they were themselves the true "*Heathens or Gentiles*."[32] The same unapologetically controversial approach characterized his many conversations with the Narragansett about "the Creation of the World, and mans Estate, and in particular theirs also" reported in the *Key*, which he described, significantly, as a "preparatory Mercy to their Soules."[33]

Indeed, Williams was indefatigable in "fighting the fight of faith" with Americans and Englishmen alike, and he evidently pulled no punches.[34] The *Key*'s preface recounted how he had acquainted Wequash "with the *Condition* of *all mankind*, & his *Own* in particular," "how *Man* fell from *God*, and his present *Enmity* against *God*, and the *wrath of God* against *Him* untill *Repentance*."[35] The dialogue about damnation included in the chapter on religion provided English readers with further helpful vocabulary for expanding upon this theme: "*Friend, when you die you perish everlastingly. You are everlastingly undone. God is angry with you. He will destroy you. For your many Gods. The whole world shall ere long be burnt.*"[36] In response to the native question, "What then will become of us?" Williams replied, "*God commandeth. That all men now repent.*"[37]

Williams took his duty to spread news of the "written word of God" and counteract the deceiving words of false evangelists like that "grievous wolf" John Eliot very seriously.[38] In this, his Indian dialogues and controversial pamphlets were of a piece. This same focus on preparation and conversion, as we shall see, defined Williams's evangelical approach to toleration.

EVANGELICAL TOLERATION

For modern readers, the radical scope of Williams's toleration is its most appealing feature. Yet it was precisely this aspect that so scandalized his contemporaries. Unlike John Milton or Locke, Williams argued that even Catholics must be tolerated alongside Protestants, Jews, Muslims, and Native Americans.[39] For him, this list had an immediacy informed by personal experience. In addition to his dealings with American "Pagans," he claimed to have "converse[d] with some *Turks, Jews, Papists* and all sorts of *Protestants*" alike "from my Childhood" and "by Books to know the *Affairs* and *Religions* of all *Countries.*"[40] The importance of knowledge about other (especially non-Christian) cultures was a persistent theme in his toleration writings, and he pursued it to the end of his life.

Recent efforts among his partisans to place Williams's lifelong interest in other religions at the heart of his openness to radical diversity are well placed. Yet this globalizing push makes their studied *disinterest* in the evangelical arguments underlying this inclusiveness all the more striking. To deny Williams's evangelical efforts and expectations is to fundamentally misunderstand his vision of a tolerant society as one that not only permitted religious diversity but also promoted robust religious conversation and controversy. "If regenerate and truly repenting English thus come forth from the unregenerate and unrepenting, how would . . . good meanes [be] practiced toward the convincing and saving of [their] soules?"[41] In *The Hireling Ministry None of Christ's* (1652)—a work that undermined the legitimacy of Eliot's particular mission and that of an ordained and state-supported clergy altogether—Williams boasted of his own informal "labour in *Europe*, in *America*, with *English*, with *Barbarians*, yea and also I have longed after some trading with the *Jewes* themselves."[42]

The argument that toleration and proselytism were complementary was more than just rhetorical window-dressing; it shaped Williams's understanding of the former as both an individual and institutional obligation. To see this, one must first notice how Williams himself practiced toleration. While refusing to interrupt the Narragansetts' "Divell" worship, he was forthright in expressing his disapproval of their polytheism and "argued with them about their Fire-God."[43] Similarly, he routinely used the epithet "Antichristian" to refer to Catholics, a slur even Locke would eschew. In an elegant cross-cutting of aversions, the *Key* explained Native American ritual feasting to an English audience by comparing it with Catholics' idolatrous celebration of Christmas, "a Feast, especially in Winter, for then (as the Turke faith of the Christian, rather the Antichristian,) they run mad once a yeare."[44]

For Williams, toleration had a sharp critical edge. The protection of free exercise of religion and free expression must go hand in hand as two essential elements of the liberty of conscience. Together, they afforded individuals the freedom to live, worship, and go to hell in their own fashion, along with the freedom to converse, engage, and criticize others for the same. Unlike medieval proponents of *tolerantia*, Williams did not espouse an attitude of mere indifference or grudging forbearance. Evangelical toleration required instead that the tolerated be actively included and engaged in social life in order to ensure their "*civill converse* and *conversation*" with godly evangelists like Williams.[45] To deny a "civill life or being" to nonbelievers would be to exclude them from the "preparatory mercies" of evangelical conversation and controversy, the best—indeed, the only—means of "propagating and spreading of the Gospel" available to saints in the wilderness.[46] This agonistic evangelism was a messy, unconstrained, and altogether uncertain enterprise that depended upon conversations rather than catechisms. The evangelized must be left to judge for themselves "according to their *Indian* or *American consciences*, for other *consciences* it cannot be supposed they should have."[47]

Williams's insistence that critical conversation was the core of toleration can be seen not only in his endless public controversies but also in his decision to frame *The Bloudy Tenent* and its sequel, *The Bloody Tenent Yet More Bloody* (1652), as dialogues between Truth and Peace. The *Key* reveals that he extended this dialogical approach to non-Christians as well. After hearing of the creation of Eve from Adam's rib, his Narragansett interlocutors responded with a creation story of their own.[48] When he talked to them about hellfire, they talked back—and he listened. To his assertion that "*English-men, Dutch men, and you [Americans] and all the world, when they die . . . that know not this God . . . goe to Hell or the Deepe [and] shall ever lament*," the Americans responded, "*Who told you so?*"

Williams's answer—"*Gods Booke or Writing*"—acknowledged that his own word was inadequate, and he noted this critical questioning with approval.[49] On several occasions, he commended the Americans for their "Berean Civilitie," a reference to the Acts of the Apostles and St. Paul's flight from persecution in Thessalonica to Berea, where the inhabitants "received the Word with all readiness of mind, and searched the Scriptures daily, whether those things were so. Therefore many of them believed."[50] Williams held the "noble" Bereans as exemplars of civility both in taking in the exiled evangelists and participating actively in their own evangelization. The parallel to Williams's own exile and evangelical conversation among the Narragansett underlying this scriptural allusion was obvious.[51]

Williams believed that the Americans, like the Bereans before them, must be prepared for conversion by judging for themselves with their "American consciences" and engaging critically with scripture. Evangelization and toleration were thickly intertwined. Upon his second return to London in 1651, Williams carried a petition from the Narragansett to "the high Sachims of England"—that is, Parliament—"that they might not be forced from their Religion." This plea for toleration was necessitated, he explained, by the "dayly visit[ations]" and "threatenings" they received "by Indians that came from Massachusetts, that if they would not pray they should be destroyed by war."[52] Williams feared the spiritual and civil damage Eliot's Indian proselytes might do if permitted to intimidate the unrepentant Narragansett into false conversions. He, too, desired "the glorious conversion of the Indians in New England" and pursued the same "by his own Lights." But warfare and evangelism would ever be at odds; toleration was the key to true conversion because it created the civic conditions most conducive to it.

Far from being a proto-multiculturalist handbook, the *Key* modeled an engaged and dialogical toleration that was evangelical in nature and in which criticism and controversy flowed both ways. The only dialogue in the text in which Williams did not participate took the form of an overheard conversation between the Narragansett sachim Miantonomo and a "Qunnihiticut Indian" who complained that the Englishman's teachings about damnation contradicted what "our fathers have told us, that our soules goes to the *Southwest*." The sachim's reply and the ensuing exchange are suggestive:

> But how doe you know your selfe . . . did you ever see a soule goe thither? The Natiue [*sic*] replyed; when did he (naming my selfe) see a soule goes to Heaven or Hell? The *Sachim* . . . replied[:] He hath books and writings, and one which God himselfe made, concerning mens soules, and therefore *may* well know more than wee that have none, but take all upon trust from our forefathers.[53]

While Williams sought to convince his auditors of the superiority of scripture as a standard of knowledge, the dialogue highlighted the imperative that they indulge their skepticism, freely vent their objections, and come to "the Word" without coercion. To do this, they first needed to know of its existence and repent of their former errors. This in turn depended upon a double freedom: of the saints to witness *and* of the evangelized to respond.

Williams was under no illusion about the strain that continuous controversy about religion would place upon members of a tolerating society and the affective bonds between them. His intimate acquaintance with civil and spiritual discord in Rhode Island precluded any wishful thinking that these fundamental disagreements might become sources of solidarity. The attitude of engagement and inclusion that his evangelical toleration required demanded a complicated balance of spiritual criticism and civil acceptance, and this ethic needed to be supplemented by institutional arrangements designed to ensure the free flowing of the Word among the "Briars" of the wilderness, despite the upset and alienation that might follow. If true conversions depended upon "the free proclaiming or preaching of Repentance and forgiveness," a society devoted to evangelical toleration needed to protect its members' evangelical liberty above all.

EVANGELICAL LIBERTY

The most famous institutional innovation associated with Roger Williams remains the "wall of separation" between church and state first described in *Mr Cottons Letter Lately Printed* (1644) and later realized in the Rhode Island charter's unprecedented disestablishment. But next to disestablishing religion, Williams's commitment to liberating men's tongues in religious matters was by far the most radical feature of his toleration arguments. As portrayed in *The Bloudy Tenent*, toleration had two distinct requirements: first, the "permission of the most *Paganish, Jewish, Turkish,* or *Antichristian consciences* and *worships,*" and second, "that they are onely to be *fought* against with that *Sword* which is only (in *Soule matters*) *able* to *conquer*: to wit, the *Sword* of *God's Spirit,* the *Word* of *God.*"[54] In order for this spiritual warfare to proceed, evangelistic activities must receive the same "free exercise and enjoyment" as any other form of worship.

This provision for evangelical liberty as a freedom to proselytize and admonish others for their spiritual errors drew on a long-standing Christian metaphor of the two swords frequently employed in Williams's writings. The first sword was a sword of law and legal punishment belonging to the civil magistrate. The second was "the *sword of Gods Spirit,* expressly said to be the *Word of God.*"[55] Applied in the cause of conversion, the former became an instrument of persecution resulting in a "steelie hardness" of their hearts and a "prison of unbeleefe . . . [un]to eternity"; the sword of speech, by contrast, softened and rendered "more humane and mercifull the eare and heart."[56] For Williams, the two swords were fundamentally different in kind and needed to be kept separate. While the first was justly wielded by the state in "civil" matters, the second sword was carried in the mouths of Christ's servants, and they needed the space to swing freely.[57]

Still, it should be noted that Williams did maintain the need for legal restrictions on seditious and libelous speech, as did other contemporary advocates of the liberty of conscience like Milton (*Areopagitica*, 1644). But unlike his friend, Williams denied the magistrate's right to punish blasphemy. As a violation of the first table of the Decalogue, which outlined men's duties to God alone, blasphemy was beyond the magistrate's purview. Moreover, *The Bloudy Tenent* pointed out that civil laws directed against uncivil tongues or "vehement" evangelism were usually covert forms of persecution that impeded "the sword of God's Spirit" in its most important work.[58]

> When a kingdome or state, towne or family, lyes and lives in the guilt of false God, false Christ, false worship,: no wonder if sore eyes be troubled at the appearance of the light, be it never so sweet . . . if persons sleepy loving to sleepe be troubled at the noise of shrill (though silver) alarums.[59]

Accordingly, laws targeting evangelism or robust religious disagreement as "uncivil" would, in fact, preclude "all true preaching of the Gospell or glad newes," which was properly done in an *"immoveable, constant,* and *resolved"* way.[60]

Two episodes from Williams's career most clearly illustrate his determination to put evangelical liberty into practice—first, his objections to the so-called Humble Proposals of 1652, and second, his public debate with several leading Quakers in Newport in 1673. Presented to the Rump Parliament as a template for disciplining "the propagation of the Gospel" and reforming the Church of England, the Humble Proposals called for the licensing of preachers through a combination of civil "approval" and ecclesiastical ordination.[61] This provision for increasing civil oversight over the state-supported ministry deeply offended Williams, who attacked the proposals in several pamphlets published during his second return to London. The licensing provision—not to mention the preservation of a national church as such—violated his principle of separation while placing unacceptable limitations on the essential evangelistic activities of preaching and teaching, competing for converts, and gathering churches. Unlike his fellow Puritans in Parliament, Williams viewed the propagation of the gospel as a duty not only of the ministry but of all Christians. Hence, he sought to extend the privilege of evangelical liberty beyond professional clerics to ensure the unimpeded witnessing of the true saints—wherever and whenever they appeared.[62]

In his endorsement of lay or "mechanick" preaching, Williams contributed to an erosion of the distinction between clergy and laity that represented one of the most striking spiritual and social developments of England's civil war years. This dismantling of religious hierarchies was vividly illustrated by the emergence of many new sects inclined to egalitarian "enthusiasm" and decidedly uncivil forms of evangelical expression. Foremost among these were the Quakers, who suffered horrible persecution in both New and Old England. Many sought refuge in Rhode Island, and Williams's ongoing struggles with Quakers in his colony challenged his commitment to putting his radical ideas about evangelical liberty into practice.

Today, the Quakers are best known as early and stalwart defenders of the liberty of conscience, with William Penn's colony of Pennsylvania being the chief competitor to Williams's Rhode Island as the New World's haven for dissent. What is often downplayed, however, is the behavior that made the early Quakers so shocking in the first place. Not only would they refuse to "doff and don" their hats, but their doctrine of the "Inner Light" also demanded that they witness for their faith by engaging in behaviors deliberately offensive to political order and social mores. They were notorious for going naked in public as a sign of their spiritual nakedness and interrupting church services by shouting down the minister, banging pots, and demanding to know "by what authority" the minister preached. [63]

Williams viewed the Quakers' extreme spiritual egalitarianism and conscientious incivility as serious threats to his lively experiment. Specifically, he argued that their use of "grievous" and "insulting" language against their spiritual opponents—justified by the inspiration of the Inner Light—demonstrated their belief "by principle and practice, that there are no men to be respected in the World but themselves as being Gods and Christs." [64] This antinomian partiality and pride, he argued, violated the "Bond of *Civility*" essential to the viability of a tolerating society. [65]

Given his own penchant for uncompromising public criticism of others' sins, the temptation to deny the Quakers their evangelical liberty might seem to betray more sensitivity—and less tolerance—toward beliefs and practices in others than he so rigorously demanded for himself. Regardless of whether one finds Williams's arguments persuasive, his failure to follow through on his suggestion that "a due and moderate restraint and punishing of [Quaker] incivilities" might be "a Duty and Command of God" is revealing. [66] Laws banning religious insults were enacted in other English colonies committed to toleration, including Pennsylvania. [67] Rhode Island remained the exception, and although he complained about it heartily, Williams never followed through in prosecuting the Quakers for their evangelical incivility. Instead, he challenged several of their leading members to a public debate later described in his anti-Quaker polemic, *George Fox Digg'd Out His Burrowes* (1676), the only work by Williams to be published in the New World during his lifetime. Due to his advanced age and poor health, Williams sometimes had to be carried into the venue; nevertheless, he spent three days trying to convince his Quaker opponents of their theological errors.

This debate, and Williams's determination to publish the results, represents a fitting vindication of his principles. His colony would remain a notorious safe haven for Quakers, as well as Jews, Turks, and infidels, well into the eighteenth century.

CONCLUSION

In the "latrine" of Rhode Island, the riffraff and castoffs of the colonial periphery came together to conduct a lively, if unlikely, experiment to test whether Williams's vision of radical inclusion and unconstrained evangelical liberty could long endure. That it did so presents a direct challenge to Jean-Jacques Rousseau's contention that "it is impossible to live at peace with those we regard as damned."[68] Indeed, it was precisely the concern to save others from damnation that undergirded the unprecedented scope of tolera-tion and other institutional innovations pioneered in the colony. Everyone, Williams insisted, must have the right as well as duty to bear witness for their beliefs while engaging—and castigating—others concerning theirs. "He that is a briar, that is, a Jew, a Turke, a Pagan, [or] an Anti-Christian today, may be . . . a member of Jesus Christ tomorrow"—but if and only if "the Word of the Lord runs *freely*."

The rejection of restrictions on evangelical speech in favor of uncon-strained conversation and controversy first articulated in *The Bloudy Tenent* represents one of Williams's most radical—and influential—contributions to the distinctive development of religious freedom in America. In treating constant witness, unlicensed preaching, and sectarian competition as essen-tial elements of free exercise, Williams posited a connection between the liberty of conscience and broader freedoms of expression and association that today are often taken for granted. This essential compatibility of religious freedom with free speech is a fundamental tenet of America's "First Amend-ment Faith" and helps to explain why the laws banning hate speech and religious insult advanced under the banner of "tolerance" in other Western democracies seem so problematic, even fundamentally at odds with the American constitutional order.[69]

Williams's insistence on a universal evangelical liberty is in stark contrast with the many other historical theories and practices of toleration in which the permission of religious difference was assumed to depend on restricting proselytism and competition between sects. While evangelical liberty was taken up by some radical Protestants—including the Quakers Williams loathed[70]—this nascent connection between religious freedom and free ex-pression was explicitly rejected by most other early modern tolerationists, who quite reasonably viewed the enthusiastic witnessing and uncivil preach-ing on the part of sectarians as obstacles, rather than inducements, to coexis-tence.

When viewed in this light, Williams's exceptional evangelical toleration presents an early version of the American polity's unique and somewhat paradoxical combination of religious disestablishment and a religiously charged public sphere. It is surely misleading to imply a direct line of descent from the Rhode Island charter to the First Amendment or to credit Williams with the creation of an "American tradition" of religious liberty, as recent scholarship has done. Still, the counterintuitive idea that religious toleration entails disestablishment, as well as sectarian competition and individual rights of conscience, can be traced at least in part to the relative density of competing strands of evangelical Protestantism in British America, of which Williams was an extreme example.

One need not read Roger Williams as a prophet of modern civil libertarianism to see that scholars who portray him as a secular liberal or proto-multiculturalist today have categorically misunderstood one of the central themes of his life and works. Justifying toleration as a partner to evangelism, as he did, is far different from the respect or recognition of other faiths they and others associate with tolerance. Yet, for that very reason, it can underwrite a commitment to diversity and fundamental disagreement that does not rely on blithe certainties or pious wishes for solidarity. In an age of deep diversity and increasing religious and political polarization, Williams's evangelical insights into the dynamics of believing and belonging are more important than ever—although not, perhaps, in the way his modern revivers might hope.

NOTES

1. "Charter of Rhode Island and Providence Plantations—July 15th, 1663," The Avalon Project, Yale Law School, accessed March 30, 2014, http://avalon.law.yale.edu/17th_century/ri04.asp.

2. See John Coffey, *Persecution and Toleration in England, 1558–1689* (London: Longman, 2000), 207–8, and Perez Zagorin, *How the Idea of Religious Toleration Came to the West* (Princeton, NJ: Princeton University Press, 2003), 196–208.

3. *Documents of the Senate of the State of New York* (Albany: New York State Legislature, 1902), 14:400.

4. Duncan Bell, "What Is Liberalism?" *Political Theory* 42, no. 6 (2014): 1–34, accessed 21 September 2014, doi:10.1177/0090591714535103.

5. For recent popularizing works, see John Barry, *Roger Williams and the Creation of the American Soul: Church, State, and the Birth of Liberty* (New York: Viking, 2012); James C. Davis, ed., *On Religious Liberty: Selections from the Works of Roger Williams* (Cambridge, MA: Belknap Press of Harvard University Press, 2008), and *In Defense of Civility: How Religion Can Unite America on Seven Moral Issues That Divide Us* (Louisville, KY: Westminster John Knox Press, 2010); and Martha Nussbaum, *Liberty of Conscience: In Defense of America's Tradition of Religious Equality* (New York: Basic Books, 2008), and *The New Religious Intolerance: Overcoming the Politics of Fear in an Anxious Age* (Cambridge, MA: Harvard University Press, 2012).

6. Nussbaum, *Liberty of Conscience*, 57.

7. Roger Williams, *The Bloudy Tenent of Persecution* [1644], in *The Complete Writings of Roger Williams*, 7 vols. (New York: Russell & Russell, 1963), 3:3.

8. "Williams's experience of finding integrity, dignity, and goodness outside the parameters of orthodoxy surely shaped his evolving view of conscience." Nussbaum, *Liberty of Conscience*, 47. See also Jonathan Beecher Field, "A Key for the Gate: Roger Williams, Parliament, and Providence," *New England Quarterly* 80 (2007): 353–82; Jessica R. Stern, "A *Key* into *The Bloudy Tenent of Persecution*: Roger Williams, the Pequot War, and the Origins of Toleration in America," *Early American Studies* 9, no. 3 (2011): 576–616.

9. Williams, *Bloudy Tenent*, 95.

10. By "evangelical" I do not mean Protestant arguments about the voluntary nature of belief, but rather the activity of evangelism itself, for which "evangelistic" might be a more precise term.

11. "The Charter of Massachusetts Bay—1629," The Avalon Project, Yale Law School, accessed March 30, 2014, http://avalon.law.yale.edu/17th_century/mass03.asp.

12. Nussbaum, *Liberty of Conscience*, 54. According to Perry Miller, "because" Williams was free from missionary care, he "could treat the Indian culture with respect." Miller, *Roger Williams: His Contribution to the American Tradition* (Indianapolis, IN: Bobbs-Merrill, 1953), 49–52.

13. In 2012, researchers at Brown University managed to "crack the code" and decipher a previously unreadable treatise written by Williams in shorthand in the margins of another book. Written sometime between 1679 and 1683 and titled "A Brief Reply to a Short Book Written by John Eliot," it refuted Eliot's criticisms of an English Baptist, John Norcot, on infant baptism. See Linford Fisher and Lucas Mason-Brown, "By 'Treachery and Seduction': Indian Baptism and Conversion in the Roger Williams Code," *William & Mary Quarterly* 71 (2014): 175–202.

14. Jeremy Waldron, *The Harm in Hate Speech* (Cambridge, MA: Harvard University Press, 2012), 29.

15. "Locke's major contribution may have been to reduce the rambling, lengthy, and incoherent exposition of the New England 'firebrand' to orderly, abbreviated, and coherent form." Winthrop S. Hudson, "John Locke: Heir of Puritan Political Theorists," in *Calvinism and the Political Order: Essays Prepared for the Woodrow Wilson Lectureship of the National Presbyterian Center, Washington, D.C.*, ed. George Hunt and John T. McNeill (Philadelphia, PA: Westminster Press, 1965), 117–18. See also Nussbaum, *Liberty of Conscience*, 41, and Barry, *Roger Williams*, 392.

16. See Teresa M. Bejan, "'The Bond of Civility': Roger Williams on Toleration and Its Limits," *History of European Ideas* 37 (2011): 607–26; Field, "A Key for the Gate," and Stern, "A *Key* into *The Bloudy Tenent*."

17. Quoted in Field, "A Key for the Gate," 376. The patent ultimately secured by Williams from Parliament in 1643 likewise justified its grant with reference to the colonists' efforts to settle near and befriend the Narragansett as laying "a sure foundation of happiness to all America." "A Patent for Providence Plantations—March 14th, 1643," The Avalon Project, accessed March 30, 2014, http://avalon.law.yale.edu/17th_century/ri03.asp.

18. Roger Williams, *A Key Into the Language of America* [1666], in *The Complete Writings of Roger Williams*, 1:80.

19. Williams, *Key*, 1:86.

20. Fisher and Mason-Brown, "Treachery and Seduction," 180. See also Richard Cogley, *John Eliot's Mission to the Indians before King Philip's War* (Boston: Harvard University Press, 1999), 16; Field, "A Key for the Gate"; and Stern, "A *Key* into *The Bloudy Tenent*," 596.

21. Field, "A Key for the Gate," 374.

22. Roger Williams, *Christenings Make Not Christians* [1645], in *The Complete Writings of Roger Williams*, 7:36–37.

23. Williams believed that the divinely authenticated form of the church had been lost and would be recovered only at Christ's return. All existing churches were therefore tainted by centuries of "converse" with the unregenerate. See W. Clark Gilpin, *The Millenarian Piety of Roger Williams* (Chicago: University of Chicago Press, 1979), 127.

24. Williams, *Key*, 1:220–21.

25. Ibid., 1:221.

26. Williams's millenarian eschatology dictated that the apostolic succession had been interrupted with the conversion of Constantine; hence missionaries like Eliot who gathered churches did so without a proper commission and "sending" from Christ. Eliot's nickname, "the Apostle to the Indians," must have particularly rankled.

27. Williams, *Christenings*, 7:39. The treatise decoded by Fisher and Mason-Brown confirms that the "first *grounding* to prepare one's soul before conversion" remained central to Williams's views on Indian evangelization until his death. He accused Eliot of having "pre-

pared" his proselytes "in error": "They might speak [or] do some[thing] as they are taught," but "surely we be cautious of such conversions." Quoted in Fisher and Mason-Browne, "Treachery and Seduction," 202.

28. Roger Williams, *The Hireling Ministry None of Christs* [1652], in *The Complete Writings of Roger Williams*, 7:168–69.

29. Williams, *Bloudy Tenent*, 3:59.

30. Williams called the Massachusetts charter a "national sin" and offended his fellow religious refugees at every opportunity by accusing them of spiritual uncleanness. He was called repeatedly before the assembly before they finally exiled him in 1635. The decision to deport him to England was due to his unwillingness to stop preaching his heterodox opinions to others, even after his earlier censure and conviction.

31. Roger Williams, *Mr. Cotton's Letter, Examined and Answered* [1644], in *The Complete Writings of Roger Williams*, 1:321; Gilpin, *Millenarian Piety*, 96, 150.

32. Williams, *Christenings*, 7:35.

33. Williams, *Key*, 1:215.

34. Williams, *Bloudy Tenent*, 3:59.

35. Ibid., 3:86–87.

36. Ibid., 3:221. I have omitted the Narragansett translation.

37. Ibid., 3:221.

38. Quoted in Fisher and Mason-Browne, "By Treachery and Seduction," 195.

39. Nussbaum mistakenly assumes that "antichristian" was a reference to atheists rather than a popular Protestant pejorative for Catholics. Nussbaum, "The First Founder: the American Revolution of Roger Williams," *New Republic*, 10 September 2008, accessed 30 March 2014, http://www.newrepublic.com/article/books/the-first-founder. Williams never mentioned atheists directly; nevertheless, his failure to explicitly *exclude* them from toleration placed him at the far edge of the radical fringe.

40. Roger Williams, "To the People Called Quakers," *George Fox Digg'd Out his Burrowes* [1676], in *The Complete Writings of Roger Williams*, 5:i. Although we know little about his life before his removal to Massachusetts, many of these conversations—as well as his knowledge of Dutch and his mastery of shorthand—would have stemmed from his upbringing as the son of a merchant tailor in London.

41. Williams, *Mr Cotton's Letter*, 1:362.

42. Williams, *Hireling Ministry*, 7:168. Ordained as an Anglican minister, Williams soon renounced the ministry and continued to preach informally. His final surviving letter reports his efforts to solicit Eliot's help in publishing a collection of his sermons. "To Governor Simon Bradstreet, 6 May 1682," in Roger Williams, *The Correspondence of Roger Williams*, 2 vols., ed. G. LaFantasie (Hanover and London: Brown University Press/University Press of New England, 1988), 2:777.

43. Williams, *Key*, 1:217.

44. Ibid., 1:211.

45. Williams, *Bloudy Tenent*, 3:117.

46. Ibid., 3:94; Williams, *Hireling Ministry*, 7:150.

47. Williams, *Bloudy Tenent*, 3:250, 354.

48. Williams, *Key*, 1:210. "They will say, Wee never heard of this before: and then . . . relate how they have it from their Fathers, that *Kautantowwit* made one man and woman of a stone, which disliking, he broke in pieces, and made another man and woman of a Tree, which were the Fountaines of all mankind." Ibid., 1:217–18.

49. Ibid., 1:218–19. Throughout, he stressed the Bible's inherent attraction for the Americans: "They have no Clothes, Bookes, nor Letters . . . and therefore are easily perswaded that the God that made English men is a greater God, because Hee hath so richly endowed the English above themselves." Ibid., 1:83.

50. Acts 17:10–12 (King James Version).

51. Williams, "Letter to Mrs. Anne Sadleir, ca. Winter 1652/53," in *Correspondence*, 1:375.

52. Williams was frustrated by attempts by Eliot and his allies in London to "publikely brand" the Narragansett as "refusing to pray and be converted." Williams, "Letter to the General Court of Massachusetts Bay, 5 Oct. 1654," in *Correspondence*, 2:409–10.

53. Ibid., 2:219–20; my emphasis.

54. Williams, *Bloudy Tenent*, 3:3.

55. Ibid., 3:160.

56. Williams, *The Bloody Tenent Yet More Bloody* [1652], in *The Complete Writing of Roger Williams*, 4:496; Williams, *Bloudy Tenent*, 3:148; Williams, *Mr Cotton's Letter*, 1:316.

57. Williams, *Yet More Bloody*, 4:229.

58. Williams, *Bloudy Tenent*, 3:160.

59. Ibid., 3:74, 79–80.

60. Ibid., 3:75–77.

61. Gilpin, *Millenarian Piety*, 139. The system of "Triers" and "Ejectors" adopted as part of the Cromwellian church settlement put this proposal into practice. Jeffrey Collins, "The Church Settlement of Oliver Cromwell," *History* 83 (2002): 18–40.

62. Gilpin, *Millenarian Piety*, 84.

63. In one memorable case, a Quaker man reportedly took off his pants and prostrated himself on the communion table. However, it is difficult to distinguish between accurate reports of the Quakers' conduct and the spurious accusations of their opponents. Alexandra Walsham, *Charitable Hatred: Tolerance and Intolerance in England, 1500–1700* (Manchester, UK: Manchester University Press, 2006), 144.

64. Williams, *George Fox*, 5:306–7.

65. Williams, *Bloudy Tenent*, 3:74.

66. Williams, *George Fox*, 5:307.

67. The Maryland Toleration Act (1649), Great Law of Pennsylvania (1682), and the Fundamental Constitutions of Carolina (1669) all included religious insult provisions.

68. Jean-Jacques Rousseau, *The Social Contract and Other Later Political Writings*, ed. Victor Gourevitch (Cambridge: Cambridge University Press, 1997), 4:8.34.

69. Waldron, *Harm in Hate Speech*, 29.

70. According to the Quaker leader George Fox, liberty of conscience demanded the "universal liberty for what people soever . . . let him be Jew, or Papist, or Turk, or Heathen, or Protestant, or what soever, or such as worship sun or moon or sticks and stones, let them have liberty where every one may . . . [and] have free liberty to speak forth his mind and judgement." Quoted in Gilpin, *Millenarian Piety*, 55.

Part II

Toleration, Revival, and Enlightenment in the Long Eighteenth Century

Chapter Five

Muslims, Toleration, and Civil Rights from Roger Williams to Thomas Jefferson

Denise Spellberg

Roger Williams, the founder of Providence, Rhode Island, was the first North American to articulate a plan for the toleration of Muslims. His tract *The Bloudy Tenent of Persecution* (1644) was a pivotal part of a longer arc of transatlantic thought about the toleration of all religions, including that professed by the "Turkes" (as Williams and his contemporaries referred to adherents of Islam). Yet Williams was not the first or last citizen of the larger Anglo-Atlantic world to support a universal toleration inclusive of all religions. His professed willingness to tolerate Muslims, along with his denunciation of government authority over individual liberty of conscience, may be traced backward to the first English Baptists as well as forward to Thomas Jefferson.

And yet, contrary to modern expectations, Williams's commitment to universal toleration coincided with an unalloyed belief in what he took to be the "true" faith, the severe form of Protestant Christianity that he espoused for much of his life. This was also apparent when it came to his views on Islam. Williams's most vigorous defenses of Muslim religious liberty coexisted with his condemnation of Islam and his prediction that Muslims, like their Prophet, were destined for hell. Of course, this double-edged pattern in his written expression was not restricted to Muslims. While individual liberty of conscience proved always precious to him, so was his commitment to the idea that the path toward salvation was restricted, narrow even for other Protestants. But it was in his approach to Islam and its adherents that Williams's peculiar combination of tolerance and intolerance manifested itself.

This chapter considers Williams's argument about Muslims and toleration. It addresses one basic question: Why, despite his criticism of Islam as a religion, did Williams consistently opt to include Muslims in his vision of toleration? The chapter begins with the writings of the early English Baptist Thomas Helwys (c. 1575–c. 1614), who preceded Williams in including Muslims within the legitimate scope of religious toleration. It then surveys commercial and cultural exchanges between England and Islamic realms before examining Williams's advocacy for the toleration of all believers, including Muslims, both imagined and real.

Williams's approach to Muslims can best be understood as he treated them in his first treatise on religious toleration written in 1644, and later in 1672, in conjunction with his treatment of Quakers, a group he reviled and confronted, yet also tolerated. Toward the end of his life, Williams publicly and privately challenged the Quakers to defend their religion and civic behavior in his Rhode Island colony. Importantly, it is only at this historic juncture that he claims to have met and spoken with Muslims. The reason appears to be that Williams's polemic against the Quakers linked them, in his view, to Muslims in important ways. But this raises another question: If there were Muslims in his colony, would he have behaved toward them as he had toward the Quakers, publicly expressing disapproval of their beliefs?

I

Decades before Williams wrote about Muslims and toleration, Helwys addressed the same issue in a tract that may have influenced the founder of Providence (for a few months, Williams embraced Helwys's Baptist faith[1]). It is not unlikely, then, that Williams knew of and had read the work of Helwys. While both men invoked Muslims in their tracts on religious liberty in the abstract, both would have been well aware of the considerable contact between England and the Islamic world, which made their inclusion of Muslims a provocative, yet predictable, reflection of seventeenth-century cultural realities.

Persecuted for his beliefs, Helwys fled London for Holland in 1608, where he wrote and published *The Mistery of Iniquity* in 1612. The work was a plea for England's King James I to end persecution of all religious minorities who dissented from the Church of England, whether Christian or otherwise: "Let them be heretics, Turks, Jews or whatsoever, it appertains not to the earthly power to punish them in the least measure."[2] Even before the appearance of *The Mistery of Iniquity*, English authorities had considered Helwys a heretic because of his Baptist beliefs. When he returned to England shortly after the book's publication, this written plea to King James rendered him a traitor in the eyes of the state.

Helwys stressed in his tract, as Williams later would, that the magistrate should exercise only civil, not spiritual, power over his subjects. In language anticipating Williams, as well as Locke and Jefferson, Helwys insisted that his king deserved obedience only in "earthly" not spiritual matters, arguing that faith was a private matter between God and the believer.[3] Imprisoned for his beliefs shortly after he founded England's first Baptist church in 1612, Helwys died in London's Newgate prison around 1614.

For Helwys, the easier road would have been to defend the rights of only Christian minorities, leaving non-Christians outside the ambit of government toleration. Indeed, such a position was hardly uncommon in the seventeenth century. But Helwys chose a different and more challenging conception of toleration, one that included Muslims, a stance that marked his sphere of religious toleration as universal. One reason may have been that he suffered religious persecution himself, as Williams would, and therefore allowed no exceptions when it came to proscribing spiritual coercion and violence.

Given the Christian memory of Ottoman military expansion into Europe since the fifteenth century, the inclusion of Muslims represented a striking statement on behalf of universal toleration. Most seventeenth-century Christians viewed non-Christians such as Muslims and Jews as "infidels" and perceived both groups as a threat to Christian society.[4] Even authors of seventeenth-century treatises on toleration often paired the two groups and described them in similarly pejorative terms. Yet the Western Christian perception of Muslims as uniquely dangerous resonated; unlike Jews, Muslims remained politically as well as religiously threatening.[5] Thus, when Helwys and Williams included them in their vision of a harmonious civil polity, it was more than culturally symbolic; it affirmed the universality of their toleration.

Significantly, for both Helwys and Williams, the inclusion of Muslims was not purely theoretical. To some extent, it reflected actual contact with adherents of Islam, including complex diplomatic relationships with North Africa and the Ottoman Empire. The latter also enjoyed important commercial exchanges with England. These interactions resulted in both accurate and inaccurate understandings of Islam, which may have influenced the way Helwys and Williams understood the faith.

While the Ottomans remained adversaries to the Catholic Habsburg regime, besieging Vienna first in 1529 and a second, final time in 1683, the English developed cordial relations with this powerful Islamic dynasty. In 1581, Elizabeth established the "Turkey Company," later known as the Levant Company, which had a monopoly on English trade with the Ottoman Empire.[6] By 1605, when Roger Williams was two years old, forty thousand people were employed by the Levant Company in England, most weaving for export a heavy fabric of cotton and flax known as *fustian*.[7]

In 1636, the year Williams fled persecution in Massachusetts Bay for Providence, Oxford University established its first chair in Arabic.[8] Cambridge University, Williams's alma mater, had done so four years earlier, the year after Williams first sailed to Boston.[9] There were theological and intellectual reasons for pursuing the study of Arabic in seventeenth-century England. The language proved useful as a corollary to the biblical study of Hebrew and the investigation of still important scientific works not fully translated from Arabic to Latin.[10] In 1649, five years after Williams's first return to England, Alexander Ross provided the first English translation of the Qur'an, an act for which his publisher was briefly imprisoned on charges of propagating Islam.[11]

At the same time, there were pressing political reasons to study Arabic, which became important in English negotiations with the corsairs of North Africa, including Morocco and the Ottoman regencies of Algiers, Tunis, and Tripoli.[12] (The rulers of the last three powers were of Turkish descent, another reason that Englishmen misleadingly referred to all Muslims as *Turks*, a term then associated with cruelty and barbarism.)[13] The necessity of forging treaties guaranteeing the safe passage of English commercial vessels prompted protracted negotiations during this period. English captives frequently defined themselves as "slaves" in Islamic North Africa.[14] However, in Islamic terms, these men were technically "captives," prisoners of war, who might one day be ransomed.[15] By embracing Islam (or "turning Turk," to use the contemporary phrase), some Englishmen chose a more direct path toward manumission. So many seafaring Englishmen faced this dire choice in North African captivity that its long-term consequences for the nation's mariners remained hotly debated in the seventeenth century, before the British navy dominated the eastern Atlantic or the Mediterranean.[16] In 1662, the year before Charles II granted Roger Williams his royal charter, "300 slaves in Algiers petitioned" the same king for aid with their ransom.[17]

Nonetheless, as we have seen, not all contacts with the Islamic world were characterized by either conflict or ideological hostility. For example, during Williams's second return to London from America, the first coffeehouse, purveyor of the "Mahometan [Muslim] berry," opened its doors in 1652.[18] There were thus multiple ways to appreciate aspects of Islamic culture in seventeenth-century England. Williams was heir to that complex cultural legacy.

II

Roger Williams shared Helwys's interest in Islam, but unlike the English Baptist, the former also claimed to have personally met Muslims on at least two occasions. This is something that, as Teresa M. Bejan notes, has "received little attention from his biographers."[19] Williams indicated generally when and where these encounters took place, and additional passages in his biography suggest that he had a more direct connection to the Islamic world than we have heretofore appreciated.[20] For example, in his tract of arguments against the Quakers in 1672, Williams notes that "my Brother [was] a *Turkey-Merchant*," who had brought him back a Bible written in Hebrew from a trip to the Ottoman Empire.[21] Thus, the Muslim ports of Istanbul, Izmir, and Aleppo were not so very distant for Roger Williams or his family. Indeed, fraternal trips to these destinations demonstrate that contact with the Islamic world was a family matter, which may have enhanced Williams's understanding of Islam.

Williams also claimed direct contact with Muslims in a letter he addressed "to the People Called the Quakers," a preface to his polemical objections to their faith, which culminated in 1672 with a three-day-long public dispute with them in Newport, Rhode Island. However, Williams noted that all his encounters with Muslims took place in England, *not* North America:

> The true *Lord Jesus*, to his *Holy Scriptures*, &c. his infinite Wisdome hath given me to see the City, Court and Country, the Schools and Universities of my *Native Country*, to converse with some *Turks, Jews, Papists*, and all sorts of *Protestants*, and by Books to know the *Affairs and Religions of* all *Countries*, &c.[22]

He does not tell us in which of these English contexts he conversed with "some Turks," or when, but there were varied possibilities for such encounters. Nor does Williams ever specify in what language these exchanges took place. But, as Nabil Matar argues, Muslims were "everywhere" in England, "not just in the literary imagination of English dramatists and poets, but in the streets, the sea towns, the royal residences, the courts, and the jails."[23] We know, for example, that among London Turks who were former captives freed from English jails, two became shoemakers, two menders, two button makers, and one, most curiously, a solicitor.[24] We don't know if these Muslims established a place of worship for themselves, and we don't have particulars about how a Muslim reportedly became a "solicitor" or what he knew of English law.[25] Nevertheless, there were more Muslims in London in the mid-seventeenth century than Jews. Their presence was even recognized in important ways, with one legal ruling saying of Muslims that they are not "perpetual enemies" and that "they are Creatures of God and of the same kind as we are, and it would be a sin in us to hurt their persons."[26]

The reason Williams mentions meeting Muslims in the context of his polemic against the Quakers—only, we might add, at the age of seventy— may be found within his tract against the latter, wherein he notes in the margin, *"The Mahumetans & Quakers considered and found one."*[27] (Some variation of *Mahumetan*, meaning Muslim, had been used in English since the sixteenth century; most Europeans seem to have wrongly assumed that Muslims worshipped Muhammad and not God.) Williams conflated the two groups, reproving both for what he asserted were false claims that God directly inspired their leaders. Indeed, he repeated the oft-told Christian polemical tale about the Prophet's base trick, in which a trained dove was said to represent the "Holy Spirit" (which is nonexistent in Islam), resulting in the "pretended" revelation of the Qur'an.[28] Similarly, Williams accused the Quakers of replacing the Holy Spirit by relying upon their allegedly "infallible" individual Inner Light, which superseded the true "Word of God" and, in his estimation, rendered these arrogant believers comparable to "walking Gods."[29] Williams insisted upon this very error during the third day of his public disputation with the Quakers at their meetinghouse in Newport. By this time, his voluble harangue had rendered him "hoarse," a state his adversaries alleged was the product of intoxication rather than oratorical vigor.[30]

Williams seldom hesitated to condemn Quaker beliefs, which he considered errant, either publicly or privately. This raises the question of whether Williams would, by analogy, have treated any actual Muslims in his colony as tolerantly as he did Quakers. A second letter, written by Williams four months later, in July 1672, hints at an answer. Addressed to a former friend named John Throckmorton of Providence, Rhode Island, a newly converted Quaker, Williams writes of his neighbor's beliefs in a passage acknowledging their mutual, public accusations of *"Condemnation"* and *"Damnation,"* adding, "But my *Knowedg* [*sic*] tells me that amongst *Jews* and *Turks*, *Papists* and *Protestants* and *Pagans* (with all of which I have conversed) I never met with such a Judging Censuring Reviling *spirit* as is the *spirit* of the *Quakers.*"[31] Quite a forceful accusation from one of the pioneers of North American religious liberty, but one that reveals a mutuality of denunciations! It is thus not surprising that Williams ends a letter to other Quaker opponents in March 1672 with the hope that *"some of you may live to see flung into the Lake that burns with Fire and Brimstone"* both the "Pope and Mahomet."[32]

While it is unlikely that Williams met or welcomed any Muslims to his Rhode Island colony, he did allow Quakers to reside there twelve years after four had been hanged on Boston Common in the neighboring colony of Massachusetts Bay.[33] Muslims, like Quakers and Catholics, may have been abhorrent and bound for hell in Williams's mind, but on earth in his Rhode Island colony, he would not persecute them for their aberrant beliefs. However, he clearly did not think that his "conference or dispute" with the Quakers contravened his support for their toleration, which included his right to rebuke these neighbors for their misguided theology and deplorable behavior, such as women stripping in public.[34]

Williams claimed to have been aware of Quaker beliefs, based on their writings, and he also attested to learning about Islam from books. He criticized the Muslim faith, but he also demonstrated familiarity with many of its key tenets. For example, he accurately recorded that Muhammad is considered by Muslims as the seal of the prophets, superseding the revelations of both Moses and Jesus.[35] He correctly noted that they "acknowledge *Christ a great Prophet*, yet affirme [him] less than *Mahomet*."[36] But this understanding did not prevent him from denouncing the Prophet's final destination as hell, conforming to the commonplace Christian belief that Muhammad was an impostor leading his followers to a fiery eternal fate.[37]

Nonetheless, Williams refused to persecute Muslims. Instead, in *The Bloudy Tenent*, his first treatise of 1644, he repeatedly promised them liberty of conscience. This pattern of censuring Islam while simultaneously defending the liberty of conscience of its adherents marks the start of a crucial pattern, one repeated in the writings of John Locke and Thomas Jefferson. Moreover, if his dispute with the Quakers represents a viable precedent, Williams also would have reserved the right to publicly rebuke Muslim beliefs and ritual practices. Thus, what Williams advocated was a rough—and robust—form of liberty for a wide variety of faiths.

Unlike his denunciation of the Quakers late in life, Williams's earliest references to Muslims in *The Bloudy Tenent* emphasized instead his plan for their religious toleration. Among the more than ten references to *Turkes* or the *Turkish* in his tract, Williams writes, "It is the will and command of *God*, that (since the coming of his Sonne the *Lord Jesus*) a permission of the most Paganish, Jewish, Turkish, or Antichristian consciences and worships, bee granted to *all* men in all *Nations* and *Countries*."[38] His insistence on *all* the world's inhabitants is noteworthy because, throughout his work, his appeal for toleration remained decidedly universal. Although he continues to explain that these non-Christians should never be violently threatened or coerced, averring that "they are onely to bee *fought* against with that *Sword*" (meaning "the *Sword of Gods Spirit*, the *Word* of *God*"), he thereafter rejects "our desires and hopes of the *Jewes conversion* to *Christ*," presumably also precluding similar intentions toward Muslims.[39]

Williams consistently linked Native Americans (referred to as *Pagans*), Jews, and Turks in his work. This triad is important, not just for its consistency but also because it illustrates the universality of his vision. More than one historian has suggested that by placing Muslims in the mix with Jews, Williams denigrated the latter as "the stereotypical alien outside the pale of Christianity."[40] But this is not his strategy. For Williams, all non-Christians deserved toleration, a civic policy that protected dissenting minority groups, including *both* Jews and Muslims, from governmental interference.

Williams's antipathy for the coercion and violence directed toward non-Christians prompted him to excoriate his fellow believers ("two *mountains* of crying *guilt* lye heavie upon the back of All that name the name of *Christ* in the eyes of *Jewes, Turkes*, and *Pagans*"), condemning their "bloody irreligious and inhumane *oppressions* and *destructions* under the maske or vaile of the Name of *Christ*, &c."[41] Being a better Christian meant living up to the ideal of Jesus's nonviolent example, but this did not mean Williams chose to ignore theological differences in writing or be silent about them in person.

Williams also knew that Muslims did not persecute those of other faiths in their dominion, and, like many fellow Christians had since the sixteenth century, he critiqued his coreligionists' violence toward one another by contrasting it with the toleration practiced by the Ottoman Turks. He wrote, "Nay it [persecution for cause of conscience] is not practiced amongst the *Heathen* that acknowledge not the *true God*, as the *Turke*, *Persian*, and others."[42] Other Europeans in the seventeenth century critiqued their own societies by referring to the example of the Ottoman Empire, where resident minorities of Christians and Jews were not forced to convert to Islam but were permitted to practice their faith, albeit while acknowledging their civic inferiority.[43]

In contrast, Williams explained that religious persecution was rife in England and Roman Catholic countries.[44] He also singled out *"New England Churches,"* where to "worship *God* after their consciences" was not permitted.[45] He vividly remembered the persecuting nature of the Puritan theocracy of Massachusetts Bay, from which he had fled to Providence during a bitter New England winter in 1636.

Indeed, Williams's *The Bloudy Tenent* challenged Massachusetts Bay minister John Cotton, who had written in his earlier *Discourse about Civil Government* that neither Christian "heretics" nor Muslims should be allowed to govern. Not even the Ottomans differed on this principle, Cotton asserted: "Yea, in Turkey itself, they are careful none but a man devoted to Mahomet bear publick Office."[46] What he believed essential in a "true" Christian commonwealth was "a form of Government as best serveth to Establish their Religion," as the only one "Established in the Civil State."[47] It was this sort of government-sponsored, coercive religion that Williams wished to bar from his own colony.

Citing the Gospel of Matthew, Williams argued against Cotton's paradigm. He declared that only God could decide upon the final separation of the human "tares," or weeds, from the garden, not an earthly government. Only with the imminent Second Coming would Christian heretics and non-Christian "tares" be separated from the "wheat," the true Christian faithful: "Christ commandeth to let alone the *Tares* and *Wheat* to grow together unto the *Harvest*. Mat 13.30.38."[48] Cotton's response to this analogy declared in 1647 that Williams's policy allowed "dangerous" and "damnable infection" to spread to the body politic.[49]

In contrast to Cotton, Williams argued that the proper purview of government should be limited to the second "Table" of the Ten Commandments, "which concerne our *walking* with man (viz. *Thou shalt not kill, Thou shalt not commit adultery, Thou shalt not steale, Thou shalt not beare false witness, Thou shalt not covet*: and if there be any other Commandment, to be briefly comprehended in this saying, namely, *Thou shalt love thy neighbor as thy selfe.*[)]"[50]

This invocation of the Golden Rule also reverberated in the description of his potential loyal non-Christian neighbors. He believed such religiously plural communities already existed on earth, a reference, perhaps, to Holland, where religious diversity flourished at the time. Indeed, his words anticipate *The Flushing Remonstrance*, a 1657 statement by Dutch colonists defending the practice of Quakers, Baptists, and Muslims, among others.[51] Thus Williams wrote:

> And I ask whether or no such as may hold forth other *Worships* or *Religions* (*Jews, Turkes,* or *Antichristians*) may not be peaceable and quiet *Subjects,* Loving and helpfull *neighbours*, faire and just *dealers*, true and loyall to the *civill government*? It is cleare they may from all *Reason* and *Experience* in many flourishing *Cities* and *Kingdomes* of the World, and so offend not against the *civill State* and *Peace*; nor incurre the punishment of the *civill sword*, notwithstanding that in *spiritual* and *mysticall account* they are ravenous and greedy *Wolves*.[52]

Despite his designation of non-Christians and heretics as "wolves," meaning those who "speak perverse things" about religion, Williams found no "*word* of *Christ* by way of *command, promise,* or *example*, countenancing the Governors of the *civill State* to meddle with these *Wolves*, if in *civill* things *peaceable* and *obedient*."[53]

Having identified Muslims as worthy of religious toleration in 1644, Williams included them in his metaphorical ship of state (and thereby the universal ambit of his toleration) while acting as president of Providence Plantations in 1655: "It hath fallen out sometimes, that both papists and protestants, Jews and Turks, may be embarked upon one ship; upon which supposal I affirm, that all the liberty of conscience, that I ever pleaded for, turns upon two hinges—that none of the papists, protestants, Jews or Turks, be forced to come to the ship's prayers or worship . . . if they practice any."[54] But even here, he asserts that there were limits to public behavior that needed to be enforced for the common social good: "I further add, that I never denied, that notwithstanding this liberty, the commander of the ship ought to command the ship's course, yea, and also command that justice, peace and sobriety, be kept and practiced, both among the seamen and all passengers."[55] These acceptable public practices had to be demarcated by the ship's commander, and Williams would condemn the Quakers for what he deemed questionable civic behavior seventeen years later.

III

Though the influential political philosopher and theorist of religious toleration, John Locke, was only twelve when Williams published *The Bloudy
Tenent*, he, too, included Muslims as tolerated believers and reached seemingly similar conclusions about the separation of government from matters of
individual religious belief. As Edwin Gaustad observes, "[So] Locke, in
echoing and often clarifying the sentiments of Roger Williams, became the
chief channel of those once unsettling ideas regarding religious liberty."[56]
Like Williams and Helwys, Locke included Jews and Muslims in *A Letter
Concerning Toleration* (1689).[57] But unlike these two predecessors, Locke
worried about the loyalty of Muslims (as well as Catholics). He wrote, "It is
ridiculous for anyone to profess himself a Mahumetan in his Religion, but in
every thing else a faithful Subject to a Christian Magistrate, whilst at the
same time he acknowledges himself bound to yield blind obedience to the
Mufti of Constantinople; who himself is intirely [*sic*] obedient to the *Ottoman* Emperor; and frames the feigned Oracles of Religion according to his
pleasure."[58]

Locke was wrong about all Muslims owing loyalty to either the grand
mufti or the Ottoman sultan. By this time, Moroccans had their own dynasty
and even Algiers, Tunis, and Tripoli remained only nominally subject to the
Ottoman ruler.[59] In any case, after venting this anxiety about Muslims
(which some scholars believe was actually meant to indict Catholics), Locke
advocated that Jews and Muslims be granted not merely toleration but also
full civil rights.[60] Locke did not borrow his reference to Muslims from Roger
Williams, instead finding a precedent closer to home. He cited Edward Bagshaw's 1660 treatise in defense of Christian dissenters: "'tis agreed that a
Christian magistrate cannot force his religion on a Jew or on a Mahomedan,
therefore much less can he abridge his fellow-Christian in things of lesser
moment."[61] Like Bagshaw, Locke sought to defend Christian dissenters in
England, but he inverted the premise. Locke argued that if all Christians
deserved to worship freely, without the ruler's interference, then so did non-
Christians.

In Locke's first Latin edition of the *Letter*, the key sentence runs this way:
"Indeed, to speak the truth, and as becomes one man to another, neither
Pagan nor Mahometan nor Jew should be excluded from the commonwealth
because of his religion."[62] However, two powerful new words, *civil rights*,
appeared in the first English edition of Locke's *Letter*, also published in
1689.[63] In subsequent letters, he repeatedly defended the application of this
phrase to Muslims. In addition, in his final, posthumous letter of 1706, Locke
critiqued the condemnation via religious polemic that Roger Williams had
embraced. He cautioned his own adversaries about the futility of such an
approach, admonishing his opponents, "Try when you please with a Brah-

min, a Mahometan, a Papist, Lutheran, Quaker, Anabaptist, Presbyterian, etc., you will find if you argue with them, as you do with me, that the matter will rest between you, and that you are no more a judge for any of them than they are for you."[64]

When it came to the treatment of Islam and Muslims, the American political founder and slave owner Thomas Jefferson echoed Locke, not Williams. Jefferson's interest in Islam began in 1765, when, at the age of twenty-two, the Virginian bought a Qur'an, the first directly translated from Arabic into English.[65] It included the translator George Sale's two-hundred-page "Preliminary Discourse," which provided the reader with the most balanced presentation of Islam's history and beliefs then available.[66] Jefferson, a law student at the time, probably bought the sacred text as a legal source, which had been the narrow European view of the text since its first translation into Latin in the twelfth century. There is no evidence of Jefferson's immediate reaction to the Qur'an, because he left no notes documenting his response. This may be because a fire destroyed all his books and papers five years after the purchase of the Qur'an. We cannot prove for certain that Jefferson purchased the sacred text a second time, though the fact that his copy survives in the Library of Congress suggests that he may have.[67]

Jefferson's engagement with Islam and its adherents spanned his entire life. Like Williams and Locke, he displayed a double-edged tendency, expressing mostly (but not exclusively) negative views about Islam while defending the rights of Muslims. His earliest notes illumine this phenomenon. For example, in 1765, the year in which he purchased the Qur'an, Jefferson recorded the seventeenth-century English legal ruling cited earlier in this chapter, which declared that Muslims were not "perpetual enemies" and that they should not be persecuted as "Creatures of God."[68] At about the same time, Jefferson recorded the French philosopher Voltaire's adage that Islam repressed scientific inquiry.[69]

While Jefferson was a careful reader of Locke, he never owned a single volume by Roger Williams in what became the largest private library in the United States.[70] Moreover, a few months after writing the Declaration of Independence in 1776, Jefferson copied a key reference to Muslims from Locke's *A Letter Concerning Toleration* (1689), writing, "[He] sais: 'neither Pagan nor Mahometan nor Jew ought to be excluded from the civil rights of the Commonwealth because of his religion.'"[71] However, unlike Locke, Jefferson also publicly expressed the view that Islam "repressed free enquiry."[72] His intent, ironically, was to abolish the established Anglican faith of his native state. However, Jefferson never feared a potential double loyalty among Muslims (or Catholics). Instead, he paraphrased Locke's language about civil rights and put an end to state meddling in religious beliefs in his landmark Virginia legislation, "A Bill for Establishing Religious Freedom." Jefferson moved beyond toleration and demanded more: disestablishment and political equality regardless of religion. In this pathbreaking legislation, he wrote, "Our civil rights have no dependance on our religious opinions."[73] This uniquely American concept of government went far beyond Locke's ideal of a tolerant but still dominant Anglican establishment, prefiguring the prohibition of a religious test for public office in Article VI, Section 3 of the Constitution and the First Amendment.

In his bill, Jefferson deliberately removed Locke's multiple references to the Gospel—and Jesus—for the Virginian's political mission never included the salvation of souls; rather, he insisted on creating a new polity in which religion would not determine civic standing. As part of that legal intent, he explicitly included Muslims. Jefferson recalled that the bill "still met with opposition; but with some mutilations in the preamble, it was finally passed; and a singular proposition proved that its protections of opinion was meant to be universal."[74] His "universal" intent is reflected in his description of a last-ditch effort in 1785 to resist the insertion of the words *Jesus Christ*. He recalled in his autobiography of 1821, "Where the preamble declares, that coercion is a departure from the plan of the holy author of our religion, an amendment was proposed, by inserting the words 'Jesus Christ,' so that it should read, 'a departure from the plan of Jesus Christ, the holy author of our religion.'"[75] He rejoiced in the ultimate rejection of those two pivotal words: "[T]he insertion was rejected by a great majority, in proof that they meant to comprehend, within the mantle of its protection, the Jew and the Gentile, the Christian and Mahometan, the Hindoo, and Infidel of every denomination."[76]

Jefferson's principle of religious equality also deliberately included Muslims. His 1784 *Notes on Virginia* strongly suggests that unlike Williams he would never have engaged in the public condemnation of anyone's beliefs, famously insisting that "the legitimate powers of government extend to such acts only as are injurious to others. But it does me no injury for my neighbor to say there are twenty gods or no God. It neither picks my pocket nor breaks my leg."[77] Indeed, this noninterventionist religious tolerance later caused Jefferson's political opponents to defame him as an "infidel," a term synonymous since the sixteenth century with the designation of not just a bad Christian but also a Muslim.[78]

The tolerationist arguments of Helwys, Williams, Locke, and Jefferson reveal that Muslims have been woven into the fabric of North American ideals about religious and civil rights since the seventeenth century. Muslims, imagined and real, certainly demarcated the outer boundaries of religious pluralism in the Anglo-Atlantic world. However, in contrast to Locke and Jefferson, Williams might very well—if presented with the opportunity—have publicly condemned Muslims, as he had Quakers, for their religious errors and public behavior. This conjecture is grounded in Williams's own conflation of Muslims and Quakers as believers in false revelations.

As Williams conceived them in the seventeenth century, the boundaries of a qualified religious toleration expanded to include Muslims while allowing for individual censure of their beliefs. Today, with an estimated Muslim U.S. citizenry of three to seven million, public condemnations of Islam and its adherents remain a common part of our national religious and political discourse.[79] In contrast, similar public invective lodged against the Quaker minority, or any other religious group, would now be considered bigoted. Thus, Williams's precedent in public religious defamation might still attract anti-Islamic followers today, albeit ones who would most certainly embrace an idea that the founder of Providence never would: that this country should be exclusively Christian.

NOTES

1. He briefly joined the Baptist confession in 1638, helping to build the first Baptist church in Rhode Island. See Edwin Gaustad, *Roger Williams* (New York: Oxford University Press, 2005), 52–53.
2. Thomas Helwys, *The Mistery of Iniquity* (London: Kingsgate Press, 1935), 69. I have adapted the original spelling. See also John Marshall, *John Locke, Toleration, and Early Enlightenment Culture: Religious Intolerance and Arguments for Religious Toleration in Early Modern and "Early Enlightenment" Europe* (Cambridge: Cambridge University Press, 2006), 150. For a broader discussion of Helwys, Williams, Locke, and Jefferson, see Denise A. Spellberg, *Thomas Jefferson's Qur'an: Islam and the Founders* (New York: Alfred A. Knopf, 2013), 53–120.
3. Helwys, *Mistery*, 69.
4. This is a paraphrase first asserted by Benjamin J. Kaplan, *Divided by Faith: Religious Conflict and the Practice of Toleration in Early Modern Europe* (Cambridge, MA: Belknap Press of Harvard University, 2007), 296. For a history of the word *infidel*, as applied to Muslims and Jews, see "Infidel," in *Oxford English Dictionary*, 13 vols. (Oxford: Clarendon Press, 1970), 5:260.
5. Kaplan, *Divided by Faith*, 296; Perez Zagorin, *How the Idea of Toleration Came to the West* (Princeton, NJ: Princeton University Press, 2003), 5–6.
6. G. A. Russell, "The Impact of *Philosophus Autodidactus*: Pocockes, John Locke, and the Society of Friends," in *The "Arabick" Interest of the Natural Philosophers in Seventeenth-Century England*, ed. G. A. Russell (Leiden: E. J. Brill, 1994), 8.
7. Nabil Matar, *Islam in Britain, 1558–1685* (New York: Cambridge University Press, 1998), 10.
8. Russell, "Impact of *Philosophus Autodidactus*," 187.
9. Charles Melville, introduction to *Faith and Fable: Islamic Manuscripts from the Cambridge University Library*, 3, accessed 1 August 2014, http://www.lib.cam.ac.uk/deptserv/neareastern/Faith_&26_Fable.pdf.
10. One example is the voluminous *Qanun fi al-tibb*, or *Canon of Medicine*, written in Arabic by the doctor and philosopher Ibn Sina (d. 1037), known as Avicenna in Europe. It would be used in Europe throughout the seventeenth century as a medical handbook in Latin, but not all of it had been translated from Arabic.
11. Ziad Elmarsafy, *The Enlightenment Qur'an: The Politics of Translation and the Construction of Islam* (Oxford: Oneworld Press, 2009), 8–9. See also Nabil Matar, "Alexander Ross and the First English Translation of the Qur'an," *Muslim World* 88 (January 1998): 81–92.
12. Matar, *Islam in Britain*, 1–49.

13. C. A. Patrides, "'The Bloudy and Cruell Turke': The Background of a Renaissance Commonplace," *Studies in the Renaissance* 10 (1963): 126–35.

14. Linda Colley, *Captives: Britain, Empire and the World, 1600–1850* (London: Jonathan Cape, 2002), 43–73, 99–134.

15. Robert C. Davis, *Holy War and Human Bondage: Tales of Christian-Muslim Slavery in the Early Modern Mediterranean* (Santa Barbara, CA: Praeger, 2009), 15. For Qur'anic verses about captives or prisoners taken during war as different from slaves, see Jonathan E. Brockopp, "Captives," in *Encyclopaedia of the Qur'an*, ed. Jane D. McAuliffe, 6 vols. (Leiden: E. J. Brill, 2001), 1:289–90, and Brockopp, "Slaves," in McAuliffe, *Encyclopaedia of the Qur'an*, 5:56–60.

16. Matar, *Islam in Britain*, 9, 15–19.

17. Ibid., 9.

18. Ibid., 110.

19. Teresa M. Bejan, "'The Bond of Civility': Roger Williams on Toleration and Its Limits," *History of European Ideas* 37 (2011): 409n4. My thanks to Dr. Bejan for pointing out this key piece of information.

20. Ibid.

21. Roger Williams, *George Fox Digg'd Out of His Burrowes*, ed. J. Lewis Diman, vol. 5 of *The Complete Writings of Roger Williams* (New York: Russell & Russell, 1963), 146.

22. Roger Williams, "To the People Called Quakers," in *George Fox*, first page of letter cited, which has no internal pagination.

23. Nabil Matar, *Turks, Moors & Englishmen in the Age of Discovery* (New York: Columbia University Press, 1999), 39.

24. Ibid., 30.

25. Ibid.

26. William Salkeld, *Reports of Cases Adjudg'd in the Court of the King's Bench* (London: E. Nutt and R. Gosling, 1717), 1:46. The reference to the original case dates to the reign of King Charles I (r. 1625–1649).

27. Williams, *George Fox*, 5:125, in the margin.

28. Ibid.

29. Ibid.

30. Quoted in J. Lewis Diman, introduction to *George Fox*, 5:xxxiii.

31. Roger Williams, "To John Throckmorton, ca. 23 July 1672," in *The Correspondence of Roger Williams*, ed. Glenn W. LaFantasie, 2 vols. (Hanover, NH: University Press of New England, 1988), 2:664.

32. Roger Williams, "To those many Learned and Pious Men . . . Mr. Richard Baxter, Mr. John Owen &c.," 10 March 1672, in Williams, *George Fox*, vol. 5, second page of the unpaginated letter, just before "A Narration of the Conference or Dispute This last August 1672."

33. "Rhode Island was known even in Colonial times as a haven for non-traditional religious adherents such as Roger Williams and Anne Hutchinson. The presence of Jews and Muslims among its settlers, and Freemasons, is therefore to be expected." This claim is made, in the case of Muslims, without any historical evidence. It is asserted by Elizabeth Hirschman and Donald Yates, *Jews and Muslims in British Colonial America: A Genealogical History* (Jefferson, NC: McFarland, 2012), 186–87.

34. Williams, "To John Throckmorton," in LaFantasie, *Correspondence*, 2:662.

35. Williams, *George Fox*, 5:125.

36. Roger Williams, *The Bloudy Tenent of Persecution*, ed. Samuel L. Caldwell, *The Complete Writings of Roger Williams*, 7 vols. (New York: Russell and Russell, 1963), 3:93.

37. Ibid.

38. Williams, *Bloudy Tenent*, 3:3.

39. Ibid., 3:3–4.

40. Quoted in Naomi Cohen, *Jews in Christian America: The Pursuit of Religious Equality* (New York: Oxford University Press, 1992), 17. Another author suggests that by linking Turks and Jews, the latter seemed "not on the same plane with Christianity"; see Maxwell H. Morris, "Roger Williams and the Jews," *American Jewish Archives* 3 (January 1951): 27.

41. Williams, *Bloudy Tenent*, 3:11.

42. Ibid., 3:33.

43. Humberto Garcia, *Islam and the English Enlightenment, 1670–1840* (Baltimore: Johns Hopkins University Press, 2012), 1–59.

44. Williams, *Bloudy Tenent*, 3:33.

45. Ibid., 3:283.

46. John Cotton, "A Discourse about Civil Government," in *The Sacred Rights of Conscience: Selected Readings on Religious Liberty and Church-State Relations in the American Founding*, ed. Daniel L. Dreisbach and Mark David Hall (Indianapolis, IN: Liberty Fund, 2009), 129–30.

47. Ibid., 135.

48. Williams, *Bloudy Tenent*, 3:43.

49. Quoted in Gaustad, *Roger Williams*, 102.

50. Williams, *Bloudy Tenent*, 3:152.

51. "Flushing Remonstrance, 1657," in Dreisbach and Hall, *Sacred Rights of Conscience*, 108–9.

52. Williams, *Bloudy Tenent*, 3:142.

53. Ibid.

54. Roger Williams, "To the Town of Providence," in *The Letters of Roger Williams*, ed. John Russell Bartlett, *The Complete Writings of Roger Williams*, 7 vols. (New York: Russell & Russell, 1963), 6:278–79.

55. Ibid., 6:279.

56. Gaustad, *Roger Williams*, 117.

57. For the best discussion of Jews and Muslims in Locke, see Marshall, *John Locke*, 371–95, 593–617.

58. John Locke, *A Letter Concerning Toleration*, ed. James H. Tully (Indianapolis, IN: Hackett, 1983), 50.

59. Locke's anxiety about Muslims living in England ceding civil allegiance to a Christian ruler might have been assuaged if he had understood, as he probably never did, that Christian authorities would be expected by most Sunni Muslim jurists to offer Muslims in their lands an *aman*, or pledge of safe conduct. Reciprocally, Muslims in Christian lands understood that they legally "may not commit acts of treachery, betrayal, deceit or fraud, and may not violate the honor or property of non-Muslims." See Khaled Abou El Fadl, "Islamic Law and Muslim Minorities: The Juristic Discourse on Muslim Minorities from the Second/Eighth to the Eleventh/Seventeenth Centuries," *Islamic Law and Society* 1 (1994): 175; Andrew F. March, *Islam and Liberal Citizenship: The Search for an Overlapping Consensus* (New York: Oxford University Press, 2009), 183–89, 261–63. Quote is from Abou El Fadl, "Islamic Law," 175.

60. Jeremy Waldron, *God, Locke and Equality: Christian Foundations of John Locke's Political Thought* (New York: Cambridge University Press, 2002), 220–21.

61. Quoted in Nabil Matar, "John Locke and the 'Turbanned Nations,'" *Journal of Islamic Studies* 2 (1991): 68; John Locke, *Two Tracts on Government*, ed. and trans. Philip Abrams (Cambridge: Cambridge University Press, 1967), 127.

62. John Locke, *Epistola de Tolerantia: A Letter on Toleration*, ed. Raymond Klibansky, trans. J. W. Gough (Oxford: Clarendon Press, 1968), 144 (Latin), 145 (English).

63. Locke, *Letter Concerning Toleration*, 54.

64. John Locke, *A Second Letter Concerning Toleration: To the Author of the Argument of the Letter Concerning Toleration, briefly considered and answered*, in *Four Letters on Toleration by John Locke* (London: Ward, Lock, and Tyler, 1876), 387.

65. Paul P. Hoffman, ed., *Virginia Gazette Daybooks, 1750–1752 and 1764–1766* (Charlottesville: University of Virginia Library Microfilm Publication, 1967), seg. 2, folio 202; Kevin J. Hayes, "How Thomas Jefferson Read the Qur'an," *Early American Literature* 39, no. 2 (2004): 247.

66. George Sale, trans., *The Koran, commonly called the Alcoran of Mohammed, Translated into English from the Original Arabic, with Explanatory Notes, taken from the Most Approved Commentators, to which is prefixed a Preliminary Discourse*, 2 vols. (London: L. Hawes, W. Clarke, R. Collins, and T. Wilcox, 1764).

67. Spellberg, *Thomas Jefferson's Qur'an*, 81–84.

68. Thomas Jefferson, *The Commonplace Book of Thomas Jefferson: A Repertory of His Ideas on Government*, ed. Gilbert Chinard (Baltimore: Johns Hopkins University Press, 1926), 76; Spellberg, *Thomas Jefferson's Qur'an*, 93–108.

69. Jefferson, *Commonplace Book*, 10. This mistaken premise would surface in his debate notes.

70. James Gilreath and Douglas L. Wilson, eds., *Thomas Jefferson's Library: A Catalogue with the Entries in His Own Order* (Washington, DC: Library of Congress, 1989), 1; see also E. Millicent Sowerby, ed., *Catalogue of the Library of Thomas Jefferson*, 5 vols. (Washington, DC: Library of Congress, 1959), 5:438, where any indication of Williams's work is missing.

71. Thomas Jefferson, *The Papers of Thomas Jefferson*, ed. Julian P. Boyd et al., 40 vols. (Princeton, NJ: Princeton University Press, 1950–), 1:548. The editor transcribes the word for Muslim as "Mahamedan," but the actual spelling may well have been "Mahometan," which is possible from Jefferson's handwritten original.

72. Ibid., 1:538.

73. Ibid., 2:545–46.

74. Thomas Jefferson, "Autobiography," in *The Life and Selected Writings of Thomas Jefferson*, ed. Adrienne Koch and William Peden (New York: Modern Library, 1998), 45–46.

75. Ibid. There is a typo in this printed edition, where "words," referring to Jesus Christ, is incorrectly rendered "word," in contrast to Jefferson's handwritten version.

76. Ibid., 46.

77. Thomas Jefferson, "Notes on Virginia," in Koch and Peden, *Life and Selected Writings of Thomas Jefferson*, 254.

78. Spellberg, *Thomas Jefferson's Qur'an*, 213.

79. John L. Esposito, *What Everyone Needs to Know about Islam*, 2nd ed. (New York: Oxford University Press, 2011), 221.

Chapter Six

"An encroachment on our religious rights"

Methodist Missions, Slavery, and Religious Toleration in the British Atlantic World

Christopher C. Jones

On a Friday afternoon in the early spring of 1801, Methodist missionary John Brownell was summoned to the office of Robert Thomson, president of the West Indian island of Saint Kitts. "A printed address was there put into my hands," wrote Brownell in his journal, "from the general conference in America to the people called Methodists, requesting them to petition the Legislative Body to Abolish the Slave-Trade." That document, published the previous year in Baltimore, decried slavery as an "enormous evil" and called for "the gradual emancipation of the slaves." Unsurprisingly, the address "caused no small alarm" among colonial officials on the small, sugar-producing island. "The Counsil," Brownell continued, "viewed us as so many Spies, whose object it was to see the nakedness of the Island, raise an insurrection, & cover the land with blood."[1]

Brownell tried to assuage the colonial officials' concerns, first expressing doubt as to "the authenticity of the address" and then, when convinced of its legitimacy, by "endeavor[ing] to distinguish between the English & the American Methodists." The distinction between the Wesleyan Methodist Church in Great Britain and the Methodist Episcopal Church in the United States was likely lost on anyone not intimately familiar with the internal dynamics of the Methodist movement. Although clearly addressed in large, bold letters to "Brethren and Friends in the United States," the address did briefly mention the Caribbean, blaming "the small number of adventurers from Europe, who visit the West Indies for the sole purpose of amassing fortunes" for perpetuating "the enslaving and destroying of the human race." That the document bore the signature of Thomas Coke, the well-known superintendent of British Methodist missions throughout the West Indies who also served as bishop of the Methodist Episcopal Church, further complicated the distinction between English and American Methodists. Downplaying the antislavery address's implications, Brownell patiently explained that "the Methodists were not unanimous respecting the Abolition of Slavery, nor was it made a condition of communion amongst them." He pointed out that a number of West Indian Methodists themselves owned slaves, and concluded by making it clear that "the intention of the English Conference in funding missionaries to the West Indies was not to abolish slavery" but rather to "bring people to a Knowledge of God." This proved satisfactory to the president, now reassured that Brownell and his fellow missionaries posed no imminent threat to the island's social stability.[2]

Brownell's run-in with colonial officials came at a pivotal moment in the history of both Methodism and the Atlantic world. The previous four decades had seen Methodism expand from a reform-minded society within the Church of England to become an independent church and transatlantic religious movement. It was also an unparalleled period of political and social disruption in the early modern Atlantic world. Revolution in North America shook the political foundations of the British Empire; the slave rebellion turned revolution in Saint Domingue and the several subsequent uprisings it inspired threatened to disrupt the labor system upon which European empires depended; and the emergence of a recognizable antislavery movement offered a formidable intellectual and legal challenge to the slave trade.

The Methodist experience demonstrates the central role that missionary efforts to free an enslaved people of color played in forging toleration in the Age of Revolution. Methodists were caught up in the era's epochal developments in the mission fields of the West Indies, North America, and Africa. The period's revolutionary disruptions facilitated Methodism's expansive growth, which, in turn, attracted vociferous resistance.[3] The opposition Methodists encountered in their earliest missions to the Caribbean and West Africa was inextricably linked to debates over slavery and often assumed racially charged overtones. Authorities in the West Indies restricted missionary access to the enslaved, as well as the worship of all people of color. Sierra Leone Company officials similarly sought to constrain the religious rights of black Methodists in Freetown by revoking the preachers' rights to perform certain rites. Proselytizing is almost always a fraught exercise. It was particularly so in an age of evangelical expansion, political revolution, and antislavery agitation. As the most aggressive missionary force of the eighteenth and nineteenth centuries, Methodists played a formative role in shaping the legal and religious limits of toleration in the British Atlantic world.

BEGINNINGS

The first Methodist missionaries to reach the Caribbean arrived by accident, when a storm blew their Nova Scotia–bound ship off course, forcing them to reroute to Antigua, where they landed in December 1786. Led by Thomas Coke, the missionaries made the most of their unexpected opportunity, capitalizing on the pioneering work of Antiguan planter Nathaniel Gilbert, his brother Francis, shipwright turned lay preacher John Baxter, and thousands of free and enslaved people of color. The latter spread the Methodist message through kinship and communication networks largely inaccessible to whites and thus formed the lifeblood of the movement. When Coke departed from the West Indies in 1787, he left missionaries stationed on three islands and organized additional classes on two others. Over the next decade, more missionaries followed, and their collective efforts to evangelize the islands turned them into Methodist strongholds. In 1798, Coke estimated that "there are about forty thousand, or from that number to fifty thousand, who regularly attend the ministry of our preachers. . . . Out of these, near ten thousand are members of our society."[4]

The Methodists, of course, were not the first to attempt the systematic conversion of the Caribbean's enslaved population. Roman Catholic missionaries had proselytized among slaves in Spanish, Portuguese, and French colonies as early as the sixteenth century, and the Society for the Propagation of the Gospel in Foreign Parts began dispatching Anglican missionaries in 1701. More successful than the Anglicans were the Moravians; missionaries from this German-speaking pietist sect began work in Saint Thomas in the 1730s, eventually spreading to other Danish and British colonies in the Caribbean, North America, and West Africa. The Anglicans and Moravians alike condoned slavery and profited from the labor of slaves, including many who worked on church-owned plantations.[5] It was not until the later decades of the eighteenth century, though, that a substantial number of slaves converted to Protestant Christianity. While their attitudes toward the morality of slavery varied widely, many evangelical-minded white Baptists, Methodists, and Presbyterians readily welcomed African American and Afro-Caribbean converts as their coreligionists and spiritual equals.[6]

The mass conversion of free and enslaved people of color to evangelical sects raised new questions about the already vexed matter of religious toleration. While the Anglican establishment in England grew concerned about the explosive growth of dissenting groups throughout the British Empire, planters and colonial officials worried about the effects of evangelical preaching on the enslaved. Political revolution in North America and the slave rebellion turned revolution in Saint Domingue amplified those concerns, as did the participation of several evangelical leaders in the emergent antislavery movement. John Wesley's *Thoughts Upon Slavery*, which was published in 1774 and circulated widely throughout the Atlantic world, accused slave traders, merchants, and owners of "villainy, of fraud, robbery and murder."[7] The antislavery writings of other Methodists in England and the United States further complicated the efforts of missionaries to convince West Indian authorities that their aim was neither to preach politics nor to incite rebellion, but rather, as John Brownell explained, to offer salvation to the souls of the enslaved. Methodist missionaries struggled to mollify those suspicious of their claims, and in the coming years, they fought back against the West Indian plantocracy, which sought to suppress Methodist activities.

EARLY OPPOSITION IN THE WEST INDIES

The earliest efforts to restrict the activities of Caribbean Methodist preachers occurred not in one of Britain's colonial outposts but on Dutch-controlled Sint Eustatius, and they took aim not at itinerant English missionaries, but rather at black Methodist slaves. Thomas Coke and his traveling companion arrived in January 1787, after learning that "some serious free Blacks" there had "joined together to bear the expense of supporting us." Upon his arrival, Coke was surprised to discover that "the Lord raised up lately a negro-slave whose name is Harry . . . to prepare our way." "Formerly a member of [the Methodist] Society" in North America, Harry had been "sold to a Mr. Godette" in Sint Eustatius.[8] Upon his arrival, he began holding prayer meetings among the slaves, eventually "rais[ing] up a little body of people" to whom he preached "whenever he had spare time allowed him." Even the island's governor, Johannes Runnels, eventually came to hear Harry. Although Runnels initially "approved of him," he began to grow concerned over the slave preacher's growing audience and influence on other slaves. When Runnels "called a second time to hear" Harry preach, the number of listeners had "increased considerably" and the governor bristled at the sight of a black slave calling the people to repentance. He worried about reports that "the poor slaves were so affected under the word, that many of them fell down as if they were dead," and grew concerned "this man would make the blacks too wise."[9] Runnels summoned Harry to his office and forbade him from preaching, under the threat of imprisonment. When Coke arrived shortly thereafter and secured permission for Methodist missionaries to preach, he apparently assumed that the approval extended to Harry and other lay preachers as well. Upon departing from the island two weeks later, Coke left three classes "to the care of Harry, two to [a] North American sister, and one to a black named Samuel."[10]

When Coke returned in 1789, things had taken a decided turn for the worse. A law aimed at forbidding public prayer had been passed, disrupting Methodist preaching and leaving the classes in a state of disarray. Harry was found guilty of "the unpardonable sin of praying with the people," received thirty-nine lashes, and was banished from the island. This "diabolical persecution" infuriated Coke, who described the law in his journal as "the first instance known among mankind, of a persecution openly avowed against *religion itself.*" It was particularly shocking, he wrote, "in this liberal and tolerating age." Leaving it to God to "carry on his blessed work" in the Dutch islands "by the means of secret Class meetings," Coke departed "this place of tyranny, oppression, and wrong," returning to Saint Kitts and "blessing God for a British constitution and a British government."[11]

The protections afforded Methodists under the British constitution and government would soon be tested, though, as missionaries met vigorous opposition in Jamaica, Barbados, and Saint Vincent. Much of the initial animus echoed well-rehearsed anti-Methodist arguments in the British Isles and North America. Newspapers in Barbados and Jamaica derided the Methodists' "depraved appetites," "profligate absurdities," and "canting hypocrisy."[12] The first Methodist preaching in Jamaica met with modest success, but it also attracted the unwanted attention of "the young Bucks and Bloods of the town." When Coke reached the island on a second visit in 1791, he noted with despair that opposition in Jamaica "very far exceeds all the persecutions we have met with in the other Islands unitedly considered." In addition to routine interruptions of preaching and the occasional antagonistic article, he reported threats made on the lives of preachers and an attempt to burn the newly constructed Kingston chapel; William Hammet was left "worn almost to a skeleton with opposition and fatigue." Following one final threat made on Hammet's life and the acquittal of those charged with ransacking the chapel, Coke and Hammet made immediate plans to leave the island.[13]

After their departure on January 25, a debate broke out in the local press over the alleged dangers of Methodist preaching. A letter published in the *Daily Advertiser* from an anonymous "Store Keeper" sought to expose the threat the missionaries' "dark activity and zeal" posed to Jamaican society. "Such nonsense as this," he wrote, "has already turned the brains of many of our negroes and made them useless to their masters and dangerous to the community." Alluding to the 1760 rebellion of more than one thousand slaves on the northeastern coast of the island, the author sounded a warning: "In this country, where the spirit of insurrection is but with difficulty held in by the strong hand of superior knowledge . . . we anxiously watch to prevent a repetition of those horrid scenes."[14] The letter provoked a response from an unidentified "Friend to Moderation," who defended the Methodists. Instead of inciting slaves to rebellion, he replied, the missionaries were trying to "civilize the negroes, to give them by the simplest methods of instruction a just conception of their interest in another world, to implant in their minds a fixed and rooted detestation of vice, and . . . to inculcate the propriety as well as necessity of a submission to the will of their masters."[15]

Although Methodist missionaries had mixed views on the subject of slavery, they were no idle threat in the minds of Jamaican planters. The letters in the *Daily Advertiser*, and those that followed in response, appeared alongside the standard series of runaway slave advertisements and news from both Europe and elsewhere in the Americas. The earliest reports of the incipient rebellion in nearby Saint Domingue heightened fears of insurrection and underlined the dangers posed by evangelizing slaves. In September 1791, the newspaper relayed news of a "great slaughter" in Cape François that left more than ten thousand dead. There were, according to the paper, "among the prisoners . . . several Ecclesiastics, who had disguised themselves as negroes, and who, it is supposed, incited the mischief that has taken place."[16] When a group of free people of color, led by several "elders of the Methodist church," petitioned the Jamaican Assembly in 1792 for the revocation of restrictions on several of their (nonreligious) rights, the petition was rejected. Planter Simon Taylor accused the "worthless Methodists" who backed the petition of utilizing "the exact plan that was first used at Hispaniola, to make divisions between the whites and people of colour there, and then to stir up the rebellion."[17] The effects of the rebellion in Saint Domingue reverberated throughout the Atlantic world, and provoked colonial officials in Jamaica and elsewhere to take the first legal steps toward curbing the missionaries' influence.

Local officials grew increasingly suspicious of Methodists and, over the course of the final decade of the eighteenth century, enacted several measures to restrict their religious rights. In Barbados, Benjamin Pearce lamented that "my enemies are many, and some of them men in power." After a mob interrupted one of his sermons and pelted the newly constructed chapel with stones in September 1789, Pearce "applied to a magistrate for redress." Though "the charges were proved with the most unquestionable certainty" and the judge promised "to do us justice," Pearce explained, "all the redress we could obtain was the following:—'*The offense was committed against Almighty God; it, therefore, does not belong to me to punish!*'"[18] In nearby Saint Vincent, rioters vandalized the Methodist chapel one night in 1791, "seized the Bible, took it to the public gallows, and hanged it [there]; where it was found hanging the next morning." Thomas Coke's appreciation for the initial efforts to catch the perpetrators turned to exasperation in January 1793, when he received word that Matthew Lumb, stationed on the island since 1789, had been imprisoned for preaching "THE GOSPEL TO THE NEGROES IN OUR OWN CHAPEL, built with our own Money, and on our own ground!" The local legislature, he was informed, had enacted a law specifically targeting Methodism's itinerant missionary force, forbidding public preaching by anyone "that had not previously resided for twelve months on the Island." "How unparalleled a Law in these modern times," wrote Coke in his journal, "and under a government called Protestant; and which boasts of the liberty of its subjects." In his mind, persecution of the Methodists in the colonies was intimately connected with the opposition they faced from the Anglican establishment at home. "The Government that would persecute us in the extremes of its Empire," he concluded, "would undoubtedly persecute us to its centre."[19]

RELIGIOUS RIGHTS IN SIERRA LEONE

While Coke continued to split his time between Europe and America during these years, navigating the sudden reality of Methodist independence from the Church of England, he also continued his search for fertile mission fields in other "extremes of the Empire." In a 1791 letter to Ezekiel Cooper, Coke excitedly reported that "we are going to send Missionaries to Sierra Leone in Africa, where the English are establishing a very capital settlement." Melville Horne, whom Coke described as "a zealous Methodist preacher," arrived in 1792 with the intention of establishing a mission to the native Temne people. Instead, he remained in Freetown for almost his entire fourteen-month stay in Africa, ministering to a group of recently arrived former slaves from Tidewater Virginia and coastal Carolina. These black loyalists had escaped to British lines at the outbreak of the American Revolution, taken up arms for the king's army, and then briefly settled in Nova Scotia before journeying across the Atlantic to found the abolitionist-led settlement of Freetown on Africa's Windward Coast.[20] Among their number, as Horne quickly learned, were several hundred Methodists, organized into classes and congregations and led by identifiable leaders.

Some of those leaders, like "Daddy" Moses Wilkinson, had been preaching Methodism longer than Horne himself had. Moses was among the first converts made by Robert Williams, a lay Irish preacher who introduced Methodism to Norfolk and Portsmouth, Virginia, in 1772. After escaping his enslavement, taking up arms against the American colonists, and surviving an outbreak of malaria and smallpox that left him blind and severely disabled, Wilkinson migrated to the British maritime province of Nova Scotia in 1783. There he worked alongside fellow black evangelists Luke Jordan, Boston King, and Nathaniel Snowball, as well as white Methodist preachers Freeborn Garrettson and William Black, in ministering to the province's steadily growing Methodist community. Harsh winter weather, crippling poverty, and broken promises from government officials, though, persuaded most of Nova Scotia's black Methodists to take advantage of abolitionist John Clarkson's 1791 offer to resettle in West Africa. Moses's congregation, along with those of fellow Methodists Henry Beverhout, Luke Jordan, and Boston King, agreed to go, as did the followers of black Baptist preacher David George and the Huntingtonian congregation led by Cato Perkins.

If the settlers expected to find a land of milk and honey in their new home, they were sorely disappointed. Their long-sought promised land was nothing more than the shoddy remains of the recently razed Granville Town, situated just upriver from the notorious slave-trading fort on Bunce Island. Matters were made worse by ongoing disagreements with Sierra Leone Company leaders. Just months after their arrival, they protested to Clarkson that several promises had not yet been kept; the company leader dismissed their petitions as "strange notions" respecting "their civil rights."[21] When Clarkson returned to London in July for a brief leave, the headstrong Zachary Macaulay, a former slave manager on a West Indian plantation turned abolitionist, replaced him. Together with William Dawes, the new governing council of the Sierra Leone settlement attempted to further restrict the rights of the former slaves. While Clarkson had proved less than helpful in achieving the full range of rights promised the former slaves, he at least allowed them some autonomy in religious matters. By contrast, Macaulay and Dawes refused to tolerate the Methodists' religious enthusiasm (or "reigning folly"), including their belief in the efficacy of "dreams, visions, and . . . ridiculous bodily sensations." Macaulay and Dawes instituted mandatory catechism classes for children, revoked the rights of Methodist preachers to marry their congregants, and imposed harsh quit-rents on the lands allotted to the settlers. In 1793, Isaac Anderson and Cato Perkins embarked for London to petition the Sierra Leone Company's directors in person, at which time they compared the actions of Dawes and Macaulay to overzealous plantation overseers and complained that "the manner you have treated us has been just the same as if we were slaves."[22]

At the very time they were presenting their case, Thomas Coke was in London, petitioning the British government for relief in the West Indies. In November 1793, he rejoiced that "our best of Kings, with the advice of his council, had disallowed the persecuting law of St. Vincent's. It is no more—Glory be to God!"[23] The victory led to a relatively prolonged period of peace for Methodists in the Caribbean. Persecution continued in the Dutch West Indies; Coke's appeal to Dutch authorities on behalf of the Methodists in Sint Eustatius and Saba during a 1794 visit to The Hague was unsuccessful, and missionaries would not return to those islands until 1811.[24] Methodists on British islands, by contrast, enjoyed freedom from harassment by colonial officials, and the movement thrived in the final years of the eighteenth century. The same could not be said for Methodists in West Africa. Anderson and Perkins's petition was rejected, and the two men returned to Africa without securing any commitments to improve conditions there.

Relations with Methodist leaders in England, meanwhile, proved mixed. British leaders were more interested in potential missions to unconverted Africans than they were in supporting the Sierra Leone migrants. To that end, they invited the Carolina-born former slave Boston King to England, where he enrolled at Kingswood School and received training for a mission to local tribes in West Africa. King's experience convinced him that "many of the White People . . . are our friends, and deliverers from slavery, as far as their ability and circumstances will admit."[25] But those who remained in Sierra Leone bristled at Melville Horne's treatment of them as children "in need of his religious and moral tutelage." As Suzanne Schwarz has noted, "Horne failed to understand how the settlers' experience of enslavement had created a fierce determination to lead an independent life."[26] That spirit of independence grew stronger in the coming years as black settlers became even more disillusioned with company leaders.

Convinced that their religious and civil rights were endangered, black Methodist leaders and laity turned to John Clarkson, who now seemed far preferable to his successors. They wrote to the former director in London, begging him to "leave us Not in the Wilderness to the Oppressing Masters— but be Amongst us."[27] Company officials had other plans and refused to reappoint Clarkson to Sierra Leone. Zachary Macaulay threatened to send any discontented settlers back to Nova Scotia or, worse, allow them to be "exposed to the treachery of the slave-traders . . . doomed to groan chained in the hold of a slave-ship, or drag out a miserable life under the smart of a West Indian whip."[28] He dismissed Daddy Moses's congregation as "mad Methodists" and criticized "their government" as "pure democracy, without subordination to anyone."[29] When a new law was passed in 1796 that stripped black preachers of the right to marry and enjoined all children to attend Anglican catechism classes, the Methodists had seen and heard enough. A group of 128 settlers identifying themselves as "the Independent Methodist Church of Freetown" sent a letter to Macaulay, rejecting the new law "as an encroachment on our religious rights." "Your advertisement is very disgusting to us," they continued, "for we are Dissenters, and esteem it our privilege to be so, and as such we consider ourselves a perfect Church, having no need of the assistance of any worldly power to appoint or perform religious ceremonies for us," concluding that "we cannot persuade ourselves that politics and religion have any connection, and therefore think it not right for a Governor of the one to be meddling with the other."[30]

In both tone and content, the black Methodists' proclamation went far beyond anything articulated by British Methodists; the contrast with Coke's address to King George the previous year is striking. In response, Macaulay charged the former slaves with "the spirit . . . of rebellion itself." He called the Methodist meetinghouse "a kind of Jacobin club," thereby linking the settlers with French revolutionaries and triggering still more threatening images of the racial violence in Saint Domingue, where "Black Jacobins" were waging war against the white landholding class and French government.[31] Some disgruntled Methodists took their resistance a step further. Nathaniel Snowball and Luke Jordan led a group of at least several dozen black Methodists to an outpost called Pirate's Bay, negotiating the terms of purchase themselves with local African rulers. Others, urged to moderation by company officials and British Methodist leaders alike, remained in Freetown, trying to achieve their aims through peaceful means. But full-fledged rebellion broke out in 1799 in response to Macaulay's renewed efforts to enforce payment of quit-rents, leading to Macaulay's departure in December, the banishment or execution of at least forty black settlers, and the return of William Dawes in 1800.[32] The prospect of religious toleration for Methodists in Sierra Leone looked dim at the close of the eighteenth century.

CONTINUED CONFLICT IN WEST INDIAN COLONIES

Meanwhile, relations between Methodists and colonial officials in the West Indies were also worsening. After half a decade of détente with colonial officials, tensions between the two groups reemerged at the turn of the nineteenth century. Local governmental leaders and planters alike grew increasingly concerned at the substantial success of Methodist missionaries throughout the islands. By 1800, there were over twelve thousand Methodists in the West Indies, with twenty missionaries stationed on at least fifteen different islands. Up to seventy thousand regularly attended Methodist services.[33] The increased number of missionaries allowed the Methodists to spend more time preaching to slaves on the large sugar plantations inland, and much of their growth in the final years of the eighteenth century occurred there. The growing number of converts, together with Methodist movements into new areas, provoked heightened opposition.

As John Brownell's experience in Saint Kitts demonstrates, some of that opposition occurred in traditional Methodist strongholds where missionaries had always enjoyed relatively good relations with colonial officials. In the months following his summons to the president's office, Brownell noted that "a heavy cloud hung over the Society" as fears of persecution remained acute. In July 1802, the missionary described in his journal "a Strange event [that] has taken place": Several slaves on a large plantation had solicited the assistance of an unidentified "White man" to write to local authorities and notify them of their overseer's "cruel usage" and "ill treatment." The slaves' actions violated the island's slave code, and two of them "were taken up & sent to Jail." When the rest of the slaves protested by "refusing to work for a day or two," soldiers were dispatched to round up any who persisted and throw them in jail. "The Methodist Preachers," Brownell recorded, "bore the blame." In order "to Save the whole Society from a Severe Persecution," he continued, "I was under the necessity of expelling . . . all those who had left their Work on those two days."[34]

Things in Jamaica, where the Methodist presence had always been fraught with tension, were even more precarious. The Jamaican legislature passed three separate acts aimed at undermining Methodist activity in the first decade of the nineteenth century. The first, passed in 1802, sought to restrict the ministerial labors of "persons not duly qualified by law." It targeted those who, "under pretence of being a minister of religion, presume to preach or teach in any meeting or assembly of negroes or people of colour within this island." Those found guilty of violating the law faced fines, imprisonment, and a period of "hard labour."[35] In both intent and effect, the law limited the rights of ordained Methodist missionaries and the free and enslaved people to whom they preached. In fact, it was Methodism's fairly elastic notions of *preachers* and *preaching* that made the law so effective. Methodists carefully distinguished between ordained clergy—those given charge of a circuit and qualified to administer sacred sacraments—and the much larger number of local preachers, exhorters, and class leaders (a category that included both men and women) who carried on the day-to-day work and worship of the congregations and classes in the absence of the itinerant missionaries. In effect, all members of society "preached," bearing testimony, exhorting their coreligionists to righteousness, and taking turns leading the singing of hymns in their class meetings and other small gatherings.[36]

Ironically, the 1802 law relied on a similarly broad definition of preaching to restrict Methodist activity. The very act of preaching, especially when the preacher was an enslaved or free person of color, was a threat to the established social order, and local magistrates interpreted the law expansively enough both to reject the credentials of regularly ordained British preachers like Daniel Campbell and to sentence one "Mr. Williams, a free man of colour" to one month's imprisonment and "hard labour in the work-house" for "singing a few hymns, and praying."[37] In April 1804 the British government disallowed and annulled the law, and for three brief years, Methodist missionaries again operated openly in Jamaica.

By 1807 Jamaican legislators were again attempting to restrict Methodist activity. The British Parliament's "An Act for the Abolition of the Slave Trade" incensed West Indian slaveholders, and a decision by the Wesleyan Methodist Church's missionary committee to forbid missionaries to own slaves or to marry a slave-owning woman further persuaded colonial officials more than ever that the missionaries were not to be trusted. In June 1807, the Common Council in Kingston passed an ordinance repeating much of the now-annulled 1802 Act, but also made illegal "public worship . . . earlier than the hour of six o'clock in the morning, or later than sun-set in the evening."[38] The impact of the ordinance was far reaching because the enslaved inhabitants of the island spent the entirety of the daylight hours working. In effect, the time restrictions banned the daily class and prayer meetings that formed the foundation of Methodist worship and community. Then, in November 1807, as part of the island's newly revised slave code, the Jamaican Assembly clamped down even harder on the rights of the missionaries. This time they singled out the Methodists by name, providing "that no Methodist Missionary, or other sectary, or preacher, shall presume to instruct our slaves, or to receive them into their houses, chapels, or conventicles," essentially prohibiting all Methodist preaching on the island.[39] Church leaders in London again petitioned the king, decrying the "grievous religious persecution" and "the antichristian principle on which it is founded." Meanwhile, missionaries stationed in Jamaica were denied permission to preach and all Methodist chapels and preaching houses were closed. The law was disallowed in April 1809; the Committee of Council for Trade and Foreign Plantations annulled its implementation and enforcement on the grounds that it was "in direct contravention of the rights and privileges secured to [Preachers and Teachers dissenting from the Established Church of England] by the Toleration Act."[40] In August, after nearly two years, Methodist missionaries resumed preaching in Jamaica.

Several months after the passage of the 1807 law, and still some time before it was disallowed, Thomas Coke wrote to his close friend Ezekiel Cooper, a prominent Methodist preacher in America. "I am come here from London," Coke wrote, "on acct. of a dreadful persecution which has arisen in Jamaica against our People." Whereas years earlier Coke had thanked God for the religious protections provided by the British constitution, he now envied Cooper's country. "O what a blessing it is," wrote the veteran preacher, "to be in a country where there is no danger of persecution."[41] The intervening years had made Coke much more skeptical toward Britain's avowed commitment to toleration, especially in the colonies. While historians have rightly concluded that during "the second decade of the nineteenth century . . . the climate for mission work began to improve," the final years of Coke's life (he died in 1814) did little to relieve his skepticism. When the second of his three-volume *History of the West Indies* went to press in 1810, Coke added a footnote informing readers "that the persecution in Jamaica still continues, notwithstanding his Majesty's gracious interference."[42] Although the new Toleration Act passed by Britain's Parliament in 1812 afforded the Methodists and other dissenting preachers renewed protection, and no missionaries were denied a license to preach by Jamaican authorities after 1815, suspicions persisted. In the coming years, Methodist missionaries found themselves accused of inciting slaves to insurrection following revolts in Barbados (1816), Demerara (1823), and Jamaica (1831). The codification of toleration in law, no doubt important, did not always guarantee the experience of tolerance or social acceptance.[43]

CONCLUSION

As in the United States, the proselytization and conversion of free and en-slaved people of color throughout the British Empire impacted the trajectory of religious toleration.[44] In an age of protest, rebellion, and revolution, Methodist missionaries and their thousands of nonwhite converts in overseas colonies worried government officers and planters alike. Fearful of their potential impact, colonial officials implemented efforts to restrict the Methodists' most basic religious rights to preach, worship, and proselytize. These restrictions in the West Indies and Sierra Leone forced government officers in London to reconsider religious toleration and its limits throughout the British Empire and beyond.

As Methodism continued its rapid growth throughout the Atlantic world through the early nineteenth century, the tens of thousands of free and en-slaved converts in the West Indies and Africa assumed an increasingly visible role in the ongoing struggle for religious toleration, suffering alongside the white missionaries in that quest. Some kept the faith alive in the absence of missionaries, continuing to meet, as one Sint Eustatius woman revealed in 1819, in secret "country places and behind the mountains."[45] Others remained active as exhorters, class leaders, and Sunday school teachers, raising up and preparing future generations of local Methodist leadership. Still others, including most of the Methodist settlers in Sierra Leone who had hoped to leave their "Children free and happy," died before they fully realized their own religious freedom. On both sides of the Atlantic, black Methodists and the white missionaries who labored among them succeeded in preparing the next generation to continue the struggle for full religious liberty.[46]

NOTES

1. John Brownell, "A Journal of the Methodist Missions in the Island of St. Christophers West Indies," 10 April 1801, Wesleyan Methodist Missionary Society Archives, School of Oriental and African Studies, University of London (hereafter cited as Brownell Journal); *The Address of the General Conference of the Methodist Episcopal Church, to all their Brethren and Friends in the United States* (Baltimore, 1800).

2. Brownell Journal, 10 April 1801; *Address of the General Conference*.

3. Dee E. Andrews, *The Methodists and Revolutionary America, 1760–1800: The Shaping of an Evangelical Culture* (Princeton, NJ: Princeton University Press, 2000); David Hempton, *Methodism: Empire of the Spirit* (New Haven, CT: Yale University Press, 2005).

4. Coke to London Missionary Society, 26 February 1798, in *The Letters of Dr. Thomas Coke*, ed. John A. Vickers (Nashville, TN: Kingswood Books, 2013), 230.

5. Travis Glasson, *Mastering Christianity: Missionary Anglicanism and Slavery in the Atlantic World* (New York: Oxford University Press, 2012); Jon Sensbach, *Rebecca's Revival: Creating Black Christianity in the Atlantic World* (Cambridge, MA: Harvard University Press, 2005).

6. Sylvia R. Frey and Betty Wood, *Come Shouting to Zion: African American Protestantism in the American South and British Caribbean to 1830* (Chapel Hill: University of North Carolina Press, 1998).

7. John Wesley, *Thoughts Upon Slavery* (London: R. Hawes, 1774), 26.

8. Thomas Coke, *The Journals of Dr. Thomas Coke*, ed. John A. Vickers (Nashville, TN: Kingswood Books, 2005), 82; "Some account of Harry the Black, mentioned in Dr. Coke's History: taken from a recital of a Black Woman in St Bartholomew," Wesleyan Methodist Missionary Society Archives, West Indies, Correspondence, 1817–1819, School of Oriental and African Studies (hereafter cited as "Some account of Harry the Black").

9. "Some account of Harry the Black," 1–3; Coke, *Journals*, 83–84.

10. Coke, *Journals*, 84.

11. Ibid., 109–14 (italics in original). Coke and Harry were reunited in 1796 in the United States. See Donald S. Ching, *Harry's Children: Methodist Origins in the Dutch West Indies* (Kingston, Jamaica: Methodist Book Steward, 1961), 9–11.

12. *Barbados Gazette, Or General Intelligencer*, 13 December–18 December 1788; *Daily Advertiser* (Kingston), 4 February 1791, 26 February 1791.

13. Coke, *Journals*, 149. See also William Hammet Diurnal, 2 September 1789, William Hammet Papers, South Caroliniana Library, University of South Carolina, Columbia, South Carolina.

14. *Daily Advertiser*, 2 March 1791.

15. *Daily Advertiser*, 4 March 1791.

16. *Daily Advertiser*, 5 September 1791.

17. Simon Taylor to Chaloner Arcedeckne, Spanish Town, 5 December 1792, accessed 17 June 2014, http://slaveryandrevolution.soton.ac.uk (original in Cambridge University Library); David Geggus, "Jamaica and the Saint Domingue Slave Revolt, 1791–1793," *The Americas* 38 (October 1981): 229.

18. Cited in Thomas Coke, *A History of the West Indies, Containing the Natural, Civil, and Ecclesiastical History of Each Island: With an Account of the Missions Instituted in Those Islands, from the Commencement of Civilization; But More Especially of the Missions Which Have Been Established in that Archipelago by the Society Late in Connexion with the Rev. John Wesley* (London, 1810), 2:146.

19. Coke, *Journals*, 151, 180–82.

20. Coke to Ezekiel Cooper, 22 November 1791, in Coke, *Letters*, 157.

21. John Clarkson Journal, 19 May 1792, 221–22, John Clarkson Manuscripts, 6 August 1791–4 August 1792, New York Historical Society Digital Collections, Manuscript Collections Relating to Slavery, accessed 25 September 2014, http://cdm16694.contentdm.oclc.org/cdm/ref/collection/p15052coll5/id/28295.

22. Anderson and Perkins to Henry Thornton, November 1793, in Anna Maria Falconbridge, *Two Voyages to Sierra Leone, During the Years 1791–2–3, In a Series of Letters* (London: 1794), 265.

23. Coke to William Black, 7 November 1793, in Matthew Richey, *A Memoir of the Late Rev. William Black* (Halifax, Nova Scotia: William Cunnabell, 1839), 303.

24. John A. Vickers, *Thomas Coke: Apostle of Methodism* (Nashville, TN, and New York: Abingdon Press, 1969), 168–69; "Some account of Harry the Black," 4–7; Coke, *Journals*, 178–79.

25. Boston King, "Memoirs of the Life of Boston King, A Black Preacher," *Methodist* magazine (June 1796), 264.

26. Suzanne Schwarz, "'Our Mad Methodists': Abolitionism, Methodism, and Missions in Sierra Leone in the Late Eighteenth Century," *Wesley and Methodist Studies* 3 (2011): 125.

27. Hutcherson and Murray to John Clarkson, 24 May 1796, in Christopher Fyfe, *Our Children Free and Happy: Letters from Black Settlers in Africa in the 1790s* (Edinburgh: Edinburgh University Press, 1991), 51.

28. Proclamation of the Governor and Council, 22 June 1794; Council minutes, 22 June 1794; as quoted in Cassandra Pybus, *Epic Journeys of Freedom: Runaway Slaves of the American Revolution and Their Global Quest for Freedom* (Boston: Beacon Press, 2007), 179.

29. Zachary Macaulay Journal, 26 November 1794, 13 September 1793, Huntington Library, San Marino, California (hereafter cited as Macaulay Journal).

30. "The Independent Methodist Church of Freetown to the Governor and Council," in Viscountess Knutsford, *Life and Letters of Zachary Macaulay* (London: Edward Arnold, 1900), 145–46.

31. Macaulay Journal, 14 July 1796, 21 July 1796.

32. Pybus, *Epic Journeys of Freedom*, 200–202.

33. *Minutes of the Methodist Conference, from the First, Held in London, by the Late Rev. John Wesley, A.M., in the Year 1744* (London: John Mason, 1863), 2:50, 54; Coke, *History of the West Indies*, 1:433.

34. Brownell Journal, 27 April 1801, 11 June 1802.

35. *Journals of the Assembly of Jamaica*, vol. 11, *1802–1807* (London: Alexander Aikman, 1809), 74; Coke, *History of the West Indies*, 1:444–46.

36. See Coke, *History of the West Indies*, 1:433.

37. Ibid., 1:447–53. See also Mary Turner, *Slaves and Missionaries: The Disintegration of Jamaican Slave Society, 1787–1834* (Urbana: University of Illinois Press, 1982), 15–16.

38. Coke, *History of the West Indies*, 2:15–17. See also James Knowlton to Coke, 23 June 1807, Wesleyan Methodist Missionary Society Archives, West Indies Correspondence, 1803–1816, box 112, School of Oriental and African Studies.

39. Coke, *History of the West Indies*, 2:19–20; *Journals of the Assembly of Jamaica, 1802–1807*, 611, 644–47.

40. Coke, *History of the West Indies*, 2:27–30.

41. Coke to Ezekiel Cooper, 1 March 1808, in Coke, *Letters*, 547.

42. Sylvia R. Frey and Betty Wood, *Come Shouting to Zion: African American Protestantism in the American South and British Caribbean to 1830* (New York: Oxford University Press, 1998), 138; Turner, *Slaves and Missionaries*, 18; Coke, *History of the West Indies*, 2:33.

43. Turner, *Slaves and Missionaries*, 19–21; David Lambert, *White Creole Culture, Politics, and Identity during the Age of Abolition* (Cambridge: Cambridge University Press, 2005); Emilia Viotti da Costa, *Crowns of Glory, Tears of Blood: The Demerara Slave Rebellion of 1823* (New York: Oxford University Press, 1997).

44. Jon Sensbach, "Slaves to Intolerance: African American Christianity and Religious Freedom in Early America," in *The First Prejudice: Religious Tolerance and Intolerance in Early America*, ed. Chris Beneke and Christopher S. Grenda (Philadelphia: University of Pennsylvania Press, 2011), 216.

45. "Some account of Harry the Black," 3.

46. Robert Glen, "Methodists in the Caribbean: Educational Initiatives in the Slave Era," *Wesley and Methodist Studies* 3 (2011): 135–45; Schwarz, "Our Mad Methodists," 121–33.

Chapter Seven

"Between God and our own Souls"

The Discussion over Toleration in Eighteenth-Century America

Keith Pacholl

In October 1789, the *Gentlemen and Ladies Town and Country Magazine* began publishing "The Friar's Tale," a didactic story describing the religious adventures of Albert and Matilda. Throughout the story the protagonists encounter several religious characters, some committed Christians and others unabashed hypocrites. The abbess Sister Theresa harasses Matilda to the point that the latter questions her own religious convictions. Albert's experience, which includes killing his nemesis, drives him to curse religious orders as a violation of God's natural laws. Ultimately, it is left to a humble monk to reveal the real essence of religion, an altruistic moral code that transcends particular denominations and doctrines. "True religion," concludes the monk, "howsoever it may vary in outward ceremonies or articles of faith, will always teach you to do good, to love, and help each other."[1] The story presents religion as essentially an ethical endeavor: true religion, regardless of denomination, privileges moral action over theological orthodoxy.

The "Friar's Tale" series was emblematic of larger changes sweeping eighteenth-century magazine literature. Periodicals circulated widely throughout the eighteenth century, fashioning and disseminating cultural trends as they offered an expansive public venue for a broad array of voices.[2] This was especially true regarding religion and religious toleration. Periodicals allowed literate Americans to develop understandings of religion and religious toleration apart from, and often at odds with, the professional clergy who had long dominated theological and moral discussion. Arising out of the polemics surrounding the religious revivals known as the Great Awakening in the early 1740s, magazines were overwhelmingly supportive of toleration from their inception. That support peaked in the 1790s, amid the partisan political wrangling that followed the American Revolution. Throughout the last half of the eighteenth century, magazines consistently embraced a relatively secularized and ecumenical conception of toleration that viewed religion as a system of ethics rather than a well-defined body of orthodox beliefs and practices. Their chief end was to foster social harmony through universal principles of morality that transcended cultural particularities—sectarian, ethnic, and otherwise.

With the backing of elites who financed the publications, periodicals thus inculcated a shared conception of civic identity through which toleration assimilated the different peoples and groups in society to common cultural standards. Because of their number and wide readership, periodicals may have been the most important venue in eighteenth-century America through which contemporaries constructed an emphatically ethical view of religion and a distinctly civic-republican understanding of religious toleration. During the eighteenth century, these magazines' publishers and writers, most of whom were lay people, contested traditional notions of religion that had been previously controlled by religious institutions and clergy. They fostered ecumenical attitudes that downplayed the civic importance of sectarian commitments. Their particular understanding of toleration often conflicted with those who advocated toleration while maintaining strong commitments to denominational identities, such as many Revolutionary-era evangelicals. The magazine publishers and writers' amalgamation of tolerance into the civic-republican tradition prepared the groundwork for important trends in liberal Protestantism for generations to come.[3]

The *American Magazine* and the *General Magazine* were the first magazines published in America. They appeared, not coincidently, at the height of the Great Awakening controversy in 1741. The Great Awakening, which consisted of a series of religious revivals that swept across America, created social fissures in churches where the revivals had their greatest impact. Itinerant preachers, called New Lights, embraced the revivals and challenged the authority of Old Light clergy who opposed the Awakening. New Light ministers such as Gilbert Tennant called on congregations to break away from their own "unawakened" or "unconverted" clergy for refusing to preach revivalism in their churches. Old Lights, in turn, denounced the limited training of itinerant preachers along with the excessive emotion associated with the revivals. The Great Awakening thus caused religious schisms and social tensions in the myriad communities where it spread.[4] Many elites responded by turning to magazines as a vehicle to stem the revivals' disruptive impact. With the assistance of magazine editors, they affirmed the values of social harmony and order by deemphasizing points of religious contention.[5] Often didactic in approach, editors inculcated among their readers a generic version of Christianity that they hoped most readers could support. In reality, their distinctly rational vision of religion sought to persuade readers that the civic norms needed for their eighteenth-century society were independent of particular denominational commitments or sectarian claims of orthodoxy. In this vein, the August 1744 edition of the *American Magazine* blamed Great Awakening polemics on those who demanded strict adherence to a particular denomination. The magazine charged that those who "rank themselves under Names of Party distinction, and affect to be call'd after this or that Sect" have been the main source of "infinite Mischief in the World." It concluded that only through the use of "sober modest reason" could the "pure Doctrines of Christianity" be practiced by all Christians.[6]

The rational Christianity of eighteenth-century periodicals was premised on the notion that sectarian attitudes bred intolerance, and thereby social disorder. To counteract this discord, writers consciously sought to reshape the public's attitudes about religious differences. During the Great Awakening, the *American Magazine and Historical Chronicle* published several articles that promoted rational, civic-minded ecumenism, including a 1744 address by the Library Company of Philadelphia. The address depicted the library as a civic institution for acquiring knowledge and promoting social intercourse, welcoming adherents of all denominations to participate in its distinctly nonsectarian public endeavors. The authors lamented how the "unhappy Divisions and Animosities of late have too much interrupted that charitable and friendly Intercourse which formerly subsisted among all Societies in this place." They defined the company's mission as fostering common social mores and the shared pursuit of useful knowledge unobstructed by sectarian differences. They prayed that one day "Men of all Denominations will mutually assist in carrying on the publick Affairs in such Manner as will tend to the Peace and Welfare of the Province."[7]

Similar attempts to cultivate nonsectarian sensibilities among literate Americans peppered the pages of the *American Magazine and Historical Chronicle* at mid-century. In 1743, an anonymous author decried the social discord precipitated by religious schisms in "A Dissertation on the State of Religion in North America." The author denounced those on both sides of the Great Awakening controversies, Old Lights and New Lights, who sowed social discord through inflammatory debates. He found these divisive habits particularly unbecoming of Christian ministers, who, he lamented, had attacked each other "with much Bitterness, and have not attended to that Justice, Charity, and Impartiality" expected of religious leaders. The author called for the moderation of religious fervor as the solution to religious differences, insisting that charity and impartiality were common traits shared by all Christians. To illustrate this point, the printers included documents from both sides of the debate to illustrate how both Old and New Lights had contributed to divisive behavior. Pastors against the revivals charged the New Lights with "the Spirit and Practice of Separation" because they "censured and condemned their Brethren." Conversely, New Light ministers warned Old Lights "not to despise these Out-pourings of the Spirit, lest a holy God be provok'd to withhold them, and instead thereof to pour out upon this People the Vials of his Wrath." Ministers from both sides, concluded the author, were guilty of "Ambition and Pride" and consumed by "the Power of human passions."[8]

The cultivation of nonsectarian sensibilities among the reading public continued well beyond the revival firestorms of the early 1740s and influenced future discussions about toleration by emphasizing rational and ecumenical conceptions of virtue. Responding to a variety of social and political conflicts over the succeeding decades, periodical authors propagated a rational and ethical Christianity as a solution to the social ills they viewed as rooted in religious divisions. In the 1750s, for example, the New York lawyer William Livingston opposed the plan to create a new Anglican-dominated college in New York. In the *Independent Reflector*, Livingston decried this kind of sectarian thinking among those who "imagine their own Profession, on the whole, more eligible and scriptural than any other." He viewed such sectarianism as having long contributed to social and political instability by creating "that Heat and Opposition, which animate the Breasts of many Men." In contrast, Livingston suggested that core religious teachings could be grasped and shared by all. To him, moral teaching, shorn of sectarian particularities, formed the basis for a broadly inclusive civic identity. "Does not every Persuasion," Livingston queried, "produce Men of their Worth and Virtue, conspicuous for Sense, and renown'd for Probity?" On the basis of this presumed overlapping moral consensus, Livingston espoused an "equal TOLERATION of Conscience," a toleration that sought to diminish denominational discord by demanding virtuous behavior.[9]

Until the American Revolution (when military conflict and the skyrocketing cost of paper and printing temporarily halted the publication of most periodicals), magazines continued to publish articles that connected ecumenical ethics to religious toleration. In 1774, the *Royal American Magazine* published an essay that explored the merits of generosity. "A generous mind may justly be considered as the noblest work of the Creator," the author contended, as "it is perhaps the most singular of all moral endowments." Tellingly, the article suggested that such a moral sensibility was missing from those who were poisoned by "the narrow prejudices of sects or parties." Ultimately, strong sectarian attachments resulted in "forced and unnatural productions of timid obedience," a "slavish" adherence to authority rather than a self-governing moral capacity. The author concluded that as "generosity sanctifies every passion, and adds grace to every acquisition of the soul," it confers "a lustre upon the whole circle of moral and intellectual qualities."[10] In 1775, the *Pennsylvania Magazine* sounded a similar note in a series of articles about education that defined true religion in terms of virtuous behavior. The author enjoined his readers to "pay the strictest attention to [their] visible conduct." And in reference to their children, he further warned that instilling sectarian passions could be detrimental to a child's development, resulting in the inculcation of fear rather than the development of moral sensibility. "The real dignity of religion," concluded the author, was its cultivation of social virtue.[11]

After the upheaval of the American Revolution, magazines picked up where they left off. In fact, the disruptions caused by the Revolution made calls for social order and harmony more urgent than ever. As upstart denominations like Baptists and Methodists pressed for equal rights during and after the Revolution, established churches fought to retain their privileges.[12] With so much in flux, magazines provided a vehicle for concerned individuals to reassert social stability. The connection between religious toleration and rational ethics thus became more pronounced in the 1780s and 1790s in an attempt to mitigate religious friction and social discord. Most Americans agreed that morality was an essential part of religion, and practicing religion made one a more virtuous person. In this sense, periodicals joined in the postrevolutionary chorus connecting religion to good citizenship and morality.[13] In its initial prospectus, the *Philadelphia Magazine and Review* promised to uphold the three pillars of civilization: "religion, morality, and social order" were, according to the editors, the foundation for the "glory and welfare" of the United States.[14] A 1794 article titled "On the entrance into Life, and the conduct of early Manhood" illustrates the kind of ethical religious education a reader could find in magazines. The author began the essay by observing that "there seems to be a peculiar propriety in addressing moral precepts to the rising generation." The key, according to the essayist, was firm reliance on the lessons that religion offers, particularly the taming of youthful passions and the art of virtuous living. The article addressed a long list of behaviors that were pleasing to God and helped control negative youthful tendencies. It was no surprise, for example, that sexual temptation would be strong, and the author encouraged early marriage to a virtuous woman. Until then, restraint was a necessary virtue, even if those practicing it were mocked for their celibate living. Readers were encouraged to be truthful, sincere, honorable, and forgiving, to live a life of moderation, and to apply their faith: "Let the beautiful Christian graces of meekness and benevolence shine most conspicuous. Wherever you can, relieve distress, prevent mischief, and do good."[15]

Thomas Reese, pastor of a Presbyterian church in Salem, South Carolina, agreed that Christian worship would have a considerable influence on the morals of the public. Reese contended that "a purity of morals" found in the worship of "that pure and immaculate Being" would "promote the happiness of civil society." In the case of America, Christianity had taught people to have "an aversion from vice, and a love of piety and virtue." Every facet of Christian worship, he wrote, "enforces purity of manners, and serves to restrain men from those vicious courses, which, in the natural stream of things, tend to the destruction of civil government." Baptism, for example, emphasized moral purity. The Eucharist embodied the notion of unparalleled love, as seen in the sacrifice offered by Jesus. For those still failing to see the light, Reese argued that a more compelling reason existed for moral behavior. Christianity also promised eternal damnation to immoral sinners. When confronted with the prospect of enjoying eternal paradise in heaven as opposed to stewing in the fires of hell, surely one would make the right choice.[16] In the *Dessert to the True American*, the penman "Moralist" reached a simple conclusion: "The sole preservative of popular morality is religion."[17]

Magazines differed, however, with other voices advocating toleration. On one end of the spectrum, they challenged the small but growing voices of skepticism and atheism that demanded toleration of every individual, including those who publicly challenged any sort of institutional church. This movement included Elihu Palmer, a former Presbyterian minister, who attacked institutional Christianity and argued that "revealed religion . . . was neither true nor divine."[18] Periodical writers quickly countered such assertions by insisting that all denominations provided basic truths (not specific to any one group) and fostered ethical behavior. In a letter to the editor of the *Dessert to the True American*, "Philoctetes" dismissed religious skeptics who denigrated the value of Christianity and argued that magazines offered a salutary alternative to this destructive view by reinforcing "religion and sound morals" within their pages. Through inculcating virtue in the reading public, Philoctetes concluded, the United States could avert the moral disaster taking place in Europe, where print was unfortunately used to advance "skepticism, infidelity, and irreligion."[19] The author of "Religion and Infidelity Contrasted" critiqued adherents of an irreligious ilk in a poem published in the *Philadelphia Magazine and Review* that highlighted the pitfalls that were associated with a lack of faith:

> When virtue's light no longer shone,
> When love and charity were flown . . .
> She [infidelity] strove to teach the poor distempered soul,
> To disbelieve eternal joy,
> To spurn at heaven's benign control,
> And grasp at pleasures that destroy.[20]

Toleration, as Philoctetes suggested, could only be extended so far, and certainly not to those who refused to recognize the ethical nature of Christianity.

Magazines also found fault with those on the other end of the spectrum, primarily evangelical Christians. When periodical editors and writers campaigned for social virtue as the basis of a civic-minded religiosity that would preserve social order in the new nation, they were advocating a distinctly nonsectarian, generic kind of civil religion. To them, sectarian attachments associated with evangelical denominations obscured the true essence of religion by privileging doctrinal views of grace over a general profession of civic, ethical behavior. For some authors, evangelical Christianity actually promoted intolerance by creating divisions among Christians (despite some evangelicals being strong advocates of toleration). An essayist in the *Boston Magazine* criticized the "narrow" views of such evangelicals and the negative consequences that ensued from their theological perspectives. "There is nothing more truly contemptible," the author wrote, "than for a narrow fouled bigot to bewail that others do not believe as he believes, and worship as he worships."[21] Philo-Aletheias specifically singled out evangelical Christians for their purported divisiveness and spent the better part of eleven pages in the *United States Magazine* outlining how they threatened political liberty and "true religion" in America. The author referred to these types of Christians as "enthusiasts" who refused to acknowledge the moral foundation of religion because of their focus on the experience of God's grace rather than obedience to civil and moral laws. "This prejudice of theirs overturns the foundations of morality," he declared, and their "mystic piety is a large fountain of delusion." Philo-Aletheias ultimately concluded that authentic religion was a middle path between the extremes of "irreligion" and "enthusiasm" and that "true Christianity" was built on the foundations of rational thought and moral behavior.[22]

Magazines then took the next step of connecting the health of a nation with its stance on toleration. Postrevolutionary magazine writers criticized the deleterious effects of intolerance because active persecution led to social discord, and stability could only be attained by eliminating such intolerance. Periodicals moved to the fore in the defense of religious toleration by demanding tolerance as a political imperative for national stability. At times, authors would use the historical past to reinforce their message. In 1796, the magazine *The Nightingale* ran a series titled "Christians and Heathens Contrasted." In a display of republican classicism, the anonymous author favorably compared the tolerant attitude of ancient heathens to the sectarian discord among many contemporary Christians. "What barbarous country was ever disunited in religion?" queried the author. "We hear of no battles fought among them, on account of religion; we hear of no persecution, for conscience sake." The author espoused the ethical superiority of classical toleration, suggesting (not unlike the great Enlightenment philosopher Jean-Jacques Rousseau) that Christians of his day had regressed on this crucial point: "Oh, merciful toleration, oh heathenish ages, how different from modern Christian times! Hail happy, heathenish ages, well were ye called golden. Hail universal toleration, when man could worship his deity as he pleased, fearless of an inquisition, regardless of that modern word—Heretic." Invoking the ancients' toleration was a popular practice among neoclassicists. Like the essayist from *The Nightingale*, they used the reference to criticize contemporary forms of religious intolerance in their quest for a res publica in which religious differences bore little on civic identity. They envisioned a broadly shared sense of civic belonging grounded in universal principles of morality and thus independent of narrower forms of commitment. The ancients had understood this, according to the series author: "No dissention disturbed them, no sons were disinherited on account of religion; much less were forty thousand victims sacrificed at once, as Heretics."[23]

A 1789 poem in the *Gentleman and Ladies Town and Country Magazine* echoed these neoclassical aspirations to a civil morality independent of sectarian divisions. The poem was titled "On the Various Sects of Religion." Its author pointed out how sectarian ways of thinking corrupted social relations. He satirized Christian denominations for privileging belief in their sectarian doctrines over concern with the moral conduct of their adherents:

> The English Church, by Athenasius breed,
>   Damn all on earth who don't to that give heed.
> So Calvin caus'd Servetus to die,
>   Because he could not with his creed comply . . .
>
> 'Tis you are wrong I know, and I am right,
> I have God's spirit, I have got the light,
> And he that joins in sentiment with me,
>   Although in works be quite immoral be,
> Stands fairer to enjoy the bless'd possession,
>   Than moral men, who're not of my profession.

Ridiculing churches for preferring creeds over virtue was standard fare among eighteenth-century critics of Christian orthodoxy. The criticism militated in favor of toleration by poking fun at those who judged others according to their belief rather than their behavior. The author of the poem sought to undermine such affiliations by appealing to Christian scripture against the divisions wrought by theologians. He invoked the gospel model of a historical Jesus who personified virtue, not orthodoxy:

> My soul! come follow Jesus and his laws,
>   Virtue and holiness adorn his cause;
> It matters not so much the form of creeds,
>   All will be judg'd according to their deeds.[24]

In order to promote an ideal of civic unity that marginalized sectarian differences, printers also hearkened to a mythic past in which harmony was prevalent and dissension minimal. In 1792, the *American Apollo* published a 1718 letter from Cotton Mather to Lord Barrington that stressed the unity of all Christian groups in Boston. Mather described a godly community full of piety where all "Calvinists with Lutherans, Presbyterians with Episcopalians, Pedo-Baptists with Anabaptists [are] beholding one another to fear God" and "sit down together at the same table of the Lord." Even more direct was the inclusion of a letter written by Roger Williams, who announced that "forced worship stinks in God's nostrils . . . there is no other prudent, christian way of preserving peace in the world but by permission of differing consciences."[25] Messages like these pounded home the point that religion should serve as a unifying rather than a divisive force, and by the end of the eighteenth century, periodicals used these paragons of the American past to illustrate the potential for religious and political cohesion despite minor differences in doctrine.

Having defined the parameters of religious behavior, authors could now be magnanimous with their support of different ways of worshiping the Creator God—as long as those opinions contributed to the greater good. Conversely, religious intolerance prevented a greater good from being realized. The author "A.Z." declared that religion was a matter of personal choice and that no civil laws should interfere with "the concern of a man individually." A person "ought to have a free choice" to pursue the path he believed would procure for him "celestial felicity."[26] The author "J.F." concurred, suggesting in the *Massachusetts Magazine* that all individuals had the right to determine their own religious path. After all, he argued, "the object of all publick worship is the same, it is that great eternal Being who created every thing. The different manners of worship are by no means subjects of ridicule, each thinks his own the best." In fact, there was no standard with which to measure the accuracy of religion: "Every man seeks for truth, but God only knows who has found it." The author of "A Prayer of an Eastern Philosopher" expressed his confusion in attempting to define one standard for Christianity: "I would serve thee [God] according to thy will, but every person I consult, would have me do according to his will."[27] The author "Berean" summed up the growing trend toward toleration and the personal choice of religions:

> As Religion is the highest Importance to Mankind,
> our Enquiries about it ought to be the most free and impartial.
> For a Mistake here may prove the most fatal Consequence.
> And for this Reason, of all the Rights belonging to Mankind,
> that of private Judgment in Matters of Conscience
> ought to be held sacred, and above all Things . . .[28]

Magazine writers thus supported the idea of choice in religious practice because they had spent the past several decades deemphasizing what they considered orthodox rigidity in favor of nonsectarian ethical practice. Individual choice no longer seemed a threat to social cohesion as long as the benign dimensions of religion were touted.

Although eighteenth-century America was still predominantly Protestant, postrevolutionary tolerance included a limited but growing call for the toleration of Catholics. Thanks to the contributions of Catholic Americans and France to the Revolutionary cause, attitudes toward Catholicism were slowly changing, though with noted resistance, as Nicholas Pellegrino discusses in chapter 8.[29] In periodicals, several authors suggested that even Catholicism be reevaluated for its positive religious contributions. According to these writers, Catholics must be included if true religious toleration was to be achieved. Those who wrote in support of Catholics generally avoided any conversation about theological differences between Catholics and Protestants; rather, they focused on the difficulties Catholics faced and how they proved to be worthy American citizens. In 1787, "A Reader" from New Jersey decried the prejudice facing Catholics in his editorial to the *Columbian Magazine*. The anonymous author argued that Catholics as well as Protestants spilled blood in the cause for independence and, as such, were entitled to the same benefits (legal as well as religious) that all Protestant denominations enjoyed after the American Revolution. He called for an end to "slavish prejudices" that had marked earlier generations, declaring that

> thanks to the genuine spirit of christianity [*sic*], the United States have banished intolerance from systems of government, and many of them have done the justice to every denomination of christians . . . by placing them on the same footing of citizenship, and conferring an equal right of participation in national privileges.

Toleration, the author concluded, must be available for Catholics and Protestants alike.[30] In 1798, the long-deceased St. Vincent de Paul received praise from the *Hummingbird* for his attempts in the prior century to end conflict in Europe and raise money for those who were affected by war. The magazine concluded that his actions were meritorious even if he was a Catholic.[31] A 1796 article published in the *Nightingale* best summed up this changing attitude toward Catholicism:

> It was well observed by the venerable Judge Russell, that among all the revolutions and strange events that have taken place in the course of his long life, the establishment of a Roman Catholic Church, in Boston, is one of the most surprising. Such a revolution in sentiments and feelings of men, produced by the illuminations of science and the energy of reason, is more honorary and important, than all the conquests and victories that ever aggrandized a Nation, or gave her the command of the world. It was reserved for America, to give unlimited effect to those divine principles of universal toleration, which, in all other countries have been promulgated by the mouth of the cannon—to which, obedience has been enforced, by the spear and the sword.[32]

After years of bitter dispute, there was a growing recognition that toleration needed to be extended to groups who had been previously excluded because now all were part of a civic-minded citizenry who valued religion for its ethical contributions—or so the magazines insisted.

By the end of the eighteenth century, magazines attempted to bring stability and order to American society by developing a rational civic-minded religion that, bereft of sectarian trappings, promoted an ecumenical ethics suited to the nation's republican institutions. Without this kind of religion to instill virtue, magazines suggested, the fate of the United States was in peril. George Washington reinforced this point in his Farewell Address when he declared that "of all the dispositions and habits which lead to political prosperity, religion and morality are indispensable supports. . . . Cultivate peace and harmony with all. Religion and morality enjoin this conduct."[33] Writers demanded toleration because they believed that it would achieve the result that Washington and others so desperately wanted: order and stability in the nation. In 1794, the *Monthly Miscellany* claimed as much when it published an extract of a sermon that had been delivered in Massachusetts during the American Revolution. The sermon declared that without the moral underpinnings of enlightened and mild religion, the republican experiment of the United States would fail. The orator concluded that religion

> gives to all the most solemn and awful threatenings against impiety, which undermines the main pillars of society; against vice, which more openly attacks it; and the spirit of contention, party and faction, which tends with still greater force to pull down the whole fabric. How admirable the religion which while it seems only to have in view the felicity of another life, constitutes the happiness of this [life]. A free and equal government cannot have any support on which it may with more certainty rely, than what it will find in the genius, spirit, doctrines, and laws of so pure, mild, and benevolent a religion.[34]

By 1800, American periodicals had become important advocates of religious toleration. They could do so because their vision of religion minimized denominational differences and creeds in order to maximize a shared conception of civic-minded virtue. Their message of toleration could safely be promulgated throughout all ranks of society because periodicals had defined religion in benign and generic ways that could no longer threaten the social stability of the nation. By the end of the eighteenth century, periodical writers felt confident that they had found the solution to America's future, one that provided a middle ground between evangelicals, on the one hand, and radical deists, on the other. Like many similarly minded rationalists, though, they failed to anticipate the surge in religiosity that characterized nineteenth-century America.

NOTES

1. *Gentlemen and Ladies Town and Country Magazine*, October 1789–January 1790; quotes from January 1790, 639. I would like to thank Chris Beneke and Chris Grenda for their invaluable feedback. This chapter has benefited significantly from their comments and suggestions.

2. This chapter will focus specifically on magazine literature of the eighteenth century, and the term *periodicals* will be used interchangeably with *magazines*. Although periodicals, like newspapers, also disseminated religious content, they did so in different ways. See Keith Pacholl, "Bearers of the Word: Religion and Print in Early America" (PhD diss., University of California, Riverside, 2002), chap. 3.

3. The magazines reviewed for this chapter will not include specifically Christian magazines published during the eighteenth century. Frank Lambert has already offered important insights into the nature of evangelical magazines in *Inventing the "Great Awakening"* (Princeton, NJ: Princeton University Press, 1999). The magazines used in this chapter are not affiliated with a particular denomination and represent the mainstream magazines that were available throughout the eighteenth century. The findings here will complement Lambert's research on evangelical magazines.

4. See Thomas Kidd, *The Great Awakening: The Roots of Evangelical Christianity in Colonial America* (New Haven, CT: Yale University Press, 2009); Lambert, *Inventing the "Great Awakening"*; Mark Noll, *The Rise of Evangelicalism: The Age of Edwards, Whitefield, and the Wesleys* (Downer Grove, IL: InterVarsity Press, 2010); Timothy Hall, *Contested Boundaries: Itinerancy and the Reshaping of the Colonial American Religious World* (Durham, NC: Duke University Press, 1994).

5. For a discussion of the elite nature of American periodicals, see Pacholl, "Bearers of the Word," chap. 3.

6. *American Magazine*, August 1744, 486–87.

7. *American Magazine and Historical Chronicle*, January 1744, 210–11.

8. *American Magazine and Historical Chronicle*, September 1743, 1–13; quotes found on pages 5, 7, and 13.

9. "An Address to the Inhabitants of this Province," *Independent Reflector*, 26 April 1753, 87–90. William Livingston, along with two other colleagues, ran a series of letters opposing the charter of King's College as an Anglican-run institution. See also "Remarks on our intended College," *Independent Reflector*, 22 and 29 March 1753. Their attempts failed, and in 1754, King's College opened its doors as an Anglican college.

10. *Royal American Magazine, or Universal Repository of Instruction and Amusement*, February 1774, 49.

11. *Pennsylvania Magazine, or American Monthly Museum*, September 1775, 399; January 1776, 14. The series began in summer of 1775 and concluded in early 1776.

12. See Thomas Kidd, *God of Liberty: A Religious History of the American Revolution* (New York: Basic Books, 2012), and Frank Lambert, *The Founding Fathers and the Place of Religion in America* (New Haven, CT: Yale University Press, 2006).

13. For accounts discussing the importance of virtue in the Revolutionary era, see Gordon Wood, *Creation of the American Republic* (Chapel Hill: University of North Carolina Press, 1969); Linda Kerber, *Women of the Republic* (Chapel Hill: University of North Carolina Press, 1997); Christopher Grasso, *A Speaking Aristocracy* (Chapel Hill: University of North Carolina Press, 1999); Richard Brown, *The Strength of a People* (Chapel Hill: University of North Carolina Press, 1999); and Lance Banning, *The Jeffersonian Persuasion* (Ithaca, NY: Cornell University Press, 1980).

14. *Philadelphia Magazine and Review*, January 1799, ii–iv.

15. *Monthly Miscellany, or Vermont Magazine*, April 1794, 27–31.

16. *American Museum, or Universal Magazine*, September 1790, 121–23.

17. *Dessert to the True American*, 23 March 1799.

18. As quoted in Kerry Walters, *Revolutionary Deists* (Amherst, NY: Prometheus Books, 2011), 187.

19. *Dessert to the True American*, 6 April 1799, 3.

20. *Philadelphia Magazine and Review*, April 1799, 231.

21. *Boston Magazine*, December 1783, 60.

22. *United States Magazine*, October 1779, 411–21.

23. *Nightingale*, 7 July 1796, 303–6.

24. *Gentlemen and Ladies Town and Country Magazine*, March 1789, 104–5.

25. *American Apollo*, 6 January 1792, 105–6, 275–84.

26. *Columbian Magazine*, May 1787, 402.

27. *Massachusetts Magazine*, May 1789, 283; *Philadelphia Minerva*, 28 November 1795, 43.

28. *American Magazine and Historical Chronicle*, August 1744, 485.

29. For a concise and effective discussion of changing attitudes toward Catholics, see Chris Beneke, *Beyond Toleration: The Religious Origins of American Pluralism* (New York: Oxford University Press, 2006), 180–86.

30. *Columbian Magazine*, December 1787, 881.

31. *Hummingbird, or Herald of Taste*, 9 June 1798, 19–20.

32. *Nightingale*, 16 July 1796, 357.

33. George Washington, *Washington's Farewell Address to the People of the United States* (Washington, DC: U.S. Government Printing Office, 2000), 20, 22.

34. *Monthly Miscellany, or Vermont Magazine*, May 1794, 100–101.

Part III

Divisions Within: Protestants and Catholics in the New Nation

Chapter Eight

"Enlightened, Tolerant, and Liberal"

Mathew Carey, Catholicism, and Religious
Freedom in the New Republic

Nicholas Pellegrino

In the autumn of 1792, a letter appeared in a newspaper that accused a local
bishop of overstepping his authority. The author, who identified himself as
"Liberal," insisted that by signing a pastoral letter "John, Bishop of Baltimore," the Roman Catholic bishop John Carroll was suggesting that his
jurisdiction included all the inhabitants of that city. This was, the letter writer
contended, an assault on the civil and religious rights of non-Catholics.

Carroll expressed astonishment at the way Liberal interpreted his signature, musing that it afforded "much room for ridicule." But this was no
laughing matter. The bishop took particular notice of another one of Liberal's
charges—that Carroll "absolutely excludes from the honourable appellation
of Christians, all who are not within the pale of his Church." Ignoring the
papal decrees that partially substantiated Liberal's claim, Carroll denied that
Catholics excluded Protestants from the community of Christians and then
inverted the original accusation by demonstrating how intolerant and illiberal
it was to slander another religion. According to the bishop, Liberal was
attempting to restrict others from speaking in "the language of our respective
Churches." The result, Carroll averred, was an un-American constraint on his
freedom of speech and religious liberty. Asserting his right to exercise his
faith, "which our free constitution grants," Carroll signed his response the
same way he had his original. This time, however, he capitalized it: "JOHN,
BISHOP OF BALTIMORE."[1]

Bishop Carroll's exchange with Liberal took place at a pivotal moment in
American religious history and demonstrates how critical Roman Catholics

133

were to the early meaning of American religious liberty. The First Amendment had been ratified just months earlier and the meaning and application of its religious protections remained uncertain. The Maryland Constitution, which itself provided for religious exercise and belief, had also not yet been given precise definition in the courts. In these and other ways, understandings of religious freedom in the new republic were fluid, and exchanges like the one between Liberal and Carroll were fraught with broader implications for religious minorities in general and Roman Catholics in particular.

Despite the intensity of Protestant-Catholic conflict throughout much of early modern Europe and America, Catholics tend to go missing in American religious freedom historiography until the mid-nineteenth century. When Catholics do appear, they are often characterized as passive victims of the anti-Catholic prejudices within American culture. Philip Hamburger has famously argued that anti-Catholicism remade church-state relations in America while virtually ignoring what Catholics thought and said about religious freedom at this time.[2] David Sehat has highlighted the difficulties that religious minorities faced as mainstream Protestants consolidated moral and social authority in the early republic; yet he overlooks Catholic efforts to resist that authority.[3] The consensus among scholars is that, when it came to the meaning of religious liberty in America, Catholics did not take an active role in shaping it until the "School Question" debates of the 1840s.[4] But as Bishop Carroll's exchange with Liberal suggests, Catholics were important agents in defining religious liberty in the United States much earlier than that.

During the Founding era (c. 1760s–1790s), Catholics battled anti-Catholic prejudices and challenged Protestant assumptions about religious freedom in creative ways. First, they engaged in a process of cultural definition by isolating and reframing anti-Catholic attacks as violations of religious freedom, unsuited to an enlightened, republican, and Christian nation. They insisted that alongside religious liberty came a responsibility to respect other faiths. Tacit limitations on free speech, in other words, were necessary for the enjoyment of religious freedom. How could they exercise their rights, conduct business, or become virtuous members of the republic, Catholics asked, if their countrymen held them in contempt? Instead of seeking legislative solutions to their troubles, Catholics argued that informal limitations on uncivil speech were a necessary precondition to the free exercise of religion. When confronted with anti-Catholic speech, they tried to shame Protestants (with some success) into retracting their statements. Second, when Protestants criticized the intolerance of the Catholic Church, Catholics routinely discounted such claims, ignoring the Holy See's stance on religious liberty. They instead emphasized the persecution that Protestant establishments in America had inflicted on religious minorities. Where those establishments still existed, as in Massachusetts, Catholics stressed the continued restrictions on their civil and religious freedom.

ROMAN CATHOLIC RIGHTS IN THE AGE OF REVOLUTION

A revolution in religious liberty took place as the American states achieved independence from Great Britain and forged new state and federal constitutions. Religious minorities, including Roman Catholics, were the leading beneficiaries.[5] The 1787 federal constitution forbade religious tests for holding office. Many states followed suit. The revolution in liberty, however, was unevenly distributed across religious groups and left a patchwork of policies that still impinged on religious conscience. No group better embodied the complexity of early American religious liberty than Catholics. Eleven of the original thirteen states continued colonial patterns by prohibiting Catholics from holding public office. Massachusetts, New Hampshire, Connecticut, New Jersey, and North Carolina upheld that practice several decades into the nineteenth century. Despite these colonial inheritances, Catholics gained newfound liberties throughout the Union, such as the freedom to worship, evangelize, and vote. However, even where Catholics enjoyed legal equality, as they did in Pennsylvania by 1776, they continued to encounter prejudices that undermined their social standing. Presented with this combination of challenges and opportunities, American Catholics were instrumental in dismantling what they viewed as the remnants of religious intolerance in an otherwise enlightened nation.

Catholic efforts on this score coincided with those of Protestant dissenters. Led by Isaac Backus and John Leland, the Baptists were the most vocal of those evangelical Protestants demanding expanded religious rights, mainly by petitioning local and state authorities to terminate the vestiges of church establishment.[6] Deists also questioned prevailing church-state relations and challenged the boundaries of tolerable religious expression.[7] But Catholics made few attempts to cooperate with those groups, partly because of the different challenges that they faced and partly because many Protestants—even stalwarts of religious liberty like Backus—did not always support equal civil and religious rights for Catholics.[8] The Catholic population confronted unique negative stereotypes, such as their supposed inability to separate religion from politics and their slavish devotion to a foreign prince (the pope). These distinctive prejudices, however, allowed them to capitalize on barefaced displays of bigotry in ways that Protestant dissenters could not. While Baptists advanced their efforts in local assembly halls or courthouses and constructed their arguments for religious freedom on theological foundations, Catholics articulated their grievances in literary tracts and built their arguments on historical foundations. To remove the stigma against their faith, they used pamphlets, books, and newspapers to depict anti-Catholic intolerance as a social pathology. Bishop Carroll led this effort in the wake of the Revolution, combatting opponents when the opportunity arose.[9] During this period, he received support from several leading Catholics. None of them did more to contest anti-Catholicism than a young Philadelphia printer named Mathew Carey.

DEFENDING THE OLD FAITH IN THE NEW REPUBLIC

Born in Dublin, Ireland, in 1760 to a successful baker, Mathew Carey was one of five boys raised in a Roman Catholic family. He grew up under Britain's penal laws, which deprived Catholics of rights to worship in public, vote, and hold political office. Affluent but not privileged, Carey joked late in life that he was "wonderfully-slow developing my faculties," and that "I was, truly, an extremely dull boy." Prone to false modesty, Carey in fact excelled in school and developed an insatiable appetite for learning, reading John Locke, James Harrington, and Algernon Sidney as a youth. That intellectual precocity was unintentionally cultivated by a nurse who dropped Carey when he was baby. The fall crippled his foot, which he later described as a "disadvantage" that he felt "almost every day of my life." While his brothers were playing physically demanding games on the streets of Dublin, Carey digested historical tracts that documented "the horrible oppression of the Irish Catholics." He admitted that while alone in his room, he "read every book and pamphlet I could procure, respecting the tyranny exercised on them."[10]

Carey spent his adult life attempting to shine a spotlight on the dark underbelly of English and Protestant history. Misconceptions about the past, he argued, provided the foundation for continued discrimination against his coreligionists. While still a teenager, he wrote his first essay defending Catholic freedoms. His subsequent writings on religious toleration set off a firestorm of controversy in Dublin. The backlash became so fierce that Carey was forced to flee—donning a wig and dress to conceal his identity—to the United States in 1784. Just months after his arrival, he opened a printer's shop in Philadelphia. There Carey developed cordial relationships with the most prominent men of the age—Benjamin Franklin, George Washington, Thomas Jefferson, James Madison, and Bishop Carroll—and became the most prolific publisher in the United States. Although he, like Carroll, recognized and praised the legal protections afforded Catholics in America, he pressed for further reforms by pointing out the remaining religious intolerance around him. He devoted especially careful attention to the cultural inequities that Catholics endured, which, Carey insisted, stemmed from misrepresentations about the history and doctrines of his church.

In 1792, the same year that Carroll penned his rejoinder to Liberal about the inclusivity of the Roman Catholic Church, the *American Daily Advertiser* quoted Pennsylvania assemblyman Miers Fisher, a prominent lawyer and antislavery activist, in an article about an upcoming vote on the institution of a state lottery. Fisher drew Carey's ire when the paper reported that the assemblyman opposed the measure because he thought the lottery was "very similar to the Pope's indulgencies, forgiving, and permitting sins to raise money."[11] Hoping to provoke a debate about religious discrimination in the new republic, Carey used the indirect slight to launch a printed assault on the unsuspecting Fisher.

The ensuing debate captured the attention of the national capital for the next three months. Several newspapers printed the exchange, including the *National Gazette* and *Federal Gazette*. As one of those captivated, Bishop Carroll privately encouraged Carey not to prematurely withdraw from the controversy, reasoning that Protestants "who indulge themselves in venting every absurd tale & imputation against us, ought to be made to feel [the consequences], or they will never cease."[12] At the request of another Catholic, a printer named Robert Walsh, Carey bound the debate into a single volume and published it in late 1792.[13] The controversy occurred just three weeks after the ratification of the First Amendment. And like Carroll's tangle with Liberal a few weeks earlier, it served as a kind of rhetorical barometer, measuring how tolerant the new nation's religious culture would be.

Carey addressed his opening salvo to the *American Daily Advertiser*'s editor, William Dunlap. He claimed that Dunlap's "aspersion must be the offspring of ignorance or illiberality" and constituted "an unwarrantable attack on those who had offered him no offence." The Irish Catholic noted how odd it was for Fisher, a Quaker—whose "own sect" labored under "slander and persecutions"—to have engaged in such conduct. History, Carey affirmed, "should have taught him not to lend a too ready ear to the voice of calumny." Steering the conversation toward greater issues of injustice, Carey characterized Fisher's remarks as part of a disconcerting trend in American culture, as his review of American sermonic, political, and literary writings showed. According to Carey, "the conduct of many pulpit declaimers, haranguers in senates, and LIBERAL writers, not of the past age only, but of the present warrants [my] interference." He explained that Catholics were "so long accustomed to calumnies of this kind, that they seldom excite" a rebuttal. "But," Carey continued, in order "to effect a cessation of hostilities" between denominations, he encouraged Catholics to defend themselves more forcefully.[14]

Carey extracted an apology from Fisher the following day. The ecumenical climate of the Revolutionary era compelled Fisher to acknowledge the illiberality of his remark, explaining that he did not intend to "wound the feelings of any individual, much more of a whole society." Fisher professed that he was "not conscious of having ever *intentionally* said any thing, that could produce such an effect."[15] Carey's response, in short, elicited the kind of contrite reaction he had sought. Yet, even though Fisher apologized, Carey pressed ahead because—with Catholics such as Carroll and Walsh privately encouraging further action—he wanted to use the opportunity to highlight the odious assumptions Protestants had about his faith and the persistent cultural injustices that afflicted his coreligionists.

Carey proceeded with a didactic account of the transgressions that Protestants committed against the Catholic faithful. Perhaps the worst of these, Carey argued, occurred when Protestants deprived Catholics of their civil and religious freedoms during the Revolutionary War, an especially egregious infraction given how many Catholics had gallantly served their country. "At the close of the eighteenth century, among the *enlightened, tolerant,* and *liberal* Protestants of America," Carey began, "when the American soil was drinking up the blood of Catholics, shed in defence of her freedom . . . the constitutions framed in several states, degrad[ed] those very Catholics, and exclud[ed] them from certain offices. O shame!"[16] Carey had thrown down the gauntlet. While Americans were celebrating the ratification of the Bill of Rights, he recounted Catholic contributions to America's War of Independence to shame his countrymen into granting Catholics their full rights, including the right to hold public office.

After these initial volleys, Carey carried the assault further by indicting Protestant America for its soft bigotry. That accusation and the responses that it provoked shed light on important changes in American culture. In a religiously pluralistic country that claimed robust freedoms for speech and religion, even minorities like the Irish Catholic immigrant Carey were willing and able to engage in intense debate to defend their faith. His charge that Americans had a false sense of their own liberality invited new participants into the fray. Robert Annan, a Scottish-born Presbyterian minister, exchanged blows with Carey soon after Fisher apologized. Francis Fleming, a resident priest in Philadelphia, rushed to Carey's defense. Their discussion enumerated both the legal and cultural forms of discrimination directed toward Catholics. After firing several shots, Fleming explained why Catholics were sensitive to verbal slights like those uttered by Fisher. He conceded that "legislative wisdom can do no more . . . to unite as good fellow citizens, men of every religious persuasion." But the law, Fleming cautioned, only went so far. There were "as yet among us some persons who counteract the benevolent spirit of our legislature, and endeavour to stop the growth of liberality and mutual good will, by imputing to one description of citizens"—namely, Catholics—a set of beliefs that were "inimical to civil society." Addressing Philip Freneau, the editor of the *National Gazette*, which had been printing the debate, Fleming pointed to the logical consequences of spreading misinformation about Catholic indulgences: "Would you Mr. Editor, think it safe, to form any friendly or commercial intercourse with men professing a religion, which teaches, that a licence, a permission, an indulgence to commit crimes may be purchased?"[17] Fleming reasoned that even though the law did not discriminate against Catholics, the prejudices that lingered within the culture circumscribed their economic, political, and religious rights. How could Catholics truly possess civil or religious freedom, Fleming asked, if their countrymen suspected them of holding such malevolent and dangerous beliefs? Soft prejudice was prejudice nonetheless. And for Catholics like Fleming, it had damaging real-world consequences.

The Catholic campaign against public bigotry did not end there. Catholics consistently responded to anti-Catholic assaults that they found in the press and took measured steps to combat stereotypes against their faith, which, they insisted, posed constant dangers to their civil and religious liberties. Carey privately complained to one correspondent that remaining silent before attacks on their religion would lead to "consequences not only disgraceful and injurious to the Roman Catholics but hurtful to the community at large."[18] Others sought out Carey's help to combat prejudices against their faith.[19] The favored tactic in nearly every instance was to publish a defense in newspaper, pamphlet, or book form. In 1795, the editor of the *Carlisle Gazette* came under assault for running excerpts from a book that predicted the "overthrow of Papal Tyranny" and insisted that the Catholic Church was the Antichrist. A Catholic respondent accused the author of planting the "seeds of violent hatred against Roman Catholics" and desiring to "raise up hostile hatred and violent animosities against a numerous body of Christians as dutiful to the laws and inoffensive to their fellow citizens as any in the United States."[20] In 1805, Father Stephen Badin followed suit, publishing *The Real Principles of Roman Catholics, in Reference to God and Country* in order "to soften down Protestant prejudice" on the Kentucky frontier.[21] In nearly every instance—whether in Philadelphia, Baltimore, Boston, or on the frontier—Catholic reformers used aspersions on their faith to invert anti-Catholic assumptions and build limitations on uncivil speech, a tactic that challenged prevailing understandings of religious freedom.

The American Revolution ushered in a period of relative ecumenism during the last decades of the eighteenth century and the first decade of the nineteenth. Nonetheless, American Catholics endured a particularly egregious rhetorical assault in 1808. In that year, Reverend John Mason's *Christian's Magazine* printed a biographical sketch of John Rogers, a Protestant martyr struck down by Queen Mary in 1555 for denying a number of Catholic doctrines. After outlining Rogers's imprisonment, trial, and execution, Mason questioned the wisdom of granting Catholics civil and religious freedom. "Can we reasonably suppose," Mason wondered, "that the Papists of the present day, who announce the same creed with their bloody forefathers, will not, when it is in their power, be found in their forefathers' cruel practices; especially when through ignorance or superstition, they believe *that while they kill you, they do God's service?*[22] Mathew Carey confessed that when he first read the article he "heaved a sigh." "I could hardly believe," he gasped, "that I had read a publication" like that in modern America.[23] Protestants had been citing what they deemed intolerant papal decrees since Pius V issued *Regnans in Excelsis* in 1570, which instructed Catholics not to obey Queen Elizabeth's civil authority. But the American Revolution had, Carey hoped, extinguished the flames of fanaticism. Mason's libel cast doubt on that hope.

By the time Carey read Mason's attack, he was on his way to becoming the most outspoken advocate of Catholic rights in the United States and had assembled a small army of allies who helped answer charges against their faith.[24] After alerting his partners that a "most illiberal attack has been made upon the Roman Catholics," he requested their assistance and fired off nearly two dozen open letters.[25] Hoping to "set the question at rest for a long time to come," he wanted his letters to be distributed "to liberal protestants" in cities throughout the country.[26] If Protestants insisted on questioning Catholics' integrity, Carey and his allies made sure that those accusations would not go unchallenged. Cleverly casting anti-Catholic attacks as un-American and anti-Christian, Carey hoped to silence his critics by publicly shaming those who used intolerant rhetoric against his religion. That effect, Carey reasoned, would finally cleanse American culture of its anti-Catholic heritage. The Dublin native charged Mason with acting "in a very *unchristian spirit*" and recommended that the minister acquaint himself with historical and literary books composed by Catholic scholars. Doing so would not only disabuse him of his mistaken beliefs but also serve "as a good model for the editor of a Christian Magazine, on the style in which he ought to treat other Christians."[27]

The letters that followed turned Anglo-America's standard Catholic-Protestant history on its head. In a brazen overturning of widely accepted facts, Carey emphasized the persecutory history of Protestant establishments and the magnanimous record of American Catholics.[28] Challenging the mainstream understanding of the Protestant origins of American freedom, Carey located the roots of America's religious liberty in Catholic soil before he debunked the romantic belief that the Protestants who migrated across the Atlantic were committed to religious freedom. "During the all-devouring rage of persecution, which was exercised in England with unceasing violence against every species of dissenters," Carey reminded the minister that the Catholic founder of Maryland, "Calvert, Lord Baltimore . . . established a glorious system of liberty of conscience." Against the Catholic model in Maryland—which set a "godlike example of religious liberty"—Carey juxtaposed the intolerant settlements of the seventeenth century. "While the *enlightened* and *tolerant* PROTESTANT EPISCOPALIANS in Virginia were *proscribing the Presbyterians*, and preparing the GALLOWS *for the hapless Quakers*," he wrote, "the equally enlightened and tolerant Presbyterians in New England, were persecuting each other and every different denomination, and actually cropping and hanging the Quakers."[29] Even while he jabbed Protestants for their intolerance in favor of Catholic liberality, Carey was helping to make American religious liberty less sectarian and more universal.

Carey believed that Catholics would not have to defend themselves from libelous attacks in the press or advocate for their religious freedom if Protestants were better students of history. Yet he purported to seek only mutual forgiveness on each side. He and his coreligionists, Carey observed, "make no reproaches against the protestant or presbyterian of the present day" for acts of aggression that were "inflicted [by] their ancestors" because they understood that those transgressions were due to the "fanaticism of the time." They merely sought "to bury the whole in oblivion." But if American Catholics were to extend an olive branch, they expected Protestants to return the favor. Writing on behalf of his coreligionists, Carey explained that Catholics "consider themselves entitled to an equal forgiveness" for the persecutions they faced under British Protestants.[30]

For their efforts, the champions of Catholic equality generally received what one Boston priest called "silent contempt" from Protestant precincts, but they also obtained laudatory letters from their coreligionists.[31] During the autumn of 1808, Catholics from around the nation thanked Carey "for [his] virtuous effort to rescue our holy religion from disgrace" and praised his "laudable pursuit" of truth.[32] By that time, the Catholic clergy, led by Bishop Carroll and Fathers Badin, Anthony Kohlmann, and Louis Dubourg, had joined forces with the laity, led by printers Carey and Walsh, in creating an incipient network of Catholic voices in American print culture.[33] What began as an essentially solitary effort by Bishop Carroll to defend Catholic rights from those he suspected of plotting to undermine his liberties had, by the beginning of the nineteenth century, become a communal effort for Catholics across the country.[34] Anti-Catholic slurs continued to appear in the mainstream press, but Catholics answered in kind, letting the defamers of Roman Catholicism know that they could not attack with impunity.

NEW THREATS TO THE OLD FAITH

As the nineteenth century gathered steam, the U.S. Catholic population faced a number of new challenges. First, their numbers grew at a blistering pace. As a result, Catholic immigrants of Irish, French, and German heritage began competing with native-born Americans for employment, creating tensions between the Catholic minority and Protestant majority.[35] Second, the American church was short on priests. Bishop Carroll reluctantly welcomed foreign clergy who were unaware of the customs and values shared by Americans of all religious persuasions. That created a rift between priests, their parishioners, and the episcopacy. Splintered into rival ideological and ethnic factions, Catholics fought each other for ecclesiastical and civil authority within and outside the church. Such protracted disputes reflected poorly on the American church, which left Catholics open to accusations that their faith was incompatible with American institutions and ideals. Third, Protestant reformers began blurring the distinction between national and religious commitments by equating Protestant and American values. As evangelical revivals swept over the country, Catholics became still more alienated from mainstream Protestant culture.[36] Institutional changes within the papacy also made Americans more suspicious of their Catholic neighbors. Part of the reason that Protestants were willing to ignore Rome at the end of the eighteenth century was that the Holy See's power had waned. The French Revolution and rise of Napoleon Bonaparte, who kidnapped Pope Pius VI and his successor, limited the papacy's power and influence. Rome was also in the middle of what scholars have called the "Catholic Enlightenment" at that time. Many American Protestants recognized Rome's more liberal stance and felt that it no longer posed a substantial threat to their liberties.[37] Those relatively warm sentiments lasted until the College of Cardinals elected a series of more conservative popes in the 1820s. Collectively, these developments placed American Catholics under a level of scrutiny that they had not experienced since the colonial era.

Amid these changes, Protestants once again began to prophesize about the impending "popish" overthrow of America's republican institutions. Isolated hostilities during the early republic therefore turned into existential and institutional threats during the second and third decades of the nineteenth century. Unflattering and sometimes salacious novels about Catholic priests and nuns appeared in bookstores, while Protestants and Catholics clashed in Philadelphia, Boston, and New York. Religious periodicals like the *Boston Recorder*, the *Christian Watchman*, and the New York *Observer* regularly published mean-spirited articles about the Catholic faithful.[38] Meanwhile, journalists, ministers, politicians, and intellectuals increasingly warned, as did John Pierce at Harvard's annual Dudleian lecture in 1821, of the "dangerous, aspiring pretentions of the Romish Church."[39]

Catholics answered these attacks by reaffirming their constitutional and natural rights. They also emphasized their church's compatibility with republican values through pro-Catholic editorializing in newspapers like Charleston's *U.S. Catholic Miscellany* and the New York *Truth Teller*. Along with several prominent Catholics, Mathew Carey formed the Society for the Defense of the Catholic Religion from Calumny and Abuse in 1826. Their raison d'être was that "an envenomed warfare is unceasingly carried on against the Roman Catholics by bigoted and illiberal members of various other religious denominations." Carey's society, which included nearly two hundred members, published tracts to correct the "utter disregard of historical truth" found in the pulpit and the press.[40]

One episode of "envenomed warfare" that the society answered was initiated by a book published in 1826 by Joseph Blanco White, a Spanish-born priest of Irish descent who had abandoned the Catholic Church. White argued that *"sincere* Roman Catholics cannot conscientiously be *tolerant"* and deduced from this premise that "the only security of *Toleration* must be a certain degree of intolerance," similar to how "prisons in the freest governments are necessary for the preservation of freedom." He also warned that Catholics were "striving to obtain direct influence in this Government," and strict measures would have to be taken to avoid that end.[41] Upon publication, thirty-two religious leaders from a variety of denominations endorsed White's work.

Several pro-Catholic papers, such as the *Baltimore Gazette*, condemned White's "peculiarly scandalous" book and the clergymen who recommended it to their "discordant flocks," once again following the script that Bishop Carroll had composed at the end of the eighteenth century. The *Gazette* sought to shape cultural sensibilities by associating anti-Catholic sentiments with anti-American and anti-Christian values. The paper explained that if White's supporters were "resolved to continue arrayed in hostility to a large portion of their Catholic brethren . . . an exact, impartial, and rigorous criticism will be passed on its contents." The forthcoming responses, the *Gazette* promised, would prove that White's work was "profane and impious as regards Christianity, illiberal and antisocial in its antipathies to Catholic freedom . . . and a mere party engine to prop up a Church establishment by law."[42] A medley of Catholic writers, including Carey, responded similarly to White's claims. They insisted that the book aimed to deny a peaceful body of citizens their civil rights and perpetuated the erroneous stereotypes that threatened their liberties.[43]

Carey replied with an essay that reinforced the same moral and historical claims he had made throughout his career. He informed his countrymen that religious intolerance was equally distributed among denominations and throughout history. Until the American Revolution, Carey wrote, most Protestants "regarded a general toleration . . . as an utter abomination."[44] History proved that all religious groups coerced others whenever they gained the power to do so. If Americans had been better educated in history, Carey wrote, they would not "dare to upbraid the Roman Catholics with their intolerance or their persecuting spirit."[45]

By again pointing to the dangers of Protestant establishments, Carey aimed to strip American religious liberty of its sectarian assumptions. He recounted the oppression that Catholics and dissenting Protestants suffered under the Anglican Church in England and Virginia as well as under the

Congregational establishment in New England before moving on to Continental Europe—all of which suggested that prejudicial histories unfairly singled out the Catholic Church. Deeply read in the history of religious persecution, Carey once again fused cultural biases with legal disabilities and conflated the past with the present by informing his readers that he was "at a loss to conceive why the holding of certain religious doctrines" continued to have any "connexion with civil or social duties," and he recommended that all jurisdictions remove religious intolerance from their code of laws. [46]

By the time Carey penned his response, he had already developed a close relationship with another Irish American radical: Bishop of Charleston John England. They first met during the spring of 1821, shortly after the bishop arrived in the United States. Along with Carroll, Walsh, and Fleming, England became one of Carey's closest allies in the struggle for Catholic equality. The bishop confessed to Carey that he was "anxious to vindicate our religion from the misrepresentations of libellers who are called Historians" and asked Carey to print his rejoinders to White's book. [47] The Irishmen frequently discussed strategies to cleanse the church's soiled reputation; kept each other abreast of recent books, pamphlets, and other apologetic materials in the press; and critiqued each other's writings. Their objective was to expand Catholic freedoms and mitigate anti-Catholic bias in America, so when England learned about White's anti-Catholic screed, he composed his own refutation.

Like many Catholics who witnessed the rise of anti-Catholic sentiments in the 1820s, England was concerned about America's flagging commitment to religious tolerance. The support that White's book received was especially disheartening. In the letters he published in response, England explained that the main reason he moved to America "was not merely the excellence of its political institutions, but, as I flattered myself, the absence of bigotry. I was led to believe that, although men differed from each other in religion," religious toleration was a universal value in the United States. "I must confess," England lamented, that "I have been disabused" of such a belief. The problem for England, like Fleming before him, lay not in America's political or legal structures, but rather in the fact that "a Roman Catholic, though legally and politically upon a level with his fellow-citizen, was however too often looked upon, by reason of his religion, as in some degree morally degraded." Still more troubling, England discovered that this kind of intolerance "was by no means considered a want of liberality, on the part of Protestants." If a Catholic "even insinuated any thing derogatory to the Protestant religion, he was marked out as a shocking bigot," but Protestants like White had license to employ "the harshest and most offensive terms" when writing about "*Popish* priests," the "*Romish* Church," and its adherents. [48] The bishop thus illuminated the double standard under which many nineteenth-century American Catholics lived.

For Bishop England, like Carey, anti-Catholic bigotry began with the history that Protestants learned in school. He complained that "under English teachers," American youths were indoctrinated into believing "English fabrications" about the Catholic Church, including the mistaken notion that Catholics could not be "good republican citizens."[49] Battling the "gross misrepresentations which are miscalled English history," the bishop sought to correct what he viewed as the historical and theological inaccuracies in American culture in general and White's book in particular.[50] Distortions in English history, then, explained why so many American clergymen who celebrated White's book sought "to prove that Roman Catholics ought not to be admitted to an equality of civil and political rights with their fellow-subject."[51]

Like Carey, the Irish bishop used White's anti-Catholic assault to highlight the discriminatory statutes still in effect in the United States, as well as the shortcomings of so-called Protestant liberty. Ignoring historical and contemporary examples of Catholic intolerance toward Protestants, England declared that throughout the British Empire "Protestant governments were and are intolerant." Official policy in New England, Virginia, Maryland, the Carolinas, Georgia, and New York, according to England, exhibited intolerance toward dissenters of all persuasions. Moving from past to present, England noted that "at this day the Protestant governments of North Carolina and of New Jersey are intolerant . . . which allow no choice of Catholicism without disqualification." The bishop was referring to the surviving constitutional prohibitions against non-Protestants holding office in those two states, which he compared with the magnanimous experiment in religious liberty under "Maryland Catholics," who granted Protestants "an equality with themselves" until rapacious Protestants overthrew the government in 1689.[52] Like Carey and others, England's expressed objective was "to silence, if possible, those who charge the Catholics with intolerance and persecution."[53] By answering charges against their faith, England and his coreligionists aimed to rebuke, refute, and even suppress anti-Catholic speech, which, they calculated, would create a more tolerant religious climate and less discriminatory laws.

CONCLUSION

During the nation's first decades, American Catholics sought to expand notions of religious liberty in ways that included themselves. They argued that civil speech was a necessary precondition to the full exercise of that freedom. However, in order to address charges against their faith, Catholics had to employ the same tactics with which they charged their adversaries: criticizing Protestant church-state establishments throughout history and accusing Protestants of gross injustices. When discussing the past, Catholics were rarely forthright about their church's own history of persecution or the Holy See's resistance to the doctrine of religious liberty. Nonetheless, their writings made Catholics powerful agents in America's cultural development nearly half a century before they are generally understood to have made an impact. Leading Catholics such as Carroll, Carey, Fleming, and England challenged acceptable forms of religious speech, forced Americans to confront alternative interpretations of their own history, and contributed to the growth of a pluralistic society.

Though the United States went well beyond previous models of religious equality at the end of the eighteenth century, American Catholics continued to confront ingrained prejudices. Their experiences remind us that religious freedom was not equally distributed during the early republic and that its meaning was never fixed. Nor was it self-implementing. Catholics sought to fashion the concept of religious freedom to include cultural understanding, and even respect, among religious groups, even while they publicly assailed Protestants and their history in the process. They attempted to publicly shame those who misrepresented Catholicism and they actively defended their rights in the hopes of earning equal respect from their fellow citizens. Catholics relentlessly assaulted the prevailing historical narratives scattered in newspapers and books throughout the culture and repeatedly attacked the anti-Catholic assumptions underpinning American religious liberty.

NOTES

1. John Carroll, "An Answer to Strictures on an Extraordinary Signature, November, 21, 1792," in *The John Carroll Papers*, ed. Thomas O'Brien Hanley, 3 vols. (Notre Dame, IN: University of Notre Dame Press, 1976), 2:69–71 (hereafter *JCP*).

2. Philip Hamburger, *Separation of Church and State* (Cambridge, MA: Harvard University Press, 2002).

3. David Sehat, *The Myth of American Religious Freedom* (New York: Oxford University Press, 2011).

4. Steven Green, *The Second Disestablishment: Church and State in Nineteenth-Century America* (New York: Oxford University Press, 2010).

5. Chris Beneke, "The 'Catholic Spirit Prevailing in Our Country': America's Moderate Religious Revolution," in *The First Prejudice: Religious Tolerance and Intolerance in Early America*, ed. Chris Beneke and Christopher S. Grenda (Philadelphia: University of Pennsylvania Press, 2011), 265–85.

6. William McLoughlin, *New England Dissent, 1630–1833: The Baptists and the Separation of Church and State* (Cambridge, MA: Harvard University Press, 1971).

7. Christopher Grasso, "Deist Monster: On Religious Common Sense in the Wake of the American Revolution," *Journal of American History* 95, no. 1 (June 2008): 43–68; Eric Schlereth, *An Age of Infidels: The Politics of Religious Controversy in the Early United States* (Philadelphia: University of Pennsylvania Press, 2013).

8. McLoughlin, *New England Dissent*, 1:610–12; 2:736, 1266–67.

9. See *JCP*, 1:82–144, 259–61, 366–69, 2:69–71.

10. Mathew Carey, *Autobiography of Mathew Carey* (Philadelphia: Historical Society of Pennsylvania, n.d.), 1–4.

11. *American Daily Advertiser*, 6 January 1792.

12. Carroll to Carey, 7 March 1792, in *JCP*, 2:23.

13. Robert Walsh to Carey, 18 March 1792, box 27, folder 2, Edward Carey Gardiner Collection (hereafter ECGC), Historical Society of Pennsylvania (hereafter HSP).

14. Mathew Carey, *The Calumnies of Verus* . . . (Philadelphia: Johnston & Justice, 1792), 7–9.

15. Ibid., 8.

16. Ibid., 10–11.

17. Ibid., 40, 47.

18. Carey to Reverend Sir, 7 November 1791, in Mathew Carey, *Miscellanies*, 7 vols. (Philadelphia: Joseph R. A. Skerrett, 1826), 2:7. See also Carey to Carroll, New York, 6 April 1789, Letterbook, vol. 1, Lea and Febiger Collection (hereafter LFC), HSP; Carey to Carroll, 27 March 1791, box 27, folder 4, ECGC, HSP.

19. Patrick Smyth to Carey, 17 March 1788, box 26, folder 5, ECGC, HSP; William Harold to Carey, 20 May 1790, box 26, folder 3, ECGC, HSP.

20. *Carlisle Weekly Gazette*, 29 July, 5 August, 12 August 1795; Martin Griffin, ed., *The American Catholic Historical Researches* 11 (January 1894): 133–34.

21. Martin Spalding, *Sketches of the Early Catholic Missions of Kentucky from their Commencement in 1787 to the Jubilee of 1826–7* (Louisville: B. J. Webb & Brother, 1852), 125. For more titles addressing anti-Catholic prejudices, see Robert Gorman, *Catholic Apologetical Literature in the United States, 1784–1858* (Washington, DC: Catholic University of America Press, 1939), 7–26.

22. John Mason, "John Rogers, the Proto-Martyr under Queen Mary," *Christian's Magazine* 2 (1808): 151.

23. "Twenty Letters to the Reverend John Mason, D.D., of New York," in Carey, *Miscellanies*, 2:149–50.

24. Margaret Abruzzo, "Apologetics of Harmony: Mathew Carey and the Rhetoric of Religious Liberty," *Pennsylvania Magazine of History and Biography* 134, no. 1 (January 2010): 5–30.

25. Carey to Walsh, 8 September 1808, Letterbook, vol. 25, LFC, HSP. Carey's letters to his associates are located in the same volume. For the other side of the correspondence, see Walsh to Carey, 3, 17, 25, 29 October 1808, in *Records of the American Catholic Historical Society of Philadelphia* 10 (1899): 109–11 (hereafter *RACHSP*); Kohlmann to Carey, 18 October, 9 and 12 December 1808, in *RACHSP* 11 (1900): 67–68; DuBourg to Carey, 7 November 1808 in *RACHSP* 13 (1902): 244–45.

26. Carey to Walsh, 8 September, 18 October 1808, Letterbook, vol. 25, LFC, HSP.

27. "Twenty Letters," in Carey, *Miscellanies*, 2:169, 158.

28. As noted above, Baptists and deists had been highlighting the evils of Protestant establishments for some time. See Isaac Backus, *A History of New England with Particular Reference to the Denomination of Christians Called Baptists* (Boston: Edward Draper, 1777–1796); Thomas Jefferson, *Notes on the State of Virginia* (Richmond: J. W. Randolph, 1853), 168–73.

29. "Twenty Letters," in Carey, *Miscellanies*, 2:215.

30. Ibid., 2:151.

31. John Thayer, *A Controversy between the Reverend John Thayer, Catholic Missionary of Boston, and the Reverend George Lesslie* . . . (Newburyport, MA, 1793), 167. Carey complained that his writings did not receive more support in the press. See Carey to Kohlmann, 10 December 1808, Letterbook, vol. 25, LFC, HSP.

32. Chas. Kenny to Carey, 16 December 1808, *RACHSP* 11 (1900): 213; Kohlmann to Carey, 12 December 1808, *RACHSP* 11 (1900): 68.

33. The first Catholic newspaper was the New York *Shamrock* in 1810. For more pro-Catholic activism regarding religious freedom, see William Lucey, *Edward Kavanagh: Catholic, Statesman, Diplomat from Maine, 1795–1844* (Francetown, NH: Marshall Jones, 1946), 34–38.

34. The effort was in fact transatlantic. See Thomas Jodziewicz, "John Fletcher's *Reflections on the Spirit of Religious Controversy* and John Carroll: Apologists Both," *American Catholic Studies* 119, no. 2 (2008): 71–90.

35. Jay Dolan, *The American Catholic Experience: A History from Colonial Times to the Present* (Notre Dame, IN: University of Notre Dame Press, 1992), 103.

36. On these developments in general, see Ray Allen Billington, *The Protestant Crusade, 1800–1860: A Study on the Origins of American Nativism* (New York: Rinehart, 1952); Jon Gjerde, *Catholicism and the Shaping of Nineteenth-Century America* (New York: Cambridge University Press, 2012).

37. See John Lathrop, *A Discourse on the Errors of Popery* . . . (Boston: S. Hall, 1793), 29, writing that "the usurpations of the Romish church are by no means so threatening to the liberties and happiness of mankind, as they were at the time when our fathers separated from her."

38. Billington, *Protestant Crusade*, 43.

39. John Pierce, *The Right of Private Judgment in Religion, Vindicated Against the Claims of the Romish Church and All Kindred Usurpations* (Cambridge, MA: Hilliard and Metcalf, 1821), 3.

40. Constitution of the Society for Vindicating the Roman Catholic Religion from Calumny and Abuse, 31 October 1826, box 27, folder 12, ECGC, HSP.

41. Joseph Blanco White, *Practical and Internal Evidence against Catholicism* (Georgetown, DC: James C. Dunn, 1826), iv–v. The "government" he referred to was in England, but Americans seamlessly appropriated his ideas to their own country.

42. *Baltimore Gazette*, 11 September 1826.

43. Sacredos [pseud.], *An Address to the Flocks of the Reverend Approvers of Blanco White's "Internal Evidences against Catholicism"* (Baltimore: Fielding Lucas, 1826).

44. A Catholic layman, *A Roland for an Oliver: Letters on Religious Persecution* (Philadelphia: Bernard Dornin, 1826), vii.

45. Ibid., 29.

46. Ibid., 53.

47. John England to Carey, 23 June 1823 and 14 April 1827, box 22, folder 5, ECGC, HSP.

48. "Letters on the Calumnies of J. Blanco White against the Catholic Religion," in *The Works of the Right Rev. John England, First Bishop of Charleston*, ed. Ignatius Aloysius Reynolds, 5 vols. (Baltimore: John Murphy, 1849), 1:106.

49. Ibid., 1:107.

50. Ibid., 3:514.

51. Ibid., 1:112.

52. Ibid., 1:184–85.

53. Ibid., 1:182.

Chapter Nine

Making an American Church

Communal Toleration and Republican Governance in
Early National Charleston and New York

Susanna Linsley

In the spring of 1819, Charleston newcomer Caroline Howard Gilman wrote a letter to her sister reporting that "the City is on fire with Clerical disputes."[1] Fires were a perennial problem in Charleston, as in all early American port cities, but so were clerical disputes, or conflicts over religious governance. Gilman was particularly attuned to notice these crises that turned communities presumed to be united by faith into factions that separately vied for power and influence. While the particular dispute she mentioned concerned other churches, Gilman had just been at the center of a crisis in her own denomination. Gilman and her husband, Samuel, had recently relocated to Charleston from Massachusetts to serve the new Unitarian congregation that had splintered from the Circular Congregational Church in 1817, taking about 40 percent of the Circular Church's members and half of its property.[2] Gilman noted that theological questions between churches were "scarcely known" among her neighbors. Instead, the dominant religious questions for Charlestonians occurred internally, within individual congregations, and involved "church government and personal animosities."[3]

By the early nineteenth century, Charlestonians already had a long history of negotiating conflicts between churches. A vibrant and diverse religious community, Charleston had been fed by immigration from England, Northern Europe, New England, the Caribbean, and Africa. Its inhabitants included Huguenots, Quakers, Scotch Irish Presbyterians, Sephardic and Ashkenazi Jews, German Lutherans, Methodists, Irish Catholics, and those of West African faiths. Though toleration was one of South Carolina's founding principles during the colonial era (the colony's Fundamental Constitution, most likely penned by John Locke in 1669, extended civil and political rights to nonconformists), the Anglican Church establishment regularly asserted its authority.[4] In the wake of the American Revolution, South Carolina's dissenting churches capitalized on their support for the patriot cause to secure the promise of Anglican disestablishment. South Carolinians first replaced the colonial church-state system with a general Protestant establishment before moving fully toward a system of voluntarism in 1790.[5]

Conflicts over religious governance took a fundamentally different shape under republican auspices than they did under monarchical rule. Building on the premise that all religious exercise should emanate from voluntary wishes, Americans began to insist that church doctrine should be derived from social contracts rather than tradition or scripture. This was as true in Charleston as in other regions of the new nation. As Charlestonians became accustomed to disestablishment, they faced new challenges about how to govern their local religious affairs. Issues that seemed to fall squarely under the jurisdiction of ecclesiastical authority—such as whether a minister could update traditions, the language of worship services, and whether a congregation could lend its support to a civic celebration—became hotly contested as democratic partisans within congregations insisted that all decisions should be made by elected representatives.

By the time Caroline Howard Gilman noted the heated local debate about clerical disputes in the Presbyterian Church, Charlestonians had developed a habit of making their congregations testing grounds for the practices of representative democracy. On a near-weekly basis, religious societies had to determine how to use space, how to manage funds, and how to organize the substance of worship services. Even more important, religious societies had to figure out who had the authority to decide these matters: clergy, lay leaders, congregants, or some combination thereof. Gilman's particular attention to "clerical disputes" highlighted a simple but fundamental truth about early national religious communities: the most pressing issues that religious societies encountered were less the attention-grabbing disputes that would preoccupy subsequent generations, such as nativism, revivalism, and the explosion of new millenarian sects, than the more mundane, yet crucial, contests over political procedure and the question of how intracommunal dissent would be managed.

While scholars have identified how early national religious societies redefined the principles of toleration as they competed in a voluntary church system, the problem of "internal toleration" (or rather the daily strategies and ideologies Americans used to govern themselves and manage dissent within the intimate spaces of their congregations) has long been neglected.[6] Focusing on two examples from Charleston and one from New York City, a region with a very similar history of clerical disputes and religious and ethnic diversity, this chapter demonstrates that many early national Americans were preoccupied with a very particular type of internal toleration, one that involved negotiating community-based conflicts through a republican framework.[7]

As republican institutions took root in early national United States, religious societies were one of the chief sites where Americans of diverse backgrounds and conflicting views interpreted constitutions, exercised voting rights, and tested the limits of legitimate opposition and dissent. The conflicts that beset these seemingly unassuming religious societies and the ways in which partisans resolved them paralleled larger political controversies and revealed how republican norms would shape social and institutional life in the new nation.

I

On the surface, the conflict that Gilman observed was nearly as old as Christianity itself. Where did the power to interpret church doctrine reside: with the clergy or the laity? The crisis in Charleston began when Aaron Leland, the minister of First Scots Presbyterian Church, took it upon himself to change the order of some of the prayers and hymns during one of the Sunday services.[8] First Scots Presbyterian, the church in question, was a socially distinguished congregation with a rich history. It was founded in 1731 when Scottish settlers broke off from the Congregationalist Church to form a religious society where they could worship according to the traditions of Scottish Presbyterianism rather than New England Congregationalism.[9] Gesturing to their long-standing Scottish traditions, the elected board of lay leaders, called the Session, condemned Leland's presumption in altering the service and rejected "innovation in the forms of worship." While the members of the Session had conceded that a blind devotion to "modes of worship [and] particular forms of prayer and of praise" was "unessential and unnecessary," they nonetheless insisted that their unique traditions were the reason they continued to have an important place in the city's religious life.[10]

Leland was convinced that the Session did not really care about the order of hymns and that the real objection was personal, nothing more than a "cruel attempt made to impeach [his] morals."[11] Leland's suspicions were not unfounded. The Session men had made no secret of their concern about Leland's New England origins and their conviction that he was conspiring to "undermine the Scotch interest in the Church" by "gradually introducing [his] own countrymen." In fact, they had accused him of trying to build a "Yankee majority" that would "revolutionize the congregation and make it a Yankee Church."[12]

What made this internal disagreement different from past clerical disputes, and more than a mere sectional debate, was that Charleston Presbyterians filtered the conflict through the lens and language of republican government. While they quibbled about tradition and innovation, their larger quarrel concerned interpreting and executing laws that had been adopted through a representative system. Session leaders explained that in 1784, members of the church adopted "Bye-laws" to govern the congregation "both in secular and ecclesiastical affairs." Those bylaws granted the Session the power over "the regulation of our times and modes of worship, and the general management of the spiritual affairs of the Church." According to the Session, when Leland changed the service without consulting anyone, he had broken the laws of the church. The Session insisted that Leland was "well acquainted" with those laws but nonetheless disregarded them, "thinking the Session incompetent to act in that capacity, without his presence."[13]

Though Leland had little use for the Session, he, too, viewed the disagreement through a republican lens. Leland believed that he was the one protecting the church's system of popular representation from an assault by the oligarchical Session men. In his eyes, the Session did not represent the will of the people because even its members acknowledged that "two thirds of the Congregation [was] very much attached to [Leland's] ministry." The Session complained about his services, but, as Leland had observed, "for months, none of the Elders except one attended Church at all."[14] To him, it looked like an elite group of men more interested in power than in worship had subverted a republican process. While they could claim to represent the people on the basis of the election to office, they were exploiting public trust. Despite Leland's protests, the Session's constant abuse eventually took its toll. In 1819, Leland resigned and took a position at Charleston's Second Presbyterian Church, where he continued to "enflam[e]" the tensions among Charleston's Presbyterians.[15]

The Charleston conflict derived from personal enmity, sectional and ethnic identity, and ecclesiastical innovation. However, nearly all of these divisions manifested themselves as problems of republican governance. In this, Charleston's Presbyterians shared a great deal with churches and synagogues across early America. In the years following the American Revolution, religious communities repeatedly invoked the principles and language of representative government as they managed dissent within their own ranks.

Like their Presbyterian colleagues, Charleston Episcopalians used political procedures to frame a crisis over religious governance in republican terms. In 1816, roughly coterminous with the Presbyterian crises, the vestry boards of St. Philips and St. Michaels Episcopalian churches unanimously approved a petition from a group of worshipers requesting a change to the "tedious" and "fatiguing" communion service. According to the liturgy (the sacred routine that churches follow in their worship services), the clergy were required to recite a lengthy blessing before serving the consecrated bread and wine to each person who desired to take communion. Since the number of communicants, or people authorized to take communion, was "estimated at four hundred and fifty," attendees at the communion service were "usually assembled for four hours, and upwards." Pointing to the great length of the Sunday service, the petitioners stated that they spoke on behalf of "aged, and infirm persons" who could not manage to attend, as well as the rumbling stomachs of virtually everyone else, who were "regularly inconvenienced by [the services] encroaching on the allotted time in which most private families dine." [16]

The vestrymen offered what they saw as an easy solution that would speed things along while still preserving the church's sacred doctrine. They proposed that when reciting the communion blessing, the clergymen could use the plural "thee," rather than the singular "thou," and thus recite the blessing one time to apply to the entire congregation. They believed that their solution would increase the piety of "the many," since the mindless repetition of the communion prayer 450 times only led to "listlessness & inattention." [17] The clergymen saw it differently. After considering the resolution and the petition, the St. Michaels and St. Philips clergy summarily rejected them.

The lay leaders who supported innovation used a republican approach to frame their next move. They insisted that their churches were "mere voluntary associations" and, as such, the participants had the right to make any changes that suited the needs of the community. While the clergy and the ecclesiastical hierarchy certainly played an important role in religious life, that role was largely "recommendatory," and "no other deference is due than such as each Individual Church is disposed to give them." [18] The vestrymen also argued that the moment their church split from the Church of England in the American Revolution, it was bound by republican mandates. Invoking the Declaration of Independence, they contended that "when in the course of Divine Providence these American States became independent with respect to Civil Government, their ecclesiastical Independence was necessarily included." Ultimately, "it is the happy and almost singular advantage of the Citizens of the United States, that in matters of Government, whether civil or Religious, every one enjoy the privilege of enquiring & determining for himself." [19] What began as a humble measure to get Episcopalians home in time for lunch had become a spirited defense of republican practices.

By the early nineteenth century, Republican norms had penetrated church government so completely that even orthodox clergy had to accede to them. While insisting on their commitment to tradition, St. Philips ministers Thomas Frost and Christopher Gadsden and St. Michaels rector Theodore Dehon employed methods that acknowledged the sovereign role of the people in governance, including the circulation of their own petition. [20] The clergy stipulated that people in their profession should generally not resort to such tactics. But it was necessary in this case because the vestrymen had suggested that they (the vestry) represented public opinion. [21]

While the clergy hoped that their own petition would demonstrate the lay leaders' hypocrisy, they only succeeded in revealing how completely republican doctrine now permeated church governance and the management of intradenominational dissent. According to the clergy's interpretation of the survey results, the vestry had been "misinformed" about how many people supported its proposed reforms to shorten the communion service. Through their inquiry, the clergy found that "300 of our Communicants have expressed to us their wish, that there should be no alteration in the mode of Administering the Lord's Supper." Virtually all of the clergy's petition signers were women (by contrast, no women signed the vestrymen's petition). [22] For the clergy, this discovery was their silver bullet. They insisted that the lay leaders could not claim that their proposed reforms had popular support if they refused to accede to the wishes of the church's majority. As one clergyman remarked, "I should not have thought it just or reasonable that the [125 males who supported reform] in this case should outweigh the opinions of 275 women." [23] While foreswearing a representative church government, the clergy still felt compelled to shroud their views in a veil of republican legitimacy.

The clergymen's arguments were largely disingenuous. Their real intention in noting the preponderance of women who opposed the measure was to illustrate the absurdity of governing churches through republican principles. To them, the whole situation underlined the necessity of religious tradition and orthodoxy as bulwarks against anarchy. Ultimately, the clergy pushed the vestry into a compromise. Instead of changing the text of the service, the two churches agreed to modify the space. St. Michaels and St. Philips both enlarged the area where communion was served and employed more ministers to take part in the ceremony. Tacitly, then, the clergy addressed the form of the vestry's concerns (that communion took too long), but not the substance (that lay people had the right to decide how to worship). [24] Nevertheless, the strength of their argument came through their appeals to popular opinion. Though it was not their intention, the clergy reinforced the notion that internal dissension had to be addressed through republican practices.

Contemporary Americans were redefining legitimate governance in many other domains of early national culture—experimenting with political parties, expanding the franchise, determining the bounds of loyal opposition, and so on. But, as these Charleston disputes demonstrate, religious societies regularly formed the vanguard when it came to managing differences within republican institutions.

II

While Charleston religious societies practiced communal toleration by citing bylaws and popular opinion, New York City's churches were much more overt in their use of party politics to frame their local contests over governance. Indeed, it's no coincidence that many local, state, and national political leaders also served as lay leaders in New York's churches.[25] The large Episcopal and Presbyterian congregations that dominated the city's religious life were more than just houses of worship; they were complex organizations that adhered to popularly determined bylaws and governed in a federated system of clergy (executive), lay leaders (legislative), and members (voters). And in the early nineteenth century, as they redefined popular governance and expanded the franchise, these churches became crucibles of partisan politics and thereby sites of both heated religious *and* political dissension.

An illuminating instance of partisan-inflected religious dissent took place in 1801 when members of the Collegiate Dutch Reformed Churches sparred over a question of when to ring the church bells. In February 1801, a "committee of citizens" from the Collegiate Dutch Reformed Churches composed a petition signed by members of the congregation and submitted to the consistory (the Dutch Reformed elected board of lay leaders). The petition had broad support in the congregation. It asked the consistory for permission to ring the church bells in honor of Thomas Jefferson's inauguration during celebrations planned for the following week. The church had rung the bells to commemorate George Washington's inauguration in 1789, but had not renewed the practice for John Adams seven years later. Opponents argued that Washington's inauguration had been unique, marking "the momentous event of the adoption of our present Constitution," and should not be repeated.[26]

Most likely, the Dutch Reformed bell ringers' interest in Jefferson's election was an expression of the broader enthusiasm for the Democratic-Republican politics then sweeping through evangelical circles. Though Thomas Jefferson is recognized as one of the great advocates of church and state separation, his presidential victory owed much to widespread support from evangelical Protestants. As Amanda Porterfield has documented, the same factors that led to the upswing in religious practice in the early nineteenth century created a broad new coalition sympathetic to Jeffersonian reforms. Despite the prevailing belief that religion should be "a cohesive moral agent transcending party," Jefferson's presidency witnessed the rise of religious organizations that aligned themselves with political parties.[27]

As illustrated in the New York Dutch Reformed churches, the partisan divide did not always conform to denominational lines, and it regularly refracted congregations' immediate struggles to govern their communities in a world where understandings of power, authority, and participation were rapidly changing. The consistory of the Collegiate Dutch Reformed Churches considered the petition of the "committee of citizens" requesting the celebra-tion of Jefferson's inauguration, and it was narrowly defeated. The vote was split, with eight in favor and eight opposed. Therefore the consistory was forced to turn to the congregation's constitution, which gave the presiding minister the privilege of casting the deciding vote. The minister voted in the negative, which meant that the Collegiate Churches of New York would not formally acknowledge Jefferson's inauguration.[28]

In keeping with republican politics in general, and Jeffersonian politics in particular, the "committee of citizens" refused to accept the consistory's decision. They rallied the congregation, sparking three days of protest that "disturb[ed] the peace and harmony" of the community. After "great uneasi-ness and discontent," the consistory gave in to popular demands. On the day Thomas Jefferson was sworn in as the nation's third president, the Collegiate Churches' bells rang throughout New York City.[29]

Even though the Collegiate Churches resolved the conflict over the inau-guration, they did not ultimately determine what to do when members and supporters made requests on church space and resources as citizens and congregants. As a result, the situation repeated itself three years later when a new committee submitted a petition to ring the bells to commemorate the Louisiana Purchase. Though different individuals were involved, the vote was again split, and the presiding minister rejected the proposal, forcing the Collegiate Churches to sit out the festivities.[30]

The faction opposing the influence of Democratic-Republican political victories in their internal congregational affairs took the opportunity to try to make a definitive policy about the sorts of public statements the churches would make in the future. The consistory men who had voted against the proposal resolved that the churches would not ring their bells for any occa-sion marking a civil celebration—with two exceptions: Independence Day and whenever the City of New York specifically requested their participa-tion. Again, the Jeffersonian bell ringers were outraged. The consistory, swayed by the disproportionate influence of the clergy, had denied a request that enjoyed broad popular support.[31]

Undeterred, the Jeffersonian-inspired bell-ringing proponents insisted that the church embrace more lay-driven, representative measures and put more decision-making power in the hands of the people. The bell-ringers resented the fact that ministers, not elected lay leaders, had generally legislated for the church. They stressed the Collegiate Churches' charter provision that "none of the ministers" were "Members of the Consistory" and therefore had "no right to vote" with the consistory on any temporal business. Despite their impassioned appeal, the proposal to strip clergymen of their right to vote with the consistory was narrowly defeated.[32]

Then, a few months later, something notable happened: The church re-ceived an application from the Society of the Cincinnati to use one of its sanctuaries for an oration to pay homage to Alexander Hamilton, who had recently died in his famous duel with Aaron Burr. While all previous requests for the civic use of church space supported Democratic-Republican causes, this one originated from an organization supporting a Federalist cause. The consistory, which had only just voted to restrict virtually all public uses of their facilities, voted unanimously to open up the space for the Society of the Cincinnati's commemoration of Hamilton. Even more tellingly, the consistory men reconsidered the previous proposal about ministers voting with the consistory. They overturned the resolution they had made only months earlier and unanimously agreed to strip ministers of their vote on issues involving civic and material affairs.[33] The faction that opposed ringing the bells to celebrate Democratic-Republican victories such as Jefferson's inauguration and the Louisiana Purchase bowed to their own partisan sympathies when they were asked for the use of their space to promote a Federalist project to commemorate Hamilton.

In early national New York as elsewhere, local and national contests over politics were thus intertwined with internal debates about how to govern faith communities and how, in particular, to manage the dissent that emerged from within them. The New York Dutch churches were among the first institutions in which people could confront authority figures and manage disagreement in a republican society.[34] They performed some of the earliest trials of republican government as they struggled to operate according to the sometimes divergent principles of popular sovereignty and scriptural fidelity.

CONCLUSION

In the wake of disestablishment, churches were no longer directly connected to the mechanisms of government power and no longer reliant on government funding. They remained, however, key civic institutions where heated discussions about partisanship, representative government, and popular sovereignty now infused the approaches taken toward church governance and intradenominational dissent. Given the preponderance of republican sentiment in the new nation, even people who wanted to preserve traditional structures of power and prevent churches from succumbing to democratic sentiment had to use novel procedural arguments to justify their positions. In these and other ways, early national churches were crucial sites for the testing of republican practices outside the halls of strictly political institutions. This experiment in disestablishment reshaped citizens' expectations about both governing and dissent in an increasingly boisterous religious culture that bore not a little resemblance to Roger Williams's original vision.

NOTES

1. Caroline Howard Gilman to Mrs. Ann Marie White, 24 May 1819, Caroline Howard Gilman Papers, South Carolina Historical Society (hereafter cited as Gilman Papers).

2. George Edwards, *A History of the Independent or Congregational Church of Charleston South Carolina, Commonly Known as Circular Church* (Boston: Pilgrim Press, 1947), 60–64. Edwards estimates that eighty-nine active members stayed at the Circular Church and sixty-two left to join the Unitarian Church. The new Unitarian Church also claimed one of the two congregational meetinghouses.

3. Gilman to White, 24 May 1819, Gilman Papers.

4. Though it was never ratified, the Fundamental Constitution helped to establish the intent of South Carolina's founders and reflected a reality of pluralism in colonial South Carolina. Walter Edgars, *South Carolina, a History* (Columbia: University of South Carolina Press, 1998), 43; John Wesley Brinsfield Jr., *Religion and Politics in Colonial South Carolina* (Easly, SC: Southern Historical Press, 1983), 31.

5. William Tennent, *Mr. Tennent's Speech, on the Dissenting Petition, Delivered in the House of Assembly, Charles-town, South Carolina, Jan 11, 1777* (Charlestown: Peter Timothy, 1777); Travel Journal and Album of Collected Papers of William Tennent (1740–1777), University of South Carolina, Thomas Cooper Library, Digital Collections Dept., 2008.

6. For example, see Chris Beneke, *Beyond Toleration: The Religious Origins of American Pluralism* (Oxford and New York: Oxford University Press, 2006); Jon Butler, *Awash in a Sea of Faith: Christianizing the American People* (Cambridge, MA: Harvard University Press, 1990); R. Laurence Moore, *Selling God: American Religion in the Marketplace of Culture* (Oxford: Oxford University Press, 1994); and David Sehat, *The Myth of American Religious Freedom* (Oxford and New York: Oxford University Press, 2011).

7. On the eve of the American Revolution, New York City had more than eighteen houses of worship from at least ten denominations: Anglican/Episcopalian, Presbyterian, Dutch Reformed, Lutheran, Huguenot, Quaker, Anabaptist, Moravian, Methodist, and Jewish. Carl Bridenbaugh, *Mitre and Sceptre: Transatlantic Faiths, Ideas, Personalities, and Politics 1689–1775* (New York: Oxford University Press, 1962), 116–18; Brinsfield, *Religion and Politics*, 31.

8. *Documents Relative to the Controversy in the First Presbyterian Church of the City of Charleston which Terminated in the Resignation of the Pastor* (Charleston, SC: A. E. Miller, 1817), 30.

9. Erskine Clarke has observed that the Reformed churches in Charleston were crucibles for debates about sectionalism and unionism well before the conversation preoccupied the nation. "The Reformed churches did not encourage a withdrawal from political activities," Clarke explains, "but provided the region with some of its most influential political leaders. To a remarkable extent, Unionist political sentiment was present in the Reformed Churches of Charleston." Erskine Clarke, *Our Southern Zion* (Tuscaloosa: University of Alabama Press, 1996), 163.

10. *Documents Relative to the Controversy*, 6–7, 8–9.

11. Ibid., 24.

12. Ibid., 33–34.

13. Ibid., 8–10.

14. Ibid., 30, 33–34.

15. Ibid., 9, 33–34.

16. 11 August 1816, Vestry Journals, St. Philips Church, 1812–1822, book 6, pp. 61–63, South Caroliniana Library, University of South Carolina Libraries.

17. Ibid.

18. Ibid., 16 October 1816, 71–72.

19. Ibid.

20. Ibid., 11 August 1816, 69–71, 75; 2 August 1816, Minute Book, St. Michaels Church, 1759–1824, p. 383, South Caroliniana Library, University of South Carolina Libraries.

21. 16 October 1816, Vestry Journals, St. Philips Church, 68–79.

22. Ibid., 70.

Making an American Church

159

23. Ibid., 74–79.

24. Ibid., 11 August 1816, 61–63; 10 November 1816, 78–79; 25 February 1819, 103–4.

25. In New York, three of the four signers of the Declaration of Independence served on church vestry boards. Philip Livingston was an elder and a deacon at the Dutch Reformed church, and Lewis Morris and Francis Lewis would go on to hold seats on the Trinity Church Board of Trustees. Scanning the lists of men providing lay leadership to Protestant churches is like reviewing lists of influential state politicians. Among them are Jays, DeLancys, Livingstons, Burrs, Bleekers, Tompkins, Kings, Schuylers, Van Rensselaers, and Rutgers. Lay leaders in Jewish synagogues also held bureaucratic offices. Jewish merchants, with experience in shipping and with extensive networks of contacts in ports throughout the world, were invaluable to the new government. National, state, and city governments readily commissioned Jews into positions such as port officers, navy officers, Indian agents, consular agents, and diplomats. "The First Jews in American Politics," in *The Jews of the United States 1790–1840: A Documentary History*, vol. 2, ed. Joseph Blau and Salo Baron (New York and London: Columbia University Press, 1963), 306–7. Also, in the early decades of the nineteenth century, Jewish printers and newspaper editors—most notably Naphtali Philips and Mordecai Noah of New York, Isaac Harby of Charleston, and Isaac Leeser of Philadelphia—contributed to and sparked political debates through the press.

26. 28 February 1801, Minutes of the Consistory of the Reformed Protestant Dutch Church in the City of New York, Liber H 1795–1807, Collegiate Church Corporation.

27. Amanda Porterfield, *Conceived in Doubt: Religion and Politics in the New American Nation* (Chicago: University of Chicago Press, 2012), 148.

28. 28 February 1801, Liber H 1795–1807, Minutes of the Consistory.

29. Ibid.

30. Ibid., 11 May 1804.

31. Ibid., 7 June 1804.

32. Ibid., 5 July 1804. They did acknowledge that the "president" had the right to make the casting vote. This likely meant that of the several ministers who served the church, only one at a time, when serving in a primary administrative role, could have anything to do with elections. They could not unite as their own faction.

33. 23 July 1804, Liber H 1795–1807, Minutes of the Consistory.

34. 3 August 1797, 2 May 1800, Liber H, Minutes of the Consistory. At the end of the eighteenth century, the Collegiate Churches began to phase out the use of Dutch in their services and rely exclusively on English. For a detailed look at religious toleration within the colonial Dutch Reformed Church, see Evan Haefeli, *The New Netherlands and the Dutch Origins of American Religious Liberty* (Philadelphia: University of Pennsylvania Press, 2012).

Chapter Ten

The Nineteenth-Century "School Question"

An Episode in Religious Intolerance or
an Expansion of Religious Freedom?

Steven K. Green

No organizing theory has had a greater impact on the way we conceptualize the intersection of religion and politics in America than the principle of separation of church and state. Since the nineteenth century, judges, politicians, educators, and even religious leaders have embraced church-state separation not only as central to church-state relations but also as a cornerstone of American democracy (albeit frequently disagreeing over the meaning of that principle). The Supreme Court borrowed the phrase "a wall of separation between church and State" from Thomas Jefferson, who used it in his famous 1801 letter to the Danbury Baptists. In the 1879 Reynolds case, the court averred that the principle "may be accepted almost as an authoritative declaration of the scope and effect of the [First] amendment."[1] Not until the mid-twentieth century, however, with the application of the Bill of Rights to the states, did the principle of separation begin to have major practical effects. In the modern court's first establishment clause holding, *Everson v. Board of Education* (1947), Justice Hugo Black wrote:

> The "establishment of religion" clause of the First Amendment means at least this: Neither a state nor the Federal Government can set up a church. Neither can pass laws which aid one religion, aid all religions, or prefer one religion over another. . . . No tax in any amount, large or small, can be levied to support any religious activities or institutions, whatever they may be called, or whatever form they may adopt to teach or practice religion. . . . In the words of

Jefferson, the clause against establishment of religion by law was intended to erect "a wall of separation between Church and State."[2]

For approximately fifty years following *Everson*, separation of church and state served as the touchstone for religion clause jurisprudence and was endorsed by liberal and conservative justices alike. Early invocations of the principle were almost wholly unqualified. Supreme Court justices insisted that separation must be "absolute," "uncompromising," "high and impregnable," and "complete and permanent," though they, like scholars, disagreed on exactly what these terms meant. (Black's *Everson* opinion, for instance, allowed public funding of transportation to parochial schools.) While some people disagreed with such rhetorical absolutism, few (if any) contested the legitimacy of the underlying principle.[3]

Beginning in the 1940s, justices employed separationist reasoning to invalidate a host of activities concerning the government's use of religion. While the display of the Ten Commandments in public school classrooms garnered some attention, the most frequent application of the principle was in two related areas: government funding of religious institutions (chiefly parochial schools) and religious exercises in the public schools. Approximately two-thirds of the court's separationist rulings between 1947 and 1993 went against school prayer and the public funding of religious entities. Of the two areas, the "no funding principle" had a constitutional pedigree reaching back into the early nineteenth century. Few people, aside from Catholic school officials, questioned its legitimacy. As with the broader principle of separation, most disagreement arose from questions over its meaning and application. For example, the modern court has ruled that some publicly funded secular services in parochial schools are permissible under the no-funding principle. This type of funding is intended to help students and includes paying for secular textbooks, testing, remedial services, and equipment such as computers. However, other uses of public money that benefit students less directly are not permissible, such as paying the salaries of parochial school teachers.[4] Despite divergent views on those questions, few people disputed the core principle. In fact, in the *Everson* case, even the amicus brief filed on behalf of the Catholic bishops expressed no disagreement with separation of church and state or the no-funding rule in principle.[5]

The American public has also consistently supported the principle of church-state separation, at least in theory. Opinion polls continue to indicate significant support for "maintain[ing] the separation of church and state," with approximately 70 percent of people answering favorably. At the same time, people's opinions, like those of judges, have diverged when it comes to applying the principle in practice. For instance, approximately the same percentage of Americans support organized prayer in public schools, regardless of the court's holdings to the contrary. Yet the principle generally remains popular.[6]

Beginning in the 1980s, the consensus surrounding separation of church and state began to unravel. First, scholars challenged the Jeffersonian model of church-state separation affirmed in *Everson*, arguing that it was not representative of attitudes during the founding period and that Jefferson had played no role in drafting or ratifying the First Amendment. These scholars further argued that founding Americans chiefly advocated "disestablishment," a model of church-state relations that allowed greater accommodation of religion in public than the strict separation model. Such accommodation, they contended, is more consistent with American traditions and values, a view popularized by Stephen Carter's *The Culture of Disbelief* and John Neuhaus's *The Naked Public Square*. To these arguments, religious conservatives such as Neuhaus added that separation of church and state was inimical to religion and people of faith, marginalizing their perspectives in American public life. Both sets of arguments draw from a larger intellectual critique of the once-prevalent conviction that modern societies were on an ineluctable secularizing path. This postsecularization critique maintains that American culture has never been strictly secular and that the Supreme Court's mid-twentieth-century rulings reflected neither the realities of American history nor a twentieth-century democratic consensus.[7]

Before long, conservative members on the Supreme Court embraced this critique. Justice William Rehnquist was among the first, arguing in 1986 that the practices of the founding period (e.g., legislative chaplains, thanksgiving proclamations) demonstrated that few early Americans accepted the Jeffersonian model of church-state separation. "There is simply no historical foundation for the proposition that the Framers intended to build the 'wall of separation' that was constitutionalized in [1947]," Rehnquist wrote. In siding with the exponents of separation, the court, Rehnquist claimed, had engaged in "bad history." The gauntlet thrown down, the cornerstone of church-state separation, the no-funding rule, soon came under attack. Conservative justices, at times buttressed by liberal colleagues, revised earlier court precedents, opening the door to greater public funding of religious schools through indirect, neutral methods such as tax credits and vouchers.[8]

However, the most vehement opponents of church-state separation were not content to simply redefine the scope of the no-funding rule or scale back its application. They attacked the legitimacy of the principle itself. Inspired by scholarly work like Philip Hamburger's influential 2002 book, *Separation of Church and State*, conservative scholars have challenged separationism, arguing on the grounds that the concept not only was alien to members of the founding generation but also emerged as a legal doctrine during the nineteenth century as a way of maintaining Protestant dominance of American culture at the expense of Catholics and other religious minorities. That dominance was manifested chiefly through Protestant control of the public schools and the refusal to fund Catholic schooling based on its "sectarian" content. Under this accounting, church-state separation is not simply ahistorical but also a profane, illiberal concept.[9]

Court conservatives have picked up on this theme, with Justice Clarence Thomas charging that "hostility to [providing] aid to pervasively sectarian schools has a shameful pedigree." As evidence, Thomas argues that opposition to funding parochial schools reached a high point in the 1870s debate over adoption of the Blaine Amendment, which would have amended the Constitution to bar any aid to sectarian institutions. "Consideration of the amendment arose at a time of pervasive hostility to the Catholic Church and to Catholics in general," Thomas insists, "and it was an open secret that 'Sectarian' was code for 'Catholic.'" In short, Thomas concluded that nothing in the establishment clause required government to exclude religious schools from receiving public funds. The no-funding principle and the "pervasively sectarian" doctrine were "born of bigotry, [and] should be buried now." This revisionist account of church-state separation and the no-funding rule, one that views both concepts as corrupt due to their purported historical legacy, has attracted a large following among conservative legal and religious scholars, as well as Republican politicians.[10] This critique thus raises an important question: Does the fact that church-state separation was used to justify a Protestant-dominated public school system and to deny the extension of public tax funds for Catholic schools mean that the principle is forever corrupt?

THE CRITIQUE

This new critique about the origins and legitimacy of church-state separation is not simply a disagreement over interpreting history; it affects contemporary legal analysis. Whether deserving or not, justices have asserted that "no provision of the Constitution is more closely tied to or given content by its generating history than the religion clauses." To delegitimize the origins and early applications of separationism is to undermine fifty years of modern church-state jurisprudence. This is one of the areas where history truly matters.[11]

The charge that the principle of separation has been associated with anti-Catholicism is not without merit. Within the education context, the concept of church-state separation has frequently advantaged the position of Protestants at the expense of Catholics. Throughout much of the nineteenth century, the common schools promoted a generic Protestant curriculum termed *nonsectarianism*. Protestant prayer and readings from the King James Bible were common practices in many public schools, although over time they became increasingly pro forma. Protestant educators regularly denied Catholic children the privilege of reading from the Douay Bible while also refusing to excuse them from participating in the Protestant religious exercises. Ironically, most educators saw little conflict between separationist principles and Protestant-oriented instruction in the public schools. For them, separating church and state meant prohibiting the funding or teaching of "sectarian" instruction in schools, which they equated with Catholic education, not the "nonsectarian" instruction that educators (blindly) believed affirmed universal Christian values that could not offend Catholic sensibilities. Separation of church and state thus legitimized Protestant dominance of public schooling while it served as a handy retort for turning aside Catholic requests for a proportional share of the state educational funds for their parochial schools. [12]

In addition to raising church-state separation as a defense for the no-funding rule, some nineteenth-century Americans used the principle to delegitimize Catholic schools, as well as the Catholic Church itself. As Nicholas Pellegrino illustrates in chapter 8, Protestant leaders argued that the hierarchical structure of the Catholic Church was inconsistent with democratic values. Authoritarian and autocratic, the Catholic Church looked "dangerously un-American partly because [it] did not harmonize easily with the concept of individual freedom imbedded in the national culture."[13] In contrast to the Catholic Church's top-down interpretation of doctrine, Protestantism had a tradition of unmediated interpretation of scriptures, which, Protestants asserted, was more consistent with freedom of conscience. The Catholic hierarchy only solidified such intuitions by issuing edicts that condemned democratic movements and religious toleration, including the principle of church-state separation. Protestant Americans also believed that Catholic clergy, with their absolute authority over matters of Catholic doctrine, interfered with the ability of rank-and-file Catholics to develop the independence of thought necessary to participate in republican governance. In contrast, Protestantism, with its congregational polity under lay control, was seen as more consistent with the principles of democratic self-governance.[14] Protestant nativists quickly embraced this view of church-state separation, becoming some of its strongest proponents, using separationism to legitimize their campaign of religious and ethnic bigotry. Thus, Hamburger and like-minded historians argue that church-state separation fueled a pervasive anti-Catholicism in America for over one hundred years, reinforcing and perpetuating suspicion, if not outright hostility and intolerance, toward Catholics and the Catholic Church. At the same time, it perpetuated a form of Protestant hegemony over the culture, ensuring that Catholics remained second-class citizens.[15]

While historians are generally agreed on many of these points, Hamburger makes several related historical claims that are more contentious: that church-state separation did not become a popular concept or legal principle until the middle of the nineteenth century; that it arose as a concept chiefly in response to Catholic challenges to public education; and that it was inherently linked to corrosive forms of religious intolerance. These are considered in turn.

CRITIQUING THE CRITIQUE

First, Hamburger asserts that separation of church and state arose as a popular concept in the middle of the nineteenth century chiefly in reaction to the massive influx of Catholic immigration. People embraced the concept not out of a commitment to principle, Hamburger contends, but chiefly to legitimize a pervasive anti-Catholicism. Yet the American legacy of anti-Catholicism reaches back to the earliest days of colonial America. The Protestant settlers of British colonial America defined themselves by the degree to which they rejected Catholic doctrines, and Protestants universally condemned what they viewed as the corruptions of the Catholic Church. The anti-Catholic sentiments expressed in the letters of many of the Founding Fathers are shocking and unsettling to modern ears. In a letter to Thomas Jefferson, John Adams once wrote that he had "long been decided in opinion that a free government and the Roman Catholic religion can never exist together in any nation or Country." Nonetheless, there were still notable examples of the toleration of Catholics during the founding period, with General George Washington forbidding his troops to celebrate Guy Fawkes Day or engage in other anti-Catholic activities.[16]

Though anti-Catholicism certainly existed in the early republic, as Pellegrino shows, its popular form remained relatively dormant until the mid-1830s. During that decade, a massive influx of Catholic migrants—initially Irish, and then Germans and Italians—arrived on American shores. Protestant Americans grew alarmed at their numbers as well as their cultural habits, perceiving Catholics as being clannish, living in isolated communities, and refusing to assimilate into the larger American society. Americans also feared the growing political influence of the Catholic Church in the United States. As noted above, for many nineteenth-century Americans, Catholicism represented a threat to core republican values, just as communism did a century later. As a result, popular anti-Catholicism surged during the 1840s–1850s, with outbreaks of violence occurring in Philadelphia, Boston, and New York, among other cities. In 1844, two days of bloody riots swept Philadelphia over the question of whether to read the Catholic Bible in heavily Catholic wards. Nativists invoked Bible reading and parochial school funding to galvanize their supporters while announcing their undying allegiance to the principle of church-state separation. This initial phase of nativism peaked in the mid-1850s with rise of the Know-Nothing (or American)

Party. In addition to defending Protestant Bible reading, the Know-Nothings proposed disbanding convents and imposing a twenty-five-year residency requirement for citizenship and voting. While nativism may have had as much to do with ethnic and economic tensions as religious animus, anti-Catholicism was a central nativist theme.[17]

As it happened, Catholic immigration and the upsurge in nativism coincided with the rise of public schooling. The common school movement, with its goal of universal, nonsectarian education, was still in its nascent stages in the 1830s–1840s. Advocates of public schooling perceived several direct threats from Catholic immigration: that Catholics resisted assimilating their children into the Protestant common schools (and in committing their children to the American project), and that a competing system of Catholic schools undermined the ideal of universal public education and thereby threatened the common school monopoly over the state school funds, further weakening the common school movement. While these perceptions were no doubt fueled by Protestant suspicions of Catholicism, they also represented the sincere concerns of educators who were committed to the goal of universal public education. Yet in defending public schooling and opposing the diversion of funds to Catholic schools, based on church-state separation, educators contributed to the larger wave of religious intolerance against Catholics. Protestant nonsectarian public education and the funding of Catholic schools thus became a focal point in the growing conflict between immigrant Catholics and the Protestant majority.[18]

While Hamburger's account of mid-nineteenth-century anti-Catholicism is largely correct, it is crucial to emphasize that the doctrine of church-state separation arose prior to the significant influx of Catholic immigrants at mid-century. As early as the 1760s, the Scottish Whig James Burgh invoked the metaphor of "an impenetrable wall of separation between things sacred and civil." Jefferson borrowed from Burgh in penning his famous letter to the Danbury Baptists, and years later, in 1819, James Madison wrote of how both civil society and personal piety had "been manifestly increased by the total separation of the Church from the State."[19]

Yet more important than the use of the metaphor in treatises and letters was the fact that the earliest controversies over religious school funding in the nineteenth century did not even involve Catholics. In two early controversies arising in New York in the 1820s–1830s, officials used principles of church-state separation to turn back funding applications from Baptist and Methodist schools. In both cases, the New York Common Council declined to fund any religious school (in this case, sectarian Protestant schools), with its legal committee asking rhetorically, "Can we, without violating the Constitution, appropriate any public funds to the support of those schools or institutions in which children are taught the doctrines and tenets of religious sectarianism?" Here, sectarianism was equated with the doctrines of any denomination, not solely Catholicism. To fund any "Methodist, Episcopalian, Baptist, and every other sectarian school" would result in the "unnatural union of Church and State," wrote the council. These cases helped to establish the legal principle against funding religious schooling. [20]

Moreover, the principle of separation was also applied in cases that had nothing to do with religious exercises, parochial school funding, or the Protestant-Catholic conflict. At the mid-century point, judges and lawyers invoked separation in matters ranging from church property disputes and estate challenges to cases concerning the enforcement of Sabbath laws and religious oath requirements. For example, in 1846, the Vermont Supreme Court refused to settle an internal church property dispute, declaring that "civil courts in this country have no ecclesiastical jurisdiction. . . . This doctrine inevitably results from that total separation between church and state . . . which is essential to the full enjoyment of the guaranteed rights of American citizenship." In the same year, a South Carolina judge refused to convict Jewish merchants of violating a Sunday law, remarking that they lived "in a community where there is a complete severance between Church and State, and where entire freedom of religious faith and worship is guaranteed to all its citizens alike." Similarly, in the 1850s, the California Supreme Court struck down a Sunday law, asserting that the state constitution guaranteed "not only complete toleration, but religious liberty in its largest sense— a complete separation between church and state." [21]

These cases, from New York in the 1820s to California in the 1850s, demonstrate that judges applied principles of separationism to controversies over education funding in which Catholics were not involved and to controversies having nothing to do with education funding at all. Thus, when conflicts did arise over nonsectarian education and the funding of Catholic schools, educators and judges applied an existing legal principle to their situation. To be sure, by mid-century most sectarian Protestant schools had either closed or been integrated into the common schools—excepting Lutheran schools that continued for ethnic and language reasons—so that the no-funding rule came to be applied chiefly with respect to Catholic schools.

Protestant-Catholic tensions reignited after the Civil War over issues of parochial school funding and Bible reading. Educators and Protestant clergy circled the wagons around public schooling, while Republican politicians seized upon the so-called School Question for political gain. In 1875, Republicans proposed a constitutional amendment to expressly prohibit religious school funding, commonly called the Blaine Amendment. Separation of church and state again became the rallying cry of a new anti-Catholicism. Yet while some used the concept to appeal to baser motives, others viewed it as an important principle that ensured the integrity and independence of both religious and government institutions and as a way to finally settle the ongoing Protestant-Catholic conflict. [22]

A related claim advanced by Hamburger and conservative jurists is that people employed the rhetoric of church-state separation solely for the benefit of Protestants and to the detriment of Catholics. In essence, the argument is that proponents applied the principle inconsistently: separation condemned the sectarianism of the Catholic Church, but it did not apply to the purportedly nonsectarian religious activities of the common schools. In so doing, separationism perpetuated a Protestant hegemony over the culture. This claim also deserves a closer look.

Without question, Protestants exercised something approaching cultural dominance in nineteenth-century America. Spurred on by a series of revivals and camp meetings in the early 1800s, evangelical Protestantism became the dominant form of religious expression in the United States. Evangelical Protestant attitudes and values also permeated many American institutions, including public education. Historian Robert Handy summed up the phenomenon: "In many ways, the middle third of the nineteenth century was more of a Protestant Age than was the colonial period with its established churches."[23]

Although Handy's critique is correct on one level, it oversimplifies the dynamic nature of nineteenth-century religious culture. Though representing the dominant form of religious expression, evangelical Protestantism faced competition not only from Catholics but also internally from heterodox movements such as Mormonism, Adventism, and Transcendentalism. Before long, contemporaries started challenging the truncated version of separationism that reinforced the Protestant dominance over the culture and its institutions. This trend was evident in the law. Whereas early on courts reaffirmed Protestantism's favored status by upholding Sabbath and blasphemy laws, frequently on religious grounds, over time lawyers and judges sought to make the law more professional and responsive to a developing economy by divorcing it from its moral and religious trappings. Contract law stopped assessing which party was at fault in a breach, focusing instead on the agreed-upon price for a default. The failure to fulfill a contract or some other financial obligation was no longer seen as a moral failing but merely as a business matter. Probate law abandoned its prohibition against honoring "irreligious" bequests deemed inconsistent with Christian principles. Blasphemy prosecutions, which courts consistently affirmed during the first third of the century, died off due to a growing discomfort over the law punishing expressions of religious heterodoxy. No longer would the law protect the dominant majority's religious sensibilities in the absence of a true public disturbance (i.e., disorderly conduct), which late-century courts measured objectively. And over time prosecutions for "profaning the Sabbath" decreased, and the justifications for Sunday laws shifted from religion to health and safety rationales. This secularizing impulse helped change not only the substance and institution of the law but also the way in which people envisioned the law's role in reinforcing religious norms. While remnants of morality remained in a handful of legal fields, such as criminal and domestic law, well into the twentieth century, overall the law was largely disentangled from moral questions. As an institution, the law became amoral.[24]

This transformation in the law led jurists, intellectuals, and religious leaders to reevaluate the meaning of religious liberty and church-state separation, with more inclusive conceptions of both emerging. In particular, courts began to employ ideas of separationism to undermine pro-Protestant practices and assumptions. The most significant example of using church-state separation to challenge Protestant dominance over the culture occurred in the famous Cincinnati Bible case of 1869. That year the Cincinnati school board voted to rescind its practice of daily prayer and Bible reading, with the intention of attracting more Catholic children to the public schools. Conservative Protestants objected and succeeded in obtaining a court injunction to reinstate the practice. However, one judge opposed the reinstatement. Judge Alphonso Taft, father of the future president and chief justice, argued that the state constitution required "absolute equality before the law, of all religious opinions and sects." To hold that Protestants were "entitled to have their mode of worship and their bible used in the common schools . . . is to hold to the union of Church and State," Taft wrote. On appeal, a unanimous Ohio Supreme Court agreed with Taft, holding that prayer and Bible reading were inconsistent with church-state separation, much to the chagrin of evangelical Protestants.[25]

The number of cases striking down Bible reading in the nineteenth century was not large—only one other significant case exists—but the decisions indicated that public and legal attitudes were evolving. In response to complaints by Catholics, Jews, and freethinkers, a significant number of urban school districts abandoned their religious exercises, while a growing number of educators and liberal ministers called for abolishing the practices. The nation's most prominent minister, Henry Ward Beecher, urged ending prayer and Bible reading in the schools, writing that it was "too late to adopt the church-state doctrine." Schools, he wrote, have "no business to teach religion, or to show partiality to one or another sect." In supporting these measures, educators, politicians, and liberal clergy made the case for church-state separation without any reliance on anti-Catholicism.[26]

By the latter part of the nineteenth century, the actions of school boards eliminating religious exercises, supported by a handful of court decisions, created the perception that public schools were becoming secularized. A national survey conducted by the Woman's Christian Temperance Union (WCTU) in 1887 confirmed the perception, noting that the Bible was not being read in schools in 175 counties out of 254 reporting. Among those schools that maintained the practice, the WCTU report lamented, Bible reading frequently was "not so generally read as formally [*sic*]." A series of late-century reports by the U.S. commissioner of education documented this phenomenon, noting that not only was religious instruction in decline but so was the use of the Bible as a textbook for teaching morals or literature. In his 1895 government report, Commissioner William T. Harris concluded that

> [outside of] New England there is no considerable area where [the Bible's] use can be said to be uniform. This condition has come about as much by indifference as by opposition. . . . There has been a change in public sentiment gradually growing toward complete secularization of the Government and its institutions. . . . Secularization of the schools is accepted or urged by many devout people who deem that safer than to trust others with the interpretation of the laws of conscience.[27]

Summarizing the trend of the previous decades, a 1912 Columbia Teachers College study stated that "over the century there has been a gradual but widespread elimination of religious and church influences from public education." In every state, the study continued, "religious instruction was either entirely eliminated or else reduced to the barest and most formal elements." The study attributed this transformation to two factors. The first was a "conviction that a republic can securely rest only on an educated citizenship." The second was "a sacred regard by the state for the religious opinion of the individual citizen." Thus, by the last quarter of the nineteenth century, separation of church and state was increasingly being identified as promoting the secularization of the culture, to the dismay of conservative Protestants. Even though Catholic officials also eschewed the growing secularism of the time, they were now the beneficiaries of church-state separation, at least with respect to the decline of Protestant religious exercises in the public schools. Meanwhile, educators and liberal Protestants and Jews came to embrace this more expansive understanding of church-state separation.[28]

This broader view of nineteenth-century history demonstrates that separation of church and state, in a sense, was an equal-opportunity offender. For Catholics, it meant that the government would not fund religious education. For Protestants, it increasingly meant that the public schools had to stop affirming Protestant values and become secular. To be sure, separationism was never used as a cudgel for attacking the legitimacy of evangelical Protestantism, as nativist groups did against Catholics during the nineteenth century. In the twentieth century, Catholic officials softened their condemnation of church-state separation, although most still argued that the no-funding rule promoted a form of discrimination against Catholic schools. At the same time, evangelical Protestants found themselves increasingly at odds with the courts' application of the principle to other contexts, such as religious exercises in the public schools and government-sponsored religious displays. Today, most criticism of separationism comes from conservative Protestants who argue that it has diluted the culture's religious values.

CONCLUSION

The Hamburger narrative wisely cautions against venerating any constitutional value. It demonstrates that history is never simple or sanitized. Still, we should resist condemning any constitutional value because previous generations held narrow or even illiberal views of that value—if that were the case, freedom of speech would never have survived the 1798 Sedition Act. Intolerance of alien religious and ethnic groups has long been a part of our history as we have struggled as a society to settle on what it means to be "American." As David Byron Davis once observed, Americans have long feared that new groups and ideas would subvert fragile American values and institutions, rather than enrich them. The road from mere tolerance to equality has never been straight or without obstacles, nor has it always been linear. Many political values we now hold dear—racial and gender equality—have taken a long time to evolve. In the same way that we should not condemn equality because of its earlier imperfect applications, we should not condemn separation of church and state. This is particularly true given that the history of separationism is much more ambiguous than its critics suggest. As Justice Sandra Day O'Connor wrote poignantly in her final church-state opinion, "Those who would renegotiate the boundaries between church and state must answer a difficult question: Why would we trade a system that has served us so well for one that has served others so poorly?"[29]

NOTES

1. *Reynolds v. United States*, 98 U.S. 145 (1879).
2. *Everson v. Board of Education*, 330 U.S. 1, 15–16 (1947).
3. *Everson*; *McCollum v. Board of Education*, 333 U.S. 203 (1948); *Zorach v. Clauson*, 343 U.S. 306 (1952).
4. *Mitchell v. Helms*, 530 U.S. 793 (2000).
5. Steven K. Green, *The Bible, the School, and the Constitution: The Clash That Shaped Modern Church-State Doctrine* (New York: Oxford University Press, 2012), 246.
6. Mariana Servin-Gonzalez and Oscar Torres-Reyna, "The Polls-Trends: Religion and Politics," *Public Opinion Quarterly* 63 (Winter 1999): 592–621, 603, 616; *Engel v. Vitale*, 370 U.S. 421 (1962); *Abington School District v. Schempp*, 374 U.S. 203 (1963); *Lee v. Weisman*, 505 U.S. 577 (1992).
7. Stephen L. Carter, *The Culture of Disbelief: How American Law and Politics Trivializes Religious Devotion* (New York: Basic Books, 1993); Richard John Neuhaus, *The Naked Public Square: Religion and Democracy in America* (Grand Rapids, MI: William B. Eerdmans, 1984); James Davidson Hunter, *To Change the World: The Irony, Tragedy, and Possibility of Christianity in the Late Modern World* (New York: Oxford University Press, 2010).
8. *Wallace v. Jaffree*, 472 U.S. 38 (1985); *Mueller v. Allen*, 463 U.S. 388 (1983); *Witters v. Washington Dept. of Services for the Blind*, 474 U.S. 481 (1986); *Zelman v. Simmons-Harris*, 536 U.S. 639 (2002).
9. Philip Hamburger, *Separation of Church and State* (Cambridge, MA: Harvard University Press, 2002).
10. *Mitchell*, 530 U.S. at 828–29.
11. *Everson*, 330 U.S. at 33 (Rutledge, J. dissenting).

12. Green, *The Bible, the School, and the Constitution*, 45–91.

13. John Higham, *Strangers in the Land: Patterns of American Nativism, 1860–1925* (New York: Atheneum, 1955), 6.

14. Ibid.

15. Hamburger, *Separation of Church and State*, 192–251.

16. John Adams to Thomas Jefferson, 3 February 1821, in *The Founders on Religion*, ed. James H. Hutson (Princeton, NJ: Princeton University Press, 2005), 41, 43; Chris Beneke, "'Not by Force or Violence': Religious Violence, Anti-Catholicism, and Rights of Conscience in the Early National U.S.," *Journal of Church and State* 54 (2012): 5–32.

17. Green, *The Bible, the School, and the Constitution*, 71–91.

18. Ibid.

19. James Burgh, *Crito, or Essays on Various Subjects* (London, 1767), 2:115–21; James Madison to Robert Walsh, 2 March 1819; Alexis de Tocqueville, *Democracy in America* (1835). All reprinted in Daniel L. Dreisbach and Mark David Hall, eds., *The Sacred Rights of Conscience* (Indianapolis, IN: Liberty Fund, 2009), 525, 595, 618.

20. Green, *The Bible, the School, and the Constitution*, 47–54.

21. Steven K. Green, *The Second Disestablishment: Church and State in Nineteenth-Century America* (New York: Oxford University Press, 2010), 170, 205–47.

22. Ibid., 179–223.

23. Robert T. Handy, *A Christian America*, 2nd ed. (New York: Oxford University Press, 1984); Handy, "The Protestant Quest for a Christian America, 1830–1930," *Church History* 22 (1953): 8–20 (quote is from page 12).

24. Green, *The Second Disestablishment*, 173–203, 205–47.

25. Robert G. McCloskey, ed., *The Bible in the Public Schools: Arguments in the Case of John D. Minor, et al. versus The Board of Education of the City of Cincinnati, et al.* (Cincinnati, OH: Robert Clarke, 1870), 414–16 (citations refer to the De Capo edition); *Board of Education v. Minor*, 23 Ohio St. 211, 250–54 (1873).

26. *New York Tribune*, 3 December 1869, 5.

27. William T. Harris, *Report of the Commissioner of Education for the Year 1894–1895* (Washington, DC: Government Printing Office, 1896), 2:1656.

28. Green, *The Bible, the School, and the Constitution*, 236–43.

29. *McCreary County v. ACLU*, 545 U.S. 844 (2005).

Part IV

Pluralism and Its Discontents: Late Nineteenth- and Early Twentieth-Century Contests over Religious Difference

Chapter Eleven

"There is no such thing as a reverend of no church"

Incarcerated Children, Nonsectarian Religion, and Freedom of Worship in Gilded Age New York City

Jacob Betz

In late January 1871 in New York City, the Methodist Preachers' Association assembled to hear a lecture by a Reverend Dr. Curry. After a theological discussion on the origin of sin, the conversation turned to political matters. Just weeks earlier, a New York state senator had proposed a bill prohibiting the city's charitable juvenile institutions from instructing their wards in any religion other than that practiced by their parents. These Methodist ministers attributed the proposed legislation—referred to by its proponents as the Freedom of Worship Bill—to the specter of Roman Catholicism; it was, they felt, a blatant attempt to force Catholicism into Protestant charitable institutions, specifically the infamous House of Refuge on Randall's Island in the East River. Reverend L. R. Dunn decried the fact that "the children themselves are prohibited from choosing any form of faith they please by this bill, which is cunningly devised to compel the education of the pauper children of the City in the Roman Catholic religion."[1] It was, Dunn added, a "most obnoxious and hateful" bill and he encouraged the preachers' association to take immediate action. A Dr. Ferris, however, warned against hasty action, arguing that patience would best serve the Methodists' cause. The Catholics, he decreed, would soon overplay their hand and reap a powerful Protestant counterreaction:

> Let them [Catholics] go on . . . the faster they drive the sooner will they come to ruin. The end of their rope is not very far off, and it will soon break. They

will run on until they arouse the Protestant sentiment of this State and of this
country, and when they do their utter overthrow will be but the question of an
hour.[2]

The evening's lecturer, Dr. Curry, was less certain of Protestant victory.
Though he was wary of ministers entering politics, he "believed that a dangerous fallacy lay beneath" any hesitation in confronting what he viewed as
nefarious Catholic designs. Thus, though the Methodist preachers were unified on the bill's dangers, they split over the best course of action. The
meeting adjourned inconclusively.

Others were less reserved in their denunciation. In a letter to the *New York
Times*, a concerned citizen, "Viator," dubbed the bill an "Act for the establishment of a Spanish Inquisition in the State of New-York." Viator, however, took heart (as well as a jab at the Catholic Jesuit order) in observing that
the bill's proponents had "inherited the spirit of Ignatius Loyola without his
genius."[3] What angered Viator was that Catholic immigrants in America
enjoyed the bounty of the rights of citizenship, yet now repaid their new
home by undermining its cherished freedoms and endeavoring to transfer
control of its republican institutions to the Vatican.[4] Catholics' demand for
the inclusion of their "sectarian" faith in what Protestants claimed was a
"nonsectarian" institution threatened the civic order of the nation.

The proposed Freedom of Worship Bill, as well as the reaction from
Methodists and Protestants more generally, provides a window into how
certain religions in late nineteenth-century America were coded "nonsectarian" and thus salutary while others were labeled "sectarian" and thus problematic. From the early 1870s until the bill's passage in 1892, Catholics' quest
for accommodation of their faith alongside Protestant "nonsectarianism" in
public institutions laid bare the shifting sands of religious liberty.

Because Catholics made up such a large percentage of the inmates at the
House of Refuge (about 60 percent), Catholic clergy and laity were eager to
have Catholic Mass and the sacraments performed for these inmates in the
asylum. Protestants, meanwhile, argued that such intrusions were unnecessary. They hung their collective hat on the House of Refuge's existing religious ceremonies, which they championed as "nonsectarian." The principle of
nonsectarianism had emerged during the antebellum era as a way to assuage
theological differences among the various Protestant denominations.[5] Late
nineteenth-century mainline Protestants understood nonsectarianism as a rational religious belief system available (and agreeable) to all self-professed
Christians. As Protestantism coalesced into an ecumenical coalition, its adherents exerted a cultural hegemony powerful enough to link their faith with
American culture writ large.[6]

In this environment, Protestants and Catholics viewed interreligious conflict as a zero-sum game; a victory for one denomination was a loss for the

other. For their part, New York Catholics saw the Freedom of Worship Bill as a necessary tool to maintain the Catholic faith (however nominal) of those children incarcerated as wards of the state. Protestants sought to inculcate their wards with notions of religious morality—what the House of Refuge chaplain called "fundamental truths"—from which the children could then make a specific theological choice. Protestant partisans assumed that a Protestant denomination would be the likely choice, since Protestantism, in their view, represented the freest form of religiosity. Protestants argued that a baseline religious morality existed independent of sectarian thinking and that instilling this morality through public institutions was necessary for creating responsible citizens. They viewed such a foundational morality as particularly important in the case of youths incarcerated for theft, vagrancy, and various other crimes. Either way, they saw no need and felt no legal obligation to accommodate a religious minority that viewed "nonsectarian" Protestantism as highly sectarian.

In response, New York Catholics countered that Protestants' fundamental truths were not universally applicable and sought to carve out a space of their own in New York society. Catholics rejected both the theological claim that Protestant nonsectarianism was agreeable to all Christian believers and the civic claim that nonsectarianism was the only religious instruction that could benefit incarcerated youth. They countered that nonsectarianism, although cloaked in a neutral language, was in fact highly sectarian. Much to Protestants' consternation, Catholics used the civic language of American religious liberty to argue for the accommodation of their faith. The Freedom of Worship Bill mandated what its proponents called a "dual system" of Protestant and Catholic services side by side.[7] Catholics not only demanded recognition of the particularity of their beliefs but also insisted that civic space be created to accommodate them; true religious liberty, in their eyes, required nothing less.

Catholic demands for religious accommodation thus delineated a new type of religious liberty claim. New York Catholic clergy and laity rejected the Protestant assumption that a child's incarceration was indicative prima facie of failed religiosity. What the prisoners needed, Catholics argued, was not a new morality derived from so-called universal religious truth. Rather, what was required to avoid recidivism was continued pastoral care in the faith of a child's baptism, which meant the faith of their parents.

BACKGROUND

The Freedom of Worship Bill had as its primary target the city's notorious juvenile asylum: the House of Refuge. Conceived by the Society for the Reformation of Juvenile Delinquents, the House of Refuge opened its doors in 1825 as an intended solution to the growing problem of poverty, crime, and vagrancy among the city's youth.[8] In the mid-1850s, the asylum moved to its new building on Randall's Island in the East River.[9] The land had been donated to the society by the city, and, beginning in 1863, the asylum received public funds for its operation. Demographically, the House of Refuge reflected the socioeconomic patterns of antebellum New York City; in 1840 the inmates were almost 50 percent Irish.[10] By 1880, the House of Refuge's youth population numbered approximately 750 boys and girls, roughly 60 percent of whom were Catholic.[11]

Religion and religious liberty became a major locus of concern at the House of Refuge after the Civil War. In early 1872, a series of violent inmate revolts rocked the House of Refuge, and subsequent investigation isolated religion as the cause. On March 17, 1872, inmate Justus Dunn attacked and fatally wounded fellow inmate Samuel Calvert. During Dunn's trial, his defense lawyer argued that Catholic inmates were deprived of their spiritual instruction and forced to attend Protestant services. He suggested that the violation of Dunn's conscience had provoked him. The lawyer posited, "If they [the inmates] strike that blow for the religious liberty which is to save their souls, then the revolt is just."[12] Two months later, inmate Thomas McDonald led a revolt that wounded the adult foremen of the penitentiary workshop. The youth claimed that "his conscience had been violated by the food provided on Fridays."[13] Yet another outbreak occurred in early July.

In the wake of these disturbances, the press leveled numerous charges against the institution, including the allegations that it provided insufficient rations, imposed cruel and unusual punishments, and demanded strenuous work to meet labor contactors' demands. A final, telling complaint was that House managers "neglected to provide religious instruction for said inmates, and have by corporal punishment inflicted upon those refusing to attend the services in the chapel on Sunday, compelled them to take part in the worship prescribed by the rules of the institution."[14] In the end, it was this accusation of religious discrimination against the House of Refuge that stuck.

Faced with a public uproar, the New York State Commissioners of Public Charities launched an investigation into conditions at the House of Refuge. For four days in late July and early August 1872, the commissioners heard testimony from House of Refuge staff and inmates, as well as Catholic clergy. At the hearings, Catholics attributed the institution's recent spate of violence to unjust treatment. A Jesuit priest, J. Renoud, testified that the city's parents' primary reason for keeping their children out of the House was its Protestant leanings.[15] He claimed that parents were more afraid of their children entering the House than remaining on the crime-ridden streets.[16]

House managers repudiated the various Catholic claims of religious discrimination and dismissed Catholic fears that a child attending a non-Catholic religious service committed a grievous sin. Furthermore, they accused

Catholic religious authorities of breeding religious "discontents and exciting in them a hope of escape through revolt to be attempted . . . while people of different religious are contending over them."[17] It was, according to the managers, the city's priests who had convinced the Catholic inmates of their victimhood: "We fully believe from what we know of the inmates—and we know much—that they would be quite contented with our religious services if not plied with *influences foreign and hostile to the House.*"[18]

The House managers likewise rejected Catholic claims that the New York State Constitution's guarantee of religious freedom applied to the inmates. The commissioners invoked the constitution's public safety clause to argue that rights of inmates were necessarily restricted by incarceration. Incarceration, according to the commissioners, necessarily entailed the "forfeiture of rights [so] that neither the delinquents nor their friends for them can justly claim, while under sentence of the courts, equal freedom with the rest of the community who have not violated the law."[19]

The managers concluded that there was indeed a connection between religious liberty and the recent outbreak of violence. But, they insisted, the Catholic understanding of this connection was wrongheaded. The reverse, the managers argued, was actually true. Demands by inmates for Catholic services would spark sectarian rivalry between the youths. Protestants' view of their faith as the universal and neutral baseline of Christianity had manifested itself in carceral policy. To introduce Catholicism into the institution was to invite discord and strife. It was safer, they argued, *not* to accommodate Catholic youth: "We believe the separation of these delinquents into different religious congregations would breed dissension and collusion," as it would "tend to foster pride and self-will." As evidence, the managers cited "the boy who . . . attacked without provocation and dangerously wounded two of the foremen in a shop, told reporters that his conscience had been violated by the food provided on Fridays."[20] Whereas Catholics contended that lack of religious freedom led to violent revolts, the managers responded that permitting religious freedom would only engender dangerous, and potentially violent, manifestations of religious diversity. Better, Protestants argued, to have the state in authority over the inmates' religious instruction.

IN LOCO PARENTIS: RELIGIOUS LIBERTY AND WARDS OF THE STATE

The commissioners' hearings raised several thorny disagreements. Not least of these was the Catholic claim that religious liberty extended inside the prison walls. Catholics objected to the idea that inmates be forced to attend the state's religious services. Each Sunday, the House of Refuge had mandatory religious services, usually led by a Protestant minister. The devotional manual was drawn primarily from the Episcopal Book of Common Prayer. This religious atmosphere, combined with the fact that over half of the inmates were Catholic, created a strong incentive for New York's Catholic population to assert pressure for change. Broadly speaking, Catholic fear of state intrusion had grown throughout the Atlantic world since the French Revolution and would extend at least through the Second Vatican Council (1962–1965).[21] How could a minority religious group maintain its cultural identity while its youngest generation was incarcerated within ostensibly Protestant institutions?

As the issue gained steam in mid-1870s New York, Catholic intellectuals weighed in. Catholic observer Isaac Hecker conceded that criminals did forfeit certain "rights and privileges." They were, after all, incarcerated for a reason. But they had not forfeited all of their rights.[22] Hecker cited as his answer the New York State Constitution, which stipulated that no person should be deprived of their religious freedom regardless of their circumstances.[23] Hecker understood that right as applying *even* to prisoners of the state. All grown men, even those serving life sentences, were allowed free access to the minister of their respective churches, regardless of religious affiliation. Why, Hecker asked, should those men who had forfeited their entire lives through murder convictions be granted total religious liberty but not those children whose incarceration was only temporary?

As for the nature of the inmates' religious training, Hecker granted that any attempted rehabilitation of inmates did indeed necessitate a religious grounding:

> Careful provision for the spiritual wants of so extensive and important a class [incarcerated youth] we of course approve to the full. The idea of a reformatory where no religious instruction is given the inmates would be a contradiction. The State empowers those into whose hands it entrusts the keeping of its wards to impart religious instruction—in short, to do everything that may tend to the mental, moral, and physical advancement of those under their charge. All that we concede and admire.[24]

But Catholic priests, he argued, requested access to the House precisely to ensure that Catholic inmates were not being subjected to objectionable teaching. The gaining of such access was the goal of the Freedom of Worship Bill. Hecker accused the House managers of using the public institution to inculcate their Protestant sensibilities. On entering the House, Catholic prisoners were no longer allowed to practice their faith. It was "a monstrous violation of human conscience, not to speak of the letter and spirit of the constitution of this State."[25] Hecker argued the state should see the church "as a power that has a province of its own, in the direction of human life and thought, where the state may not enter—a province embracing all that is covered by the word religion."[26] It was a separation of church and state that was markedly distinct from the Protestant ideal of separation.

In articulating his version of the separation of church and state, Hecker tapped directly into the zeitgeist of the Catholic First Vatican Council. This global meeting in Rome of Catholic prelates occurred from 1860 to 1870 and put forth a Catholic version of the proper relationship between church and state. Hecker thus went beyond carving out a protected niche for religion vis-à-vis the state—he argued that freedom of religion also entailed that the state leave religious duties to the churches, which, in this instance, extended inside prison walls to their children. In other words, the state must acquiesce to minority groups in maintaining their particular religious identity. In Hecker's pluralist vision, "No man even dreams of interfering with the worship of another. . . . Conversion or perversion, as it may be called, on any side is not attempted. . . . And the thought of a state official or an official of any character coming in and directly ordering the Catholics to become Methodists or the Methodists Jews, or the Jews either, is something so preposterous that the American mind can scarcely entertain it."[27] Yet, according to Hecker, New York officials were doing precisely that. Banishment of Catholic priests from the House of Refuge removed all barriers to it being a wholesale Protestant missionary enterprise.

It was this demand for the inclusion of Catholic religious services in the House that most appalled Protestant observers. Protestants argued that parental rights could be limited once it had been established that they had been negligent toward their wards. The *New York Times* dubbed the proposed Freedom of Worship Bill "an Act to make religion hereditary."[28] "The father or mother having abandoned their 'duties,' have lost their 'rights,' as to their children," the paper asserted. "They are not even good 'Catholics.'"[29] It envisioned a scenario in which a drunken Catholic father employs his vagrant son to steal on his behalf. After the son is arrested and sent to the House of Refuge, the father sobers up and learns of his son being "taught the simple principles of Christianity." Should the Freedom of Worship Bill pass, the paper warned, a judge would be forced to release such a child so he might resume "the worship of the Virgin, or some other dogma."[30]

Protestants repeatedly questioned the authenticity of both the parents' and the children's Catholicism. How sincere did a child's religious beliefs have to be to warrant acknowledgment by the state? How could the children truly be religious, Protestants asked, if the youth were imprisoned and their parents had clearly failed so miserably in raising their offspring? Surely, they claimed, the "young ruffians confined" in the House only "pretend to belong to the Roman Church."[31] In fact, anyone who met with these "young vagrants must be aware that no company of mortals could be more indifferent to the creed they profess."[32] This observation tapped into a larger Protestant critique of Catholicism. The perceived indifference on behalf of the incarcerated Catholic youth easily meshed with the broader Protestant perception of Catholicism as a calcified relic from the pre-Reformation era. How, Protestants wondered, could these children be given the agency of "professing" a creed, and yet profess it so half-heartedly? To them, religious liberty was a function of religious choice, and religious choice proceeded from strong conviction. These "Catholics" gave no evidence of the latter. Besides, Protestants asserted, any show of religiosity on the part of Catholic inmates was in no way sincere. The managers rejected wholesale the suggestion that any children actually desired Catholic services. It was Protestant wardens and chaplains, not outsiders, who understood what was needed to expunge the criminal inclinations out of inmates, as well as the religious needs of their inmates.[33] Thus went the argument for circumscribing the religious rights of incarcerated persons.

At times, usually with a splash of hyperbole, Protestants raised the specter of a Catholic Church that would attempt to bring large numbers of Protestant children into the Catholic fold. They feared a reaffirmation of the Catholic parish system that would assert the "spiritual wellbeing of everybody and so bring all wanderers into the fold." *Zion's Herald* asked, "Who are Catholic Children? Are men born into a Church territorially as they are within the civil jurisdiction of an earthly sovereign, or must they be born again of the Spirit?" The *Herald* anxiously queried "whether all children not specially registered as members of Protestant churches are to be assumed to be Catholics, whether they be Jews, Turks, Hindoos, or Chinese?"[34] Catholics responded to such claims through their use of petitions signed by parents of inmates, stressing that they were only asking for the spiritual well-being of the Catholic inmates.[35]

The question remained regarding whether children possessed the right to choose their own religion. This sharp distinction that Protestants constructed between their faith and Catholicism centered in many ways upon their individualistic faith and what they envisioned as the communal character of Catholic faith. The central points of contention during the 1870s swirled around the exact nature of religious freedom—and, moreover, what role parents should play in the religious beliefs of their children.[36] The Catholic notion of religious identity, which they refused to abandon at the prison gate, was different from Protestants' self-proclaimed identity. Protestants emphasized (often in an exaggerated distinction with Catholicism) that rational and free inquiry would lead religious seekers to a Protestant endpoint. In declaring Protestantism the freest form of religious belief, Protestants argued that their faith justified the greatest latitude. It seemed almost axiomatic, in Protestant eyes, that the freest religion deserved the greatest religious freedom. Catholics thought otherwise.

SECTARIAN AND NONSECTARIAN RELIGION: IN THE EYE OF THE BEHOLDER?

New York Catholics rejected the so-called neutral character of Protestant nonsectarianism, and, as a result, they objected vociferously to the idea that incarcerated children had become spiritual wards of the state and lost the freedom to choose their own religion. In Catholic eyes, there was nothing nonsectarian about Protestant religions services in the House of Refuge. Moreover, they argued, the very notion of nonsectarianism was a theological red herring. When the Freedom of Worship Bill was first proposed in the early 1870s, it asserted that the family, not the state, had primary responsibility for a child's religious beliefs. Much of the subsequent controversy centered on how much responsibility children should have in making their own religious decisions. Catholics claimed that parents, as the children's guardians, had the right to shape their children's religious instruction. Administrators at the reformatory countered that when the children found themselves wards of the state, the Catholic faith had clearly failed them, and it was now time for the state to step in with what Protestants considered a kind of neutral nonsectarian morality.

As Catholic legislators repeatedly reintroduced the Freedom of Worship Bill in the late 1870s and mid-1880s, the House of Refuge staff, as well as Protestant observers, clung to the language of "nonsectarianism" to justify the state's choice. It would be through nonsectarianism, they insisted, and not Catholic *sectarian* beliefs, that inmates' rehabilitation would occur. True rehabilitation of criminal character must come from the heart and, in taking a jab at Catholic rites and sacraments, they noted that "to look for [contrition in] religious ceremonies performed by convicted offenders without signs of repentance, is to look in vain."

The House of Refuge claimed to advance the "simple principles of Christianity," not the particular doctrines of proselytizing sects.[37] In practice, they were not terribly strict. The managers acquiesced to requests for a priest or minister from a specific denomination. This compromise, however, was moot because the managers would not relinquish their claim that none of the inmates possessed sufficient religiosity to prompt such a request. The wards were "youthful delinquents, who presumably have had no religious training that could give them denominational preference and no parental care that exhibited a regard for their spiritual well-being. As a rule they are ignorant."[38] Catholics resorted to Dickensian analogy to explain the youths' solicitude on religious matters: "It might not have been safe for a boy to complain concerning either the quality or quantity of the religious food furnished to him, or to ask for something different. The food for which Oliver Twist asked was of a material nature, but the asking was all the same, and we know what happened to him when 'he asked for more.'"[39] In Catholic eyes, the

House of Refuge's Protestant trappings had worked to silence the children's genuine beliefs.

But for Protestants, who often championed a direct causal link between faith and behavior, the logic seemed simple: the fact that the children were in the institution indicated that they lacked the moral training that would have prevented their entry into the criminal system in the first place. Once in the system, their minds, assumed to be vacant of spiritual leanings, could be cultivated to receive God's Word. The inmates' "religious instruction is simple and unsectarian . . . and they are sent forth without denominational bias, and can then adopt any form of religious faith that may suit them."[40] In this way, Protestants argued that they championed liberty and religious choice. They merely inculcated the children with a baseline of universal morality. A group of prominent Catholic laymen rejected this as a logical tautology: "The system of worship now in force in the House of Refuge is as sectarian as could possibly be invented or imagined. Therefore, it *is* sectarian."[41] In other words, Catholic observers reserved for themselves—and, by extension, anyone else—the right to reject another group's claim to religious neutrality and instead label that group sectarian. It was, then, a clear rejection of Protestantism as the default American faith, and with this rejection came a substantive demand for religious accommodation.

The House's managers conceived of their training as a nonsectarian foundation upon which a child might build a sectarian structure, depending on his/her preference. By demanding access to the institution, managers argued, Catholics were putting the cart before the horse. How could youth develop a clearheaded approach to religion if they were indoctrinated by sectarian proselytizing from the outset? The Catholic Church's response was that these children were indeed religious subjects. Furthermore, they were Catholic. And to Catholic eyes, nonsectarianism was indistinguishable from Protestant evangelizing.

Hecker and other Catholics rejected the idea that there was a Protestant nonsectarian morality that could serve as a foundation for all religious belief. Indeed, the Freedom of Worship Bill's very language permitting particularist religious instruction within the House rejected this so-called universal nonsectarianism. Hecker looked to "expose the cant and humbug" of nonsectarian religious instruction practiced by the New York Society for the Reformation of Juvenile Delinquents.

He cited the House's own chaplain, Reverend George H. Smyth, who testified that all inmates were required to attend Sunday services. In attempting to ascertain the chaplain's denomination, Hecker observed that Smyth was not found in any Catholic directory. Though Smyth might not be a Catholic, he must, Hecker declared, be *something*. The chaplain must have been raised in some religion and subsequently attended a seminary belonging to a specific denomination. Hecker declared, "There is no such thing as a reverend of no church, of a non-sectarian church."[42] After all, it simply wasn't possible to be an ordained minister of nonsectarianism. Smyth replied that

> the truths preached to these children have been those fundamental truths held in common by all Christian communions and which are adapted to the wants of the human race, and much ever be the foundation of pure morals and good citizenship. Studious care has been taken not to prejudice the minds of the inmates against any particular form of religious belief; nor has it ever been shown that such was the result to the children committed to the House.[43]

This reassurance linking a generic Christianity with morality did little to satisfy Hecker. Even more problematic was Smyth's subsequent statement:

> What delinquent children need is not the mere memorizing of ecclesiastical formularies and dogmas which they can repeat one moment and commit a theft the next. But they do need, and it is the province of the State to teach them that there are independent of any and all forms of religious faith, *fundamental principles* of eternal right, truth and justice, which, as members of the human family and citizens of the commonwealth, they must learn to *live* by, and which are absolutely essential to their peace and prosperity.[44]

Smyth reiterated the Protestant charge that Catholicism was an accretion of heretical ideas that had been grafted onto the true Christianity, which was now embodied in nonsectarianism. In response, Hecker asked what those "fundamental principles" were and who determined them.[45] The *New York Times* flipped the question, asking who was "catholic" in the truest sense of the word. Wasn't it, after all, the managers of the House of Refuge who "have never attempted to interfere with the religious faith the young offenders may chance to profess, but have made their religious instruction general and 'catholic' in the true sense of the word"?[46] In this view, it was Protestants who were the true universal *catholics*.

CONCLUSION

By the mid-1880s, the introduction of the Freedom of Religion Bill in the New York state legislature had become an annual occurrence.[47] Often it passed just one house before stalling. In 1881, the bill passed both houses; only Governor Alonzo Cornell's veto prevented its enactment. A lay organization—the Catholic Union of New York—worked closely with Archbishop Michael Corrigan to coordinate support for the measure. The union claimed to be acting "as representatives of those parents and guardians" of children confined to the House of Refuge.[48] It kept the issue in the news through constant editorials in publications like the *Catholic Review*.

Whereas the Western House of Refuge in Rochester, New York, had voluntarily opened its doors to Catholic priests in 1874, the House on Randall's Island continued to refuse them. Louis Binsse, a New York businessman and officer of the Catholic Union, wrote Corrigan in 1883 that House managers "never intended to concede anything and never will until the law compels them."[49] House manager Henry Cram seemed to confirm Binsse's sentiments when he testified before the New York Assembly in 1885 that the arrangement in Rochester was permissible only because "the [Catholic] priest is on his good behavior. . . . He is the servant, he is there by permission, and if he creates discord or disturbs the discipline, they have the power to say 'begone.' Here [if the bill should pass] he comes by the power of the State, a power transcending our own, imposing the duty on us, he is our master."[50] Much as the pseudonymous author Viator had warned in the *New York Times*, fear of priestly infiltration and control—a fear long nurtured in Protestant minds—worried the administrators of the House of Refuge.

Finally, in 1892, the bill passed both houses, and in a "sudden and expected action," Governor Roswell Flower signed it into law.[51] The new act directed that inmates "shall be allowed such religious services and spiritual advice and spiritual ministration from some recognized clergyman."[52] Acknowledging the authority of the archdiocese, the House of Refuge wrote to Archbishop Corrigan in October 1892, informing him that a "clergyman nominated by you may meet such children, inmates of the house, as are connected with the Roman Catholic Church."[53]

Protestant observers expressed shock and immediately began searching for ways to circumvent the law. Protestants countered that the bill stipulated that the request for a Catholic priest must come from the *parents*, not the archbishop. If Catholic parents cared enough about the transmission of their faith to their offspring, this Protestant measure indicated, they—and not the church hierarchy—would have to act upon it.[54]

The ultimate passage of the New York Freedom of Worship Bill meant that the city's dominant Protestantism had been forced to accommodate the minority's Catholic faith. It was a statutory indicator that religion in late nineteenth-century America could not be distilled down to a neutral common denominator. This legal acknowledgment of religious diversity—a diversity that took theological differences seriously—opened the door for an expanded form of religious liberty. This newly permitted freedom of worship granted rights to Catholic priests to enter the House of Refuge even if children had not made the initial request. The Freedom of Worship Bill's lengthy journey illustrates how Catholics took an active role in fashioning the rationale for state recognition of a religious minority predicated on Catholic rejection of universal nonsectarian religious teachings that Protestants presented as theologically neutral. Toleration of minority religious groups has expanded since the late nineteenth century, in part because of favorable court rulings that began in the 1940s.[55] Yet, as the first numerically powerful religious minority in the United States, Catholics used democratic action to force the state to acknowledge alternative civic identities through an accommodation of minority religious conscience.

NOTES

1. "An Act to Make Religion Hereditary," *New York Times*, 31 January 1871.
2. Ibid.
3. Viator also felt the New York State Constitution would prevent the bill's passage. Conversely, Catholics cited that same constitution in supporting the bill's passage. Section III, Article 1 of the New York State Constitution read, "The free exercise and enjoyment of religious profession and worship, without discrimination or preference, shall forever be allowed in this State to all mankind."
4. "An Act to Make Religion Hereditary," 2.
5. For the role of Massachusetts educator Horace Mann and nonsectarian education, see Steven K. Green, *The Second Disestablishment: Church and State in Nineteenth-Century America* (New York: Oxford University Press), 256–66.
6. It is not coincidental that this ecumenical Protestant coalition solidified at precisely the moment that the academic study of religion took shape. Some religions (Protestant denominations) were championed as rational and unadulterated, while others (Catholicism) were labeled outdated sects with cultish concern for the rituals of the body over the mind. See Robert A. Orsi, "Snakes Alive: Religious Studies between Heaven and Earth," in *Between Heaven and Earth: The Religious Worlds People Make and the Scholars Who Study Them* (Princeton, NJ: Princeton University Press, 2005), 177–204.
7. For the antebellum Catholic experience, see Jon Gjerde, *Catholicism and the Shaping of Nineteenth-Century America*, ed. S. Deborah Kang (New York: Cambridge University Press, 2012). For the rural Catholic experience, see Kathleen Neils Conzen, *Making Their Own America: Assimilation Theory and the German Peasant Pioneer* (Washington, DC: German Historical Institute, 1990).
8. For example, in 1879, a fourteen-year-old Irish immigrant received a one-year sentence to the House for the theft of one dollar. See Timothy Gilfoyle, *A Pickpocket's Tale: The Underworld of Nineteenth-Century New York* (New York: W. W. Norton, 2006), 68.
9. Robert S. Pickett, *House of Refuge: Origins of Juvenile Reform in New York State, 1815–1857* (Syracuse, NY: Syracuse University Press, 1969), 67, 140.
10. Ibid., 6.
11. *The Religious Rights of Minors*, n.d., Archbishop Michael Corrigan Collection, box 31, folder 5; Catholic Union of New York, *The Persistent Violation by the Managers of the House of Refuge of the Religious Rights of Catholic Minors Committed to that Institution* (1882), 3, Pamphlet Collection, box 4, folder 18. Both collections at Archives of the Archdiocese of New York, St. Joseph's Seminary, Dunwoodie, NY.
12. *Report of Special Committee to the Managers of the House of Refuge on the Investigation by the State Commissioners of Public Charity of Charges Made through the Public Press against the Officers and Managers of the House of Refuge* (New York: Thitchener & Glastaeter, 1872), 13, Series A2090, Annual Reports and Miscellaneous Publications, box 3, New York State Archives, Albany, NY.
13. Board of Managers of the House of Refuge, "Memorial to the Commissioners of Public Charities of the State of New York" (14 September 1872), 23, Series A2090, Annual Reports and Miscellaneous Publications, box 3, New York State Archives, Albany, NY.
14. *Report of Special Committee*, 6.
15. Ibid., 8.
16. Ibid.
17. Ibid., 16–17.
18. Ibid., 18 (my emphasis).

19. Ibid., 17.

20. Board of Managers of the House of Refuge, "Memorial to the Commissioners of Public Charities," 23.

21. See, for example, Philip Gleason, "American Catholics and Liberalism, 1789–1969," in *Catholicism and Liberalism: Contributions to American Public Philosophy*, ed. R. Bruce Douglass and David Hollenbach (New York: Cambridge University Press, 1994).

22. Isaac Hecker, "Religion in Our State Institutions," *Catholic World*, April 1875, 3. Hecker drew a direct connection between the English Magna Carta and the religious freedoms enshrined in the New York State Constitution. The constitution, he claimed, "established in their fullest sense of the civil and religious liberty of the individual [is] taken from these grand old charters of Catholic days."

23. Hecker, "Religion in Our State Institutions," 1.

24. Ibid., 7.

25. Ibid., 8.

26. Ibid., 1–2.

27. Ibid., 2. That Hecker was himself a Catholic convert apparently gave him no pause.

28. "An Act to Make Religion Hereditary," *New York Times*, 31 January 1871.

29. "Have Protestants any Rights?," *New York Times*, 3 February 1871.

30. "An Act to Make Religion Hereditary," *New York Times*, 31 January 1871.

31. "Sectarian Bigotry and the House of Refuge," *New York Times*, 26 May 1872.

32. Ibid.

33. Ibid., 18. For the long-standing connections between Protestantism and criminal reform, see Jennifer Graber, *The Furnace of Affliction: Prisons and Religion in Antebellum America* (Chapel Hill: University of North Carolina Press, 2011).

34. "The Legal Aspects of Religious Liberty," *Zion's Herald*, 24 April 1873.

35. Blank parental petition sheet, n.d., Archbishop Michael Corrigan Collection, box C-9, Archives of the Archdiocese of New York, St. Joseph's Seminary, Dunwoodie, NY.

36. This tug-of-war over children between the state and religious parents extended well into the second half of the twentieth century. See, for example, the U.S. Supreme Court victory of Old Order Amish over Wisconsin's state law mandating schooling beyond the eighth grade, *Wisconsin v. Yoder*, 406 U.S. 205 (1972).

37. "An Act to Make Religion Hereditary," *New York Times*, 31 January 1871.

38. "Catholics and Public Institutions," *New York Times*, 12 May 1882.

39. [Catholic Laymen of New York], *Hear the Other Side. Freedom of Worship: The Merits, Principles and Practicability of the Measure Explained and Vindicated* (New York: Willis McDonald, ca. 1885), 27, Archbishop Michael Corrigan Collection, box G-53, folder 3, Archives of the Archdiocese of New York, St. Joseph's Seminary, Dunwoodie, NY.

40. "Catholics and Public Institutions," *New York Times*, 12 May 1882.

41. [Catholic Laymen of New York], *Hear the Other Side*, 12 (emphasis in original).

42. Hecker, "Religion in Our State Institutions," 11.

43. *Fiftieth Annual Report of the Managers of the Society for the Reformation of Juvenile Delinquents to the Legislature of the State and the Corporation of the City of New York, 1874* (New York: Evening Post Steam Presses, 1875), 45.

44. Ibid. (my emphasis).

45. Hecker, "Religion in Our State Institutions," 11.

46. "Sectarian Bigotry and the House of Refuge," *New York Times*, 26 May 1872.

47. The bill had been introduced each year from 1880 to 1885. Some years it passed only the Assembly, while in other years it passed the Senate.

48. Catholic Union of New York, *The Persistent Violation by the Managers of the House of Refuge of the Religious Rights of Catholic Minors Committed to that Institution* (1882), 3. Pamphlet Collection, box 4, folder 18, Archives of the Archdiocese of New York, St. Joseph's Seminary, Dunwoodie, NY.

49. Louis Binsse to Michael Corrigan, 17 April 1883, Archbishop Michael Corrigan Collection, box C-6, folder 24, Archives of the Archdiocese of New York, St. Joseph's Seminary, Dunwoodie, NY.

50. *Argument of Henry A. Cram against the so-called "Freedom of Worship Bill" before the Committee of Cities of the Assembly* (1885), 21, Archbishop Michael Corrigan Collection, box G-53, folder 3, Archives of the Archdiocese of New York, St. Joseph's Seminary, Dunwoodie, NY.

51. "They Will Fight the Law," *New York Times*, 2 May 1892.

52. "An Act to Provide for the better security of the freedom of religious worship in certain institutions," 8 February 1892, Archbishop Corrigan Collection, box G-53, folder 2, Archives of the Archdiocese of New York, St. Joseph's Seminary, Dunwoodie, NY.

53. A. E. Orr to Archbishop Michael Corrigan, 8 October 1892, Archbishop Corrigan Collection, box C-29, folder H, Archives of the Archdiocese of New York, St. Joseph's Seminary, Dunwoodie, NY.

54. "Plain Violation of Law," *New York Times*, 11 November 1892.

55. For more on the court's role, see Shawn Francis Peter's chapter on the Jehovah's Witnesses in this volume.

Chapter Twelve

The Cost of Inclusion

Interfaith Unity and Intrafaith Division in the Formation of Protestant-Catholic-Jewish America

David Mislin

In 1929, hostilities erupted within the Federal Council of the Churches of Christ in America when one of its larger constituent denominations, the United Presbyterian Church, voted to slash its annual contribution to the organization in half. These Presbyterians went so far as to threaten to withdraw from the Federal Council entirely. Their reason was straightforward: during the 1920s, the ecumenical organization had grown too "liberal" and, in particular, had begun promoting interfaith cooperation. One conservative Presbyterian singled out the Federal Council's Committee on Goodwill between Jews and Christians, which sought to foster understanding among Protestants, Jews, and Catholics. The United Presbyterians lamented that the Federal Council, in its sponsored radio broadcasts, was "more favorable about Jews than about orthodox Christians," and they blamed the Goodwill Committee for this state of affairs. Other groups in the council expressed similar concerns. Samuel McCrea Cavert, the general secretary of the Federal Council, reported that he had surveyed the newspapers of several other "conservative and fundamentalist" denominations. In each, he had discovered editorials blasting the newfound "friendly and cooperative attitude toward Jews."

The Federal Council's leaders were unfazed by the criticism. They insisted that they had "no intention of discontinuing" the Goodwill Committee; indeed, they planned to expand its programs to increase understanding and cooperation between Protestants, Catholics, and Jews. In the years following the United Presbyterian Church's protest, the Federal Council gave support to a spin-off organization consisting of members of all three traditions. This group, which became the National Conference of Christians and Jews (known today as the National Conference for Community and Justice), has served as an interfaith vehicle for social justice causes ever since.[1]

The Federal Council of Churches had come into existence for the very purpose of preventing just these sorts of tempestuous disagreements among Protestant denominations. For much of American history, the major Protestant traditions—Methodist, Baptist, Presbyterian, and the like—had focused on their theological differences as often as (if not more so) on their commonalities. Even within the denominations, competing factions vied for congregants, money, and prestige. By the early twentieth century, however, the competing claims of agnostics and atheists, combined with the growing visibility of non-Christian religions in the United States, prompted many Protestants to seek a rapprochement with one another.

The Federal Council represented the largest and most influential of these enterprises. Established in 1908, it encouraged a cooperative spirit among Protestants and emphasized their common Christianity rather than denominational division. In its early years, the Federal Council met with great success. Squabbling among America's Protestant churches gave way to surprisingly harmonious relations. Local churches of various affiliations banded together for community projects such as charitable campaigns, while national denominations joined forces on larger projects, including a joint World War I venture to construct chapels at army training camps.[2]

Yet a mere two decades after its founding, the Federal Council began to split into liberal and conservative factions. The leaders of the organization largely adopted the liberal theology that was gaining sway in America's major Protestant denominations and their theological seminaries. This outlook included a professed commitment to cooperation with members of non-Protestant faiths. During the 1920s, Federal Council leaders sought to formalize their efforts to foster interfaith dialogue with Roman Catholics and Jews. Accordingly, the Goodwill Committee began with informal discussions in 1921 and became an official part of the Federal Council organizational structure two years later. "Perhaps no page of human history," declared one of the group's early reports, "bears more blots and stains upon it than that which records the relations of Christians and Jews during the past two thousand years." Federal Council leaders thus had the lofty goal of overcoming centuries of intolerance and hostility between Protestants, Catholics, and Jews. This effort was all the more ambitious given its cultural context. The 1920s saw a sharp increase in hostility toward Jewish and Catholic Americans, with the resurgent Ku Klux Klan, Henry Ford's mass circulation of the anti-Semitic *Protocols of the Elders of Zion*, and the attacks on Al Smith, the first Roman Catholic candidate for president.[3]

The Federal Council was clearly committed to liberal and inclusive principles, both in theology and politics, and this—ironically—fostered divisions within its ranks. Theologically, council leaders downplayed adherence to inherited sectarian doctrines in favor of an emphasis on social ethics. Inspired by nineteenth-century views of history and post-Darwinian evolutionary theory, they were optimistic about progress, believing not only in the potential for moral improvement in human affairs but also that religious knowledge deepened as science advanced and society evolved. They were dogged proponents of progressive policies. Though Federal Council leaders did not see their work as primarily political, Goodwill Committee members subscribed to Progressivism's core tenets. They embraced urban reform, the labor movement, and social science. Above all, they had immense faith in the ability of the new class of university-educated "experts" to manage society more effectively than ordinary Americans or party leaders, and they believed these civil servants were able to transcend the divisions of party politics. The Federal Council, with its avoidance of denominational disputes and its paid professional staff, reflected an attempt to bring the political structure favored by Progressivism to the religious world. These Progressive ideals shaped all of the organization's work. The Goodwill Committee, despite its seemingly uncontroversial goal of encouraging interfaith tolerance and understanding, was in reality bound up in a complex web of controversial theological and political commitments.

The common political and theological bonds that united Protestant, Catholic, and Jewish representatives on the committee were the very things that divided them from other members of all three faiths. For orthodox Protestants, Jews, and Catholics, the group's declaration that it would not "enter into doctrinal controversy" amounted to a dismissal of their fundamental convictions. This was most true among conservative Protestants like the United Presbyterians. For them, the historical doctrines of their church were an essential part of their religion. Thus, setting aside core theological beliefs in favor of an ecumenical and progressive understanding of religion rendered religious dialogue meaningless. By the 1920s, conservative Protestants were determined to reassert the centrality and immutability of historical doctrines. In marginalizing these views, the Goodwill Committee leaders also marginalized their coreligionists who did not share their liberal commitments.

The quarrels that erupted over the interfaith efforts of the Federal Council of Churches provide an instructive example of the complexities of American religious tolerance. It is tempting to imagine the history of religious diversity in the way that Federal Council leaders did: as a progressively unfolding process. In this view, intolerance gives way over time to greater acceptance of religious pluralism. However, the American experience, like that of the Federal Council, has not been so simple. Protestant liberals themselves occasionally revealed the limits of inclusiveness. Several members of the Goodwill Committee expressed a desire to convert Jews to Christianity. Though they quickly backtracked and apologized for their remarks, these Protestants nevertheless impeded their own cause. On other occasions, they caused additional turmoil by suggesting that Catholics were slavishly beholden to the pope or that Jews resisted adaptation to middle-class culture.[4]

The interfaith movement of the early twentieth century was intimately connected to religious liberalism, and it consequently generated as much division and discord as it mitigated. It was not merely that orthodox Catholics, Jews, and especially Protestants were theologically averse to interfaith activities, but rather that these activities were highly ideological in principle. Supporting the Goodwill Committee required endorsing a range of political and theological positions opposed by orthodox believers. Conservative Protestants bristled at the claim that doctrines were a product of society's political and cultural evolution. As the discord within the Federal Council of Churches revealed, the desire for interfaith understanding was not merely a charitable sentiment; it also reflected a broader commitment to a liberal vision of cultural assimilation and national progress led by new professionals such as Federal Council members themselves. The project of fostering tolerance was thus enmeshed in larger cultural conflicts that could not be easily resolved.

I

Efforts like the Federal Council's Goodwill Committee marked a sharp departure from nineteenth-century Protestant hostility to Catholics and Jews. After an uptick in ecumenical feelings spawned by the American Revolution, virulent anti-Catholicism reemerged with mass Irish immigration in the 1840s and 1850s. Widespread anti-Catholic rhetoric accompanied occasional eruptions of violence. During the Philadelphia riots in the spring and summer of 1844, several dozen people, both Catholic and Protestant, were killed, and thousands more Irish Catholics were displaced from their homes. Overt forms of religious hostility peaked again during the final decades of the nineteenth century. Anti-Catholicism and anti-Semitism intensified amid another wave of immigration, this time from southern and eastern Europe. The nativist American Protective Association targeted Catholics, while Jews faced increasingly overt discrimination from businesses that refused them services.[5]

Following this peak of hostility, Protestant attitudes toward Catholics and Jews began to soften considerably at the turn of the twentieth century. Many Protestant leaders reversed course, opting to combat rather than encourage anti-Catholic and anti-Semitic rhetoric. The transformation began among Congregationalists and Episcopalians before spreading to Methodists, Presbyterians, and Baptists. Given that Protestant churches were home to the nation's business, political, and cultural elite, their leaders exerted enormous social influence, and their broad-mindedness rippled well beyond the walls of their churches.

The Congregationalist minister Lyman Abbott exemplified this shift in Protestant thought. During his long career, which spanned from the 1850s to the 1920s, Abbott served as the pastor of numerous churches while also becoming a leading journalist. For several decades he edited *Outlook*, a nationally read weekly journal that offered general-interest news along with articles and commentary on religious subjects. Because of its wide reach, *Outlook* afforded Abbott the power to shape public opinion, especially among elite circles in the northeast. Under his leadership, the journal became a crucial vehicle for promulgating theological liberalism and the related message that Protestants, Catholics, and Jews were, in his words, "all seeking the same end."[6]

Those ends were primarily social in nature. Abbott championed what liberal Protestants called the "Social Gospel." According to this view, religious understanding was not derived from transcendent truths, but emerged from the social and political evolutions of history. Abbott boasted that "things which were once traditional beliefs I have cast off as errors," indicating that doctrines were historically contingent constructions. The notion that "dogmatic definitions necessarily change" with historical progress was common among Social Gospelers, who worked to transform society through collective action, hoping to more closely approximate the kingdom of God.[7] This collective consciousness would yield more equal access to economic opportunity and resources—a social end, Abbot argued, that united liberal Protestants, Catholics, and Jews. Leading colleagues thus joined Abbott in decrying Protestantism's long-standing emphasis on personal salvation. One popular clergyman called it "childish" to "shut ourselves within our little conventicles and sing and pray and have a happy time all by ourselves, saving our own souls, and letting the great roaring world outside go on its way to destruction."[8]

The Social Gospelers' assessment of earlier forms of religiosity was part caricature. Even the most ardent revivalists had placed some emphasis on improving society, and earlier generations of evangelicals had created a vast array of social reform movements. The difference was that early twentieth-century liberals considered good works an important source, not the mere fruit, of spiritual well-being. It was in social relationships, they argued, that spiritual capacities developed. These relationships equipped individuals to contribute to the emerging democratic spirit of history, which manifested itself in more robust public management of the nation's resources. The vision of progress offered by evolutionary liberals and the new social sciences suggested the possibility of actualizing elements of God's kingdom in the present life. This, leading liberal Protestants believed, was the essence of true religion.

The Baptist minister Walter Rauschenbusch gave the Social Gospel—or Social Christianity—its clearest explication. Rauschenbusch believed that all of Christian theology should be reformulated to emphasize a "social, political, solidaristic" religion because the central teaching of Jesus was that faith was essentially social in nature and thus served social needs. Anyone, Rauschenbusch thundered, who "uncouples the religious and the social life has not understood Jesus."[9]

Rauschenbusch did not live to see the interfaith movement of the 1920s, having perished in the global influenza epidemic of 1918. But the Social Gospel, with its focus on Jesus's ethical teachings and society's salvation in the progressive unfolding of God's kingdom in history, continued to occupy a central place in Protestant thought and became the guiding ideology of the Federal Council of Churches. Ultimately, the Social Gospel provided an intellectual foundation for the interfaith movement by fostering a common religious sensibility among early twentieth-century liberals, including many Protestants, Catholics, and Jews.

As Protestants developed their Social Gospel theology, prominent Catholics such as John Ireland, archbishop of St. Paul, Minnesota, conveyed a similar message. With an outgoing disposition, connections to political leaders (he, like Abbott, enjoyed a personal friendship with Theodore Roosevelt), and penchant for media attention, Ireland was arguably the most famous American Catholic from the 1880s until his death in 1918. He drew inspiration from a strand of liberal Catholic thought that emerged in the United States during the second half of the nineteenth century. Though more restrained in their view of progress than many of their Protestant counterparts, liberal Catholics nevertheless believed in the human capacity to transform society. They understood this kind of social transformation as a spiritual endeavor. It was grounded in the conviction, shared with liberal Protestants, that personal salvation was communal in nature, symbiotically tied to social salvation. The soul, Ireland explained, "is entangled in a hundred networks of most complex relations, the perils of which are its perils, the purification and elevation of which must ever be both the cause and the effect of its personal sanctification." This liberal purification of society was to foster the progressive unfolding of God's kingdom, which was immanent in history but would become manifest only as religious institutions worked to advance it through polices designed to increase social equality and economic opportunity.[10]

To be sure, liberal Catholics and Protestants drew from different strands of Christian tradition and differed considerably in their precise vision of the kingdom of God. Catholics retained strong convictions of human sin and depravity and held a less optimistic view of human potential, which tempered their optimism about the ease with which humans could advance God's kingdom. Nevertheless, the overlap in socioreligious sensibilities among the two cohorts was substantial. Ireland and like-minded Catholic leaders earned the appellation "Americanists," which reflected their view that the United States, with its new corporate economy and accompanying inequality and urbanization, provided fertile ground for efforts at social transformation.

The Americanists delighted in their agreement with Protestants about the specific policies of social reform, sharing with them a commitment to Progressive causes. Both groups touted greater equality in the control of the nation's industries and resources, the conviction that property rights must be tempered by perceived social needs, and the shifting of municipal power from political parties and party leaders to a new, university-trained class of avowedly altruistic civil servants. One liberal Catholic affirmed that his coreligionists could join Protestants "in one common and sacred cause" to "promote the welfare of the people" and "to remedy social miseries." Indeed, many Catholics viewed liberal Protestants as moving closer to Catholic positions on social and political matters. When an early proponent of Social Gospel ideals wrote a book on economic inequality in 1890s America, a reviewer in the popular periodical *Catholic World* suggested that the author's positions were nearly identical to the pope's![11]

Parallel developments occurred in the relationship between Protestants and Reform Jews. Like Americanist Catholics, many Jewish leaders saw in the Social Gospel the evolution of Protestantism toward the teachings of Judaism. One Reform rabbi, David Philipson, noted that for centuries Jews had been championing the idea of "social salvation"—now a favorite term among liberal Protestants. This meant a focus on present conditions rather than on the hereafter. Social Gospel theology echoed this long-standing Jewish perspective as it shifted its conception of the kingdom of God from transcendence to historical immanence. The newfound conviction among many Protestants about the social nature of salvation resonated with their Jewish neighbors. "If today the Christian churches have great programs of social justice," Philipson declared, "they appear to be turning to the Jewish vision of life in this respect."[12]

Early twentieth-century liberal Protestants, of course, did not view their social ideas as originating in papal encyclicals or historic Judaism. Rather, Social Gospelers understood their outlook to embody the evolution of God's revelation in tandem with the changes sweeping turn-of-the-century America. Either way, the religious sensibilities of liberal Protestants were recognizable to Jews and Catholics. Their shared belief in God combined with their mutual commitment to social action in the interest of the progressive development of God's kingdom allowed members of all three traditions to perceive that they were, in Abbott's words, in accord "upon the most important . . . articles of faith." During the early twentieth century, liberals from all three faiths sought to make reality match their rhetoric. They undertook mutual campaigns for social reform while conducting new experiments with interfaith worship services and new efforts to foster interreligious conversations throughout the United States. [13]

The Federal Council's Goodwill Committee was the most successful of several attempts during the 1920s to enact these new ideals on a national scale, and its successes were widely reported. Well-attended interfaith discussions and social events took place in cities and towns throughout the United States, as well as on college, university, and seminary campuses. It seemed that Protestants, Catholics, and Jews had taken an unprecedented step in the direction of interfaith tolerance and understanding. And in an important sense they had. Yet their efforts embodied ideological commitments that generated as many divisions and feelings of hostility as they overcame. Strong opposition to the interfaith campaign broke out within all three traditions, most forcefully among Protestants. Supporters of programs like the Goodwill Committee pursued a project of tolerance that, perhaps like all such endeavors, was enmeshed in the politics of its time—in this case, the early twentieth-century marriage of liberal politics and religion. The project thus inescapably generated its own opposition, especially among those who questioned the progressive doctrine of social salvation.

II

As liberal Protestants, Catholics, and Jews professed their shared commitment to redeeming society through the tools of progressivism, critics emerged arguing that liberals were straying too far from core beliefs. The division first appeared among Catholics. During the 1890s, conservatives attacked the modernizing Americanism of John Ireland and like-minded prelates. They blanched at Ireland's participation in the 1893 Parliament of Religions in Chicago, which brought together representatives of the world's major religious traditions to discuss their beliefs and practices. Many saw the parliament as evidence that liberal participation in interfaith efforts bred relativism. Six years later, Pope Leo XIII denounced the view articulated by Ireland and other Americanists that the United States possessed the most highly evolved political and social institutions and thus offered the most likely setting for the unfolding of God's kingdom. Leo rejected the progressive vision of the Americanists and made it clear that the Catholic Church would not support interfaith efforts that undercut its theological teachings. [14]

During the early twentieth century, another group of American Catholics argued for the progressive evolution of religious thought. They, too, insisted that their faith tracked modern values and science, and, on this basis, they sought to develop robust interfaith ties. Like the Americanists in the previous decade, these so-called Modernists soon faced censure, and worse, from the

Vatican. A papal denunciation of Modernism in 1907 left little room for accommodation or compromise. Modernists had four options: abandon Modernism, self-censor, leave the church, or risk excommunication by committing apostasy. One American Catholic theologian with Modernist sympathies, Roderick MacEachen, faced the prospect of censure in the late 1920s for rejecting the view that "revelation" was "a closed book." He argued, instead, for "progress" in the realm of the "spiritual." MacEachen indicated that he was "under suspicion and the hounds are on the trail." [15]

The opposition of the Vatican and many American bishops to theological liberalism and its perceived endorsement of relativism had consequences for interfaith efforts in the United States. Roman Catholics found it exceedingly difficult to participate in interfaith organizations informed by the spirit of religious liberalism. Despite intense lobbying by Protestant and Jewish leaders, Catholics remained aloof from the Federal Council's Goodwill Committee. The experience of a smaller interfaith group that sought to increase interreligious understanding on the nation's university campuses exemplified the difficulties that accompanied Catholic involvement. One of the group's Jewish members described how a Catholic comember temporarily withdrew because of "the prejudice of the Jesuits" (the Catholic monastic order known at the time as critics of progressive trends). Significant portions of the Catholic Church viewed the interfaith group as encouraging liberal sensibilities at odds with Catholic teaching. [16]

Because Judaism lacked Roman Catholicism's institutional hierarchy, debates between liberals and conservatives did not produce the same winner-take-all mentality. Nevertheless, pronounced divisions became evident among Jews as well. Most Jewish Americans who sought closer ties with Protestants and Catholics belonged to the Reform tradition. Much like Americanist Catholics, Reform Jews saw no inherent conflict between their beliefs and the values of the United States.

One of the most prominent Jewish leaders in early twentieth-century America, Abram Simon, made the advancement of interfaith efforts a core element of his life's work. Simon was rabbi of a major synagogue in Washington, DC, and for several years he served as president of the Central Conference of American Rabbis, the body that oversaw Reform Judaism in the United States. His interest in a range of social issues, including marriage, divorce, and birth control, exemplified the connection between religious liberalism and progressive politics. During the 1920s, he supported the Federal Council's Goodwill Committee as well as other organizations that brought Jews together with Protestants and Catholics. He even carried this commitment to his deathbed: in his last hours on December 24, 1938, Simon delivered a Christmas radio message to Christians urging them to continue their support for interreligious understanding. [17]

Yet, like Catholics, American Jews were split on general questions of assimilation and the specific issue of interfaith relations. Critics from both Orthodox Judaism and the nascent Conservative movement chastised Reform leaders like Simon for abandoning essential elements of historical Jewish practice in accommodating America's modern liberal mores. American Jews who retained more of their tradition established new institutions, such as the Conservative Jewish Theological Seminary in New York, which offered an alternative to Reform Judaism. Though the theological arguments that divided Judaism were far less acrimonious than those in Catholicism, fissures still widened in the Jewish community around the cultural issues embedded in interfaith endeavors.

However, the most divisive quarrels took place within American Protestantism. By the 1920s, most Protestant denominations had experienced liberal-conservative discord for nearly a half century. During the late nineteenth century, theological liberals won a series of contentious debates within the nation's major Protestant denominations. By the early twentieth century, they had secured the leadership of many of them. But strong opposition persisted. The revivalist tradition fostered by Dwight L. Moody during the late nineteenth century retained the older emphasis on individual salvation that contrasted sharply with liberals' argument for social salvation. In the early twentieth century, revivalism coalesced with the growing Holiness movement, which emphasized the quest for perfection through strict adherence to biblical teaching. While these alternative modes of Protestant thought contained conflicts within themselves, it was possible to see in the Holiness and revival traditions a clear and compelling alternative to liberal Protestantism.[18]

This conservative alternative received a strong intellectual foundation between 1910 and 1915 with the publication of the twelve-volume *The Fundamentals*. These short and lucid pamphlets targeted a broad audience. Their caustic assault on Protestant liberalism revealed why conservatives opposed interfaith efforts. *The Fundamentals* attacked the very basis of liberal theology, insisting that religion did not evolve in tandem with changing social and cultural conditions. "Old-time doctrine" was not, as liberals suggested, to be cast aside in the face of "new-time conditions." Rather, it represented the core of Christianity, conservatives insisted, and overlooking it to advance interfaith conversations rendered those conversations suspect. These early twentieth-century conservative Protestants were also put off by their liberal coreligionists' insistence on mixing religion and politics. Many hailed from rural areas and embraced cultural values that clashed with the progressive sensibilities popular among middle- and upper-class city dwellers and suburbanites. Even when they agreed with Progressives on specific issues, such as Prohibition, Fundamentalists increasingly preferred to avoid politics entirely. They were not seeking a spiritualized politics geared toward the transformation of society, and, as a result, they did not support the policy initiatives that united liberals across religious lines. Finally, Fundamentalists and similarly orthodox Protestants believed in the apostolic commission to proselytize. They resented that the liberal members of interfaith efforts refused to avail themselves of the close contact with Jews and Catholics to seek converts to Protestant Christianity.[19]

During the 1920s, just as the interfaith movement took shape with institutions like the Federal Council's Goodwill Committee, the "Fundamentalist-Modernist" controversy divided American Protestantism between the theologically liberal, primarily urban proponents of the Social Gospel and the theologically conservative, predominantly rural adherents of traditional Christianity. Fundamentalists within major denominations objected to the Federal Council's liberal tendencies. Like the United Presbyterians in 1929, they denounced interfaith efforts that seemed to imply that there might be greater religious value in Judaism or Catholicism than in orthodox Protestantism.

For supporters of closer interfaith ties, the perception that Protestantism, Catholicism, and Judaism all shared the same divisions helped to bolster interfaith solidarity. Abbott proclaimed that Catholic leaders like Ireland were "faithful and devoted servants" of both their church and the nation who were more committed than orthodox Protestants were to the reform of both religious institutions and American society. Whereas conservative members of his own tradition remained focused on preserving established doctrine and securing individual salvation, liberal Catholics shared Abbott's commitment to social salvation through progressive politics.[20]

Other Protestant leaders echoed these sentiments about Catholics. The noted theologian Charles Briggs derisively characterized the division within Roman Catholicism as between the modernists, whom he supported, and the "medievalists," whom he opposed. He viewed this Catholic divide as "precisely the same conflict that has been in progress all over the Protestant world." The "old lines" between Catholics and Protestants had become blurred by conflicts within each tradition that pitted liberals against traditionalists.[21]

Similarly, Abbott noted that "the divisions . . . of Protestants into orthodox and liberal, are paralleled in the divisions of Judaism." In his view, Reform Jews believed that "Judaism is not a ritual or a dogma, but a life." Abbott saw in this perception an intuition regarding religion's essential nature that closely resembled the vision of liberal Protestants. Reinhold Niebuhr, a few years before his emergence as one of the foremost Protestant theologians in the United States, likewise felt a closer connection to Reform Jews than to orthodox Christians. Noting his conviction that Jews surpassed Christians in "social sensitivity," he confessed to feeling that he had "more in common with many liberal Jews" than with many of his own faith.[22]

Catholic and Jewish leaders were somewhat more restrained in touting what they had in common with Protestants. Yet they, too, recognized that divisions between liberals and conservatives within religious traditions had begun to supplant the long-standing cleavages between Protestantism, Catholicism, and Judaism. The liberal Catholics were the most tentative, with lingering commitments to the uniqueness of Catholic teaching and a wariness about openly espousing liberal thought in the wake of their church's denunciations of Americanism and Modernism. Yet some were willing to concede that the "old controversy" between Catholics and Protestants had diminished significance given the sharp split between liberals and conservatives. And liberal Catholics like MacEachen quietly forged relationships with liberal Protestants with whom they could correspond and discuss new theological perspectives without attracting unwanted attention from the Holy See.[23]

Religiously liberal Reform Jews, who faced growing criticism within their own tradition, sought connections with like-minded Protestants to advance the cause of a religiously tolerant liberalism. Simon advocated the establishment of a "Federation of Religious Liberals," an institution in which he hoped that "Jew and Christian can not only think together . . . speak together . . . dwell together, but can also work and worship together in peace and unity." Most important, such an organization would provide a counterpoint to the claims of "Christian and Jewish Orthodoxy." Indeed, he believed that religious liberalism would provide a vehicle for an "inclusive" message that would "render impossible for all time the growth of noxious plants of hatred toward those who chance to differ in their attitude of God." One of Simon's colleagues in the Central Conference of American Rabbis and a fellow participant in many interfaith efforts, David Philipson, likewise called on liberals to transcend traditional boundaries in order to combat religious conservatives. The conflict between Fundamentalists and Modernists in Protestantism was of concern to "Jews no less than Christians." All faiths suffered, he suggested, when an emphasis on tradition divided people who might otherwise coalesce around a modern liberal message.[24]

CONCLUSION

By the 1920s, the development of a common social outlook merged with a growing pattern of interfaith interaction to produce a hitherto unknown sense of shared purpose and agreement among liberal Protestants, Catholics, and Jews in the United States. The result was a newfound commitment to religious toleration and a newfound friendliness among Americans of different faith traditions. Liberal Protestants downplayed historical doctrines, connected individual and social salvation, and proclaimed the progressive reform of society as the heart of their religious message. This turn in Protestant thought provided the basis for new feelings of commonality with those Catholics and Jews who embraced their own forms of theological liberalism and progressive social focus. After several decades of negotiation, liberal members of all three traditions cultivated a deeper appreciation of one another's beliefs and practices and came to hold the view that they had far greater similarities than differences.

Yet, just as this embrace of liberal theology created new commonalities, it also generated new divisions. It alienated orthodox Catholics, Jews, and Protestants—especially Protestants. The 1929 protests by the United Presbyterians and other conservatives reflected underlying discomfort with the spirit of interreligious comity and the liberal rejection of traditional doctrine that underlay it. The Federal Council's Goodwill Committee and related efforts revealed a larger truth—namely, that projects to foster religious tolerance and inclusion rest on a foundation of political and theological commitments. Campaigns to advance pluralism are never nonideological. In the United States of the 1920s, the ideological commitments that underlay the nascent interfaith movement were far from universally held among Protestants, Catholics, and Jews.

Thus, the interfaith movement of the early twentieth century contributed to the reshaping of the boundary lines of American religion. For religious liberals of all stripes, the once-insurmountable divide among faith traditions became far less formidable. However, already existing chasms between liberals and conservatives in Protestantism, Catholicism, and Judaism, which had grown steadily for decades, now widened significantly. Debates between the two sides became increasingly acrimonious. And thus conflict between divergent perspectives within traditions grew alongside newfound understanding across religious boundaries. As the twentieth century progressed, this reorientation would become all the more pronounced. Liberal Protestants, Catholics, and Jews would enjoy an ever-growing sense of kinship on a range of issues. Conservative members of all three traditions would likewise develop a feeling of solidarity amid the culture wars of the late twentieth century. Testifying to the complexities of the American religious landscape, the dramatic reduction of hostility fostered by the interfaith movement came at the cost of an even greater chasm between liberals and conservatives.

NOTES

1. "The Goodwill Movement Tested," 7 June 1929, folder 18, box 14, Central Conference of American Rabbis Records, Joseph Rader Marcus Center of the American Jewish Archives, Cincinnati, OH; Francis J. McConnell Letter, 25 July 1929, folder 13, box 2, series B, David Philipson Papers, Joseph Rader Marcus Center of the American Jewish Archives, Cincinnati, OH.

2. The best history of the divisiveness of denominations and the establishment of the Federal Council remains Samuel McCrea Cavert, *The American Churches in the Ecumenical*

Movement, 1900–1968 (New York: Association Press, 1968); on Protestant cooperation in World War I, see John F. Piper, *The American Churches in World War I* (Athens: Ohio University Press, 1985).

3. See the notes on the setup of the committee, reprinted in "Committee on Goodwill between Jews and Christians, Federal Council of the Churches of Christ in America," 26 October 1928, folder 18, box 10, Federal Council of the Churches of Christ in America Records, Presbyterian Historical Society, Philadelphia, PA.

4. On the tensions inherent in the movement, see Benny Kraut, "A Wary Collaboration: Jews, Catholics, and the Protestant Goodwill Movement," in *Between the Times: The Travails of the Protestant Establishment in America, 1900–1960*, ed. William R. Hutchison (Cambridge: Cambridge University Press, 1989), 215; on the specific issue of conversion, see Kraut, "Toward the Establishment of the National Conference of Christians and Jews: The Tenuous Road to Religious Goodwill in the 1920s," *American Jewish History* 77 (1988): 388–412.

5. See John T. McGreevy, *Catholicism and American Freedom: A History* (New York: W. W. Norton, 2003), 21–25, 124–26, and Leonard Dinnerstein, *Antisemitism in America* (New York: Oxford University Press, 1994), 11–23, 35–57.

6. Lyman Abbott, "The Message of the Nineteenth Century to the Men of the Twentieth," *Outlook*, 19 October 1912, 354.

7. Lyman Abbott, *In Aid of Faith* (New York: E. P. Dutton, 1886), x–xi.

8. Washington Gladden, *The Christian Pastor and the Working Church* (New York: Charles Scribner's Sons, 1898), 48.

9. Walter Rauschenbusch, *A Theology for the Social Gospel* (New York: Macmillan, 1917), 107; Rauschenbusch, *Christianity and the Social Crisis* (New York: Macmillan, 1907), 48.

10. John Ireland, *The Church and Modern Society: Lectures and Addresses* (1896; Chicago: D. H. McBride, 1903), xix; Jay P. Dolan, *In Search of an American Catholicism: A History of Religion and Culture in Tension* (New York: Oxford University Press, 2002), 68–69.

11. Augustine F. Hewit, "The Lesson of the 'White City,' Second Part," *Catholic World* 60 (October 1894): 82; Hewit, "Talk about New Books," *Catholic World* 57 (August 1893): 722. The review is of Washington Gladden, *Tools and the Man: Property and Industry under the Christian Law* (Boston: Houghton, Mifflin, 1893).

12. David Philipson, "The Humanist Movement," folder 8, box 4, series D, Philipson Papers.

13. "The Unity of the Faith," *Outlook*, 18 June 1910, 336–37.

14. Dolan, *In Search of an American Catholicism*, 105–10.

15. Roderick MacEachen to George A. Coe, Easter 1928, folder 3, box 1, George A. Coe Papers, Yale Divinity School Archive, New Haven, CT.

16. Minutes of a Meeting of the Committee on Goodwill Between Christians and Jews, 8 June 1925, folder 13, box 2, series B, Philipson Papers; Abram Simon to David Philipson, 12 May 1927, folder 19, box 1, series A, Philipson Papers.

17. On Simon's influence, see, for example, "Let Us Understand Each Other," clipping from the *Congressional Record* (1924), folder 2, box 1, Abram Simon Papers, Joseph Rader Marcus Center of the American Jewish Archives, Cincinnati, OH.

18. George M. Marsden, *Fundamentalism and American Culture*, 2nd ed. (New York: Oxford University Press, 2006), 27–39.

19. R. A. Torrey and A. C. Dixon, eds., *The Fundamentals: A Testimony to the Truth* (Grand Rapids, MI: Baker Books, 2003), 283; "The Goodwill Movement Tested"; Marsden, *Fundamentalism and American Culture*, 90–93.

20. "The New American Cardinals," *Outlook*, 11 November 1911, 607.

21. Charles Augustus Briggs, *Church Unity: Studies of Its Most Important Problems* (New York: Charles Scribner's Sons, 1909), 438, 440.

22. "The Week," *Outlook*, 28 January 1911, 138–39; Reinhold Niebuhr to Isidore Singer, 20 September 1929, folder 5, box 1, Isidore Singer Papers, Joseph Rader Marcus Center of the American Jewish Archives, Cincinnati, OH.

23. John Lancaster Spalding, *Religion, Agnosticism, and Education* (Chicago: A. C. McClurg, 1903), 184.

24. Abram Simon, "The Function of the Liberal Movement," 1923, folder 1, box 1, Simon Papers; David Philipson, "The Fundamentalist Controversy," folder 6, box 4, series D, Philipson papers.

Chapter Thirteen

Dog Tags

Religious Toleration and the Politics of American Military Identification

Ronit Y. Stahl

When the Office of the Army Chief of Chaplains received a request for additional Jewish chaplains to assist with funerals in 1944, it did not object in principle. "It is obvious," the office responded, "that there may be occasions when a Jewish chaplain is not available. At such times a Protestant or Catholic chaplain is empowered to conduct Jewish burials." This aligned with the army's general policy, which stated that "under war conditions Protestant chaplains often bury Catholic dead and Catholic chaplains bury Protestant dead. . . . There can be no guarantee for a chaplain of a particular denomination in times of extremity."[1] No matter the religious background of the chaplain available, however, the funeral was supposed to match the religious preference of the deceased. Chaplain Reuben Curtis, for example, received accolades for "providing adequate religious burial services for all faiths."[2] But how did Curtis—or any other chaplain—determine which religious rites to perform?

The short answer is dog tags. Small, engraved metallic objects, worn by every member of the armed forces for the grim purpose of identifying fallen soldiers, dog tags also signified the boundaries of religious inclusion in mid-twentieth-century America. During World War II, the military limited the available religious categories on dog tags to three options—P for Protestant, C for Catholic, and H for Hebrew (Jewish). These options reflected the tripartite religious division favored by the American armed forces at the mid-century point.[3] This limited set of choices frustrated faithful soldiers who found themselves excluded from the pantheon of American believers, such as

Buddhists, Muslims, and Eastern Orthodox, as well as those lumped together as Protestants despite significantly divergent theologies (Mormons, Pentecostals, etc.). In this way, dog tags reinforced and projected the interpretive fiction that American religion consisted of three faiths. Just as state recognition of certain racial categories and heterosexual marriages granted legitimacy and privilege to some citizens over others, so, too, did the military sanction some religious identities at the expense of others.

During the mid-twentieth century, dog tags forged literal and material connections between God, family, and country. The P-C-H options proved acceptable to many Americans but frustrated those who desired a more complete taxonomy (or none at all). Ultimately, this seemingly mundane form of military identification provided a concrete means for Americans to agitate for greater recognition of religious diversity even as willful blindness and bureaucratic inertia stymied efforts to expand the scope of American religious belonging. While the state initially rebuffed efforts to expand the range of faiths recognized on dog tags, the military eventually conceded the existence of greater religious diversity and allowed service members to choose their own religious designations. This unheralded policy change represented a major victory for individuals who had long sought more specific self-identification. At the same time, the elimination of de facto state-sanctioned categories cost minority religious groups recognition as American religions.

DOG TAGS: A SHORT HISTORY

American dog tags were born of death, specifically Civil War death. Union and Confederate soldiers pinned paper nametags on their uniforms so that, if killed, their kin would know they had fallen. "If a soldier could not save his life, he hoped at least to preserve his name," explains historian Drew Gilpin Faust. By the late nineteenth century, Chaplain Charles Pierce began reforming burial practices. Posted to Manila during the Spanish-American War, the Episcopalian priest suggested that small metal tags engraved with names would help systematize the morgue procedures, as well as death notification. In 1906, the War Department permitted soldiers to wear identifying discs under their uniforms. Within a decade, the military mandated that all personnel wear military identification—provided gratis to enlisted men and at cost to officers—that declared name, rank, and company, regiment, or corps. By the end of World War I, all American soldiers were wearing some form of identification in the field, and in the years following the Great War, the colloquially known "dog tags" expanded to include other vital information, including religious affiliation alongside one's name, rank, and blood type.[4]

The transformation of dog tags from mere nameplates to markers of religious identity represented a concession to the imperatives of both faith and bureaucracy. The chaos of war, even outside main battle arenas, had long made the task of proper burial impossible and improvisation unavoidable. Unpredictable surges of dead, sometimes thousands in a matter of days, rarely offered ideal conditions for attending to distinct backgrounds of individual servicemen. An increasingly religiously diverse nation made this project even more challenging because religions hold differing expectations about the appropriate and respectful treatment of the dead. With the inclusion of religious identity on dog tags, counting and naming the dead gave way to honoring and burying fallen service members according to the rites of their faith.

Attending to the needs of men who identified with different faiths represented a massive challenge in war. Chaplains, the official religious representatives of the armed forces and the officers responsible for handling matters of death, were ordained by their particular faith traditions and commissioned by the military to serve all men regardless of religion. While they, too, fell under the Protestant-Catholic-Jewish taxonomy, by the time of World War II, chaplains relied on informational pamphlets and bulletins developed by the armed forces to address the specific creeds and practices of many different faith groups. A 1944 memo granted chaplains "ready and authoritative information concerning the ministry desired by the several faith groups to fulfill religious obligations and bring the maximum comfort and spiritual help to patients in time of illness and danger of death." Unlike the three religions engraved on dog tags, the memo instructed chaplains about the practices of twenty-six religions and denominations, ranging from Baptists, Catholics, and Christian Scientists to Jews, Mormons, and Russian Orthodox. A subsequent memo added eleven more groups, including the Assemblies of God, Buddhists, and Quakers.[5] But chaplains could not act on this detailed guidance without accurate data. Respect for religious tradition depended on knowing the religious affiliation of the wounded and the dead. Dog tags functioned as the critical, albeit incomplete, axis of information.

The military bureaucracy's haphazard approach to religious diversity—extremely restricted on dog tags but increasingly accommodating in memos and in the field—exposed the gap between a limited state religious taxonomy and the religious identities of American personnel. Dog tags became a site of conflict precisely because they both marked and masked religious diversity. Army Chief of Chaplains Luther Miller explained how the military understood religious difference in matters such as worship and funerals. "There is no question about the necessity of allowing Catholics and Jews to attend their own services," he wrote, "because of the positive and fundamental differences of belief or practice which would make it impossible for them to join in the general chapel service with conviction." But, he continued, "it is a serious question how far a corresponding concession could be allowed to other groups when a positive matter of conscience or church government is not involved without detracting seriously from the sense of unity in high purpose which the common chapel service seeks to promote."[6] Miller articulated the fundamental challenge the state faced in managing religion in the mid-twentieth century: To what degree could—or would—the U.S. military recognize religious difference beyond the tri-faith division? Clearly demarcated as separate but almost equally American, Catholics and Jews could attend their own services without sacrificing unity. Everyone else, however, was expected to attend the common—which was to say, Protestant—chapel service, lest they fracture the American esprit de corps.

The discrepancy between the state's top-down emphasis on a tri-faith nation and the occasional admission of more nuanced religious categories exposed dueling impulses: a desire to ignore difference in pursuit of unity and a tacit acknowledgement of diverse religious needs. Between the first and second world wars, "Protestant" had become a catchall category for the American military, an elastic label that encompassed everyone who was not Catholic or Jewish. It was less a theological marker than an imprint of comingled national and religious identity. The country was indeed predominantly Protestant and, for about two decades from World War I to World War II, this capacious and imprecise terminology seemed to suffice.[7] However, during World War II, the military's tentative (albeit inconsistent) recognition of additional American religions and denominations strained against the religious impressionism that enabled the tri-faith ideal. By the 1940s, numerous religious groups branded with the Protestant P rejected bureaucratic uniformity and jockeyed instead for particularity and distinction.

THE MIXED-UP DOG TAGS OF PRIVATE LEONARD SHAPIRO

Learning that her son had been killed in France on August 20, 1944, was bad enough, but the follow-up letter devastated Rose Shapiro. It first stated that her child's "remains received respectful and reverential care," but then informed her that his grave was "marked with a modest Christian cross." Moreover, the note disclosed, "last rites of the Church were held, his grave was blessed, and Masses were being said regularly for him and the others who have made the supreme sacrifices for their country."[8] But Rose Shapiro and her fallen son were Jewish, not Catholic. The military understood that death elevated the importance of religious ministry and commemoration for soldiers and their families, and it therefore instructed chaplains on comforting dying men, conducting a variety of religious funerals, and writing appropriate condolence letters. Yet the provision of these services in a religiously diverse nation could easily go awry, as the case of Rose Shapiro's son indicates.

To bolster men on the battlefield and to comfort families on the home front, the military invoked a blend of faith and patriotism. "Make men courageous and unafraid," exhorted one pocket-sized manual designed to assist soldiers in helping their buddies. "Upon finding a seriously wounded man," the pamphlet added, "inquire at once as to the religious faith of the man concerned" and then recite the appropriate Protestant, Catholic, or Jewish prayers, and, as necessary, follow the proper procedures for temporary burials. Written by chaplains, the manual granted laymen access to religious rites in times of crisis. Even in the absence of certified clergy, the military imperative to provide the wounded and dead "spiritual comfort" persisted.[9] The arc of religious sustenance also extended to the families soldiers left behind. Parents and siblings, spouses and children, all received letters of consolation confirming that their kin departed this life with all the necessary and expected prayers and rituals.

Because the state did not track individual religious affiliation, dog tags declared the faith of soldiers silenced by death.[10] Or that was one of their intentions. Although personnel were supposed to select one of three initials (P-C-H) to indicate their religion, the rules were sometimes broken. Mormons, for example, asked to use LDS in place of a P, since, as they argued, "we are in no sense Protestants."[11] The military generally did not accommodate such requests. However, on rare occasions an enterprising Mormon managed to find "a commanding officer that maybe didn't know the rules or the regulations and he would permit LDS men to have LDS on their dog tags."[12] Periodically, printed dog tags contravened War Department policy and substituted J for H to indicate Jewish. Indeed, less than a month after the United States entered World War II, American Jewish leaders began to protest the use of the archaic racial category "Hebrew" and pled instead for the religiously associated J.[13] While Jews, like Mormons, often failed to receive the letter they preferred, sometimes individuals found a helpful commander or quartermaster and made themselves the dog tag of their choice.[14] In the face of bureaucratic inertia and glacial policy change, individual initiative could meld with diffuse state power to produce a religious accommodation.

For most Jewish soldiers in World War II, registering faith on a dog tag represented a more fraught and fateful decision than debating the relative value of an H or a J. Many deliberated whether to include their religion on their dog tags at all, concerned that, if captured by the German military, they might be treated as Jews rather than prisoners of war. Fearing torture by Nazis, some American Jews opted out of disclosing their faith and opted for the P or C as a safer form of (mis-)identification.[15] When asked how Jewish soldiers should resolve this dilemma, Jewish chaplain Charles S. Freedman remained ambivalent. On the one hand, "for many men and their families back home, it would be of the greatest importance that, should death come on the field of battle, a Jewish burial be given the deceased." On the other hand, "expediency and practicality teaches the desirability of being a live dog rather than a dead lion." Little was to be gained through martyrdom.[16]

Connecting the dead soldier to his faith was thus an imprecise science, even if the soldier fell within one of the standard religious categories. Officers assigned to ensuring proper religious burials first had to determine whether the dog tag signified the correct person. As LDS chaplain Lyman Berrett recalled, "When we would bury men . . . we would not always go by the name on the dog tags," because superstitious men believed that their dog tags marked them as targets for bullets and exchanged dog tags. This led Berrett and other chaplains to develop additional layers of verification, most often by confirming the dog tag with other records, lists, and forms of identification. When they encountered men with "the C or the P on their dog tags," Berrett explained, we "identified them as being who the dog tag actually said they were or after we got our direct identification of the body, then we would write to the parents and tell them that they had had a Christian burial service."[17]

But this multistep process still left room for mistakes. Army Chief of Chaplains William R. Arnold chastised the chaplain who penned the condolence letter to Rose Shapiro: "Mrs. Shapiro is, as the name so strongly suggests, Jewish. She is no little distraught that her son received a Catholic rather than a Jewish burial." The Catholic chief of chaplains asked several questions in an attempt to elicit how procedures went awry. Was it possible the soldier had converted overseas? And what was actually on his dog tag? If there was uncertainty regarding "his official religious preference[,] could not his buddies have supplied the necessary information?" Finally, was this incident merely a mix-up, a letter sent in error?[18] The chaplain hastened to clarify his actions, noting that in the absence of clear religious preference, he "selected names that I thought were of a Catholic faith. Inadvertently I selected the name Shapiro to be an Italian name, and one that was a Catholic."[19] Without clear information, he did the best he could and apologized for the error. Enforcing religious clarity through dog tags and personnel lists would preclude such mistakes, he asserted. The state, he argued, needed to collect better data and insist that soldiers designate religion on dog tags to prevent mishaps and errors, thus enabling chaplains to honor the dead and comfort families.

B IS FOR BUDDHIST?

Prone to fumbling to meet the spiritual needs of soldiers who fit the P-C-H framework, the military struggled mightily to accommodate soldiers whose religious identities fell outside the three accepted religious categories. In

1948, the Office of the Chief of Chaplains received a petition asking for a seemingly modest change: to allow Buddhist military personnel to designate themselves as such (rather than Protestant) on their dog tags. Many minority religious groups had at best questionable ties to the ecclesiastical definition of Protestant, and dog tags provided a means through which to lobby for recognition of distinct religious identities and an accommodation of conscience. For Buddhists and the Eastern Orthodox, the postwar effort to convince the state to acknowledge their presence in and contributions to the military extended an effort to appoint Buddhist and Orthodox chaplains that began during World War II. In steadfastly resisting these pleas through weak, pragmatic arguments, the military revealed the degree to which state officials were invested in limiting the recognition of unfamiliar faiths, especially those perceived as racially distinct.

For brief moments during World War II, it appeared that both the Eastern Orthodox and Buddhists would receive chaplains. Officially, the racial and religious composition of units was irrelevant because military policy dictated that all chaplains were commissioned to serve all men. In practice, however, racial and religious categorization mattered. In this racially segregated military, white chaplains (of any faith) could serve any unit, but nonwhite chaplains were restricted to same-race units. Just as black chaplains could serve only black units, so, too, did the chaplaincy presume that Asian American chaplains could serve only Asian American units.[20] The logic held for distinctive minority faiths as well: Buddhist chaplains might have a place with predominantly Buddhist units, and Orthodox chaplains with wholly Orthodox units.

When war came, Orthodox men were drafted into the military but wore no discernible markings of their faith and looked like the white majority. When they referred to themselves as Orthodox or Eastern Orthodox, officials generally translated that as Catholic *or* Protestant. There were also those who self-identified as Catholics—which they were, albeit not *Roman* Catholics. Still others self-identified as Protestants—which, under the military's classification scheme (which designated everyone not Catholic or Jewish as Protestant), they were as well.[21] The resulting confusion of identities and state taxonomies created a gap in religious support for Eastern Orthodox soldiers. Metropolitan Antony Bashir wrote to President Roosevelt to plead the case of his Greek Orthodox followers: "We are not Roman Catholic, nor are we any form of Protestant. . . . Our young Orthodox men are therefore either to go without Spiritual guidance and Religious Worship, or else be forced by circumstance to accept Roman Catholic or Protestant ministrations."[22] The available categories camouflaged the Eastern Orthodox, rendering them invisible and denying them the religious support they desired.

The creation of the 122nd Infantry Battalion changed everything. In January 1943, President Roosevelt issued an executive order establishing a Greek battalion tasked with parachuting or boating into Greece to liberate it from Nazi control. Its Greek-speaking immigrant and native-born commandoes were almost all Greek Orthodox, which helped the state see them as such.[23] As William Arnold had told Russian Orthodox prelate Cyril A. W. Johnson the year before, "If all members of any one denomination were in or near a certain place or unit the problem of religious ministration would be easy, simple, and most effective." Once informed about the activation of a Greek battalion, Arnold contacted Greek Orthodox archbishop Athenagoras and asked him to send one of his best priests immediately.[24] The lone Greek Orthodox chaplain represented a slight improvement in terms of religious representation, but his presence could not overcome the reality that the religion of most Orthodox men remained concealed by a dog tag that identified them as either Protestant or Catholic.

In acquiring a chaplain, the Greek Orthodox fared better than Buddhists, who were predominantly Japanese American men serving in the Japanese American 100th Battalion and the 442nd Regimental Combat Team. In 1943, the commanding general of the Third Army, which oversaw the 442nd's training at Camp Shelby, Mississippi, requested a Buddhist chaplain from the chief of chaplains.[25] Initially, Chief of Chaplains William Arnold attempted to fulfill his request. The army had commissioned Japanese American Christian chaplains but had few contacts in the Buddhist community. Arnold informed Bishop Matsukahe, the leader of the Buddhist Mission of North America, that the army would "be pleased to consider a clergyman of your faith who meets the eligibility standards" and noted that "a clergyman appointed from your faith will be assigned to a unit the majority of whose members are Buddhists."[26] Unlike other applicants, the priest endorsed by the Buddhist Mission would have to clear military intelligence, but defective vision, rather than strained loyalty, thwarted his candidacy. Around the same time, the Baptist and Methodist chaplains assigned to the 442nd asserted that no Buddhist chaplain was necessary because "the [Buddhist] men were coming to them for advice."[27] William Arnold thus acknowledged that his office had not commissioned a Buddhist chaplain, but "because of advice from various sources it seems best that none should be."[28] When pressed about the need for a Buddhist chaplain, Arnold's office responded that "the preponderance of religious adherents are Christians," though no formal census had been taken and no set threshold established.[29] While the chaplaincy accepted Japanese American Christians as chaplains, it made no room for their Buddhist counterparts.

After the war ended and the patriotic contributions of Japanese Americans became evident, American Buddhists pursued state recognition once more. In the late 1940s, about one hundred thousand petitioners, mostly civilians living in Hawaii or California, tried to amend the religious categories available on dog tags yet again by asking for a Buddhist designation. The organizers of the petition drive, the National Young Buddhists, also enlisted the aid of local, state, and national political leaders to support their effort. Yet the military proved intransigent.

The climate of opinion was changing, however. Several local political leaders added their voices to the clamor for change. The governor of Hawaii, then a U.S. territory, championed the cause, noting that a large percentage of Hawaiian soldiers were Buddhist. From Fresno, John L. E. Collier informed the Western Young Buddhist League "the faith that is so desired by the service men should be recognized, whether it be Protestant, Catholic, Jewish, Buddhist, Mohammedan or any other faith." From Los Angeles, Republican assemblyman Harold Levering, most famous for instituting a loyalty oath for all California state employees, endorsed the effort on the grounds of equity. If Protestants, Catholics, and Jews had letters of their own, he asserted, so should Buddhists and members of other religious denominations. "To do otherwise," he wrote, "is contrary to the American tradition for which so many Americans have given their lives."[30] Together, each letter and each signature on the petition made two interrelated claims: Buddhism was its own religion, and, as such, it deserved recognition from the military as a valid American religious choice.

Advocates for a Buddhist B understood the importance of dog tags as fundamental to the appropriate handling of battle deaths. The Honolulu Board of Supervisors, for example, recognized that many Hawaiian Buddhists had died for the United States during World War II. But because "these men were classified as Protestants by the Armed Forces," they "were accorded final burial rites which were not in accordance with their religious affiliation."[31] This was unnecessary given that the military bureaucracy instituted procedures to ensure that the bodies of Jewish soldiers repatriated after the war were not "deprived of burial according to rites of their faith . . . because men really Jewish in faith have not indicated the fact for fear of cruel treatment in the case of capture." Instead, they followed a procedure set up by the Jewish Welfare Board to allow next of kin to make affidavits about the correct faith and thus correct burial practice.[32] Had Buddhists been able to register their religious identities, they could have been buried in accordance with their faith as well.

Despite local and state legislative endorsement in favor of a Buddhist classification, the petition proved ineffective. Resistance arose from multiple quarters, some inspired by racially inflected religious prejudice, some focused on practical repercussions, but none swayed by the rhetoric of unity and freedom common to the era's emphasis on "the American way."[33] Reserve chaplain Sydney Croft opposed all efforts made by Buddhists to assert their religious identity in the armed forces, whether by lobbying for chaplains or requesting a dog tag designation. From his perch as the rector of an Episcopalian church in Hawaii, he asserted that "Buddhism has degenerated;

if it was a religion in the past, it is no longer a religion insofar as the draft-age group is concerned." Claiming inside information from conversations with a World War II Japanese American Congregationalist chaplain, Croft made plain his disdain for Buddhism. According to him, the religion was a "sect . . . dominated by that element of the Japanese population which seeks to perpetuate their old-country customs and practices which are unAmerican and inimical to our American way of life." At the same time, and consistent with the language of unity central to the American way, Croft carefully emphasized that his objections had absolutely no basis in race: "I am willingly serving all races of people in my work here, and we live harmoniously together and worship together . . . there has never been any question of racial discrimination."[34] Concerned with the propagation of "alien customs and practices" in an area where the Japanese and Caucasian populations were evenly matched, Croft rejected Buddhism as an American religion for reasons both racial and religious. In the Japanese American war experience, he saw a history of Christian religious revival rather than Buddhist persecution. Croft viewed Buddhism as a threat because it imperiled the expansion of his Christian community by competing with the church for members. And while Croft stood alone in his overt denunciation of Buddhism, he was part of a chorus of naysayers who refused to permit (primarily Japanese American) Buddhists to be classified as Buddhists.

Unlike Croft, most opponents of Buddhist designations on dog tags objected on supposedly pragmatic grounds. The Red Cross Home Service Committee, for example, proposed the additional classification of O for "Other." They claimed that they could not endorse B for Buddhist because B could also stand for Bahaism.[35] The Armed Forces Chaplains Board adopted this logic and stretched it to a more extreme conclusion. The problem, they alleged, with adding a new religious designation to dog tags was a practical one—it would result in "endless confusion" as "every minute fraction of a percent claiming distinct worship, or even simply belief in God, would request their own religious symbol. The letter 'B' could be interpreted as Baptist; it could mean 'Believer' for anyone who believes in God; or, under the duress of battle, it could be misread as blood type."[36] Doubtful as this reasoning was—certainly J could mean Jehovah's Witness or C could indicate the Christian Missionary Alliance, while P could refer to Presbyterians—it continued to inform military policy.

Addressing the mismatch between the categories into which the military compartmentalized its personnel and the religious identities lived by real soldiers presented a practical and ideological challenge. Luther Miller, the Episcopalian chief of chaplains, explained that it was unnecessary to change protocol because religious identification on dog tags was optional, not mandatory. As a result, he argued, limiting military personnel to three religious classifications did not violate individual rights or religious freedom. It simply reduced confusion. Allowing additional markers of religious affiliation, he warned, could lead approximately 250 denominations to seek particular notations on identification tags. Indeed, the 1936 Census of Religious Bodies enumerated 256 distinct denominations. Moreover, as of 1945, the secretary of war set chaplaincy quotas that encompassed thirty-eight religious groups (with at least one hundred thousand adherents) and an additional thirty-two denominations classified as "miscellaneous" (whose numbers likely did not reach one hundred thousand members). In other words, his office recognized seventy separate religious entities. Given an opportunity to select a specific religious identification, military personnel would probably draw on a more extensive range than the military recognized for chaplains. Whether they would have selected "Baptist" or one of the twenty-five types of Baptists enumerated in the census is unclear.[37]

Miller was not wrong to expect a surge in religious groups seeking specificity. Other religious groups squirmed under the ill-fitting dog tag P and sought more precise labels. During World War II, the Eastern Orthodox campaigned for a classification distinct from either Protestant or Catholic. In the late 1940s, as the Buddhist campaign for recognition gained momentum, the Greek Orthodox again pled their case. The "indiscriminate" designations as either Protestants or Catholics made no sense, according to Greek Orthodox leaders, because "the Orthodox Faith is practically as large as the Jewish Faith which is recognized by the proper agency as a principal denomination."[38] If numerical strength served as the determining factor in American religious classification, then the Red Cross's suggestion of O ought to refer to "Orthodox," not just "Others." Yet these efforts to drum up support for new religious designations failed to gain traction for reasons J. Willard Marriott, the head of the LDS Military Relations Committee, understood quite clearly. "Even though we do not consider ourselves Protestant, and could convince them of our distinctive position, it would be very difficult for the War Department to separate us from the smaller Christian denominations and put us in a separate category," he wrote to Mormon elders. "If they did this for our Church, it would have the same request from Christian Scientists, Southern Baptists, United Brethren and many other minority groups."[39] In trying to broadly classify, rather than splinter, American religion, the military declined to reconcile itself to the diversity of American religious life.

The push for an Orthodox O lagged behind the contest over the Buddhist B, but both groups succeeded in acquiring a new letter of sorts. In January 1949, Army Chief of Chaplains Miller recommended a new option, an X for "those soldiers whose religious affiliations does not fit any of the three principal denominations." Soldiers who elected the X could also wear another piece of stamped metal indicating their particular faith. The wire story reported that "young Buddhists in Hawaii and on the Pacific coast" asked "that a 'B' for Buddhist be provided on the tags of soldiers of Buddhist faith" and for the requisition of Buddhist chaplains.[40] But these requests went unfulfilled, yielding instead a rather nonspecific X. The X represented an imperfect compromise at best. It conceded the presence of religious faiths that did not conform to the blueprint of tri-faith America while refusing to acknowledge them as distinguishable (or perhaps even recognizable) American religions.

By the early 1950s, additional religious groups that fell outside the Protestant-Catholic-Jewish phalanx requested recognition from a variety of state representatives. During the 1952 presidential campaign, American Muslims wrote to General Dwight D. Eisenhower asking for his assistance in marking Islam on dog tags. He demurred, insisting he could do little to help, though he left open the possibility that as president he might be able to enact change.[41] But when the Romanian Orthodox Church asked for an Orthodox notation in 1955, President Eisenhower followed the lead of the military he commanded: "The Administration feels . . . that the religious classification letters on identification tags can serve the recognized purpose only if restricted to broad designation categories." That plenty of religious groups sought more than an uninformative X was immaterial. Indeed, the president's staff couched the request as trivial, concluding that no letter "would accord the Eastern Orthodox faith any greater recognition than it now enjoys, both in this country and throughout the world."[42] Yet the endorsement of the American state was not insignificant to either the church or the state. Regardless of whether an Orthodox indication on a dog tag would have increased public awareness of the church, the state's imprimatur would have undoubtedly breached the fiction of tri-faith America celebrated at mid-century. Acknowledging the presence of religious Americans outside this triptych interfered with the projection of a unified national identity that was harnessed to the acceptable diversity of three religious traditions.[43] Bureaucratic inertia in the face of religious complexity thus perpetuated a truncated and simplified religious order.

Nevertheless, over time, the petitions wore down the military. First, in 1954, the military acceded to the Jewish request to use J, rather than H, on their dog tags.[44] Larger and more significant changes followed. In 1955, the *New York Times* reported in a small, three-paragraph story that "every soldier may now have his particular religious denomination stamped on his identification tag." In its rendering, the change came about as a result of Greek Orthodox protest and Army Chief of Chaplains Patrick H. Ryan (Catholic) recommending "that any and all denominations be listed."[45] The Assemblies of God weekly, the *Pentecostal Evangel*, offered a different interpretation when it announced that "in [the] future, the name of the Protestant denomination will be shown."[46] For the Pentecostals, the value of this change had little to do with the Eastern Orthodox or Buddhist efforts to acquire a dog tag initial of their own; rather, the publication celebrated the opportunity for

Protestant servicemen to declare their specific denomination apart from a mass of undifferentiated Protestants. While the new dog tag policies acknowledged the existence of non-Protestant Americans formerly construed as Protestant, they also represented a victory for evangelicals who stood outside the boundaries of mainline Protestantism.

A NEW AMERICAN RELIGIOUS ORDER?

In November 1962, Army Regulations 606-5 made this policy change official by stipulating that religious preferences had to be spelled out on dog tags, thereby lifting the constraints caused by the use of initials.[47] The pluralization of dog tags signaled that the military acknowledged religious diversity in its midst and extended recognition even to atheists and agnostics. Although the shift to stamping dog tags with the terms *Buddhist* or *Assemblies of God, Eastern Orthodox* or *Mormon* was hardly a radical move, the policy expanded the religious accommodations offered to American military personnel. At the same time, this democratization shifted the responsibility for categorization from the state to the soldier. By placing the power of classification and identification in the hands of individual servicemen, the military also eliminated the validation that accompanied a list of officially sanctioned religious identities. Rather than legitimize Buddhists and the Eastern Orthodox as faith groups unto themselves, the new procedures individualized the naming of religions. For those concerned about death and burials, this was certainly a relief because tailored funerals became easier and more viable. For those seeking state sanction or recognition, the dog tag no longer sufficed as evidence.

Empowering individuals to proclaim their faith was meaningful and fulfilled the promise of granting all Americans access to the rituals of their particular religion or denomination. It also enabled the nonreligious to claim atheism and agnosticism and, in the late twentieth century, allowed personnel to select Wicca and Humanism as their religious preference. But in the mid-twentieth century, what was good for discrete souls was not necessarily good for the group writ large, as the change cost minority religious groups such as Buddhists and the Eastern Orthodox de facto state recognition. The perceived value of this sacrifice was neither automatic nor clear, for the abandonment of the tri-faith ideal on dog tags masked the markers of power and privilege that state sanction had provided. Inasmuch as new dog tags underscored the broad range of American religious options, they also signaled a diffusion of American believers. By making the options of religious self-identification infinite, the state simultaneously limited opportunities for group recognition and mobilization.

NOTES

1. John Monahan to Edward L. Trett, 22 January 1944, RG 247 (1920–1945), box 181, folder 211 (Jewish Chaplains), National Archives and Records Administration, College Park, MD (hereafter cited as NARA II).

2. "L.D.S. Chaplain Wins Praise, Work of Lt. Col. Curtis on Attu is Commended," 3 June 1944, in CR 33 2, scrapbook 1944–45, Servicemen's Committee, Church History Library, Salt Lake City, UT (hereafter cited as LDS-CHL).

3. In the military, the Protestant-Catholic-Jewish view of American religion began in World War I. See Ronit Y. Stahl, "God, War, and Politics: The American Military Chaplaincy and the Making of a Multi-Religious Nation" (PhD diss., University of Michigan, 2014), 1–72.

4. David McCormick, "Inventing Military Dog Tags," *America's Civil War* 25, no. 2 (May 2012): 56–59; Drew Gilpin Faust, *This Republic of Suffering: Death and the American Civil War* (New York: Vintage, 2008), 121; War Department General Order No. 204, 20 December 1906; United States Quartermaster Corps, *Price List of Clothing and Equipage* (Washington, DC: Government Printing Office, 1917).

5. First Service Corps, "Religious Coverage in Sickness and Death for Members of the Armed Forces in Posts, Camps, and Stations," supplement to October 1943, 31 January 1944; "Religious Requirements of Various Denominations in Second Army Organization," 27 March 1944, RG 247 (1920–1945), box 200, folder 293 (Funerals and Burials, vol. 2), NARA II.

6. Luther D. Miller to Kenneth D. Johnson, Memorandum for the Secretary of War re: Letter from Dr. Arthur J. Todd dated 22 April 1947, 12 June 1947, RG 247 (1946–1948), box 354, 080 (Christian Science), NARA II.

7. On the World War I origins of the tri-faith nation, see Stahl, "God, War, and Politics."

8. Kenneth C. Martin to Mrs. Shapiro, 9 October 1944, I-249, box 10, folder 60, American Jewish Historical Society, New York, NY (hereafter cited as AJHS).

9. "Brief Rituals: For Emergency Use by Laymen on the Field of Battle," 1, RG 247 (1920–1945), box 262, folder 350.001 (Lectures, vol. 3), NARA II.

10. On the stymied efforts of collecting religious data, see Kevin Schultz, "Religion as Identity in Postwar America: The Last Serious Attempt to Put a Question on Religion in the United States Census," *Journal of American History* 93, no. 2 (September 2006): 359–84.

11. Harold B. Lee to Gustave A. Iverson, 8 June 1944, quoted in Joseph Boone, "The Roles of the Church of Jesus Christ of Latter-day Saints I Relation to the United States Military" (PhD diss., Brigham Young University, 1975), 571.

12. Lyman C. Berrett, interviewed by Richard Maher, 24 October 1974, 13, Charles Redd Center for Western Studies/LDS Chaplains Oral History Project, MS-17096, LDS-CHL.

13. David de Sola Pool to Aryeh Lev, 2 January 1942, RG 247 (1920–1945), box 72, folder 080 (JWB, vol. 2), NARA II. On the state's racial categorization of Jews, see Eric Goldstein, "Contesting the Categories: Jews and Government Racial Classification in the United States," *Jewish History* 19, no. 1 (2005): 79–107.

14. Samuel Silver to Philip Bernstein, 31 March 1944, and Isaac Toubin to Samuel Silver, 5 April 1944, I-249, box 10, folder 59, AJHS.

15. Allen Sinsheimer to Solomon Freehof, 15 April 1943, I-249, box 10, folder 52, AJHS.

16. Charles S. Freedman to Philip S. Bernstein, 28 April 1944, I-249, box 10, folder 52, AJHS.

17. Lyman C. Berrett, interviewed by Richard Maher, 24 October 1974, 14.

18. William R. Arnold to Kenneth C. Martin, 9 January 1945, I-249, box 10, folder 60, AJHS.

19. Kenneth C. Martin to William R. Arnold, 11 February 1945, I-249, box 10, folder 60, AJHS.

20. When the Congregational and Christian Churches disclosed that a Chinese American pastor wanted to become a chaplain, the Office of the Chief of Chaplains advised the group that "the only place we could use a Chinese pastor would be with a Chinese unit. To the best of our knowledge and belief, the organization of Chinese units in our Army is not contemplated. Chinese in the service are in regular units of other Americans. Therefore, we have no requisitions for Chinese chaplains." Walter Zimmerman to Frederick Fagley, 15 October 1943,

RG 247 (1920–1945), box 64, folder 080 (Congregational and Christian Churches, vol. 2), NARA II.

21. John Telep to William Arnold, 22 October 1942, RG 247 (1920–1945), box 85, folder 080 (Russian Orthodox), NARA II; William Arnold to J. Warren Albinson, 29 November 1943, RG 247 (1920–1945), box 70, folder 080 (Greek Orthodox), NARA II.

22. Antony Bashir to Franklin D. Roosevelt, 1 April 1942, RG 247 (1920–1945), box 70, folder 080 (Greek Orthodox), NARA II.

23. For an explanation of how states "see" and impose their vision to create administrative order, see James Scott, *Seeing Like a State: How Certain Schemes to Improve the Human Condition Have Failed* (New Haven, CT: Yale University Press, 1999).

24. William Arnold to Cyril A. W. Johnson, 5 March 1942, RG 247 (1920–1945), box 85, folder 080 (Russian Orthodox); William Arnold to Archbishop Athenagoras, 16 February 1943, RG 247 (1920–1945), box 70, folder 080 (Greek Orthodox), NARA II.

25. William Arnold to William Scobey, 10 June 1943, RG 247 (1920–1945), box 60, folder 080 (Buddhist), NARA II.

26. William Arnold to Bishop Matsukahe, 24 March 1943, RG 247 (1920–1945), box 60, folder 080 (Buddhist), NARA II. The Buddhist Mission in North America (BMNA) represented the confluence of Japanese migration to the United States and the introduction of Buddhism to Americans at the 1893 World Parliament of Religion. In the 1920s, the BMNA began to Anglicize much of its religious terminology, which is when religious leaders became known as ministers, priests, and bishops. During World War II, about 55 percent of interned Japanese Americans were Buddhist, the majority of which affiliated with the BMNA; in 1944, a group at the Topaz relocation center suggested changing the religion's name to the Buddhist Church of America to emphasize their Americanness. Richard H. Seager, *Buddhism in America* (New York: Columbia University Press, 1999), 51–59.

27. William Scobey to William Arnold, 7 June 1943, RG 247 (1920–1945), box 60, folder 080 (Buddhist), NARA II.

28. William Arnold to William Scobey, 8 July 1943, RG 247 (Security Classified General Correspondence 1941–48), box 1, folder 080 (Societies and Church Organizations), NARA II.

29. Harry Lee Virden, 18 August 1943, RG 247 (1920–1945), box 60, folder 080 (Buddhist), NARA II.

30. Ingram Stainbeck to Ralph Honda, Kenji Onodera, Shiro Kashiwa, 26 October 1948; John L. E. Collier to Ryu Munekata, 8 November 1948; Harold Levering to National Young Buddhists, 3 December 1948, RG 247 (1946–1948), box 466, NARA II.

31. "Resolution by the Board of Supervisors of the City and County of Honolulu," 1948, RG 247 (1946–1948), box 466, NARA II.

32. Office of the Chief of Chaplains to the Quartermaster General, 20 August 1946, RG 247 (1946–1948), box 406, folder 293 (Funerals & Burials, vol. 5), NARA II.

33. On the construction of "the American way," see Wendy Wall, *Inventing the "American Way": The Politics of Consensus from the New Deal to the Civil Rights Movement* (New York: Oxford University Press, 2008).

34. Sydney Croft to Luther D. Miller, 20 November 1948; Sydney Croft to James Forrestal, 21 September 1948, RG 247 (1946–1948), box 354, folder 080 (Buddhist), NARA II.

35. Ruth Blakey to Mike Iwatsubo, 17 November 1948, RG 247 (1946–1948), box 466, folder 080 (Buddhist), NARA II.

36. The Chaplain Board to the Office of the Chief of Chaplains, 22 October 1948, RG 247 (1946–1948), box 384, folder 080 (Buddhist), NARA II.

37. Luther D. Miller to Leonard Bloom, 28 September 1948, RG 247 (1946–1948), box 384, folder 080 (Buddhist), NARA II; "Religious Bodies: 1936, Volume I, Summary and Detailed Tables" (Washington: Government Printing Office, 1941); "Data Sheet: Quotas for Chaplains," 1 May 1945, RG 220, box 8, folder 3a, Truman Presidential Library, Independence, MO.

38. Peter Chumbris to Luther D. Miller, 8 January 1948, RG 247 (1949–1950), box 471, 080 (Greek Orthodox), NARA II.

39. J. Willard Marriott to Harold B. Lee and Mark E. Petersen, 23 April 1947, quoted in Boone, "The Roles of the Church of Jesus Christ of Latter-day Saints," 571.

40. "Chief Chaplain Asks 'X' Designation on Army's 'Dog Tags,'" *Chicago Tribune*, 7 January 1949.

41. Abdallah Ingram to Dwight D. Eisenhower, 29 July 1952, Papers as President of the U.S., 1953–1961 (White House Central Files), General File, box 619, folder OF 144B-4, Eisenhower Presidential Library (hereafter cited as DDE).

42. Assistant to the President to the Bishop of the Romanian Orthodox Episcopate of America, 2 June 1955, Papers as President of the U.S., 1953–1961 (White House Central Files), General File, box 691, folder OF 118G, DDE.

43. Three decades later, the Orthodox were still petitioning "to be considered and listed as a fourth major religious body," at which point the Armed Forces Chaplain Board "approve[d] the recommendation for the use of the word 'distinctive' instead of the word 'major' when addressing the matter of religious bodies or faith groups. It was noted that 'distinctive' could be used with all faith groups." AFCB Minutes, 4 June 1975 in AFCB Minutes 1974–76, Ft. Jackson Navy Chaplain Corps Archives, Columbia, SC.

44. Deborah Dash Moore, "Jewish GIs and the Creation of the Judeo-Christian Tradition," *Religion and American Culture* 8, no. 1 (Winter 2008): 52n39.

45. "Army 'Dog Tags' to List G.I.'s Choice of Religion," *New York Times*, 28 July 1955.

46. "New Ruling on 'Dog Tags,'" *Pentecostal Evangel*, 28 August 1955.

47. Chief of Chaplains Frank A. Tobey Circular Letter, 14 August 1959, RG 247 (1954–1962), box 561, folder 312.1 (Monthly Letters, 1959), NARA II; Army Regulations 606-5, Section XII, 78d, November 1962.

Part V

Ecumenism's Paradoxes: Religious Dissent and the Redefinition of the Modern Religious Mainstream

Chapter Fourteen

"This Is a Mighty Warfare That We Are Engaged In"

Pentecostals in Early Twentieth-Century New England

Evelyn Savidge Sterne

In 1897, a group of earnest evangelicals who called themselves the First Fruit Harvesters formed a worship community in Rumney, New Hampshire. Led by Joel Adams Wright, a religious seeker who had started his journey as a Baptist minister, the Harvesters sought to re-create the purity of the early Christian church by rejecting denominational ties, following strict standards of behavior, and seeking out "gifts of the Spirit" such as faith healing and speaking in tongues. The Harvesters' choices tested the limits of New England's tradition of religious tolerance as it had developed during the eighteenth and nineteenth centuries. Not only did they worship in ways some found unusual and unsettling, but they also alienated other Christians by criticizing ordinary ministers as "hirelings," castigating popular traditions such as parish baked bean suppers, and denouncing a bewildering range of "vices" that ranged from eating white bread to reading novels. Despite the Harvesters' unconventional behaviors, they were generally tolerated in a region that valued individual religious expression and experimentation. Yet efforts to spread their "gifts of the Spirit" sometimes inspired harassment and violence. In one defining instance, the residents of Jefferson, New Hampshire, dynamited the Harvesters' chapel and ran them out of town.

The extent to which New Englanders tolerated these "Holy Rollers," as critics called groups such as the Harvesters, points to the vibrant, yet contested, nature of religious freedom in modern America. The Harvesters offer an intriguing case study of a dynamic inherent in many contests over religious freedom: the struggle by illiberal religious minorities to carve out cultu-

227

ral space within a liberalizing society. Mass industrialization and urbanization disrupted late nineteenth-century community life, challenged traditional
ideas about gender and sexuality, and introduced tempting new secular entertainments such as films and dance halls. Many rural and small-town
Americans, and not a few city dwellers, resisted such changes and held on to
older ways of living and worshiping. Some of these holdouts were evangelical Protestants who countered modern patterns of behavior by affirming the
Bible as a source of fundamental moral truths that could guide individuals
and communities through the vicissitudes of modern life. Those who embraced the radical form of evangelicalism known as Pentecostalism, as the
Harvesters did, also rejected Darwinian principles of biological evolution
and expressed skepticism about the new class of credentialed social scientists, preferring intense forms of spirituality that defied scientific methods
and measurable outcomes.

Pentecostals share the evangelical belief in a born-again conversion but
go further, arguing that true Christians undergo a second experience called
"baptism in the Holy Spirit," whereby they receive gifts such as divine healing, prophecy, and speaking in tongues (also known as glossolalia). The
craving for these gifts forms part of a deeper longing to recapture the intensity of early Christianity. Charles Fox Parham, at whose Kansas Bible school
students started to speak in tongues in 1901, is considered the founder of
modern American Pentecostalism, but it was William Seymour, briefly one
of his students, who popularized the movement. Seymour, an itinerant
African American preacher, started a mission in Los Angeles in 1906. Before
long he had launched a full-fledged revival marked by interracial crowds,
faith healings, and speaking in tongues. The Azusa Street Revival continued
until 1909, putting Pentecostalism on the map as a major destination for
religious seekers. In the following century, more than three hundred Pentecostal denominations were established in the United States, with the two
largest claiming a combined membership of nearly nine million. [1]

The extraordinary success of Pentecostalism, which combines ecstatic
spiritual experience with strict standards of behavior, testifies to the ability of
illiberal religious movements to thrive in a liberalizing society, carving out
space in which to exercise their religion. Yet, as the Harvesters' experiences
demonstrate, the history of Pentecostalism has hardly been devoid of conflict. Like the Jehovah's Witnesses whom Shawn Peters discusses in chapter
15, the Harvesters employed a confrontational form of evangelism, a caustic
verbal warfare against public institutions and leaders, that unsettled many
communities and precipitated concerns about public order. Reaction to the
Harvesters also took disorderly and even violent forms, highlighting how
susceptible liberal societies are to bouts of illiberalism and intolerance. The
Harvesters' story, then, shows that when religious exercise provokes and

offends, as it has periodically throughout American history, otherwise tolerant attitudes can give way to intolerant practices.

Many treatments of twentieth-century evangelicalism overlook its presence in New England, a region better known as the home of liberal Protestants and ethnic Catholics. Evangelicalism had been popular in nineteenth-
century New England when it was linked to liberal reform movements such
as abolitionism or women's suffrage. But according to most authoritative
accounts, evangelicalism had declined in the region by the early 1900s, as it
assumed a more conservative bent, rejecting progressive interpretations of
the Bible, forbidding amusements such as film and radio, and opposing the
teaching of evolution. Yet the First Fruit Harvesters, as well as the group's
long-lived successor the New England Fellowship and a plethora of like-
minded local groups, call attention to a vibrant evangelical presence in the
region. When we take into account their stories, we are able to see that
conservative religious minorities could both thrive and endure intolerance—
even persecution—in the generally liberal climate of New England.[2]

JOEL ADAMS WRIGHT AND NEW ENGLAND'S FLUID RELIGIOUS LANDSCAPE

The life of Harvesters' founder Joel Adams Wright illustrates the range of
options available to a religious seeker in New England. Wright was born into
a farming family in 1853 and raised in East Piermont, New Hampshire. He
had strong religious leanings from an extraordinarily young age but resisted
the evangelical call until he suffered a life-threatening case of pneumonia at
age twenty-five. As he lay in bed, convinced he was dying, he had a vision he
later described as follows: "The Holy Spirit carried me . . . many miles across
the country and opened up before me the real pit of hell. I saw the flames, the
smoke as it came vomiting out of that horrid pit." From here he was trans-
ported to the banks of the Jordan River, where he saw "a mansion of the
blest" whose doors were closed to him. At this point Wright surrendered to
God, saying, "You have conquered, I give it up," and he "fell into a peaceful
sleep to awake in a new world, everything seem[ed] changed about me, not
only was I saved but healed."[3]

Thus began Wright's life as a converted Christian, but it took the deaths
of his two oldest sons and his mother to inspire him to preach his first sermon
seven years later. In 1888, he was ordained a Free Will Baptist minister and
embarked upon the demanding life of a father, farmer, preacher, and itinerant
evangelist. Four years later he moved to the Free Methodist Church because
of its greater commitment to a theology known as Holiness. Holiness, a
precursor to Pentecostalism, taught that every Christian had the potential to
live a sinless life, urged believers to live according to strict moral standards,

and emphasized the importance of baptism in the Spirit.[4] Wright soon received his first "gifts of the Spirit." At one revival, he recalled, "Something inside of me seemed to be rolling up toward my throat. I opened my mouth and the Holy Ghost shouted through me and I was free." The Holy Ghost, Wright claimed, also cured him of ulcers and enabled him to heal others, a heady power he described as "strong currents of electricity" passing through his arms. As Wright received these spiritual gifts, he became convinced he could re-create the church as Christ had intended it by forming a community of believers without denominational ties. As he later wrote in an informal memoir, "Whom the Son makes free, is free, with all handles knocked off. I am simply free in Christ." He left the Free Methodists and, in the most important decision of his life, founded the First Fruit Harvesters in 1897.[5]

Wright's path from converted Christian to Baptist minister to Methodist preacher and finally religious innovator illustrates the vitality of religious experience and the permeability of religious borders in nineteenth-century America. It also reflects the legacy of the Second Great Awakening, the religious revivals that emboldened countless believers and spawned groups as diverse as the Seventh-day Adventists, the Oneida Perfectionists, and the Church of Jesus Christ of Latter-day Saints (Mormons). Late nineteenth-century New England was still generating new modes of faith and worship such as the Christian Science movement. At a time when Americans were used to seeing religious experiments come and go, the birth of a small worship community in rural New Hampshire attracted little attention. In many ways, this already was a familiar story.

PREPARING FOR WARFARE: THE FIRST FRUIT HARVESTERS

The Harvesters' unusual name, which apparently came to Wright in a vision, was derived from a passage in Leviticus: "Ye shall bring a sheaf of the first fruits of your harvest" (Lev. 23:10).[6] Hoping to reap that harvest, Wright bought a house and 135 acres of forest and farmland in Rumney, a town in Grafton County in central New Hampshire whose train depot would give his missionaries access to distant settlements. He filled the home with Christians who shared his commitment to spreading the gospel. For the first year the Harvesters lived as a commune, sharing living space and possessions, but they soon tired of the experiment and moved into separate homes on the property, assembling regularly for prayer meetings and Bible study.[7]

The Harvesters were neither a church nor a denomination, but rather a community of evangelists. As Wright put it, "God has planted a power house here and an armory, and every saint can . . . learn the mode of warfare." Once trained, these "Christian workers," as they called themselves, fanned out across New England, a region they considered corrupted by Unitarians and

Roman Catholics. The Harvesters spread the word by knocking on doors and holding tent meetings year-round in any community that would have them—staying anywhere from a few days to six months, depending on the response. If a revival went well, they would establish a permanent chapel run by either a Harvester or a local recruit. The high point of their annual calendar was the camp meeting held in Rumney every August.[8]

Like many early Pentecostals, the Harvesters were white, old-stock, working- and middle-class folks, and their respectability and ability to blend into the Yankee demographic of northern New England no doubt softened the reaction against them.[9] Their monthly organ, the *Sheaf of the First Fruits*, tended to identify with the poor and downtrodden, but some Harvesters were prominent members of their communities. Illustrating what historian Grant Wacker calls the "productive tension" between "the primitive and the pragmatic" impulses in American Pentecostalism, Wright never accepted a salary for his ministry, although he did give up farming for a successful career as a real estate agent.[10] Some Harvesters worried about whether Wright could "serve God and mammon." He managed to do both, and his material success both helped to keep the community running and bolstered its claim to respectability.

If the Harvesters' social standing helped them blend into their host communities, their strict lifestyle clearly set them apart. This separation in turn helped to unite them internally even as it induced friction with outsiders. In the first decades of the twentieth century, many Americans (especially those who flocked to the growing cities) were enjoying new amusements, like movies and amusement parks, and new social freedoms, such as unchaperoned dates and dances. By contrast, the Harvesters and other Pentecostal groups functioned as a countercultural minority, continually resisting the nation's liberalizing tendencies. They avoided the same vices many contemporaries condemned, such as liquor, lying, stealing, swearing, fornication, adultery, and divorce. They also frowned on indulgences that would have seemed innocuous to most: white bread, pork, shellfish, tea, and coffee; movies, radio, theater, and novels; bobbed hair and bathing suits; gossip and flirting; and tobacco (according to one *Sheaf* contributor, "A tobacco spittoon is the devil's collection box"[11]). The Harvesters also shunned the "unbiblical" holiday of Christmas, a position shared by Jehovah's Witnesses but very much out of fashion in a society that had embraced Christmas as a major religious and commercial holiday. The life of "saints," as the Harvesters called themselves, was not easy, and living as saints made their relationship to the outside world perpetually difficult.

Being a Harvester also meant being prepared to take a vow of poverty, another commitment that set the group apart in a capitalist society brimming with strivers. Even in the sleepy farm towns of northern New England, residents embraced a "Protestant work ethic" that valued hard work and upward mobility. Wright's real estate business notwithstanding, he was committed to the concept of "faith ministry," taking no salary other than voluntary donations (sometimes called "love gifts") and trusting in God to provide the rest. His missionaries often practiced the "return fare test," in which they would embark upon an evangelistic trip without money to get home and trust that the funds would appear. The *Sheaf* is filled with accounts of itinerant preachers receiving such miraculous provisions, gifts from God that belied capitalist norms.[12]

The Harvesters' commitment to a strict lifestyle united them internally, yet complicated their relationships with outsiders. Controversies abounded. "We purpose to be a pure people and though few in numbers it is our privilege to be clean," the *Sheaf* proclaimed in April 1905. Yet even as the Harvesters were proud to be a select minority, they acknowledged that some outsiders saw them as "extreme fanatics" and charged them with "tearing down the church of God." The Harvesters' inflexible positions limited their outreach. Their refusal to work with missionaries who had remarried after divorce, for example, caused problems when seeking to cooperate with groups that had looser policies. So did their condemnation of tobacco, which Wright admitted made him "very unpopular" in towns where respected preachers indulged in the habit. The evangelists' bitter opposition to Christmas must have made them particularly unwelcome. Excoriating the "professed church" for "whoring after this idolatrous practice under the garb of religion" was unlikely to win many converts. It is not surprising that Wright's informal memoir is peppered with stories of opponents seeking to discredit him with spurious rumors about his character and business dealings.[13]

New Englanders thus had good reason to both forbear and distrust the unusual group that formed in the foothills of New Hampshire's White Mountains in 1897. By the beginning of the twentieth century, the region prided itself on its individualism and spirit of tolerance. The Harvesters, moreover, were respectable Yankees who blended into the ethnic fabric of the farming communities where they evangelized. Yet they also embraced a very strict moral code and, crucially, were vocal in their criticism of those who did not. They aggressively evangelized and railed against existing churches and held conflicting ideas about capitalism—trusting God to provide for their needs while their leader ran a successful business. For the most part, the Harvesters' neighbors seem to have tolerated them without much complaint. In 1909, the *Plymouth Record*—the closest Rumney had to a local newspaper—described the evangelists as "people of good repute" who "have built up good homes here and attend to their own business."[14] But as the Harvesters' worship practices became more unusual, some New Englanders were unnerved.

"A GREAT SEPARATOR": SPEAKING IN TONGUES

The practice of speaking in tongues presented the Harvesters with both their greatest opportunity and most serious challenge. On the one hand, glossolalia was an extraordinary gift that satisfied their quest for spiritual fullness and reinforced their sense of being chosen people with a special mission. On the other, it created tensions within their own ranks, alienated outsiders who found the practice too outlandish, and, in one extreme case, sparked an explosive reaction. Many early Pentecostals agreed with Charles Fox Parham that only those who spoke in tongues were truly saved. This gift, they argued, was the distinguishing mark separating saints from mere seekers. Yet for many years Joel Wright rejected the practice. Having not received the gift himself, he repeatedly argued in his early *Sheaf* editorials that glossolalia was but one of many signs of having been anointed by the Holy Spirit.

During their August 1908 annual camp meeting, however, the Harvesters' position suddenly changed. First Wright, then almost fifty of his followers, claimed to receive the gift. As he described the event one month later, "I did not expect to speak in tongues, I only asked him to baptize me with Pentecostal fulness [*sic*]. This he did, and the Spirit immediately seizing my throat and tongue gave me to understand in a way that I cannot describe, that He would use them as he pleased and I soon found myself speaking in another tongue." Fellow Harvester J. Frank Burdick described his impression of Wright's experience: "The Spirit of the Lord came upon him in glorious power and he spoke in an unknown tongue." Coreligionist Alice Belle Garrigus offered this account: "The fight was fierce, but the Spirit gave the victory, and the leader of the work, Bro. J. A. Wright, went down among the pine needles, and received a precious baptism."[15]

Garrigus, a former Connecticut schoolteacher, had received the gift herself the previous summer at a camp meeting in Maine. The Harvesters had confronted the limits of their own internal commitment to tolerance when she returned, and they greeted her with suspicion. Now, however, they heralded her as a leader who could guide them toward spiritual fullness. Cora Barney—an active Harvester who had established a successful mission in Canaan, New Hampshire—asked Garrigus to pray with her, and after a nine-hour marathon, she, too, began speaking in tongues. Wright then asked Garrigus to do the same for his wife. When she achieved the desired result, it was an enormous relief for both spouses, who had agreed that otherwise they would need to separate. Sometimes the journey was a terrible ordeal. As Wright described one woman's experience, "It was a desperate struggle and an awful death, but God took her through." And the rewards were great. As Wright described one episode, "From the depths of my being a person that was not myself began to rise up in song . . . and such heavenly music I had never heard, as this almighty person . . . seemed to lift me up and let me float out into space." By the end of the meeting almost fifty Harvesters, virtually the entire group, were speaking (or claiming to speak) in tongues. They swiftly fanned out across northern New England, bringing their good news to potential converts. [16]

Here the Harvesters confronted the limits of New Englanders', and even their own followers', openness to religious experimentation. By late 1908, Wright reported more than thirty conversions and claimed that "nearly all of our local assemblies were the recipients in a measure, at least of this outpouring." Yet he also confessed that many supporters were "very much exercised . . . because of the thing which I have gone into." On an evangelistic trip in January 1909, he reported that out of sixty-three meetings he attended, "I was permitted to preach the gospel twenty-eight times in the fulness [sic] of Pentecost with comparatively little opposition." He summed up the situation as follows: "Some are still seeking, others desiring, others favorably inclined, while some are opposing. This is a great separator." Wright, once skeptical about tongues himself, now implored readers to keep an open mind, to reject an intellectualized form of worship for something more experiential. "Do not try to put this new wine of the kingdom into your old, dried bottles of theory. If you do, the bottles will be burst and the wine be spilled. Stop your theorizing. You know you are dry and lifeless. . . . Get down on your knees . . . to cry out to Him from the depths of your soul for the real Holy Spirit." [17]

"A MORE AGGRESSIVE WARFARE"

One town not ready for "the real Holy Spirit" was Jefferson, a New Hampshire resort town about seventy miles north of Rumney. In 1906, two Harvesters had started conducting missions there in tents, halls, and private homes. As crowds grew, the missionaries brought in more of the faithful to support their efforts. They also escalated their verbal attacks on the town's Baptist and Methodist churches, as well as popular secret societies such as the Freemasons and Odd Fellows. Tensions deepened when Wright, never one to avoid confrontation, arrived to take on churches he deemed "harlots" and rid the town of the "sect spirit coupled with that of secretism." As a reporter for the *Plymouth Record* noted, for every "convert they made they antagonized a great many churchgoers. They announced the imminent coming of Christ, and threatened with future torment all those who neglected the warning to repent. . . . By preaching against secret societies, church entertainments, etc., they aroused the ire of the community." [18]

Wright was not discouraged, however, and geared up for "a more aggressive warfare" against a town he compared to "Sodom and Gomorrah." [19] The intensity of his verbal attacks against the town's institutions suggests an ambivalence in his mission. He had formed the Harvesters as a group of missionaries committed to spreading the gospel across the region and the world. In this scenario, the Harvesters were a religious minority reaching out to reverse the liberalizing trends in American society. Yet the nature of Wright's preaching in Jefferson suggests his goal (at least in that town) had shifted from saving as many souls as possible to identifying a cadre of true believers to join his select group in renouncing a corrupt society and preparing for the final days. In the process, he and his missionaries came to be perceived as an acute source of social disruption.

By the summer of 1908, the Harvesters had attracted a small group of converts whom a reporter described as primarily female and representing "some of the best families in Jefferson." The latter observation is somewhat surprising, given the group's brash critiques of the town's secular and religious elite. According to a report in the *Coos County Democrat*, townspeople resented these verbal assaults but tolerated the Harvesters "because some of our good people were of them and no one cared to offend them." One of these "good people" was Ellen Davis, mother of a former selectman, who donated land upon which the group began to construct a permanent chapel. It was an unfortunate coincidence that the Harvesters started this work during the same summer they began to speak in tongues.[20]

Residents who had resented the Harvesters' preaching now grew concerned about their worship practices, conducted at the conclusion of nightly tent meetings open to the public. "The devotees come under some kind of a spell or enchantment and throw themselves prostrate upon the floor," a reporter observed. "Then they roll and turn and twist, sometimes uttering unintelligible gibberish which they style 'Speaking in tongues.'" Locals charged that the "Holy Rollers" embraced "practices conducive to low morals" and spent their meetings "shouting and working themselves into such a nervous frenzy that they finally collapse." These concerns may have reflected the fact that mixed companies of "as many as six or eight men and women [would] be upon the floor at a time, apparently perfectly unconscious to their condition or surroundings and . . . remain for more than two hours." Wright himself admitted to "some peculiar manifestations and demonstrations of the Spirit"—a term he frequently used to describe practices such as speaking in tongues—but he insisted the behavior was "nothing immodest or tending toward immorality."[21]

Most residents were unconvinced and remained deeply suspicious about the Harvesters' new embrace of glossolalia and its apparent implications for public order. "Many of those who were first attracted to their meetings couldn't stand this new feature and withdrew their moral and financial support and now very rarely attend," according to the *Coos County Democrat*. From the townspeople's perspective, speaking in tongues was "unintelligible babble which the brothers and sisters pretend to interpret," and the Harvesters were immoral people threatening "the happiness of homes." Their aggressive critiques of local churches and fraternal orders also threatened the town's most respected institutions and earned them some powerful enemies. By December 1908, the newspaper reported, the Harvesters had become so unpopular that their Jefferson assembly had been reduced to seven members. The Harvesters admitted that "the 'talking in tongues' has driven many from the fold" but denied that "they are over emotional and assert that all of their meetings are open to the public and that they were never guilty of degrading or demoralizing conduct."[22]

Even as the group dwindled in size, a pattern of harassment intensified. Wright charged opponents with both slander and physical threats such as rocks thrown, windows broken, and physical traps intended to trip his missionaries. "The rage of our enemies has known no bounds," he claimed. In Jefferson, he had witnessed "such persecution as I have not seen in the twenty-two years of my ministry. There are but a few who will stand this awful firey [sic] trial." It is ironic that Wright would object to such abuse, given his withering verbal attacks on the town's churches and secret societies. The fact that residents responded to the Harvesters' rhetorical onslaught with physical attacks suggests that they perceived the missionaries' verbal critiques and religious differences as a threat to law and order.[23]

The situation turned explosive—literally—the evening of December 8, when the Harvesters' brand-new chapel was destroyed. According to missionary reports, a "furious mob" of at least one hundred men bearing axes and battering rams had attacked and dynamited the newly dedicated structure. Jefferson residents refused to discuss the incident with reporters, other than to suggest that rats had caused the fire. As one reporter put it, "The good people of the town apparently retired early on [that] particular evening." They did, however, seize the momentum and circulate a "monster petition" asking the selectmen to run the sect out of town "on the ground that the public welfare demands such action." Wright responded in kind, garnering hundreds of signatures on his own petition, which asked that New Hampshire's governor investigate the incident and guarantee the Harvesters' religious freedom. A few local reporters sympathized with the group. Yet a lack of further coverage in local papers suggests that Wright's petition came to naught. Soon after, the Harvesters withdrew from Jefferson altogether.[24]

Ever resilient, Wright declared the disaster further proof the end times were near, and this sense of impending crisis made his work seem all the more urgent. "We are living in grand and awful times. The anti-christ [sic] spirit is ripening up things for the last final conflict," he declared. For the next two decades the *Sheaf* was filled with accounts of efforts—many successful—to spread the gospel and the gift of tongues around New England. As Wright wrote in 1913, "We believe that God had this in mind for us."[25]

SEPARATING FROM THE WORLD, TALKING TO GOD

Speaking in tongues empowered the Harvesters as individuals and a community even as it set them apart, alienating some potential converts (while no doubt attracting others) and sparking violent opposition on at least one occasion. When the gift descended upon an entire community, the experience could be religiously and socially transformative for some and deeply unsettling for others. As Garrigus described one meeting, "The glory filled the old barn. . . . Heavenly strains of music burst through yielded lips. Messages in many languages were given with interpretations—holy laughter and shouts of victory blended into one harmonious song of praise." For a group like the Harvesters, experiencing tongues together cemented the ties that bound them to one another, elevating already earnest feelings of devotion and reinforcing their identity as a select group with a special mission. As Wright stated, in language that mirrors the Puritans' "city upon a hill" rhetoric, "He has chosen us in the furnace of affliction that we might stand as a beacon light for the whole truth of God, more especially for New England, and also in a way for the whole world."[26]

At the same time, positioning themselves as a socially conservative minority in a modernizing nation put the Harvesters at risk of condemnation and even persecution by those they sought to convert. They were fortunate, however, to live in a region that valued individual religious expression, maintained a long (albeit contested) tradition of toleration, and conceived many new religious movements. This history no doubt facilitated the Harvesters' survival despite their condemnation of existing churches, secret societies, and social traditions that formed the backbones of the communities in which they evangelized. It also helped that the Harvesters were in good company. The early twentieth century witnessed nationwide gains by Pentecostals as well as by Jehovah's Witnesses and Mormons, who also evangelized aggressively and lived by strict moral codes. In the South, fundamentalist Christians were defying modern science by leading successful campaigns against teaching evolution in public schools. Elsewhere in New England, conservative Christians made significant gains at such venerable Boston institutions as the Tremont Temple and Park Street Congregational Church. Movements such as these constituted a vibrant minority of Americans who looked askance at liberal trends in religious and cultural sensibilities. Their ability to survive, and even thrive, suggests that the violence against Jefferson's Harvesters was the exception rather than the rule.

The Harvesters lasted another two decades after their forced exile from Jefferson. It is difficult to assess objectively how well they did, as the most significant extant source is their own newspaper, which was filled (unsurprisingly) with reports of successful revivals and momentous conversions. Yet the *Sheaf* did continue to publish and the Harvesters did continue raising churches and chapels all over New England. They also operated a Bible school, a home for single mothers, an orphanage, a retirement home, and even a small orchestra. By 1924, the group had fourteen "ordained elders," twenty-nine Christian workers, and thirty-seven chapel leaders; this staff coordinated meetings in about twenty-four centers around New England. In addition, the Harvesters' network of missionaries was active not only across the northeast but also as far afield as China.[27]

In the 1920s the group took a new direction after Wright's son Elwin assumed leadership. Feeling the group had become too sectarian in belief and worship practices, the younger Wright reoriented it toward mainstream evangelicalism, renamed it the New England Fellowship, and moved its headquarters to Park Street Congregational Church on Boston's Beacon Hill. There he worked closely with respected leaders such as Rev. Harold Ockenga to unite coreligionists in a region-wide revival. In 1943, Wright and Ockenga helped found the National Association of Evangelicals (NAE), which presented a moderate counterpart to more conservative evangelical groups. The NAE played an important role in the explosive growth of American evangelicalism in the second half of the twentieth century, and, in this way, a very large harvest was reaped from the seeds planted by Joel Wright in 1897. The New England Fellowship survives, in attenuated form, on its original campground in Rumney today.[28]

The long history of the First Fruit Harvesters and the New England Fellowship is testimony to both the vibrancy and the limits of religious toleration in New England. If one looks beyond the Catholic parishes in the city centers and the Baptist congregations and Quaker meetinghouses on the town commons, one can find—sometimes tucked into unassuming houses on the fringes of towns or storefronts in the inner cities—a multitude of evangelical churches nestled in the landscape. It certainly is an index of tolerance that these institutions have survived; yet their obscurity also is evidence of the "soft" intolerance of indifference and disdain that has characterized some places and times in American religious history. These churches and communities, along with the cultural perspectives they embody, have been overlooked in the scholarly record and underappreciated in the popular consciousness. Paying more attention to forgotten groups such as the Harvesters will enhance our understandings of how, and to what extent, illiberal religious minorities have survived in regions and eras marked by social and political liberalism.

NOTES

1. Randall Balmer, *Mine Eyes Have Seen the Glory: A Journey into the Evangelical Subculture in America*, 3rd ed. (New York: Oxford University Press, 2000), 24–25; Edward L.

Queen II, Stephen R. Prothero, and Gardiner H. Shattuck Jr., *The Encyclopedia of American Religious History* (New York: Facts on File, 1996), 48, 494, 502.

2. Margaret Lamberts Bendroth's *Fundamentalists in the City: Conflict and Division in Boston's Churches, 1885–1950* (New York: Oxford University Press, 2005) is the only full-length study to focus on evangelicals in twentieth-century New England. Even Randall Balmer's excellent *Mine Eyes Have Seen the Glory*, one of the most wide-ranging books on the topic, profiles modern American evangelicals in every region except New England.

3. Elizabeth Evans, *The Wright Vision: The Story of the New England Fellowship* (Lanham, MD: University Press of America, 1991), 1; Kurt O. Berends, "A Divided Harvest: Alice Belle Garrigus, Joel Adams Wright, and Early New England Pentecostalism" (MA thesis, Wheaton College, 1993), 33–34.

4. *Sheaf of the First Fruits*, January 1913; Berends, "Divided Harvest," 36–40; Queen, Prothero, and Shattuck, *Encyclopedia of American Religious History*, 295.

5. *Sheaf*, May, July, August 1913; Berends, "Divided Harvest," 48; Evans, *Wright Vision*, 2.

6. *Sheaf*, January 1907.

7. Evans, *Wright Vision*, 2–3; Kurt O. Berends, "Social Variables and Community Response," in *Pentecostal Currents in American Protestantism*, ed. Edith W. Blumhofer, Russell L. Spittler, and Grant A. Wacker (Urbana: University of Illinois Press, 1999), 72; Berends, "Divided Harvest," 51–52.

8. *Sheaf*, May 1914; Evans, *Wright Vision*, 2; Berends, "Divided Harvest," 56–57.

9. In this respect the Harvesters resembled the Mormons discussed by Cristine Hutchison-Jones in her chapter in this volume, "The First Mormon Moment: The Latter-day Saints in American Culture, 1940–1965." By the twentieth century, she argues, the Mormons had become more respectable for a variety of reasons that included their identity as old-stock Americans associated with the nation's heroic frontier history.

10. Grant Wacker, *Heaven Below: Early Pentecostals and American Culture* (Cambridge, MA: Harvard University Press, 2001), 10; Evans, *Wright Vision*, 3.

11. *Sheaf*, February 1905.

12. Evans, *Wright Vision*, 3; Wacker, *Heaven Below*, 131–32.

13. *Sheaf*, April 1905, January, March, December 1914.

14. *Plymouth Record*, 2 January 1909.

15. *Sheaf*, September 1908, Kurt O. Berends, "Cultivating for a Harvest: The Early Life of Alice Belle Garrigus," *PNEUMA: The Journal of the Society for Pentecostal Studies* 17, no. 1 (Spring 1995): 46.

16. Berends, "Cultivating for a Harvest," 46; *Sheaf*, October 1914.

17. *Sheaf*, October, November 1908, March 1909, October 1914.

18. Berends, *Social Variables*, 77–79; *Sheaf*, April 1915; *Plymouth Record*, 2 January 1909.

19. *Sheaf*, April 1915.

20. *Coos County Democrat*, 9 December, 30 December 1908.

21. *Coos County Democrat*, 9 December, 30 December 1908, 20 January 1909.

22. *Coos County Democrat*, 9 December, 30 December 1908.

23. *Sheaf*, October 1908; *Coos County Democrat*, 20 January 1909.

24. *Coos County Democrat*, 9 December, 30 December 1908, 20 January, 27 January 1909; *Plymouth Record*, 2 January 1909; "To His Excellency, Governor of the State of N.H.," Old Business Meeting Records, 6 June 1902 through June 1917, 98, First Fruit Harvesters Papers, New England Fellowship of Evangelicals, Rumney, NH.

25. *Coos County Democrat*, 20 January 1909; *Sheaf*, April 1913.

26. Berends, "Divided Harvest," 61; *Sheaf*, August 1916.

27. Evans, *Wright Vision*, 7–8.

28. The group now calls itself the New England Fellowship of Evangelicals. It runs a conference and retreat center, summer cottages and camps, and a year-round retirement community in Rumney.

Chapter Fifteen

How the Persecution of Jehovah's Witnesses Changed American Law and Religion

Shawn Francis Peters

Perhaps the worst outbreak of religious persecution in American history involved the Jehovah's Witnesses during the World War II era. Members of this small religious sect were targeted because many viewed their refusal to salute the flag and their reluctance to serve in the armed forces as evidence of disloyalty. Some even regarded the Witnesses as Nazi sympathizers. As a result, mobs across the United States repeatedly set upon proselytizing Witnesses. In the spring and summer of 1940 alone, anti-Witness rioting was reported in all but four states. These were not a few scattered shouting matches or minor scuffles. Rather, they involved large groups of self-styled patriots who perpetrated violent assaults in nearly every state. [1]

The persecution went beyond savage vigilante attacks to include the systematic approbation of government officials. Authorities in many states and communities enacted new laws or applied existing ones to suppress the Witnesses' religious conscience and proselytizing endeavors, thus violating what the Witnesses argued were their constitutional rights to the free exercise of their religion. Municipalities and town governments restricted their right to assemble and speak freely, while employers and coworkers regularly discriminated against them in workplaces. Expulsions of Witness pupils from public schools became so widespread that members of the faith in dozens of communities were forced to operate their own makeshift schools. Witness parents were charged with neglect or disorderly conduct following the flag-salute expulsions of their children. Some impoverished families were even denied such relief benefits as food and clothing on the grounds that their peculiar religious beliefs and practices were threats to national security.

The Witnesses did not take all of this lying down. They were nothing if not resilient. In response to systematic intolerance, they doggedly pursued judicial recognition of their conscientious objections and proselytizing endeavors as constitutional rights. Throughout the latter part of the 1930s and continuing through the following decade, they mounted a sustained legal counterattack against the myriad forms of religious discrimination that they encountered. The Witnesses' indefatigable legal efforts resulted in hundreds of favorable rulings in municipal, state, and lower federal courts. The Witnesses even gained several noteworthy victories in cases heard by the U.S. Supreme Court. Over a ten-year period, the high court handed down almost two dozen opinions in Witness-related cases.

The resulting body of law was not only massive but also transformative. In addition to recognizing the rights of the Jehovah's Witnesses, it laid important groundwork for the "rights revolution" that revolutionized American jurisprudence in the 1950s and 1960s. Although the Witnesses of the 1930s and 1940s did not anticipate this larger legal revolution, they contributed to it in critical ways as they pursued legal protections for their own civil liberties, ultimately benefiting Americans well beyond their own sect.

The Witnesses deftly capitalized on their persecution. While being reviled for their purported lack of patriotism, they portrayed themselves as ultra-Americans, brave champions of the First Amendment and other core constitutional freedoms. This recasting enabled members of the faith to move from the margins of American culture—where they were routinely derided as a pernicious "cult"—to self-proclaimed champions of American values, staking a claim to a position remarkably close to the mainstream of American society.

This chapter reexamines the persecution of Jehovah's Witnesses and its impact on religious freedom and expression in the United States. It scrutinizes how members of the faith were discriminated against and sometimes assaulted in both public and private spaces because of their unconventional religious doctrines and practices. It also details how the victims formulated their unprecedented response to intolerance, using the public forum of the courts for a dual purpose: both securing legal decisions recognizing their practices as protected civil liberties and contesting their public image as a socially divisive, and thus potentially dangerous, religious minority. In the early years of World War II, these looked like formidable tasks. By the opening of the Cold War, however, the Witnesses were well on their way to achieving both goals.

I

The Jehovah's Witnesses emerged as part of an efflorescence of American Protestantism in the nineteenth century. Distinct and innovative faiths like Mormonism, Christian Science, and Seventh-day Adventism all developed during this period. The Jehovah's Witnesses (officially the Watchtower Bible and Tract Society) originated in late nineteenth-century Pennsylvania with a man named Charles Taze Russell. Russell peddled a distinctive brand of millennialism, telling his followers that the temporal world would soon end with a climactic battle pitting Satan against Jehovah (God), in which the former would be vanquished once and for all. According to Witness doctrine, the kingdom of heaven would arise on earth for most of those who maintained fidelity to the teachings of the scriptures. A select group of others would ascend into heaven and take a seat at the right hand of God.[2]

For the Jehovah's Witnesses, aggressive proselytizing was an essential form of religious worship, one modeled on the indefatigable work of the disciples in spreading Christ's teachings. This meant going door to door, distributing tracts and Bibles, playing sound recordings, and, in their words, "preaching the gospel." Witnesses didn't regard these activities as corollaries to worship, but rather as an important form of worship itself. They intended their public canvassing to be so provocative, even harassing, that it would command attention. In the 1930s and 1940s, Witnesses would park outside Catholic churches on Sunday mornings and broadcast sermons comparing Catholicism to the "whore of Babylon" described in the book of Revelation. (A rough contemporary analogue might be the Westboro Baptist Church, which has attracted more or less universal scorn for its anti-homosexual protests outside military funerals.)

The second, and perhaps more significant, dimension of the Witnesses' public and religious lives involved their aversion to saluting the flag. Their intransigence on this issue—even in the face of violent oppression—was central to the problems that beset them in the World War II period. In abjuring patriotic rituals, members of the faith took their cue from Christian scriptures, particularly the book of Exodus (20:4), which admonishes, "Thou shalt not make unto thee any grave image, or any likeness of anything that is in heaven above, or that is in the earth beneath, or that is in the water under the earth. Thou shalt not bow down thyself to them, nor serve them."

For Witnesses living in Nazi Germany during the 1930s, there were catastrophic repercussions for their refusal to salute. Joseph Rutherford, Russell's successor as leader of the faith, decided that German Witnesses should not offer the "Hitler salute," insisting that the gesture amounted to a form of idolatry. Not surprisingly, Witnesses who heeded Rutherford's admonition and defied the Nazi regime in this overt manner were among the first religious minorities sent to concentration camps.[3]

At that time, the American flag salute was rendered in similar fashion (the only visible difference being that the palm was facing up rather than down). Rutherford underscored the similarities when he cautioned in 1935, "The distinctive doctrine of the flag-saluting cult is the deification of the flag. It not only advocates the offering of respect, service, honor, reverence and devotion to the flag, but attempts to coerce worship to its god." Following this edict, Witnesses young and old began to refrain from saluting the American flag.[4]

Although they were not packed off to internment or concentration camps, there were dire consequences for Witnesses who failed to participate in patriotic rituals and generally refused to support the American war effort. (In addition to Rutherford's warning about the flag salute, the Witnesses frequently parroted the faith's unequivocal official stance against the war.) Witness schoolchildren faced disciplinary proceedings when they refused to salute the flag in public schools. So many young Witnesses were suspended and expelled throughout the country in the late 1930s that the members of the faith established their own "Kingdom Schools" to educate the children. While these makeshift schools got off the ground, Witnesses pursued litigation in which they argued that public schools had a constitutional duty to respect their conscientious objections to saluting the nation's flag.

American Witnesses had regularly faced sporadic vigilante action when proselytizing, but what occurred in the spring and summer of 1940 was unprecedented. Developments in Europe and Asia ignited the most severe anti-Witness attacks America had ever seen. Amid the mounting crisis in Europe and Asia, Americans were told in a succession of alarming media reports that a "fifth column" of spies and saboteurs was at work in the United States and undermining the nation's war effort. In retrospect, these stories grossly exaggerated the threat posed by Axis espionage, but at the time they seemed to confirm suspicions that the Witnesses might be engaged in un-American activities.[5]

In the meantime, a legal case involving the Witnesses and the flag salute was resolved by the U.S. Supreme Court: *Minersville School District v. Gobitis*. Early in June 1940, the court ruled 8–1 that mandatory pledge exercises did not violate the Witnesses' religious liberty. "The mere possession of religious convictions which contradict the relevant concerns of a political society," the court held, "does not relieve the citizen from the discharge of political responsibilities." That the opinion was written by Justice Felix Frankfurter, who was widely regarded (perhaps inaccurately) as a champion of civil liberties, eased concerns that the court's decision lacked sufficient concern for basic constitutional rights. The fact that the decision was nearly unanimous, with only Justice Harlan Fisk Stone dissenting, gave it still more weight.[6]

Despite its high-minded qualifications and liberal sentiments, the Supreme Court's ruling was widely perceived as being an indictment of the Witnesses' patriotism. In at least some instances, the ruling appeared to sanction brutal oppression. A Southern sheriff who supervised the round-up and expulsion of Witnesses, for example, characterized the *Gobitis* ruling in terms of a preexisting sentiment regarding Witnesses. "They're traitors," he harrumphed. "The Supreme Court says so."[7]

Throughout the World War II era, and especially the spring and summer of 1940, Jehovah's Witnesses repeatedly fell victim to such tragic misapprehensions. Witness attorney Hayden Covington observed that members of the faith were "beaten, kidnapped, tarred and feathered, throttled in castor oil, tied together and chased through the streets, castrated, maimed, hanged, shot, and otherwise consigned to mayhem." Covington was not exaggerating. His laundry list of depredations is verified by the historical record.[8] It is difficult to estimate the number of vigilante actions taken against Jehovah's Witnesses in this period, but reports from the American Civil Liberties Union (ACLU) and the Justice Department archives indicate that there were 335 separate incidents of anti-Witness violence in the United States in 1940. By the end of World War II, somewhere between eight hundred and two thousand attacks on Witnesses had occurred in the United States.[9]

These numbers were highlighted by a number of observers at the time, especially the ACLU. It published a pamphlet documenting the abuse titled *The Persecution of Jehovah's Witnesses*; that document concluded, "Not since the persecution of Mormons years ago has any religious minority been so bitterly and generally attacked as the members of Jehovah's Witnesses."[10]

There were common threads connecting many of the attacks. They were often prompted by large groups of Witness proselytizers descending on small towns in sizable numbers and aggressively seeking converts to their faith. Dozens of them would blare recordings of Rutherford's dogmatic speeches, preach on street corners and public squares, and travel from door to door with their literature. Their proselytizing techniques were aggressive, even provocative, and they triggered a vicious response. Witnesses rarely shrank from confrontation. In fact, they viewed resistance to their efforts as a sign that they were doing God's work in battling infidels. And there was an undeniable public relations benefit: when their suffering was reported in the media, the Witnesses' faith received free (and often sympathetic) publicity.

When groups of Witnesses brashly sought potential converts, they often would be met by a combination of law enforcement, local patriotic groups such as the American Legion, and local vigilantes. Usually, the Witnesses were confronted and asked to salute the American flag; when they refused, they were beaten and arrested, and their literature was destroyed, often in a massive bonfire. Tensions reached a fever pitch in the spring and summer of

1940 as mobs demolished or even set fire to Witness buildings in some small towns.

A typical attack occurred in Litchfield, Illinois, in June 1940 after twenty-one carloads of Jehovah's Witnesses arrived in the town. Locals had gotten wind of their plans and prepared accordingly. Before the Witnesses knocked on a single door, "most of the men were beaten [and] the entire company was placed in the town jail," according to the *St. Louis Post-Dispatch*. One vigilante told the paper, "Why, they wouldn't even salute the flag! We almost beat one guy to death to make him kiss the flag."[11] It was not simply that the Witnesses' religion was perceived as aberrant but also that their religion was considered politically subversive—as if their faith was merely a front for anti-American beliefs and practices. The irony here is that Witnesses were, at the very same historical moment, being sent to concentration camps in Nazi Germany, already a de facto enemy of the United States.

Hostility may have peaked in the small, southern Maine town of Kennebunk, where tensions had been fueled by mounting fifth column fears and the Supreme Court's *Gobitis* flag-salute case. One beleaguered Witness said that the state police informed her and her coreligionists that "our lives were in danger and not worth a nickel out in the streets." Events reached a fiery culmination with the burning of the Witnesses' Kingdom Hall. As the *Boston Globe* reported:

> The mob made two visits and set two fires. The first burned out part of the building's interior but was extinguished quickly. The second . . . completed the destruction. Before each of the fires the mob ransacked the building . . . and removed tracts, furnishings and members' personal belongings. These were burned in piles in a street of this ordinarily placid town. A man and woman were "roughed up" in the second sacking of the headquarters . . . they were taken to the town line and released. . . . Neither was hurt, police said, but the man's shirt was torn from his back. Hours after firemen doused the last ember, club-carrying townspeople milled around the building, and someone affixed a small American flag to the charred front of the hall.[12]

Such events did not go unnoticed by contemporaries. The ACLU publicized the attacks and advocated for victims. Roger Baldwin, the organization's leader, put the attacks in the context of pervasive wartime suppression of minority groups, decrying them as "a symptom of the hysteria of the moment that Jehovah's Witnesses, of all minorities, should be so savagely and widely attacked on wholly false grounds."[13]

High-profile newspaper editorials and columnists joined Baldwin in criticizing the persecution. First Lady Eleanor Roosevelt noted abuses in her syndicated newspaper column, "My Day," in which she lamented the "unconstitutional and ill considered" activities of vigilantes who were targeting Jehovah's Witnesses. Roosevelt was especially vexed by an incident in which Witnesses in Wyoming had been pulled from their homes by vigilantes and forced to salute the American flag. "Must we drag people from their homes," she wondered, "to force them to do something which is in opposition to their religion?"[14]

Some common themes emerged from the critiques of anti-Witness attacks. One was the drawing of a causal link between the persecution of Witnesses and the irrational fifth column scare. Another was a comparison to the outrages being perpetrated by the Nazis against religious minorities throughout Europe, including Jehovah's Witnesses. It seemed both shameful and ironic to be supporting a war on fascism abroad while such persecution was being practiced at home.

There was also a frank acknowledgment of the Witnesses' role in provoking attacks. The ACLU's John Haynes Holmes offered some typical comments, conceding that the Witnesses were a "peculiarly aggressive, even obnoxious set of people" who seemed to go out of their way to court trouble. But he also lamented their suffering, saying that he could not help but think about parallels to "some of the persecutions which are going forward on a larger scale in Europe."[15]

Critics often singled out law enforcement for its inactivity in safeguarding the Witnesses. Clearly, local law enforcement authorities were complicit, turning a blind eye to the activities of vigilantes and generally failing to follow up with criminal prosecutions, which might have deterred further attacks. Often they went a step further, rounding up, arresting, and physically abusing victims—that is, actively participating in the oppression of the Witnesses, violating not only the free exercise of their religion but also their most fundamental rights to due process. In one especially egregious case in West Virginia, authorities oversaw a round-up in which Witness proselytizers were tied together with rope, compelled to salute the flag, and forced to ingest large quantities of castor oil (a form of torture popularized in fascist Italy). These were crimes both of omission and commission.

As many observers noted, the federal government—which might have been expected to take an interest in such gross violations of civil rights—did not do much for the Witnesses either. There was a nascent civil rights section in the Justice Department, but it was toothless. (Its main functions centered on the collection of data rather than law enforcement.) Solicitor General Francis Biddle did what he could by publicly denouncing the attacks. In a radio address in June 1940, he lamented that the Witnesses "have been repeatedly set upon and beaten." Tellingly, he concluded, "We shall not defeat the Nazi evil by emulating its methods."[16] Fortunately, these public and private abuses waned significantly during the latter stages of the war. By 1944, the harassment and violence directed at Jehovah's Witnesses had come to a virtual halt. The intolerance diminished for a variety of interrelated reasons, including the changing course of the war. As World War II slowly turned in the Allies' favor and it seemed that spying and sabotage would not be decisive factors in the conflict, fifth column fears abated. And there was also the fact that the Witnesses became more familiar, less alien, and somewhat less assertive and annoying. There was, in short, a cooling off.

Finally, and perhaps most significantly, the Supreme Court changed course on the flag salute. In 1943, just three years after the *Gobitis* flag-salute case, the court effectively reversed course in *West Virginia v. Barnette* (a ruling handed down, appropriately enough, on Flag Day). "Those who begin coercive elimination of dissent," Justice Robert Jackson wrote in the court's majority opinion, "soon find themselves eliminating dissenters. Compulsory unification of opinion achieves only the unanimity of the graveyard."[17] It was clear that the violent response to *Gobitis* was partly responsible for the court's change of heart. Various sources indicate that several justices were appalled that their decision had yielded such disastrous results.

As *Barnette* shows, the outburst of intolerance directed at the Jehovah's Witnesses during the World War II years produced some paradoxical results. One of these was an invigorated First Amendment. We think of the era of the Warren Court (1953–1969) as the era of the "rights revolution," when courts began safeguarding individual rights. But the dawn of the rights revolution actually occurred somewhat earlier, and the persecution of the Jehovah's Witnesses in the 1940s was at its center. Their plight during World War II forced courts at all levels to engage in unprecedented scrutiny of the parameters of constitutional protections for fundamental individual rights, including freedoms of religion, speech, press, and assembly. Nothing comparable had transpired in the history of America's civil liberties.

II

In response to the onslaught of intolerance directed at them during World War II, the Witnesses pursued judicial recognition of their rights, mounting a sustained legal counterattack against all forms of religious discrimination. The Witnesses' legal efforts resulted in hundreds of favorable rulings in municipal, state, and lower federal courts. A group of Witness attorneys worked tirelessly in courtrooms throughout the country to combat the manifestations of religious bigotry that plagued adherents.

While their numerous lower-court victories were significant both practically and symbolically, the Witnesses' most noteworthy accomplishments came before the final arbiter of American constitutional rights: the U.S. Supreme Court. From 1938 to 1946, the high court handed down twenty-three opinions covering a total of thirty-nine Witness-related cases. Such decisions profoundly affected the evolution of constitutional law by helping to bring minority and individual rights into the forefront of constitutional jurisprudence. Such were its successes that Witnesses' legal department should be mentioned in the same breath at the NAACP's vaunted "Inc. Fund," which brought so many cases before the Supreme Court in the 1950s and 1960s. In a private letter to a colleague, Justice Harlan Fiske Stone summed up the Witnesses' contributions in this period. Stone wrote (only half in jest), "I think the Jehovah's Witnesses ought to have an endowment in view of the aid which they give in solving the legal problems of civil liberties."[18]

Cantwell v. Connecticut (1940) was a particularly significant Witness case of this era. Prior to *Cantwell*, the U.S. Supreme Court's opinion in *Reynolds v. United States* (1878) controlled its religious liberty jurisprudence. Under *Reynolds*, religious beliefs were inviolable, but religious conduct could be subject to state regulation. This doctrine essentially removed religious conduct from the purview of the First Amendment. Impeded by the *Reynolds* precedent, litigants pursuing safeguards for religious conduct were forced to seek shelter under other constitutional protections.[19] The Jehovah's Witnesses were particularly successful in evading the strictures of *Reynolds* and gaining judicial protections for their religious conduct. But when the members of the U.S. Supreme Court shielded Witnesses' practices, they typically cited the protections afforded by the First Amendment to speech, press, and assembly rights. In *Cantwell*, however, the court more directly addressed a religious liberty claim brought by a Witness.

The *Cantwell* case originated in New Haven, Connecticut, when police arrested Witness Newton Cantwell and his sons Jesse and Russell in 1938 for disturbing the peace and soliciting money for a charitable cause without having first received approval of the state's public welfare council. They were convicted on both charges in local court, and Connecticut's highest court upheld all of their convictions on the permit requirement charge. Witness attorney Hayden Covington appealed the Cantwells' convictions to the U.S. Supreme Court. There was no guarantee of success. At that point, the First Amendment still applied only to actions by the federal government. In two previous cases involving Witness appellants—*Lovell v. Griffin* (1938) and *Schneider v. New Jersey* (1939)—the court had continued its piecemeal incorporation of First Amendment freedoms into the due process clause of the Fourteenth Amendment. Those cases, however, had involved speech and press freedoms; the right to free exercise of religion had not yet been incorporated.[20]

In an auspicious move for Witnesses, the Supreme Court went further in *Cantwell*, barring states from abridging the right to free exercise of religion. However, Justice Owen Roberts's majority opinion still cleaved closely to the reasoning in *Reynolds*. According to Chief Justice Waite, the free exercise clause encompassed "two concepts—freedom to believe and freedom to act. The first is absolute, but in the nature of things, the second cannot be."

In short, the state might exercise control over some forms of conduct even though they were motivated by an individual's religious beliefs. In the context of the Witnesses' proselytizing, this regulation might involve the nondiscriminatory regulation of the time, place, and manner of their public solicitation.[21]

Where *Cantwell* differed from *Reynolds* was in the level of scrutiny applied to the actions taken by the state to regulate religious conduct. The court indicated that it would now subject state regulation to heightened judicial scrutiny, wherein authorities would have to demonstrate that the application of statute to religious conduct served a compelling state interest. Using this more rigorous standard, the court determined that the application of the permit requirements to the Cantwells' religious conduct represented an unconstitutional infringement on their religious liberty. Although the Connecticut permit law at issue was neutral on its face, Justice Roberts wrote, it was so broadly drawn that public officials had wide latitude to take actions infringing on religious liberty.

Cantwell thus marked a major turning point for religious liberty. Never before had the Supreme Court recognized constitutional protections for religious conduct. As a consequence, much of modern free exercise jurisprudence flows from the proselytizing spirit of the Jehovah's Witnesses. Their provocations and legal efforts invited the court to reconsider and ultimately redefine constitutional safeguards for religious conduct.

That the oppression of Witnesses compelled the courts to bolster these formal protections says something about the sometimes uneasy relationship between religious expression and religious toleration. For the most part, when individuals practice their faiths in private spaces with fellow believers, it is not especially difficult for others to tolerate them. Toleration becomes far more complex and challenging, however, when those practices are not only public but also (in the view of nonbelievers) socially aberrant and intentionally provocative. Critics tend to maintain that such unconventional iterations of faith are not recognizably or authentically religious, and thus unworthy of toleration. The Witness cases made that position harder to sustain, while also demonstrating the critical role that state and federal courts could play in guaranteeing religious liberties.

There were other unexpected results flowing from the persecution of the Jehovah's Witnesses. One was that the Witnesses experienced a kind of legitimization through litigation. By going to court and participating in the political system, they were perceived as less alien and more "American." It also helped that they modified their manner of "preaching the gospel" in public, gradually toning down some of their more confrontational proselytizing activities. Once persecuted as potential enemies of the state, they now were grudgingly hailed as exemplars of the First Amendment. It was a remarkable turn of events.

Moreover, the Witnesses looked upon their martyrdom in this period as a galvanizing event, something to be viewed with pride. They made meaning out of the shared experience of their suffering on the streets. Most official histories of the faith include an extensive discussion of this period and celebrate how the Witnesses rose above their tribulations in order to further serve their faith. Such narratives continue to be an integral part of their collective memory.

Today, the Jehovah's Witnesses remain religious outsiders in American life. But if they still are a peripheral group, they are also a thriving one, boasting more than seven million adherents worldwide. A catalytic event in this growth was their suppression during the late 1930s and early 1940s. In the general public's eyes, it ennobled them; internally, it fortified them. And the nation's approach to religious and civil liberties would never be the same.

NOTES

1. This chapter expands upon my book *Judging Jehovah's Witnesses: Religious Persecution and the Dawn of the Rights Revolution* (Lawrence: University Press of Kansas, 2000).

2. For a full view of Witness history and doctrine, see M. James Penton, *Apocalypse Delayed: The Story of Jehovah's Witnesses*, 2nd ed. (Toronto: University of Toronto Press, 1997).

3. Among the best accounts of these matters is M. James Penton, *Jehovah's Witnesses and the Third Reich* (Toronto: University of Toronto Press, 2004).

4. Peters, *Judging Jehovah's Witnesses*, 27.

5. The best account of this topic is found in Francis Michael MacDonnell, *Insidious Foes: The Axis Fifth Column and the American Home Front* (New York: Oxford University Press, 1996).

6. *Minersville School District v. Gobitis*, 310 U.S. 586 (1940).

7. Buelah Amidon, "Can We Afford Martyrs?" *Survey Graphic*, September 1940, 457–60.

8. Peters, *Judging Jehovah's Witnesses*, 8.

9. Peters, *Judging Jehovah's Witnesses*, 8–10.

10. Peters, *Judging Jehovah's Witnesses*, 99–100.

11. *St. Louis Post-Dispatch*, 17 June 1940.

12. *Boston Globe*, 10 June 1940.

13. Baldwin quoted in Peters, *Judging Jehovah's Witnesses*, 81–82.

14. *New York World-Telegram*, 22 June 1940.

15. John Haynes Holmes, "The Case of Jehovah's Witnesses," *Christian Century*, 17 July 1940, 896–98.

16. American Civil Liberties Union, *The Persecution of Jehovah's Witnesses* (New York: American Civil Liberties Union, 1941), 22.

17. *West Virginia State Board of Education v. Barnette*, 319 U.S. 624 (1943).

18. Peters, *Judging Jehovah's Witnesses*, 294.

19. *Reynolds v. United States*, 98 U.S. 145 (1878).

20. *Lovell v. City of Griffin*, 303 U.S. 444 (1938); *Schneider v. State of New Jersey*, 308 U.S. 147 (1939).

21. *Cantwell v. Connecticut*, 310 U.S. 296 (1940).

Chapter Sixteen

The First Mormon Moment

The Latter-day Saints in American Culture, 1940–1965

Cristine Hutchison-Jones

Much was made during the years surrounding the 2008 and 2012 presidential elections of the nation's so-called Mormon Moment. Mormons seemed to be everywhere in the early twenty-first century. Former governor of Massachusetts and faithful Latter-day Saint Mitt Romney was first a leading candidate for and then the winner of the Republican nomination for the presidency. Trey Parker and Matt Stone took the Tony Awards and the nation by storm when they put the fascination with Mormons often displayed in their animated television show, *South Park*, to music in *The Book of Mormon*. And popular television shows, from the award-winning HBO drama *Big Love* to the reality series *Sister Wives*, centered on the lives and beliefs of fundamentalist Mormons—who, unlike the far more numerous members of the Church of Jesus Christ of Latter-day Saints, practice polygamous marriage—inviting viewers to judge these peculiar practices for themselves. But despite the nation's seemingly newfound interest in understanding rather than simply condemning the Latter-day Saints and their unique beliefs and behaviors, this was not America's first Mormon Moment.

The first "moment" came in the middle of the twentieth century. In that era, despite the U.S. government's concerted efforts to present the nation as a united Judeo-Christian community, in direct contrast to its mid-twentieth-century communist enemies, a number of American religious groups continued to be subject to significant prejudice and discrimination.[1] Yet it was in the midst of this climate of suspicion that the Latter-day Saints—one of the nation's most reviled outsiders well into the twentieth century—reached the zenith of their acceptance in American culture. At the end of the nineteenth century the federal government had attempted to disband the church for its refusal to embrace American political and cultural norms, including the separation of church and state, market capitalism, and monogamous marriage. In a radical reversal of Mormonism's popular image, only half a century later America's first Mormon Moment saw the Saints lionized in fiction and on the silver screen, praised in the national press, and welcomed into the nation's halls of power.

The American embrace of the Latter-day Saints in the mid-twentieth century stands as a case study of successful religious assimilation. How did this long-despised group move, in just over fifty years, from near destruction to admission into the inner circles of national culture and politics? At its core, the story of the Latter-day Saints in the first half of the twentieth century is one of assimilation on the part of the minority followed by increasing acceptance on the part of the broader culture.[2] As sociologist Armand L. Mauss explains, the Latter-day Saints purposefully "Americanized," abandoning or suppressing their most unique practices—including polygamy, theocratic blending of church and state, and economic communalism—to such an extent that their non-Mormon neighbors could tolerate their remaining muted differences.[3] In addition to ridding themselves of practices and beliefs that many non-Mormon Americans opposed, the Latter-day Saints, led by their church's hierarchy, embraced and publicized the aspects of their religion that they shared with America's largely Protestant population. By mid-century they had succeeded in this assimilationist project to such an extent that non-Mormon Americans were willing to acknowledge the Latter-day Saints as upstanding fellow Americans.

I

In one fell swoop in 1890, Mormon prophet Wilford Woodruff's manifesto publicly divested Mormonism of its most "un-American" practices: plural marriage, economic communalism, and direct church involvement in politics and state government.[4] The question of whether a person could be a good Mormon *and* a loyal American was apparently resolved in the Mormons' favor in the Senate investigation sparked by Mormon apostle Reed Smoot's election to that body. The debate over whether a high-ranking Mormon could serve the nation despite his loyalty to his religion created a national sensation. The Senate compelled testimony from prominent Mormons, including the president of the church; non-Mormon citizens organized letter campaigns and petitions calling for Smoot's dismissal and the banning of Mormons from national office; and newspapers across the nation printed dozens of front-page headlines and endless pages of type reporting on Smoot and his religion. The hearings ended in 1907 with Smoot, supported by President Theodore Roosevelt, retaining his Senate seat, marking a major shift in acceptance of a Mormon presence on the national political stage.[5] Less than a decade later, the church and its members proved their loyalty to the nation through their support of American military efforts in both the Mexican Revolution and World War I.[6]

The Saints' public image improved not only due to such proofs of commitment to American values but also as a result of a number of national cultural trends. First and foremost, while many minority religious communities were still associated with immigrant ethnic groups well into the twentieth century, Mormon immigration was primarily from northern and western European countries, whose (white) racial and (Protestant) cultural heritage Americans favored. Moreover, by the early twentieth century, Mormon immigration had all but ceased in response to the leadership's call to converts not to gather in the Mormon Zion of America's intermountain West, but rather to build Zion where they were. Finally, the closing of the frontier in 1890—the same year in which the Saints began to make earnest efforts to assimilate wider American norms—sparked a national craze for romanticized stories of the American West and the pioneers who "tamed" it. The Mormons, who had settled the intermountain West and made the desert "blossom as the rose," were poised to take advantage of the national mood.

But the Saints still had to fight an uphill battle to prove themselves to an American public steeped in anti-Mormon rhetoric. Before the First World War, national newspaper coverage was almost entirely negative, and popular books featured Mormons only as stock villains. Arthur Conan Doyle's first Sherlock Holmes mystery, *A Study in Scarlet* (1887), included a story of the LDS Church hierarchy's forced conversion and ruthless destruction of an innocent Gentile (non-Mormon) pioneer and his adopted daughter.[7] Harry Leon Wilson's widely advertised and well-reviewed epic Western *The Lions of the Lord* (1903) retold the Latter-day Saints' story from the anti-Mormon mob destruction of the Mormon city of Nauvoo, Illinois, after founding prophet Joseph Smith's death in 1844, through the aftermath of the Mountain Meadows massacre in 1857. In that act of reciprocal violence, a group of Mormon settlers and Indians killed more than 120 American pioneers in a wagon train traveling through southern Utah.[8] After the massacre, Wilson's main character—the only good Mormon, who nevertheless participated in the violence—was driven to madness and death by the realization that he had helped murder the pioneers out of loyalty to a false religion.[9] Popular author Pansy, who wrote novels for young ladies that one *New York Times* reviewer noted were destined for "the Sunday School libraries," wrote a lurid and pathetic tale the same year about one woman's victimization under the secret system of polygamy in contemporary Utah.[10] And Zane Grey's popular Westerns, most notably *The Riders of the Purple Sage* (1913), featured an assortment of power-hungry, cruel, and lecherous Mormons. In *Riders*, the Mormons are prevented from destroying two innocent young Gentiles and the lone independently minded Mormon in one southern Utah settlement only by the timely intervention of a heroic Gentile cowboy.[11] Little wonder that reviewers expected such books to inspire "a spirited little anti-Mormon revival."[12] The Mormons were so unpopular among their non-Mormon fellow citizens that, upon Utah achieving statehood status in 1896, the *New York Times* declared the possible addition of church president and early Utah governor Brigham Young to the Hall of Statues in the U.S. Capitol "wildly absurd" and "monstrous."[13]

Popular representations of the Mormons began to soften after the Saints demonstrated their resolve to eliminate polygamy with repeated affirmations of President Woodruff's 1890 manifesto[14] and proved their patriotism through support of the nation's military efforts in Mexico and Europe between 1915 and 1920.[15] In the face of unprecedented economic and military threats in the 1930s and 1940s, Americans began to overlook their religious differences in order to emphasize national unity. The Saints' well-publicized efforts at community self-sufficiency in the midst of the Great Depression in the 1930s and support of America's wars against all enemies, whether fascist or communist, in the 1940s and 1950s went over well with non-Mormon Americans. As a result, the Saints' popular image shifted from that of a deviant, un-American sect to one of a community of descendants from self-reliant—albeit somewhat eccentric—pioneer ancestors who opened the West for all of America.

This upward trend in the Mormon public image was spearheaded by a cadre of writers from the intermountain West. Nationally recognized and critically acclaimed novelists like Vardis Fisher, Virginia Sorensen, and Maurine Whipple and popular historians like Bernard DeVoto and Wallace Stegner all produced works in the 1930s and 1940s that presented the Latter-day Saints in a more positive light.[16] While some, like Fisher and Whipple, tended to lionize the early Saints, DeVoto and Stegner both presented more critical but still fair portraits of early Mormon belief, practice, and community building. None of these writers depended solely on the wicked, lustful, polygamous villains of earlier American gothic novels and melodramas, nor did they resort to the lionized men and angelic women of typical Mormon hagiography. They presented the Saints as people whose strange marital practices resulted from deeply held religious beliefs that average Saints struggled daily to fulfill in spite of the personal and social hardships such practices created.[17]

In 1939 Vardis Fisher, a former Mormon and director of the Idaho Federal Writers Project, wrote a story of his religious ancestors. *Children of God: An American Epic* won the 1939–1940 Harper Novel Prize.[18] But some non-Mormon critics accused Fisher of taking Joseph Smith too seriously and absolving the Mormons of their fair share of guilt in their early nineteenth-century conflicts with their non-Mormon neighbors.[19] Fisher's interpretation of the persecution of the Saints is relatively unnuanced—his Joseph Smith simply "wanted a life of peace and study and reflection"—but Fisher didn't merely accept Smith as God's prophet.[20] Rather, the book begins with an understated effort to explain the origins of Smith's prophetic mission in terms of folk Christian beliefs, religious upheaval, and economic hardship. Divinely inspired or not, Fisher's Smith was not the monster of earlier depictions, and his followers were neither blind dupes nor bloodthirsty tyrants. But they were also not wholly good. Fisher's Smith neither founded nor approved of the Mormon vigilante group known as the "Danites," but he knew that such movements existed among the Saints and attributed them to the "hell of persecution and death" visited on them by their Gentile neighbors.[21] In Fisher's telling, the Mormons were not entirely to blame for resorting to violence, which was often done in self-defense. Rather than denying Mormon militancy, Fisher blamed it on the non-Mormon Americans who viciously expelled the Saints from state after state and the government forces that sometimes joined anti-Mormon mobs and always failed to intervene to protect Mormon citizens from harassment and violence. Regardless of whether Smith was a true prophet, Fisher suggested, he led people who wanted to live and worship freely and who were driven to violence by the depredations practiced on them by their neighbors.

Fisher's book focused almost entirely on rehabilitating the image of early Mormon men. Other writers were more interested in the early Mormon women who labored in the Mormon Zion under the yoke of polygamy. Utahan Maurine Whipple received an award from publisher Houghton Mifflin to develop *The Giant Joshua*, her novel of the building of the city of St. George in southern Utah. Published in 1941, the book was a Mormon *Gone with the Wind*.[22] One reviewer called it an "oddly exciting novel" about "an heroic, dogged people, often wayward, often erring, who made a specialty of performing the impossible."[23] The story centered on young, beautiful, headstrong Clory McIntyre, the third wife of an elder sent by Brigham Young to establish the settlement of St. George. In the midst of Clory's several romances, Whipple told the story of her pioneer ancestors who founded a city in a harsh desert and the sometimes harsher dictates of the church that enforced the unity required of a community in order to tame that desert. But Whipple did not condemn the church for its sometimes painful and even unreasonable demands on members. In her telling, Apostle Erastus Snow succinctly explained, "Some day [the Saints] would be strong enough to afford dissenters—now salvation lay only in complete and disciplined togetherness."[24]

The following year Mormon novelist Virginia Sorensen published a remarkably sympathetic portrayal of the most taboo of all Mormon practices: polygamy. *A Little Lower Than the Angels* (1942) illustrated the sometimes painful costs of such togetherness in her imagined story of one of the first

Mormon women to accept a second wife into her home at Nauvoo in the early 1840s. Heroine Mercy Baker embraced Mormonism and moved across the plains out of love for her devout husband, and she likewise accepted her husband's second wife for his beliefs and not her own.[25] But while Sorensen painted a painful picture of the agony that some plural wives endured at sharing their husbands, their homes, and their children, her exploration of the lives of Mormons on the frontier also demonstrated how hardworking, ingenious, faithful, and deeply decent these early Saints were. Not surprisingly, her richest portraits were of the women who gave birth on the move, made comfortable homes out of the rude cabins they helped their men erect on the frontier, and embraced the difficult and complicated consequences of plural marriage out of devotion to their husbands and their church. Thus, while plural marriage dominated Sorensen's narrative, the novel's primary theme was the strength and faith that carried the Saints across the plains in search of a place to build Zion. While they may have sacrificed aspects of personal fulfillment, they gained a tightly bound community dedicated to shared beliefs and goals. Despite their peculiar marital practices, Sorensen's Saints were the ultimate Americans, taming hostile lands to build a safe place where they might practice their religion and make a better future for their families.

The popular domestication of Mormonism's polygamous past extended to nonfiction as well. In 1951, Samuel Woolley Taylor—son of Apostle John Taylor, who was excommunicated after the Second Manifesto in 1907 for his refusal to abandon plural marriage—published the memoir *Family Kingdom*, in which he presented an insider account of Mormonism's peculiar institution.[26] Not surprisingly, Taylor's account of life in a polygamous family garnered significant attention. Vardis Fisher recommended the book to readers of the *New York Times* as "a remarkable story . . . delightfully told."[27] Taylor related the story of his parents: a former apostle and son of nineteenth-century LDS president John Taylor and his third wife. When Apostle Taylor approached his three wives about adding two young sisters to the family after the 1890 manifesto forbidding new plural marriages, the author's mother feared the impact of new wives and children on her financially strained family. Further, she understood the potential for excommunication and even criminal charges against her husband. Despite these reservations, Taylor eventually took three additional wives and, as a direct result, was forced out of the church. Thus divided from his contacts in the Mormon community, he could not support his families, and each wife had to fend for herself and her children. But while the author condemned his father for his decision to take new wives and his resultant inability to care for his family, he also presented a sympathetic portrait of people who "had gone through too much for the principle to deny it."[28] While he did not seek to defend polygamy, Taylor showed readers the strong religious belief on which the decision to enter plural marriage was founded—for both men and women—and described a home life dedicated to the familiar values of family and faith.

The ultimate example of the shift to a Mormon image palatable to a national audience was John D. Fitzgerald's family memoir *Papa Married a Mormon* (1955).[29] The book said little about unique Mormon beliefs and practices, focusing instead on an idealized picture of Mormon-Gentile cooperation on the southern Utah frontier. Fitzgerald, who later gained fame for writing "The Great Brain" series of children's books, narrated the story of his Roman Catholic father and Mormon mother raising an intentionally interreligious family at the physical and cultural borders of a Mormon village and a non-Mormon mining town. When his papa first arrived in Utah, Fitzgerald recounted, he determined to "judge men by the contribution they made to science, culture, social and economic progress, tolerance, patriotism, spiritual leadership, and their regard for the well-being of their fellow-men."[30] By all of these measures, his Mormon neighbors were respectable men and women. While he initially wondered at some of the Saints' peculiar beliefs and worried whether he ought to associate with them, he reflected that every religion undergoes a "baptism of ridicule and persecution" before it achieves wider acceptance and decided that one false tenet does not a false religion make.[31] This realization allowed him to fall in love with and marry a good Mormon girl, and later, in part because there was no Catholic church nearby, to send his children to Mormon Sunday schools and have them baptized as Latter-day Saints. In the absence of representatives of his own religion, Fitzgerald's father saw Mormonism as an acceptably Christian substitute. When the children were old enough, their parents allowed them to choose their own faith: one followed his mother into Mormonism, completed a mission, and married a local Mormon bishop's daughter; the other three embraced their father's Roman Catholicism. This interfaith understanding extended well beyond the Fitzgerald household. There was still no Catholic church in the area when his father died, so the Mormon bishop had a Catholic altar installed in the local tabernacle. A Catholic priest presided at a funeral where a Mormon choir performed the Catholic mass to mourners of all faiths. According to Fitzgerald's recollections, even in the Mormon kingdom's strictest days in the late nineteenth century, the Saints were kind and tolerant toward anyone who settled among them, ever ready to be good neighbors and friends.

While books demonstrated and advanced this more all-American Mormon image, they could not penetrate popular consciousness the way movies did. In this first Mormon Moment, Hollywood, too, celebrated Americans' embrace of the Mormons. The first major example came in the lead-up to the 1947 centennial of the Saints' settlement of Utah Territory with the film *Brigham Young: Frontiersman*. Helmed by well-known director of westerns Henry Hathaway, the film starred Dean Jagger as a stoic, heroic Young; Vincent Price as a sympathetic Joseph Smith; and Hollywood heartthrob

Tyrone Power as an idealistic young member of the first party of Mormon immigrants to enter the Salt Lake Valley. The film was big on budget and short on any hint of the harsh criticism that defined earlier depictions of Mormonism in American culture. In fact, critics accurately complained that the film ignored the most controversial aspects of Mormon history—especially polygamy—in favor of boring platitudes about struggle and sacrifice for religious freedom.[32] In stark contrast to earlier depictions of the Latter-day Saint prophets, this Young was not a closed-minded zealot and religious bigot but a religious freedom fighter. Early in the film he delivered a particularly stirring argument for tolerance during Smith's trial for treason, which included a broad-minded statement on his own tolerance for other faiths and illustrated his larger commitment to the American enterprise of religious toleration: "The whole point is whether Joseph Smith or any other American citizen has a right to worship God as he chooses."[33] Young went on to compare the Mormons to the Puritans in Massachusetts, the Quakers in Pennsylvania, the Huguenots in South Carolina, and the Roman Catholics in Maryland, all of whom, he noted, came to America in pursuit of religious freedom. This character was a far cry from the brutal dictator depicted in earlier popular stories like Doyle's *A Study in Scarlet*—itself adapted into numerous silent films before 1920—and Wilson's *Lions of the Lord*.

In a much quieter way, John Ford's classic 1950 Western film *Wagon Master* humanized Young's frontier followers.[34] The movie began with a pair of Mormon elders hiring a pair of non-Mormon horse traders as guides to lead their party into the uncharted deserts of southern Utah. The members of Ford's wagon train were average workaday Mormons: there were no polygamous wives, and the most valuable goods they carried were the seeds they meant to plant upon choosing a spot for their new settlement. A few were self-righteous and occasionally mean, but most were warm, pious, and good-natured. They cussed when they were angry, prayed when they needed help, and shared what little they had with those in need—Mormon or not. After together enduring the dangers and privations of the trail, including thirst, sickness, Indians, and outlaws, the young horse traders and the Saints arrived in the right place and together set about building a new settlement. The final scenes implied that one of the young Gentiles intended to marry a Mormon elder's daughter. In the end, Ford's story emphasized similarity over difference. These Mormons were only one part of "a bunch of people going west."[35] Ford, like so many other observers of Mormons and Mormonism in this period, was committed to an image of the Latter-day Saints that emphasized not how they differed, but rather the many beliefs, practices, and values—a common civic identity—that they shared with their non-Mormon American neighbors.

II

Increased political power followed cultural influence. Novels, films, and other popular representations of Mormons as tolerant, freedom-seeking, faithful Judeo-Christian neighbors paved the way for the Saints to be welcomed into the national halls of political power in the mid-twentieth century. One of the earliest demonstrations of their effect came as the United States endured its first great tragedy in World War II. On January 2, 1942, the government held the first official memorial service for the American men and women killed when the Japanese had attacked Pearl Harbor one month earlier. National newspapers reported that the public memorial service was brief and primarily made up of native Hawaiian observances: the service began with the singing of "Aloha Oe" and ended with the Daughters of Hawaii placing leis on graves and temporary grave markers. The only Christian prayer offered at the service was delivered by Keawe Kapellela, a native Hawaiian Mormon missionary.[36] At this most significant and solemn of national events, the Mormons were regarded as American enough to represent all Americans and all Christians.

Another signal moment occurred in 1950 when, a half-century after the *New York Times* had proclaimed Brigham Young's presence in the Hall of Statues "wildly absurd" and "monstrous," a marble sculpture of the second president of the LDS Church was unveiled in the U.S. Capitol. The statue, draped in an American flag, was unveiled with great pomp and ceremony by the sculptor, Young's grandson, along with Young's only living child and prophet and church president George Albert Smith. The speeches delivered to mark the occasion demonstrated the rapprochement Mormon and non-Mormon Americans had reached on the subject of one of the most controversial figures in the Saints' history. Senator Elbert Thomas declared that the "Utah pioneer movement . . . has left its mark on its people and in the development of American culture and traditions." Church president Smith said that Young "gave his all that this nation might persist." (He did not mention that Young once threatened to burn down Salt Lake City rather than see federal troops in the city.)[37] Vice President Alben Barkley enthused, "Brigham Young belonged in the great group of pathfinders."[38] The speakers all ignored key features of pre–World War I representations of the Mormon prophet: Young's polygamy, his theocratic rule over Utah, and his defiance of the federal government. Instead, they lauded his accomplishments as a heroic American pioneer.

Americans' tolerance for their reimaged Mormon neighbors extended not only to such significant ceremonial roles but also to granting Saints positions of real power. Two years after Young's likeness was installed at the U.S. Capitol, President Eisenhower appointed two Mormons to serve on his cabinet, cementing Mormonism's new position at the heart of American culture.

Perhaps the most powerful evidence of Mormonism's assimilation was that at the cabinet's first meeting, the secretary of agriculture and Mormon apostle Ezra Taft Benson led the cabinet in prayer.[39] In times of public celebration as in times of mourning, Mormons were granted the right to serve as the official voice of America's Judeo-Christian values.

Given this mid-century embrace of Mormonism, George Romney's career as Michigan's governor (1963–1969) and his nearly successful campaign for the Republican presidential nomination in 1968 are not surprising. Though Romney's son Mitt faced questions about his religion throughout his early twenty-first-century campaigns for the presidency, historian J. B. Haws contends that religion was a nonissue for the elder Romney. According to Haws, the elder Romney lost not because of his Mormonism but because of his then-controversial moderate position on race and his very public gaffe in 1968 when he referred to having been "brainwashed" by American generals into supporting the Vietnam War. Surprisingly, given the struggles of earlier Mormon politicians like Reed Smoot to gain acceptance on the national political scene in spite of their religion, George Romney's faith was regarded by many American voters not as a liability but as an asset.[40]

Perhaps the greatest exemplar of this mid-century Mormon Moment was the informal ambassadorial role accorded the popular Mormon Tabernacle Choir. The group was beloved in the United States by the 1950s largely thanks to its weekly radio program, which in 1954 marked its 1,300th performance and celebrated its standing as the oldest continuously broadcast nationwide radio program in the country.[41] The choir was renowned for its renditions not only of classical choral music but also of favorite Protestant hymns and patriotic music like "America the Beautiful."[42] In 1955, at the height of the Cold War, the choir carried American values abroad on a sweeping tour of major European cities. During a trip that included Scotland, England, Holland, Denmark, Switzerland, and France, American observers were less interested in the music that the choir performed than in the American and foreign dignitaries in the audiences and the critical praise the performances garnered. National newspapers reserved their most extensive coverage for the choir's Berlin appearances. Traveling on a special permit from the Soviet authorities, the choir journeyed through occupied East Germany to perform for members of the American military stationed in West Berlin. The "greatest experience of our European tour," according to the choir's conductor, was a special free concert for East German refugees in West Berlin, at which the audience called for six encores.[43] Here the Mormons both comforted those dispossessed by America's enemies and spread the patriotic, Judeo-Christian image that much of America wanted to project to the world.

The choir performed the same service from home in 1962 with a televised concert for an international audience aired as part of a demonstration of the

United States' technological and ideological superiority. Multiple American broadcasters sent several hours of programming around the globe via satellite to illustrate an approved slice of American life to the nation's friends and enemies. Programming included a press conference with President John F. Kennedy, scenes of the United Nations building and other skyscrapers in New York City, a Chicago Cubs baseball game, Indians on the Western plains, and the Golden Gate Bridge in San Francisco. Such images communicated America's commitments to and success with democracy, diversity, international cooperation, leisure, and technological innovation. But according to the *Chicago Daily Tribune*, "The climax was the Mormon Tabernacle Choir from Salt Lake City, singing 'A Mighty Fortress Is Our God.' . . . The choir was at Mt. Rushmore, S.D. While it sang, the cameras swept the stone faces."[44] Both the *Tribune* and the *New York Times* featured photos of the choir arrayed in front of the national memorial, the embodiment of the nation's talent, faith, and patriotism, as they performed a classic Protestant Christian hymn in front of one of the nation's most celebrated landmarks.[45]

III

So what did the Mormons do "right" that other minority religions did not during this period? How did they secure a measure of toleration that was frequently not accorded to other minority religious groups in the United States? They assimilated popular American values, downplaying the unique beliefs and practices that most set them apart from the Protestant majority in both the past and the present, thereby diminishing their own distance from the cultural center. They played up their contributions to the nation's nineteenth-century expansion—a history in which many smaller and more recently arrived minority groups did not share—and avidly sought to contribute to its twentieth-century defense. They were joiners who saw themselves not only *in* the United States but also *of* the United States, and who sought to adopt and reinforce rather than challenge the nation's accepted norms. And they looked and sounded the part. The Latter-day Saints were, in the mid-twentieth century, a group whose public image was dominated by patriotic white, family-oriented, middle-class Americans who went to church on Sunday and prayed publicly to an acceptably Judeo-Christian God that their neighbors and their government recognized. As the United States sought to present a united front at home and abroad, the Mormons helped bolster the national self-image. Rather than challenging mainstream American culture, they assimilated with gusto and were accordingly rewarded with a place of respect at the heart of that mainstream during this first Mormon Moment.

NOTES

1. An exemplar of the notion of "Judeo-Christian" religiosity in mid-twentieth-century America is Will Herberg's *Protestant-Catholic-Jew: An Essay in American Religious Sociology* (Chicago: University of Chicago Press, 1955). For a brief history of this much-criticized concept in its heyday, see Mark Silk, "Notes on the Judeo-Christian Tradition in America," *American Quarterly* 36, no. 1 (Spring 1984): 65–85.

2. On Mormon assimilation in the first half of the twentieth century, see Armand Mauss, *The Angel and the Beehive: The Mormon Struggle with Assimilation* (Urbana: University of Illinois Press, 1994).

3. Mauss, *Angel and the Beehive*, 21–76.

4. It was several decades before many of these practices, particularly plural marriage, were truly abandoned by the Mormon community. While the church officially disavowed the practice of plural marriage in 1890 and called on members within the United States to stop solemnizing new polygamous marriages, it took several additional actions by church leadership, including a Second Manifesto (1904) and the expulsion of two members of the Quorum of the Twelve Apostles (1906), to force the community to accept the end of the practice. The controversies over the manifesto resulted in the formation of several breakaway fundamentalist groups that continue to practice plural marriage. See Matthew Bowman, *The Mormon People: The Making of an American Faith* (New York: Random House, 2012), 159–60, 178–79. On the Saints' Americanization after the manifesto, see Thomas G. Alexander, *Mormonism in Transition: A History of the Latter-day Saints, 1890–1930* (Urbana: University of Illinois Press, 1986).

5. The definitive study of the Smoot trial is Kathleen Flake, *The Politics of American Religious Identity: The Seating of Senator Reed Smoot, Mormon Apostle* (Chapel Hill: University of North Carolina Press, 2004).

6. Preeminent historian of Mormonism Jan Shipps demonstrates an increase in positive depictions of the Mormons in popular national magazines after World War I. See Shipps, "From Satyr to Saint: American Perceptions of the Mormons, 1860–1960," in *Sojourner in the Promised Land: Forty Years among the Mormons* (Urbana: University of Illinois Press, 2000). On the importance of the Mexican Revolution in changing the American perception of the Latter-day Saints, see Cristine Hutchison-Jones, "Reviling and Revering the Mormons: Defining American Values, 1890–2008" (PhD diss., Boston University, 2011).

7. In Arthur Conan Doyle, *"A Study in Scarlet"; and, "The Sign of Four,"* Dover Thrift Editions (Mineola, NY: Dover Publications, 2003). It is worth noting that Doyle had not visited Utah prior to writing *A Study in Scarlet*. The book depends not on personal observation, but rather on the anti-Mormon tropes that Doyle would have encountered in the fiction, memoirs (some based on real experience and some entirely fabricated), and even well-regarded histories about the Latter-day Saints that were widely available in the late nineteenth century.

8. For a full account of the massacre in historical context, see Ronald W. Walker, Richard E. Turley, and Glen M. Leonard, *Massacre at Mountain Meadows* (New York: Oxford University Press, 2008).

9. Harry Leon Wilson, *The Lions of the Lord* (Boston: Lothrop, Lee & Shepard, 1903).

10. Pansy [Mrs. G. K. Alden], *Mara* (Boston: Lothrop, 1902). Contemporary readers might have encountered Pansy in L. M. Montgomery's *Anne of Green Gables* (2nd ed. [New York: Bantam Books, 1998], 116), first published in 1908, in which Anne and her school friends excitedly look forward to reading the latest Pansy novel aloud together during school lunch breaks.

11. Zane Grey, *The Riders of the Purple Sage* (New York: Grosset & Dunlap, 1913).

12. Stephenson Browne, "Boston Notes: Harry L. Wilson and Mrs. Alden on Mormonism: Some Forthcoming Books," *New York Times*, 27 June 1903.

13. "Topics of the Times," *New York Times*, 20 February 1897. Similar objections were raised to the proposed placement of a statue of Young in the Hall of Statues at the St. Louis Exposition in 1903. See "Oppose Brigham Young Statue," *New York Times*, 17 May 1903.

14. Prophet Joseph F. Smith issued what is known as the Second Manifesto, affirming the cessation of all new plural marriages, in 1904. Two members of the Quorum of the Twelve

Apostles—the church's highest authority behind only the Prophet—were asked to step down from their positions for failure to adhere to the manifesto and one, John Taylor, was excommunicated from the church. See Bowman, *The Mormon People*, 159–60.

15. Newspaper coverage during the period demonstrates non-Mormon Americans' approval of the Latter-day Saints' support for these war efforts. The *New York Times* increasingly used the phrase "American Mormon(s)"—a combination of national and religious identities absent from non-Mormon writing prior to this period—during the period of the Mexican Revolution after 1913. Coverage of the Saints' support of the national effort during World War I was exemplified by headlines such as "Mormons Give Up Wheat: Church Turns Over Reserve of 250,000 Barrels to Government" (*New York Times*, 12 June 1918).

16. Not coincidentally, all of these writers were raised in the Mormon stronghold of the intermountain West; only Stegner was not the child of at least one Mormon parent.

17. Vardis Fisher, *Children of God: An American Epic* (New York: Harper & Brothers, 1939), winner of the 1939–1940 Harper Prize; Virginia Sorensen, *A Little Lower Than the Angels* (New York: Alfred A. Knopf, 1942); Maurine Whipple, *The Giant Joshua* (Boston: Houghton Mifflin, 1941), for which Whipple received a $1,000 advance award from publisher Houghton Mifflin; Bernard DeVoto, *The Year of Decision: 1846* (New York: Little, Brown, 1943), which was a Book of the Month Club selection; and Wallace Stegner, *Mormon Country*, ed. Erskine Caldwell, American Folkways (New York: Duell, Sloan & Pearce, 1942).

18. Fisher, *Children of God*. On the Harper Prize, see "Books and Authors," *New York Times*, 16 July 1939.

19. Ralph Thompson, "Books of the Times," review of *Children of God*, by Vardis Fisher, *New York Times*, 24 August 1939.

20. Fisher, *Children of God*, 183.

21. Ibid., 187.

22. Margaret Mitchell, *Gone with the Wind* (New York: Macmillan, 1936). Like Mitchell's story, Whipple's tells a sweeping tale of a moment in American history when a group of people who established the way of life in a particular region as they face the onslaught of the dominant culture determined to eliminate a central aspect of their way of life. Whereas Mitchell's story examines the practice and eventual end of slavery in the American South, Whipple examines Mormon life in the early years of the colonization of Utah Territory and during the height of the practice of polygamy. The other obvious similarity between the two books is in their heroines: dark-haired, spunky young women who primp and simper and flirt their way through life even as they battle to maintain their dignity and protect their families in the face of overwhelming challenges and cultural change.

23. On the award, see "Book Notices," *New York Times*, 13 June 1938. The review is Edith H. Walton, "Maureen Whipple's Novel about Mormons Is an Arresting Piece of Work," review of *The Giant Joshua*, by Maurine Whipple, *New York Times*, 12 January 1941.

24. Whipple, *The Giant Joshua*, 132.

25. Sorensen, *A Little Lower Than the Angels*.

26. Samuel Woolley Taylor, *Family Kingdom* (New York: McGraw-Hill, 1951). During this period, Taylor also authored a book about contemporary Mormon fundamentalist polygamy: *I Have Six Wives: A True Story of Present-Day Plural Marriage* (New York: Greenberg, 1956). While he kept the identities of his subjects secret at the time of publication, it was later revealed that the family profiled in the book was that of Rulon C. Allred, who went on to become one of the most prominent leaders in the Mormon fundamentalist community in the middle and late twentieth century.

27. "'Incredible' Is the Word for Father," *New York Times*, 17 June 1951.

28. Taylor, *Family Kingdom*, 156.

29. John D. Fitzgerald, *Papa Married a Mormon* (Englewood Cliffs, NJ: Prentice-Hall, 1955). Fitzgerald's later children's books, "The Great Brain" series, were also based on his childhood in southern Utah; the series remains popular today. In the 1970s, the Osmond family—perhaps Mormonism's greatest twentieth-century ambassadors to wider America—produced a film version for the NBC television network: *The Great Brain*, directed by Sidney Levin (USA: National Broadcasting Company, 1978; Larchmont, NY: Media Basics Video, [release date unknown]), VHS.

30. Fitzgerald, *Papa Married a Mormon*, 51.

31. Ibid., 71.

32. "The Screen in Review: 'Brigham Young—Frontiersman' Opens at the Roxy," *New York Times*, 21 September 1940. These sentiments were echoed in "*Brigham Young* Is Worthwhile as a Spectacle," *Chicago Tribune*, 30 September 1940.

33. *Brigham Young—Frontiersman*, directed by Henry Hathaway (1940; USA: 20th Century Fox, 2003), DVD.

34. *Wagon Master*, directed by John Ford (USA: RKO Pictures, 1950).

35. Peter Bogdanovich, commentary to *Wagon Master*, directed by John Ford (USA: Warner Home Video, 2009), DVD.

36. "Honolulu's Tribute Is Paid to War Dead: Citizens Join in Memorial Service at Navy Men's Graves," *New York Times*, 2 January 1942, and "Honolulu Marks Memorial Day for Raid Victims: Services at the Graves; Churches Filled," *Chicago Daily Tribune*, 2 January 1942. The latter is an extended version of the same article published by the *New York Times*.

37. Bowman, *The Mormon People*, 119.

38. "A Tribute to Mormon Leader," *New York Times*, 2 June 1950. See also "Mormons' Leader Gets Niche Today," *New York Times*, 13 March 1950. The only apparent controversy about Young's installation was where he should be placed: Utah's governor wanted him to have a seat of honor in the Capitol Rotunda, while Young's grandson and sculptor wanted him placed near a window, for good light.

39. "Cabinet Meetings Open with Prayer," *New York Times*, 21 February 1953.

40. "When Mormonism Mattered Less in Presidential Politics: George Romney's 1968 Window of Possibilities," *Journal of Mormon History* 39, no. 3 (Summer 2013): 96–130. For a more in-depth discussion, see J. B. Haws, *Mormonism in the American Mind: Fifty Years of Public Perception* (New York: Oxford University Press, 2013), 12–46.

41. "Mormon Choir on Radio Today for 1300th Time," *Chicago Daily Tribune*, 18 July 1954.

42. See Larry Wolters, "New West via Video," *Chicago Daily Tribune*, 31 October 1955.

43. "Audience in Berlin Hails Mormon Choir," *New York Times*, 7 September 1955. See also "Londoners Get a Shock from Utah Mormons," *Chicago Daily Tribune*, 24 August 1955, and "Airmen Hear Mormons," *New York Times*, 9 September 1955.

44. "Telstar Bridges Sea for Millions in U.S., Europe," *Chicago Daily Tribune*, 24 July 1962.

45. "Telstar Program Hailed in Europe: 18-Nation Audience Placed at 100,000,000 Persons," *New York Times*, 24 July 1962. More recently, this broadcast was noted as "a high point of assimilation for the choir and the church" in Kirk Johnson, "Mormons on a Mission," *New York Times*, 20 August 2010. A brief excerpt of the choir's performance is available via the *New York Times* online at http://www.nytimes.com/video/technology/100000002842114/inblooms-vision.html?playlistId=1194812888716.

Chapter Seventeen

The National Council of Churches versus Right-Wing Radio

How the Mainline Muted the New Christian Right

Paul Matzko

On February 10, 1960, a reservist at Mitchel Air Force Base in New York showed his pastor an official training manual that included quotations from fundamentalist radio broadcasters attacking the National Council of Churches of Christ (NCC). The pastor immediately forwarded the manual to James Wine, then an executive in the Office of Interpretation at the NCC.[1] Wine shared the document with former NCC president Eugene Carson Blake, and they read page after page accusing National Council clergymen of being "card-carrying Communists."[2] The NCC immediately went on the counteroffensive. Within four months, they had extracted an apology from the secretary of the air force, set in motion the resignation of the general responsible for the manual, and convinced presidential hopeful John F. Kennedy to condemn the manual on the Senate floor.

Normally a controversy of this nature would end up a colorful footnote in an unread institutional history. Yet this seemingly minor squabble over an air force training manual incited a decade-long campaign by the National Council of Churches, with the help of the Federal Communications Commission (FCC), to force conservative, religious broadcasters off the air. The National Council of Churches targeted small, independent stations airing conservative programs with a flurry of "Fairness Doctrine" complaints to the FCC. Enough complaints and the FCC might decide that these stations were not broadcasting in the "public interest" and decline to renew their licenses. Two such stations, WLBT in Jackson, Mississippi, and WXUR in Media, Pennsylvania, fought back and lost their licenses; hundreds of other stations saw the writing on the wall and preemptively dropped conservative programming. In the end, the National Council of Churches had muted their religious competitors through one of the most successful episodes of state-sponsored censorship in twentieth-century America.

The National Council's use of the FCC to further its own interests is a reminder that state intolerance of religion in the twentieth century looks quite different from the "hard" intolerance that afflicted the colonial era. There was never any chance that the federal government or its agencies would prohibit outright the exercise of religion by fundamentalist broadcasters. Rather, this episode was an example of what might be termed "soft" intolerance as a government agency used its discretionary power to advance the interests of one private faction at the expense of another. The potential for this kind of soft religious intolerance grew in step with the modern administrative state.[3] During the New Deal, Congress created many new agencies to regulate industry and protect consumers. For the sake of efficiency, administrators were given wide latitude in setting their own rules; in practice, Congress ceded legislative power to agencies not directly accountable to the public. These developments created ripe conditions for interest group lobbying and, in this case, for the exercise of a peculiarly modern form of religious intolerance.

When Congress created the Federal Communications Commission in 1934, it gave the commission rule-making power and tasked it with protecting the "public interest, convenience, or necessity" on the airwaves. "Public interest" was an ambiguous standard left undefined by Congress. No sooner had the ink dried on the Radio Act of 1934 than industry interest groups began lobbying the FCC to define the public interest in a way congenial to themselves and injurious to their competition. The commission quickly became a revolving door; commissioners would serve a few years, leave for better compensated industry jobs, and then lobby their old counterparts. In economics, this is called "rent-seeking" behavior, an attempt to extract a competitive advantage, or "rent," from the government.[4] Religious groups are not immune to its allure: churches and denominations, no less than corporations, stand to gain from friendly government regulators. When the National Council of Churches convinced the FCC that fundamentalist broadcasters did not air in the public interest, they were engaged in rent-seeking behavior. Silencing fundamentalist broadcasters would drive religious listeners, and their donations, to broadcasts sponsored by the National Council. The fundamentalists tried to push back, but it was not a level playing field. The politically well-connected National Council of Churches, with forty-five million members in its denominations, simply outmaneuvered the conservative broadcasters, who had significantly smaller formal memberships and fewer political connections.

In recent years, scholars have paid closer attention to the history of mainline Protestantism.[5] The new historiography tends to emphasize the prophetic role played by the National Council of Churches and other ecumenical organizations in the 1960s as they protested the Vietnam War, advocated nuclear disarmament, and campaigned for civil rights legislation. This narrative suggests that a self-abnegating National Council stood for liberal justice even as mainline pews emptied of parishioners. At times, it slides into adoration, as when Gary Dorrien writes that the mainline "served as guardians of America's moral culture," "preserved the idea that the USA was a nation with the soul of a church," and "helped to liberalize American society."[6] This cheery depiction of ecumenical Protestantism glosses over the more pragmatic actions of mainline leaders, who were willing to fight hard, and sometimes dirty, in defense of their claim to represent the soul of America. The mainline's defense of liberalism could be profoundly illiberal.[7]

Among the broadcasters targeted by the National Council, two stood out: Billy James Hargis and Carl McIntire. Hargis, a Disciples of Christ minister from Tulsa, Oklahoma, founded a broadcast ministry in 1948 that later became the *Christian Crusade*. McIntire's *Twentieth Century Reformation Hour* began broadcasting from Collingswood, New Jersey, in 1955.[8] In the 1950s Hargis and McIntire had traveled together to West Germany and released fifty thousand weather balloons, laden with gospel tracts, to bombard souls behind the Iron Curtain. Both men believed that communism lurked behind every sinister development in American society, from nuclear disarmament to sex education. They stoked their listeners' wildest fears. One of McIntire's revival brochures was titled "Stalin's Agents in Camden County." Yet beneath their anticommunist rhetoric was an authentic expression of growing conservative dissent from consensus liberalism, both in politics and in religion.[9]

To Hargis and McIntire—both fundamentalists who were committed to doctrines such as the inerrancy of the Bible and the depravity of humankind—the National Council's championing of liberal theology represented a deviation from true Christianity. The errors of the National Council of Churches seemed so egregious to McIntire that he called for a second Protestant Reformation to turn back liberalism's "ecumenical blitz."[10] Likewise, Hargis's *Christian Crusade* battled against the National Council no less fervently than it did communism. Their accusations of communist sympathizing and heretical doctrine remained a minor irritant that the National Council could safely ignore during the 1950s, when the two men were broadcast on only a handful of stations in Oklahoma and New Jersey. But by 1960, McIntire aired on 108 stations across the country, a total that would more than quadruple over the next four years.[11] McIntire, Hargis, and their compatriots began to pose a serious threat to the National Council's own financially struggling Broadcasting and Film Commission (BFC); McIntire's *Twentieth Century Reformation Hour* alone had an annual income (roughly $2,040,000) more than eight times that of the BFC (roughly $250,000).[12] The National Council, representing 45 million Protestants, was being dwarfed on the airwaves by the likes of McIntire, whose American Council of Christian Churches could claim perhaps 120,000.[13] Although the National Council had won a quick victory in the air force manual controversy, conservative broadcasting now loomed menacingly.

The National Council especially worried about the influence of conservative broadcasters on mainline parishioners. After all, lay folk heard McIntire and Hargis on the radio five days a week; mainline clergy only had them for an hour on Sunday. In desperation, one pastor wrote to the FBI to say that he had instructed his parishioners to ignore the "prophets of discord on the air." But despite his best efforts, his people continued to believe that communists had infiltrated the National Council. He hoped that if J. Edgar Hoover vouched for the National Council's anticommunist credentials, they would be persuaded otherwise.[14] Concern over the effectiveness of conservative libel percolated up into the denominational leadership as well. Having received more than twenty inquiries about communist infiltration of the National Council, one denominational executive concluded that McIntire was waging a "deliberate, calculated, organized and well-financed campaign to drive a wedge between lay men and women and their ministers."[15] The danger was more than hypothetical; in 1960, under the influence of McIntire and Hargis, the largest National Council–affiliated church in Kansas, First Baptist of Wichita, voted to sever all ties with the organization and its own denomination.[16] First Baptist of Wichita was exhibit A at a meeting of the National Council's Broadcasting and Film Commission (BFC) in February 1963. After a lively debate about how the National Council should respond to the threat of conservative broadcasting, the hawkish faction carried the day, advocating aggressive countermeasures. As Methodist bishop John Wesley Lord argued, the threat could not be dismissed because "the attack is from within as well as from outside." What the National Council needed were "shock troops to meet the attacks of the virus."[17]

As the disparity in fund-raising shows, the National Council could not hope to compete with conservative Christians in the marketplace, so its members turned to government regulators. Their "shock troops" would come from the Federal Communications Commission. The goal, as one NCC executive put it, was to make the independent radio stations "watch their p's and q's concerning some kinds of broadcasts that they carry because it is a very risky business."[18] The National Council wanted to make it even riskier, encouraging regional councils and pastors to write to their local stations—with a convenient form letter provided by the NCC—to remind them that their licenses depended on their compliance with the FCC's "Fairness Doctrine" and then to encourage them to replace the offending programs with council-sponsored ones.

The Fairness Doctrine, although not so named until 1959, had its roots in the birth of the FCC. The Radio Acts of 1927 and 1934 had mandated that broadcasters use their licenses in the "public interest, convenience, or necessity"—an ambiguous phrase, yet one that the courts recognized as preceding any claim to First Amendment rights or private property by license holders. Over the next forty years, the FCC vacillated between a policy of salutary neglect and periodic attempts to crack down on noncompliant broadcasters, though noncompliance was hard to determine while the criteria remained vague and arbitrarily applied. After all, it was a rather tall order to ask a board of five nonelected commissioners, mostly lawyers with little background in radio or television, to determine what precisely was in the public interest for all Americans.

From the 1930s through the 1950s, radical groups on both the left and the right felt the sting of heightened FCC scrutiny, including labor unions, socialists, and anti–New Dealers. But it was not until a series of scandals embroiled the radio and television industry in the late 1950s that the FCC formally instituted the Fairness Doctrine.[19] The doctrine stipulated that the public interest would best be served by educational programming that covered "controversial issues of public importance" from diverse points of view. In practice, that provision of the Fairness Doctrine came into conflict with the FCC's personal attack rule. Under that rule, if a station aired a program attacking an individual or organization, the station owner was required to notify the offended party and provide them with an opportunity to respond on air. From the perspective of station owners, the 1959 Fairness Doctrine simply bred more confusion since the difference between a "personal attack" and robust disagreement remained unclear. For instance, conservative broadcasters believed that they were promoting robust disagreement when they accused the Kennedy administration of kowtowing to Moscow on nuclear disarmament. The Democratic National Committee, however, believed this was a slanderous personal attack and reported hundreds of stations for Fairness Doctrine violations in the summer of 1964. Given the lack of clarity, many station owners calculated that it was easier to avoid controversial programming altogether.

In response to the FCC's scandals during the late 1950s, John F. Kennedy appointed several young, reform-minded lawyers to the Federal Communications Commission.[20] On July 26, 1963, the FCC issued a clarification of the Fairness Doctrine that opened the door for the National Council's campaign to shut down right-wing broadcasters. The statement clearly targeted conservative broadcasters, stipulating that regardless of whether "a particular program or viewpoint is presented under the label of 'Americanism,' 'anticommunism,' or 'states rights,'" it would still be obligated to fairly represent opposing viewpoints. Stations that supported segregation on air without giving equal opportunity to civil rights activists were also put on notice.[21] The FCC had thus called out conservative broadcasters; station managers airing the likes of McIntire and Hargis would be under heightened scrutiny. In response, station owners started adding a bit of diversity to their programming—typically through listener call-in shows—but groups like the National Council would not be satisfied until they received, for free, the same amount of airtime as broadcasters like McIntire and Hargis, who had purchased their airtime. Small, independent radio stations were caught between the Scylla of financial insolvency if they did not air conservative programming and the Charybdis of Fairness Doctrine complaints (which might cost them their licenses) if they did.

The FCC's July 26 clarification gave the National Council and its allies a chance to finish what had begun with the air force manual controversy. First, the National Council sent Robert Edwin Lee—director of the BFC's West Coast office and author of *Inherit the Wind*, the Broadway play that was a thinly veiled critique of fundamentalism and McCarthyism—to meet with the FCC in Washington, DC.[22] There is no record of the discussion at that meeting, but the following year four of the seven commissioners spoke at a Washington Council of Churches meeting on broadcasting, marking the first time so many commissioners had attended an NCC-affiliated event. BFC executive director William F. Fore lauded the meeting for being "extremely helpful in establishing two-way communication between local religious broadcasters and the FCC."[23] The desire for "two-way communication" seems to have been mutual. A year later, Fore confidentially reported to the BFC that "many members of the Federal Communications Commission . . . are deeply interested in us as a force in the public arena of discussion, expressing quite openly their hope that we can be an ally in some of the FCC efforts to achieve more responsible broadcasting."[24] With a 4–3 majority on the FCC and the July 26 clarification as a mandate, the National Council could get to work.

The National Council channeled its efforts against conservative broadcasting through its regional councils and through a denominational affiliate, the United Church of Christ's Office of Communications. Having some distance between the National Council and the campaign allowed for plausible deniability. As soon as word of the FCC's July 26 clarification spread, the targeted broadcasters had begun to complain that their freedom of speech was being trampled upon. Charles Brackbill, a key regional coordinator from New Jersey with a history of animosity toward McIntire, convinced the Broadcasting and Film Commission that the National Council should not be directly involved in the campaign. In part, this was because "a frontal attack is what these birds welcome most," given how adept McIntire and Hargis were at turning controversy to their own advantage. All press is good press for those in the business of stirring up outrage; if the National Council got its hands dirty, it would be a gift to McIntire and Hargis, a David versus Goliath story with which to rouse their listeners. Isolating the National Council would also keep it from being "officially connected with any imagined suppression of free speech." An unofficial connection to actual suppression of free speech would have to do.[25]

The National Council took Brackbill's advice and turned to the United Church of Christ (UCC) and Everett C. Parker, director of the UCC's Office of Communication and a board member of the National Council's BFC. Parker was a progressive in his politics, having earlier produced programs for the Kelly-Nash Machine in Chicago. He had no love for fundamentalist broadcasters like McIntire and Hargis, who preached what he called a "theology of greed." To be sure, they were popular, Parker reasoned, but so long as "the consumer was not a real person"—meaning socially conscious in progressive terms—someone like himself needed to "force upon the people some factual material, some honest interpretation."[26] Parker's denomination, the United Church of Christ, felt the sting of conservative broadcasting even more than most of the mainliners. The UCC had been formed by a denominational merger only a few years before and some recalcitrant local churches refused to join because they listened to McIntire, who told them that the UCC was a pawn of the communist-infiltrated National Council.

The United Church of Christ had an additional reason to lead the counteroffensive against conservative broadcasting, as the church prided itself on its defense of civil rights. Parker had met with Martin Luther King Jr. during the Montgomery bus boycott of 1955–1956. The civil rights leader had asked him, "Why don't some of you do something about the way we're treated on radio and television?"[27] Indeed, conservative broadcasters typically supported segregation and frequently voiced their suspicion that the civil rights movement was a communist plot. Parker looked for a test case and found his mark in WLBT-TV in Jackson, Mississippi. The station had editorialized against James Meredith's attempt to integrate the University of Mississippi, urging its listeners to "go out to Oxford and stand shoulder to shoulder with Governor Barnett and keep that nigra out of Ole Miss."[28] Furthermore, in a town that was more than 40 percent black, the station did not employ any (nonjanitorial) black staff, gave no airtime to black clergy, and never used titles—Mr., Mrs., etc.—for its black interviewees, yet never failed to identify their race. WLBT was in clear violation of the FCC's July 26 statement.

The UCC, with amicus curiae from the AFL-CIO and the National Council's BFC, took WLBT to court. After a lengthy, expensive legal battle, the station owners lost their appeal for license renewal in 1969. Control of the license then passed to a local coalition of civil rights groups sponsored by the UCC. Even more significantly, future Supreme Court chief justice Warren Burger, then serving on a circuit court of appeals, issued a landmark ruling in

1966 that made the WLBT victory possible for the UCC and bolstered the National Council's campaign against conservative broadcasters. Previously, only those applying for station licenses themselves were granted standing before the FCC during license renewal hearings, but after Burger's ruling members of the general public could appear as well.[29] Burger's ruling cleared the way for challenges to radio station licenses by local community groups, an opportunity that the National Council of Churches and the United Church of Christ would exploit.

In 1967, Everett Parker, encouraged by Burger's ruling and with funding from the Ford Foundation and the AFL-CIO, organized a mass monitoring campaign of ninety-six stations in thirty-eight southern cities with the goal of eliminating racism in broadcasting within five years.[30] Yet the UCC did not restrict its monitoring to the South or to fighting segregation. It targeted additional stations in the West, claiming that "extremist groups and individuals such as Carl McIntire" were "concentrating in these areas in the hope of influencing the election results for the Senate and House of Representatives" during the 1968 election.[31] By threatening Fairness Doctrine complaints, the UCC convinced more than two hundred stations to air a response, produced by the National Council's BFC, without charge. It was unsubtly titled "EX-TREMISM '67" and featured a former FBI agent giving tips on combating right-wingers. By having the UCC distribute the program, the BFC had fulfilled its wish that the program "be distributed by a non-BFC agency and not be under the auspices of the NCC," again giving the appearance that the National Council was above the fray.[32]

As the United Church of Christ launched its monitoring campaign, the Greater Philadelphia Council of Churches (GPCC) began to wrest station WXUR from Carl McIntire's grip. Ever since the air force manual scandal, the GPCC wanted nothing more than to rid itself of this troublesome preacher. A noisy neighbor, McIntire taped the *20th Century Reformation Hour* at his home church in the Philadelphia suburb of Collingswood, New Jersey. In particular, Charles Brackbill, the founder of the radio arms of both the Greater Philadelphia and New Jersey councils, could not stand McIntire. Brackbill was a graduate of Princeton Theological Seminary, which McIntire had attended before leaving in protest at the seminary's liberal theology. As a pastor in New Jersey, Brackbill had intimate knowledge of McIntire's ministry. He was embarrassed that "some of the worst 'non-Council' broadcasting in the country originates in New Jersey" with Carl McIntire, who "from his kitchen in Collingswood . . . daily spews forth his invectives against Eugene Carson Blake" and the National Council of Churches. He acknowledged that attempting to silence other broadcasters put the council in a "very difficult and ticklish position" vis-à-vis freedom of speech. But that would not stop Brackbill from launching a "Truth Crusade" in 1965 when McIntire applied to the FCC for a license transfer for the recently purchased station WXUR.[33]

It was obvious to even casual listeners of the *20th Century Reformation Hour* that McIntire attacked his opponents incessantly. Anticipating that McIntire would violate the Fairness Doctrine, the GPCC sent a formal complaint to the FCC protesting the license transfer. Francis Hines, Brackbill's successor as director of broadcasting for the GPCC, wrote to FCC chairman E. William Henry, objecting that McIntire's persistent attacks on the Roman Catholic Church, the National Council of Churches, the United Nations, and the FCC itself made him "a dangerously divisive force wherever he is or is heard." Hines's argument—that McIntire's divisiveness made him dangerous—was common in Cold War rhetoric. Segregationists, including McIntire, routinely accused civil rights leaders of disrupting American unity and thus playing into Soviet hands.[34] Hines turned the same logic against conservatives, accusing them of undermining the religious and diplomatic institutions that held back the tide of communism. Indeed, the perceived threat McIntire posed to American harmony was so severe that although Hines "would not deny any man the right to free speech," he would make an exception for McIntire, arguing that free speech "carries with it a responsibility for the truth which I do not believe Mr. McIntire exercises."[35]

Dozens of other churches, denominations, and community organizations joined the GPCC's complaint and echoed Hines's logic. A Lutheran pastor in Havertown asked the FCC to deny the transfer to "this apostle of discord" because "men who make statements and accusations backed up by phony documentation should not be allowed to create a false image and thus undermine our beloved country."[36] Many of the cosigners recognized the dissonance between their repeated affirmations of freedom of speech and their request to deny a radio station license to McIntire. Frank Stroup, a self-proclaimed "ardent believer in the right of free speech" and an executive in the United Presbyterian Church, "hesitate[d] to ask that his application be turned down." Yet he did ask, because "when I consider the use to which Dr. McIntyre puts freedom of speech it appears to me that he does not exercise it responsibly."[37] The letter writers also betrayed a more pragmatic motivation for supporting the GPCC's complaint: the desire to remove an obstacle to the success of the ecumenical mainline. As Prince Taylor Jr., a Methodist minister in Princeton, acknowledged, "Those of us who work for harmony and peaceful relations among the peoples of New Jersey will be seriously handicapped by having such a powerful medium of communication in such irresponsible hands."[38] By turning down the license transfer, the FCC would rid the Greater Philadelphia and New Jersey councils of a major competitor.

Yet, in 1965, the GPCC's challenge to the license transfer failed, partly because it preceded Chief Justice Burger's ruling on standing, but mostly because denying a license on Fairness Doctrine grounds before the doctrine was actually violated smacked too much of prior restraint. So the GPCC tried again when WXUR's license came up for renewal in 1967. The FCC's hearing examiner, H. Gifford Irion, surprised everyone by siding with McIntire. Irion agreed with the GPCC that McIntire had fallen short of the letter of the Fairness Doctrine, but he preferred McIntire's "rough-and-tumble and fervent rhetoric" to the "diluted parlor chat" that characterized much American broadcasting. Irion feared that strictly enforcing the Fairness Doctrine would have a chilling effect on news coverage, thus undermining the very reason that the FCC instituted the Fairness Doctrine—to encourage robust editorializing. Irion had identified an inconsistency in the Fairness Doctrine itself. McIntire's attempt, "however inept, to allow wide-swinging utterance of all shades of thought" conflicted with the FCC's personal attack rule.[39] The FCC very rarely overturned its own examiners, especially not a veteran like Irion, but did so in the WXUR case. After six years and multiple appeals, the GPCC had won and McIntire lost his license.

McIntire's last day on WXUR was July 4, 1973. The symbolism was not lost on him. In protest, he held a "funeral" for WXUR on the lawn behind Independence Hall in Philadelphia. Pallbearers wearing judicial robes and powdered wigs laid a scale model of the station's antenna in a coffin marked "Freedom of Speech" while mourners bedecked in Revolutionary-era garb listened to Carl McIntire pronounce WXUR's last rites.[40] The following month, McIntire purchased a surplus World War II minesweeper and outfitted it with a powerful radio transmitter and a banner reading, "Radio Free America." McIntire's pirate radio station broadcast for a single day from the international waters off Cape May, New Jersey. The FCC shut it down with a court order, but not before the broadcast had interfered with signals from as far away as Salt Lake City.[41]

In the WLBT and WXUR cases, the National Council and its affiliates had won two major victories over conservative broadcasters, but the true scope of their victory was made more apparent by the U.S. Senate's investigation of right-wing broadcasting. In early 1966, Bob Lowe, a lawyer hired by the Senate Commerce Committee, contacted the National Council of Churches. The ranking Democrats on the Commerce Committee wanted to reinforce the FCC's Fairness Doctrine (of which Commerce had oversight). They commissioned Lowe to gather evidence of right-wing radicalism in the broadcasting industry. In March 1966, Lowe met with William Fore, director of the National Council's BFC. Afterward, Fore informed the head of the GPCC that Lowe had encouraged the monitoring of WXUR to continue and confided that he believed WXUR "ought to be clobbered" by the GPCC when the station's license came up for renewal that summer.[42] In May, Lowe attended the BFC's annual meeting to update them on the Commerce Committee's plan, even giving them a scoop on the FCC's upcoming revision of the personal attack rules, which would add an additional $10,000 fine per violation. After hearing Lowe's presentation, the BFC voted to send Fore to the Commerce Committee to speak in favor of the change, providing the committee cover lest the public think the hearings were a narrowly partisan ploy.[43]

The National Council further aided Lowe's investigation by compiling a list of every station in the United States that broadcast conservative "attack programs."[44] It did so through the regional councils, which saw this as an opportunity to pressure independent stations to drop conservative programming. The Minnesota Council of Churches' effort provides a compelling case study of the effect of Bob Lowe's investigation on local broadcasters. Bruce Sifford, director of the Minnesota Church Committee on Radio-Television, contacted all 103 radio and television stations in Minnesota and heard back from 96.[45] Of those stations, four carried either the *20th Century Reformation Hour* or the *Christian Crusade*. Sifford reported them to Bob Lowe. What is most interesting about the Minnesota Council's correspondence is the approach Sifford took when he contacted the stations. In the first paragraph of his letter, Sifford name-checked the Senate Commerce Committee, informing stations that the Senate was investigating compliance with the Fairness Doctrine. The implicit threat was clear. Sifford also asked the stations to air, without charge, a series of fourteen one-minute responses.[46] Most stations quickly complied, but the stations that aired either McIntire's or Hargis's shows were less forthcoming. One manager, Charles Woodward of station KSUM, agreed that "the tactics used by this man" (Billy James Hargis) were distasteful but defended airing Hargis's program because "a significant number of my listeners have indicated they want me to, and I am only attempting to live up to my promise to program 'in the public interest.'" Unfortunately for Woodward, demand for a program did not equate with the public interest—at least not according to the Minnesota Council of Churches or the FCC. After a few more threatening letters, the station caved and stopped airing the *Christian Crusade*.[47]

The Minnesota Council of Churches had used Bob Lowe's request for information to intimidate stations into compliance. Receiving a letter implying the full force of a U.S. Senate investigation carried an unmistakable message: accede to the council's demands or risk losing your license. The pressure had its intended effect. Sifford's letters show that two stations—that is, half the stations in Minnesota that reported carrying conservative programs—had dropped McIntire because of the Minnesota Council's efforts. Staying in the good graces of the Minnesota Council of Churches, the FCC, and the U.S. Senate Commerce Committee mattered more than popularity or revenue. More than two stations may have been impacted by the campaign. McIntire's records reveal that during the mid-1960s he broadcast on eight stations in Minnesota. Seven dropped him sometime before the start of 1967.[48] The Minnesota Council of Churches' campaign to intimidate local broadcasters left McIntire with a single station in the state.

As the pressure applied by Bob Lowe and the National Council of Churches mounted on independent station owners, letters poured into McIntire's office, warning him that stations would drop his program to avoid FCC Fairness Doctrine complaints. As one station manager put it, "The FCC has their teeth in my bread and butter."[49] Another station, WUNS in the hamlet of Lewisburg, Pennsylvania, regretted dropping McIntire given their amiable relationship of six years, but compliance with the new regulations would cause "many, many man-hours of work over and above the regular weekly chores of an already-under-staffed small radio station." Furthermore, the station owner was in negotiations with a "very responsible group of citizens" seeking to buy his license, and he feared that a complaint would cause the FCC to balk at the transfer.[50] There are dozens of similar letters in McIntire's archives, but the full impact of the National Council's campaign on conservative broadcasting becomes apparent from Bob Lowe's national statistics. In 1967, Lowe, in addition to his contacts with the National Council of Churches, had contacted every station in the country. He asked station managers whether they still carried right-wing programming and, if not, whether they had dropped such programs in the previous year. Unsurprisingly, a considerable number of stations dropped conservative programming between 1966 and 1967. The top secular conservative programs lost an average of 33 percent of their stations that year. The programs targeted by the National Council (including both the religious programs and the *Citizens Council Forum*) declined by 59 percent, nearly double the rate of broadly conservative programming.[51] McIntire's own station count plummeted from a high of 460 stations in 1964 to just 183 in 1967. Conservative broadcasting had taken a body blow from which it would not recover until the Carter administration's relaxation of the Fairness Doctrine in the late 1970s.

The National Council of Churches and its allies had won a major, if temporary, victory over their religious and political competitors in the New Christian Right. They had done so by convincing a sympathetic federal bureaucracy to deny licenses to stations that aired conservative broadcasters. This was not an exercise of impartial justice, but rather a targeted effort to silence an intolerant opposition. McIntire and company were indeed intolerant given their support for segregation and the paranoid extremes to which they took their anticommunism, but the central irony is that a coalition of liberal advocacy groups had used deeply illiberal methods to combat illiberalism. As media historian Heather Hendershot notes of the WXUR case, "The idea of 'free speech' was used to shut down free speech."[52] The tortured rhetoric in the letters of the various leaders of this campaign confirms Hendershot's observation. They were well aware of the discrepancy between their liberal beliefs and their illiberal acts.

That discrepancy reflected the contradictory mandates of the Fairness Doctrine itself, both to promote rigorous debate on controversial issues and to enforce civility. The Fairness Doctrine was a mess—ill conceived, arbitrarily applied, and rooted in an inchoate idea of the public interest. Yet it became a vital tool in one of the most successful episodes of censorship in modern American history, comparable in scale and effectiveness to the Second Red Scare. In the early 1950s, Senator Joseph McCarthy and other congressional Republicans made partisan hay using House and Senate investigations to intimidate leftist intellectuals. In the 1960s, McCarthy's tactics were swung around to bear on the anticommunists instead. Senate Democrats and sympathetic groups like the National Council of Churches convinced the FCC to intimidate radio stations that aired conservative programs, many of which had strong religious underpinnings.

The silencing of the New Christian Right in the 1960s is a prime example of the soft religious intolerance enabled by the post–New Deal administrative state. Toleration always has limits, of course, but the struggle to define those limits takes place everywhere the administrative state reaches, including federal agencies, municipal planning commissions, and local zoning boards. Administrative intolerance hinders religious sects on the cultural periphery more than churches that have a privileged place at the core. When Native Americans first sought to legalize peyote smoking, they faced a bewildering maze of federal regulatory hurdles and legal challenges. Since 9/11, local zoning boards have often been pressured to deny approval for Muslim mosques. Christian fundamentalists learned the same lesson during the 1960s.[53] The National Council of Churches beat them by arguing that it better represented the "public interest" because of its size and moderate stance on the political issues of the day. It framed itself as the reasonable, mainstream alternative to conservative extremism and found favor in the eyes of the FCC.

Although McIntire's *20th Century Reformation Hour* and Billy James Hargis's *Christian Crusade* were muted, their listeners did not simply disappear. Those who listened to conservative religious broadcasters in the 1960s formed the core constituency for the next generation of fundamentalist broadcasters. When the FCC began relaxing its enforcement of the Fairness Doctrine during Jimmy Carter's presidency, radio and television preachers like Jerry Falwell and Pat Robertson adopted an increasingly strident political approach in their shows. The National Council and its allies had delayed the rise of the New Christian Right for roughly a decade, a relatively brief caesura between the surge of pro-Goldwater broadcasting in 1964 and *Newsweek* naming 1976 the "Year of the Evangelical." Of course, conservative Christian activism continued to bubble just below the surface during that decade, but without access to the mass media as a tool of political mobilization, the New Christian Right remained a niche movement rather than the imposing force that it became in 1980s electoral politics.

NOTES

1. Interview with James Wine, n.d., record group 17, box 7, folder 8, Papers of the National Council of the Churches of Christ (hereafter NCC), Presbyterian Historical Society (hereafter PHS), Philadelphia, PA.

2. Air Reserve Center Training Manual, n.d., record group 17, box 6, folder 28, NCC, PHS.

3. The term *administrative state* is from Dwight Waldo, *The Administrative State: A Study of the Political Theory of American Public Administration* (New York: Ronald Press, 1948). Ever since he coined it, scholars have pushed back against the idea that the New Deal was truly new—for instance, finding the origins of the administrative state in the early republic in agencies like the post office. See Jerry L. Mashaw, *Creating the Administrative Constitution: The Lost One Hundred Years of American Administrative Law* (New Haven, CT: Yale University Press, 2012). But even if the New Deal was not qualitatively different from prior government administration, it did feature a quantitative expansion in the scope and reach of the administrative state.

4. "Rent-seeking" is a concept drawn from the public choice theory of economics. The idea comes specifically from Gordon Tullock, "The Welfare Costs of Tariffs, Monopolies and Theft," *Western Economic Journal* 5 (June 1967): 224–32. The term itself was coined by Anne Krueger, "The Political Economy of the Rent-Seeking Society," *American Economic Review* 64 (June 1974): 291–303.

5. See Jill K. Gill, *Embattled Ecumenism: The National Council of Churches, the Vietnam War, and the Trials of the Protestant Left* (Dekalb: Northern Illinois University Press, 2011); David Hollinger, *After Cloven Tongues of Fire: Protestant Liberalism in Modern American History* (Princeton, NJ: Princeton University Press, 2013); Matthew S. Hedstrom, *The Rise of Liberal Religion: Book Culture and American Spirituality in the Twentieth Century* (Oxford: Oxford University Press, 2012); Leigh E. Schmidt and Sally M. Promey, eds., *American Religious Liberalism* (Bloomington: Indiana University Press, 2012).

6. Gary Dorrien, "The Protestant Mainline Makes a (Literary) Comeback," *Religion Dispatches*, 5 August 2013, accessed 14 October 2013, http://www.religiondispatches.org/archive/atheologies/7233/the_protestant_mainline_makes_a_literary_comeback; see also Martin E. Marty, "From Declinism to Discovery," *Christian Century*, 21 August 2013, accessed 27 March 2014, http://www.christiancentury.org/blogs/archive/2013-08/declinism-discovery.

7. Historian Elesha Coffman also grapples with this complicated legacy in her study of the *Christian Century*, the preeminent publication for ecumenical Protestant intellectuals for most of the twentieth century. Coffman documents the tactics that the editors of the *Christian Century* employed to undercut evangelist Billy Graham's rocketing popularity during the 1950s, including accusing him of financial impropriety, claiming that his convert totals were inflated, and portraying his followers as dupes. Coffman ends her account in 1960, but the pattern of mainline attacks on evangelical insurgents continued. Mainline attacks on Billy Graham failed to gain traction given his immense popularity, but mainliners could hope for better results with the fundamentalist broadcasters, who were both more radical and more vulnerable than Graham. Elesha Coffman, *The Christian Century and the Rise of the Protestant Mainline* (New York: Oxford University Press, 2013).

8. There is a hole in the historical literature on both conservative and religious broadcasting post–World War II. There are excellent works covering the early years of radio from the 1920s through the 1940s, including Matthew Sutton's *Aimee Semple McPherson and the Resurrection of Christian America*; Tona Hangen's *Redeeming the Dial: Radio, Religion, and Popular Culture in America*; Douglas Carl Abrams's *Selling the Old-Time Religion: American Fundamentalists and Mass Culture, 1920–1940*; and chapter 7, "Tuning in the Gospel," in Joel Carpenter's *Revive Us Again: The Reawakening of American Fundamentalism* (Oxford: Oxford University Press, 1997). The standard work on broadcasting history during the period, Erik Barnouw's trilogy, particularly *The Image Empire: A History of Broadcasting in the United States from 1953*, barely mentions conservative broadcasting in the 1950s–1960s.

9. *Christian Beacon*, 22 April 1948, 1 (hereafter cited as *CB*); *CB*, 12 February 1948, 4.

10. Carl McIntire, *Twentieth Century Reformation* (Collingswood, NJ: Christian Beacon Press, 1944), ix.

11. McIntire kept a binder, updated through 1966, listing every station he broadcast on, its frequency, location, and the start and end dates of his relationship with it. I would be glad to make my tabulations available upon request. See "Radio Maps," n.d., box 528, folder 52, Papers of Carl McIntire, Princeton Theological Seminary Library, Princeton, NJ.

12. The disparity was even starker given that McIntire's money came almost exclusively through small listener contributions, while the BFC relied on budgeted amounts from its member denominations. The comparison between the BFC and McIntire's ministry is for 1964–1966. "Comparison of Month-End Operating Balances," n.d., rg 16, box 1, folder 26, NCC, PHS.

13. "What Is This American Council?" n.d., rg 17, box 6, folder 2, NCC. Samuel McCrea Calvert, "Information about the American Council of Christian Churches," n.d., rg 17, box 6, folder 2, NCC.

14. Freedom of Information and Privacy Acts, "Subject: National Council of Churches," HQ File: 100-50869, section 9, pp. 12, 41, 146, 150–51, 182. Hoover refused to get involved in the air force manual scandal despite the offer of a prize-winning, home-cooked blueberry pie from one Episcopal chairwoman.

15. James E. Wagner, "To Pastors and Lay-Members of the Evangelical and Reformed Church Who Have Expressed Interest and Concern with Reference to the Recent Controversy over an Air Force Manual," 1 April 1960, rg 17, box 6, folder 21, NCC.

16. Louis Cassels, "American Baptists May Leave National Council of Churches," *Lodi News-Sentinel* (Lodi, CA), 27 May 1960. The battle over control of the large church building went all the way to the Kansas Supreme Court, which finally ruled in favor of the American Baptists. See chapter 5 of Roger L. Frederickson, *The Church That Refused to Die: A Powerful Story of Reconciliation and Renewal* (n.p.: Victor Books, 1991).

17. "Notes on the Consultation between Members of the General Public Interpretation Committee and the Broadcasting and Film Commission," 26 February 1963, rg 303.2, box 17, folder 22, Papers of the United Presbyterian Church, PHS.

18. James Wine to Paul C. Combs, 14 March 1960, rg 17, box 7, folder 8, NCC.

19. Three scandals rocked the television and radio industry during the late 1950s. In 1958, the popular quiz show *Twenty One*, in which contestants competed for a $64,000 cash prize, was found to be rigging the outcomes. Several months later, the "payola" scandal broke. Record companies had been paying radio stations to air their songs without announcing their sponsorship in violation of FCC regulations. Finally, media critics worried about how the on-screen violence of television Westerns would affect child development, leading to FCC chairman Newton Minow's famous speech in 1961 condemning the "vast wasteland" of television programming.

20. Three of the Democrats on the commission in 1963—Robert Bartley, E. William Henry, and Kenneth Cox—were joined by Republican Frederick W. Ford on most of the pro-reform votes. Ford, an Eisenhower appointee, resigned at the end of 1964 to join the BFC's Government and Industry Committee. Oddly enough, the antireform faction—which included Republicans Rosel Hyde and Robert Lee—was headed by Lee Loevinger, a Democrat and Kennedy appointee.

21. Ben Waple, "Text of FCC July 26 Statement on 1959 'Fairness' Doctrine," rg MC#001, box 934, folder 7, Papers of the American Civil Liberties Union, Princeton University Library, Princeton, NJ.

22. Minutes, "Broadcasting and Film Commission Board of Managers," 6–7 May 1965, rg 16, box 1, folder 26, NCC. Parker and Brackbill were also elected to the BFC's executive committee at this meeting; Minutes, "Broadcasting and Film Commission Board of Managers," 17 February 1964, rg 16, box 1, folder 26, NCC.

23. William F. Fore, "Report of the Executive Director to the Organizational Meeting of the Broadcasting and Film Commission," 6–7 May 1965, rg 16, box 1, folder 26, NCC.

24. William F. Fore, "Report of the Executive Director to BFC Executive Committee," 5 May 1966, rg 16, box 3, folder 1, NCC. This report was marked confidential, unlike previous reports.

25. Charles Brackbill to James Wine, 11 March 1960, rg 17, box 7, folder 8, NCC.

26. George E. Korn, "Everett C. Parker and the Citizen Media Reform Movement: A Phenomenological Life History" (PhD diss., Southern Illinois University at Carbondale, 1991), 102–3.

27. Everett C. Parker, interview by William C. Winslow, in *United Church of Christ, a Four-Part DVD Collection*, 15 December 2006.

28. Fred Friendly, *The Good Guys, the Bad Guys, and the First Amendment: Free Speech vs. Fairness in Broadcasting* (New York: Vintage Books, 1977), 90.

29. "WLBT-TV and the Jackson Community Development Program," n.d., UCC 2002.19.03, Papers of the United Church of Christ Office of Communications, United Church of Christ Archives, Cleveland, OH.

30. Everett C. Parker to Thomas E. Cooney, 21 August 1967, UCC 2002.19.02, item 22, UCC; "Supplementary Report to the Ford Foundation by the Office of Communication," 5 January 1970, UCC.

31. Minutes, United Church of Christ Office of Communication Board of Directors, 11 September 1967, UCC 2002.19.22, item 11, UCC.

32. Minutes, "National Council of the Churches of Christ in the U.S.A. Broadcasting and Film Commission Board of Managers," 22–23 September 1966, rg 16, box 1, folder 26, NCC.

33. Charles Brackbill Jr., "Comprehensive Statement of Synod Radio-Television Work," 27 April 1961, rg 303.2, box 5, folder 11, Papers of the United Presbyterian Church.

34. Mary Dudziak, *Cold War Civil Rights: Race and the Image of American Democracy* (Princeton, NJ: Princeton University Press, 2011).

35. H. Francis Hines to William Henry, 20 November 1964, box 507, folder 1, Carl McIntire Papers.

36. Frederick L. Fritsch to Federal Communications Commission, 19 November 1964, box 507, folder 1, Carl McIntire Papers.

37. Frank H. Stroup to William Henry, 23 November 1964, box 507, folder 1, Carl McIntire Papers.

38. Prince A. Taylor Jr. to Federal Communications Commission, 24 November 1964, box 507, folder 1, Carl McIntire Papers.

39. H. Gifford Irion, "Report No. 4846, WXUR, WXUR-FM, Media, Pa., License Renewal Proposed in Initial Decision," 13 December 1968. McIntire reprinted and distributed the full document as "Historic Decision WXUR," box 455, folder 27, Carl McIntire Papers.

40. Photos of the event are in an envelope marked "WXUR Funeral," 4 July 1973, box 613, folder 51, Carl McIntire Papers.

41. Edward E. Plowman, "McIntire's Navy," *Liberty* 69, no. 1 (January–February 1974): 2–9.

42. William F. Fore to H. Francis Hines, 23 March 1966, rg 16, box 1, folder 13, NCC.

43. Minutes, "Broadcasting and Film Commission Executive Committee," 5–6 May 1966, rg 16, box 3, folder 1, NCC.

44. Bruce Sifford to Robert Norris, 2 March 1966, rg 16, box 1, folder 13, NCC.

45. The Minnesota Church Committee on Radio-Television was a joint venture of the Minnesota, Greater Minneapolis, and St. Paul Area Councils of Churches.

46. Bruce Sifford to Fred King, 1 March 1966, rg 16, box 1, folder 13, NCC. King was the program director at radio station KQRS, which carried the *20th Century Reformation Hour*.

47. Charles Woodward to Bruce Sifford, 2 March 1966; Bruce Sifford to Robert Norris, 3 March 1966, rg 16, box 1, folder 13, NCC.

48. Of those seven, the cancellation dates for four are unknown. KEVE-FM and KEVE-AM dropped in October 1966, suggesting that they gave false information to Bruce Sifford.

49. Emmett Alleman to Carl McIntire, 25 September 1967, box 499, folder 22, Carl McIntire Papers.

50. Carl Miller and Gloria Bailey to Carl McIntire, 8 September 1967, box 175, folder 18, Carl McIntire Papers.

51. "Some Surprises in All Those Answers: Senate Survey Shows Broadcasters Split on Fairness," *Broadcasting*, 13 May 1968, 58–61.

52. Heather Hendershot, *What's Fair on the Air? Cold War Right-Wing Broadcasting and the Public Interest* (Chicago: University of Chicago Press, 2011), 140.

53. There is a large literature on church-sect cycle typology in the sociology of religion. See L. R. Iannaccone, "A Formal Model of Church and Sect," *American Journal of Sociology* 94 (1988): S241–S268.

Part VI

Civil or Religious? The New Boundaries of Religious Tolerance

Chapter Eighteen

Pseudo Religion and Real Religion

*The Modern Anticult Movement and
Religious Freedom in America*[1]

James B. Bennett

In 1971, twenty-two-year-old Kay Rambur was riding her bike near UC
Berkeley when she passed a chorus on the street. The voices belonged to the
Children of God, a religious movement founded three years earlier. Kay had
long been interested in religion, and the members' biblical knowledge impressed her. Leaving behind a nursing career and a fiancé, she joined the
Children of God and moved to a missionary training center in Dallas, Texas,
to prepare for a life of missionary service for the Children of God. She also
curtailed communications with her parents. Stunned by her conversion and
silence, Kay's parents were convinced the Children of God had coerced her
into joining and that she remained in the movement under duress. Her father,
William Rambur, a retired navy lieutenant commander and high school history teacher in San Diego, twice tried to remove his daughter from the Children
of God. Neither attempt succeeded. Kay soon married a fellow Children of
God member, had children, and eventually moved to South America.[2]

Two years later the Crampton family had a similar experience when
nineteen-year-old Kathe Crampton left her home in Redondo Beach to join
the Love Family, a religious commune in Seattle. Kathe's mother, Henri,
who described her daughter as having "close attachments to her family" and
a strong but well-adjusted personality, claimed Kathe completely changed
within three weeks of her conversion. Kathe sent her parents a letter announcing her conversion and her new life in a "God-centered family," which
rendered her biological family irrelevant. Letters from Kathe's parents went
unanswered, and certified mail was marked "refused" and returned. When

Kathe's parents traveled to Seattle to see her, they were shocked to discover her face covered in scabs. During the visit, commune members did not allow Kathe to be alone with her parents. Worried about their daughter's health and safety, the Cramptons hired Ted Patrick, a well-known "cult rescuer," to deprogram her. Deprogramming was a legally dubious practice that involved forcibly removing Kathe and keeping her isolated until she agreed to leave the commune and return to her parents. CBS News accompanied Patrick and broadcast a three-part series on the attempted deprogramming in August of 1973. But the effort failed when Kathe escaped and returned to the Love Family home. When Kathe left the group of her own accord eight years later, she indicated that her parents' concerns were not unfounded and expressed approval for their actions on her behalf.[3]

The experiences of families like the Ramburs and the Cramptons gave rise to the modern anticult movement in the early 1970s. In the Cramptons' case, after the failed attempt to deprogram Kathe aired, and despite the broadcast's critical tone regarding the effort, hundreds of parents whose adult children had joined new religious movements contacted the Cramptons with notes of sympathy. Many also sought information about the deprogramming process. The parents disapproved of the religious choices their adult children had made, were distraught over breaks in family ties, and worried that membership in alternative religious communities would restrict their children's educational and economic opportunities. Like the Cramptons, many also had genuine concerns about the health and safety of family members, especially when religious organizations prevented families from contacting their children or refused to identify their location. Concerned about the physical and psychological consequences of membership in alternative religious communities, families like the Ramburs and the Cramptons organized support groups for families whose children had become involved in alternative religious movements, which they labeled "cults." By the early 1980s, the patchwork of local support groups coalesced into a national association, the Cult Awareness Network (CAN), which became the nation's most prominent anticult organization.[4]

As it moved toward a nationwide organization, the anticult movement also advanced efforts to deny constitutional protections for alternative religious communities. Helping parents locate and deprogram their adult children remained a focus of the anticult movement. But it also undertook efforts to delegitimize new religious movements, legally and in popular opinion, and to advance legislative restrictions against them. Through community education programs, media appearances, congressional hearings, and legislative proposals, the anticult movement warned of an impending "cult crisis" that would destroy families and threaten social stability.

These efforts to restrict American religious expression mark a distinct episode in the struggles over religious tolerance and intolerance in American history. Even in a nation whose Constitution privileges religious freedom, the modern anticult movement illustrates the challenges of defining religious freedom and the blurry boundary that separates reasonable disagreements over religious differences from impermissible intolerance. Families acted reasonably when they questioned the role of alternative religious communities about sudden changes in the behavior, health, and social relationships of their previously independent and mature adult children, especially when the religions seemed to act in a secretive or controlling manner. The judge who refused to convict Ted Patrick for his attempt to deprogram Kathe Crampton sympathized with her parents' actions, stating that "the parents who would do less than what Mr. and Mrs. Crampton did for their daughter, Kathe, would be less than responsible, loving parents."[5] But anticult organizers did not stop with their own children. They also worked to enact legal restrictions against a wide range of alternative religious communities they stereotyped as dangerous. The anticult movement used generalizations from a limited number of individual cases as the basis for describing all members of alternative religious communities and for discriminating against the religions to which they belonged. The movement thus crossed the boundary into religious intolerance when it moved from reasonable criticism based on specific and concrete evidence to advocating restrictions on the religious freedom of a broad array of diverse religious communities. While it creates little controversy to defend the free exercise of traditional churches, the anticult movement reveals the difficulty that some face in accommodating religious communities whose organization and practices contrast with or even challenge widely shared social values. As anticultists expanded their efforts from support groups to promoting government regulation, they were unable to distinguish reasonable and permissible challenges to social norms from legitimate threats to the peace, order, and safety of the nation.

DEFINING THE CULT PROBLEM

As the anticult movement expanded during the 1970s from support groups for concerned parents to advocates of state regulation, it did not precisely define what counted as a "cult." Anticultists approached the problem in a way that reflected Justice Potter Stewart's famous quip about pornography: "I know it when I see it." As president of the Citizens Freedom Foundation, William Rambur conceded there were no set guidelines for determining if a religion was a dangerous cult. "All we can advise," Rambur suggested, "is to observe the members, ask questions, inquire in the community and seek out former friends and the parents of members."[6] Religious organizations that were small and/or secretive, or whose structures challenged prevailing social values, especially the importance of family relationships, were most likely to run afoul of the anticult movement. But many other religious communities did not escape its gaze. During its quarter century of existence (1971–1996), CAN and its predecessor organizations gathered information on nearly 1,500 groups in the United States, covering a wide swathe of the American religious landscape. They ranged from religions Americans had long been suspicious about, such as Mormonism and Christian Science, to more recent innovations, such as Scientology and the Unification Church (Moonies). Yet the anticult movement's files also covered the breadth of religion in the United States, including immigrant Asian religious communities (e.g., Buddhist, Hindu, Sikh), Catholic religious orders, and many Protestant Christian denominations, from Pentecostal to mainline. With such a wide range of possible problematic religious organizations, the anticult movement could not easily distinguish the parameters that separated those it considered a threat from those it found acceptable.

The most common description the movement used was "dangerous." Religious organizations with alternative social systems were most commonly described in that way, especially if affiliation resulted in behavioral changes, such as rupturing relationships or abandoning educational, vocational, or financial hopes. Yet the structure of religious communities labeled "cults" was hardly monolithic. They ranged from communal living that remained engaged with the surrounding community, including ongoing interaction with family members, to remote separatist encampments with little or no interaction with anyone outside the religion. In addition, a single religious movement might maintain different arrangements across multiple locations.

Failing to clarify the definition of "cult" made it hard for the anticult movement to quantify the problem. The ambiguity may have been an intentional strategy to make the threat appear as widespread as possible. When anticult leaders offered statistics, their figures varied widely. In 1975, William Rambur claimed there were five thousand cults in the United States. A year later, deprogrammer Ted Patrick reported only a few hundred, but insisted their membership totaled more than three million. Neither man offered his criteria for categorizing a religion as a cult or the basis for estimating the number of members.[7] Religious studies scholars agreed there were many new religious groups. Most of the groups that both the anticult movement and religion scholars identified were small—less than a hundred members—and existed at only a single location. Scholars also stressed that the existence of such groups, and the alternative and often separatist structure that characterized many new religious movements, was not new. These forms of religious innovation have always been part of the American religious landscape, with most disappearing before being noticed and few (if any) presenting a threat to the safety or stability of civil society.

Nonetheless, anticultists insisted an unprecedented wave of dangerous new movements had begun in the late 1960s and was continuing into the

1970s. At the same time, they claimed that their campaign was not about religion and thus did not run afoul of constitutional guarantees of religious freedom. The key for the anticult movement was differentiating between belief and practice. This distinction, rooted in Western understandings of religion that privilege belief as the essential dimension of religion, has long been the basis for regulating religious behavior in the United States. Thomas Jefferson argued that while opinion (i.e., belief) is outside the government's jurisdiction, it was among "the rightful purposes of civil government for its officers to interfere when principles break out into overt acts against peace and good order."[8] Following this line of reasoning, the Supreme Court ruled in 1879 that while Mormons were free to believe in a divine revelation commanding polygamy, they were not free to put that decree into practice.[9] Subsequent First Amendment jurisprudence in the twentieth century generally followed this pattern. Government restrictions on religion were limited to practice, and even then only when it posed a clear and present danger to the civil order. The anticult movement invoked a similar logic, arguing that it was only concerned with "destructive practices," not beliefs. Its guidelines for starting new chapters noted that "our concern is the *harmful practices* of the *destructive cults*—not deviant doctrine."[10] Yet, significantly, the anticult movement did not demonstrate that the groups it opposed had, in Jefferson's words, broken "into overt acts against peace and good order." Rather, the movement invoked anecdotal evidence from parents and former members, which, troubling as some of it was, did not reveal demonstrable threats to the safety or stability of the civil order. Perhaps in recognition of this disconnect, anticult arguments remained largely in the realm of generalized claims, calling the religious organizations whose practices it condemned "pseudo religions" in the attempt to delegitimize their free exercise claims. Drawing on broad themes of family, patriotism, and conspiracy, the anticult movement hoped to enlist support for their efforts to restrict the religious rights of alternative religious communities.

CULTS AND FREEDOM

For anticultists, alternative religious communities posed a danger to civil order and safety because they used coercive or manipulative practices to recruit and retain members. Like much of the anticult rhetoric, the claim was a generalization based more on anecdotal reports than widespread verifiable evidence. Still, when religious communities prevented families like the Ramburs and the Cramptons from having unsupervised or uncensored communication with their children—if they could have any contact at all—concerns about excessive control were not unreasonable. A deprogrammer who feigned interest in joining the Children of God in order to infiltrate their community confirmed the strict limits on sleep and outside communication for new recruits. Yet the same infiltrator also successfully escaped after twenty-four hours, demonstrating that a voluntary exit was not impossible. [11] Kathe Crampton, whose parents refused to accept that she was ever a willing convert, eventually walked out of her own accord when she decided to leave the Love Family eight years after joining. Nonetheless, the accusation that cults "manipulate their members through psychological and physical control" remained one of the anticult movement's central claims and a primary justification for advocating limits on religious liberty. [12]

As evidence of coercion, anticultists invoked the specter of brainwashing, a form of psychological manipulation they also called "mind control." The anticult movement accepted brainwashing as a real and effective technique. Typical was a pamphlet that asserted "there is a growing number of enslaved victims because of the misuse of mind control techniques." [13] For parents who struggled to understand their children's religious choices, brainwashing not only explained otherwise incomprehensible behavior but also shifted blame and responsibility away from both the converts and their parents. After Henri Crampton visited her daughter, she was convinced Kathe's conversion and her changes since joining the Love Family could only be explained "by methods of brainwashing [that] Love Israel, the cult leader employs." [14] The anticult movement relied on the testimony of a handful of psychologists to support its brainwashing claims, but most social scientists remained skeptical. In 1987, the American Psychological Association, through its Board of Social and Ethical Responsibility, rejected brainwashing as an explanation for religious behavior or as a tactic used by new religious movements. Other professional organizations reached similar conclusions. As a result, courts no longer accepted as expert witnesses the handful of psychologists who insisted on the validity of religious brainwashing. [15]

The preponderance of professional opinion notwithstanding, the anticult movement maintained that coercion, exemplified through brainwashing, was evidence of a threat to the stability of public order that necessitated government intervention. Anticultists were confident that once Americans became aware of such practices, they would support investigations and regulations limiting the activities of alternative religious communities, if not eliminating them altogether. In response, the targeted religions insisted that the anticult movement misrepresented their practices. Of course, criticisms of religious groups, while they might damage a religion's standing or create obstacles to recruiting, are inevitable in a liberal democracy and have long characterized competition in the American religious marketplace. But once anticult activists pursued government-enforced restrictions on alternative religious communities, they crossed into constitutionally problematic efforts to limit religious free exercise. When alternative religious communities and their allies protested these legislative efforts, anticultists insisted that they themselves, not the religions invoking the First Amendment, were the true defenders of American freedom. This anticult conception of freedom did not concern constitutionally delineated particulars such as religion, speech, or assembly as much as a generic conception of freedom, an abstract ideal, which alternative religious communities purportedly threatened.

CULTS AND FREE CHOICE

Free choice was the clearest expression of freedom for the anticult movement. The anticult organizations stressed the freedom of individual choice as a fundamental value undergirding a liberal, democratic state in general, and the American Constitution in particular. The priority was evident in the names that anticult groups chose, nearly all of which included some form of the world "free." The Citizens Freedom Foundation, the parents' group that William Rambur helped to organize, declared as one of its foundational beliefs that "each person . . . should be capable of making his own decisions."[16] In a subsequent newsletter editorial, Rambur claimed that people's "inability to make a simple decision" signaled that "their civil liberties are being denied them."[17] Rambur and others did not specify what choices were at stake, though criticisms most often focused on communication with family members and the ability to come and go at will. Elsewhere, Rambur insisted that, as a result of Kay's participation in the Children of God, "my daughter does not have a free will . . . she does not have the right to choose her own way," and that "this certainly is not the intent of the Constitution."[18] When religious communities restricted a member's free choice, the anticult movement considered the religion and its leaders unworthy of constitutionally protected toleration.

Contemporary events bolstered the anticult movement's linkage of free choice with constitutional freedoms. After the November 1978 mass suicide of over nine hundred followers of Jim Jones and his People's Temple in Jonestown, Guyana, the anticult movement had a powerful example of the dangers of a charismatic and controlling leader who isolated his followers and demanded strict obedience. Jonestown exemplified the dangers of coercion in the name of religion. Even though Jonestown was not representative of most new religious movements, the anticult movement invoked the tragedy in order to build support for their crusade against alternative religious communities to "fight for free minds—the right of man to make his own decisions—and thus be able to enjoy the liberty and human rights which our U.S. Constitution promises."[19] In this way, anticult activists affirmed a commitment to freedom even as they promoted legislation that would restrict or even terminate some religious organizations. Among the organizations supporting the anticult movement was the American Jewish Congress, which was concerned about the Unification Church's recruitment efforts among Jews. When a reporter inquired about the contradiction of a long-persecuted religion advocating government investigations and restrictions, a spokesperson insisted his organization was "strongly committed" to religious freedom. "But," he asserted, "some cults recruit and retain members through tactics that are clearly in violation of basic civil rights."[20] As was typical in the anticult movement, the spokesperson did not specify the coercive actions or the civil rights that had been violated.

For the anticult movement, reports of ruptured social connections, especially intimate family relationships, were evidence that new religious movements both denied freedom and used mind control. Like William Rambur and Henri Crampton, parents often perceived their children's membership in a religious movement as a wholesale rejection of parental bonds. From these experiences came the anticult charge that "parents are fearful for the well-being of their children—cults are controlling and abusing them behind a façade of religion."[21] Anticultists feared that an explosion of alternative religious communities was undermining family structures, which anticultists insisted were necessary for a stable society. A small percentage of new religions did enforce restrictions on family contact. But those who joined alternative religious communities also made independent decisions to limit or cut off contact, especially when their parents criticized their new affiliation or tried to remove them. Kay Rambur, for example, in a statement made more than twenty years after joining the Children of God (now called the Family), insisted that her decision to join and remain had always been a free choice. She claimed her limited communication with her parents stemmed from their ongoing hostility, in public as well as in private, toward Kay, her family, and her religious community.[22] Yet the anticultists blamed only the religious movement and its leaders, neglecting the possibility that a convert might have initiated the rupture. Anticult accusations notwithstanding, there is no evidence suggesting young adults who joined alternative religious communities significantly differed in their relationships with family members. They maintained the same spectrum of relationships with family, ranging from close and regular contact to none whatsoever, in about the same proportion as American young adults as a whole.

Nonetheless, the anticult movement insisted the impact on family relationships was evidence of coercion and a criterion by which a religion's right to free exercise should be evaluated. Although many religious communities have argued that religion replaces family as one's primary loyalty and that fellow religionists are a convert's new family, the anticult movement insisted that "real" religions honored family ties rather than disrupting them. The anticult movement used the particular experiences of a handful of converts, such as Kathe Crampton, who declared her biological family irrelevant upon joining the Love Family, to characterize all "cults" as enemies of family relationships. According to a position statement from an anticult organization, whereas "mainline religions . . . strengthen and enrich personal and family life," cults "alienate a follower from his family and distort and destroy family values and structure."[23] Accordingly, a convert's "severance of family ties" and "an irrational change from love to hatred of family" were signs that she was a victim of coercion. "It is inconceivable," the warning continued, "that any individual can make these sudden, drastic and illogical changes in behavior and still consider it an expression of free will."[24] Families and cults were mutually exclusive categories, only one of which could be aligned with American ideas of religion and freedom.

Contrasting cults with families capitalized on insecurities about the status of domestic relations in the 1970s. Concerns about changes to the family were not unique to the era. The danger posed by new religions to the stability of American families has been a consistent charge against new religious movements, as evidenced by attacks on Mormons and Shakers in the nineteenth century. Still, real and perceived changes in family, gender, and sexual relationships that began during the preceding decade made warnings of cult-inspired family breakdown resonate in the 1970s. Anticultists were not the only Americans who interpreted these changes as threats to the stability of the nation. When anticultists claimed the question "How does one keep his family together?" was among the most pressing issues of the age, Americans across a range of religious traditions agreed.[25] And disrupting families was only the beginning. As one parent wrote, cults had to be opposed because of "their mind-controlling techniques which alienate their members from family, government, education, prior religions, and society and its viable values."[26] An editorial cartoon frequently reprinted in anticult materials depicted a boat named "U.S. family unit," which had tattered sails and was taking on water, while two sharks circled nearby, one labeled "drugs" and the other "religious cults."[27]

"Freedom" and "cult" thus emerged as the fundamental antithetical categories in the anticult perspective, though both terms remained vague. Anticultists depicted freedom as an amalgamation of family, the Constitution, and individual choice. Meanwhile, the cult label described a coercive, authoritarian, and psychologically manipulative religion that threatened American freedom and personal choice, especially through its disruption of family relationships. For the anticult movement, labeling a religious community a "cult" precluded any need to investigate a religion's particular practices or the beliefs that informed them. Simply applying the term connoted sufficiently dangerous characteristics to justify excluding a religion from the realm of protected religious status. In this manner the movement avoided quantifying the empirical evidence, which would have undercut the scope of the movement's claims. This tendency to use a limited set of examples as sufficient to define the practices of all alternative religious communities led anticultists to move from reasonable criticism to intolerance. But they rejected charges of intolerance, depicting themselves instead as defenders of freedom within the either/or paradigm of the cult/freedom dichotomy. The choice, as one parent warned, was to oppose cults and thereby defend "the values that created that First Amendment" or to tolerate them and thereby "drive another nail into the coffin of freedom."[28]

By the mid-1970s, the insistence on a looming threat to freedom, in conjunction with accusations of mind control, led anticult activists to insist that the nation faced a crisis. Those who organized the anticult movement had become parents in the decades following World War II. Their emphasis on pervasive danger may have reflected a legacy of Cold War anxieties, resulting from the Korean War and concerns about Chinese communism that dominated the news as many were beginning their families. Both anticommunism and the anticult movement stressed the need for vigilance against an often-invisible enemy. Like Joseph McCarthy's exaggerated claims of communist subversion, the anticult movement extrapolated isolated examples into evidence of widespread threats against the peace and security of the entire nation that only government intervention could prevent. Critics of the anticult movement noted the parallels to McCarthyism, suggesting that "lumping together of terms like cultists, cult champions, cult lawyers and hood-winked sounds a lot like 'Communist, Pinko, and fellow-traveler.'"[29] But anticultists maintained that their suspicions were warranted. While William Rambur in California was making his unsubstantiated claim of "thousands of cults committing crimes against our society," an anticult newsletter in Michigan insisted that "pseudo-religious cults" were "a creeping, pervasive evil [that] is stalking our country. It is growing to epidemic proportions." The newsletter also contended that the use of brainwashing compounded the threat because "no one is immune to the brain-washing technique of cults."[30] The tendency to generalize without clear definitions, and without delineating differences between religions or individual experiences with them, was especially pronounced in the rhetoric of impending crisis. Typical was the admonition of a former Moonie that "all the cults use brainwashing and they're all very dangerous."[31] Parents likewise translated the very real pain of losing their own children into warnings of a crisis of national proportions. That some Americans had succumbed to the entreaties and even manipulation of new religious movements led to fears that all young people were vulnerable. Henri Crampton closed an account of the trauma she endured when her daughter Kathe joined the Love Family by warning her readers that "your children or grandchildren may be as easily ensnared."[32]

LEGISLATIVE EFFORTS

By the end of the 1970s, anticult concerns led to a push for government involvement. Anticult activists were aware that they risked infringing on constitutional protections as they attempted to mobilize the power of the state to regulate alternative religious movements and practices. Despite the potential hazards, they insisted that after a decade of organizing parent groups and educating the public, more concrete action was necessary. In a 1980 letter responding to parents troubled by their daughter's involvement in the Unification Church, the president of the newly nationalized Citizens Freedom Foundation wrote that "education is a way to go up to a point. Then the pressure you mentioned will have to take over. The only way we will triumph is thru [*sic*] the legislative process."[33] But not all anticult leaders agreed on what form legislation should take. Some advocated explicit regulation of religion, while others supported bills that did not single out religion by name.[34] Reflecting the anticult emphasis on choice as an expression of freedom, a Michigan state legislator drafted a bill "making it a criminal offense for anyone to attempt to eliminate another person's ability to exercise his own free will." The legislator assured a local anticult group that he knew of "many legislators who share our concern about cults." But recognizing the danger of infringing on constitutional freedoms, the legislator "emphasized that we must avoid the 'religious issue.'"[35]

The earliest bills focused on regulating solicitation through permits and disclosures of fund-raising activities and donors. Such a bill passed in Minnesota, but a federal court ruling, upheld by the U.S. Supreme Court, declared the bill an unconstitutional violation of the establishment clause because the restrictions applied only to some, not all, religious organizations.[36] Other states framed legislation as "fraud bills," requiring increased financial disclosure, allowing audits, and mandating a "cooling off" period following a donation or purchase of a spiritual service (e.g., in Scientology, EST, etc.). Both California and Hawaii passed such legislation, although the California legislature later revoked the attorney general's authority to enforce the law.[37] To muster support for their legislative efforts, anticult groups also called for government hearings and investigations. Some were framed broadly to address cult dangers in general, while other hearings inquired into specific issues, including finances, the treatment of children, or (as was the case in Vermont in 1976) the use of mind control.

Toward the end of the decade, anticult activists gained the attention of federal legislators and officials. The highest-profile hearings took place in Washington, DC, in 1976 and again in 1979, both under the sponsorship of Senator Bob Dole of Kansas. Kansas had its share of alternative religious communities, and pressure from constituents led Dole to organize unofficial hearings on the issue. The 1976 event provided an opportunity for parents and anticult groups to express their concern to representatives of several federal agencies, especially regarding the Unification Church. Although still not an official Senate hearing, the 1979 event was more formal in nature. It was in direct response to the mass suicide in Jonestown, but not limited in scope to the People's Temple. Dole's framing of the event was consistent with the anticult perspective, insisting it was only about the "dangerous activities of cults" and not about religious beliefs. Despite this characterization and the seemingly favorable timing in the wake of Jonestown, Dole encountered widespread opposition, which came not only from religious organizations under scrutiny but also from many clergy, denominational leaders, and religious studies scholars, all of whom expressed concern for protecting religious liberty. The complaints forced Dole to include opponents of the anticult movement, including a national leader of the Unification Church. Many people spoke, but no plan of action emerged. Both the attorney general and the FBI refused to investigate religious organizations, citing First Amendment concerns. After the hearings, Dole pursued no further public or legislative action, although a staff member who had once been president of a local anticult group, and had been hired to deal with this issue, continued to work for his office for a few more years.[38]

State legislatures remained the most promising site to mobilize governmental support in the campaign against cults. From the mid-1970s into the early 1980s, anticult groups identified and supported over twenty-three bills in seventeen states that imposed restrictions on alternative religious organizations or immunized those who took actions against them. The earliest bills regulated fund-raising and recruiting tactics. Toward the end of the decade, the anticult movement focused on legislation to protect those who forcibly removed their adult children from religious communities that parents deemed dangerous. Although the proposed laws never used the word *deprogramming*, their purpose was to legalize the practice. In a call to redouble their lobbying efforts, the president of the Citizens Freedom Foundation reminded his members that politicians "are the ones that will ultimately tell the courts how to decide anticult cases."[39] Several bills emerged in the years following the Jonestown tragedy, indicating a brief surge of concern among politicians and the wider public. Between 1981 and 1983, seven states proposed "guardianship bills" that would allow judges to appoint a guardian or conservator for an adult, using familiar anticult criteria that focused on changes in personality and isolation from family or friends. But no guardianship bill became law. In most states, the bills never reached the governor's desk. New York came the closest: the legislature twice passed such a bill, only to have it vetoed by the governor both times. The second version had gone through over fifty revisions in consultation with anticult families and legal sympathizers.[40] While legislation had the greatest potential to achieve the anticult movement's goals, it proved the least successful of the strategies developed during its first decade.

THE DECLINE OF THE MODERN ANTICULT MOVEMENT

By the early 1980s, the modern anticult movement was a decade old. Local organizations, which were present in over half the states by that time, were coalescing into a national structure. While legislative efforts were petering out, other efforts that had emerged during the formative years continued, especially deprogramming. Deprogramming reflected the anticult perspective, which framed national civic life in terms of a struggle between the freedom essential to American liberal values and the coercive tyranny of cults. It also exemplified the irony of the anticult approach: preserving freedom necessitated limiting the freedom of some individuals and religions, despite the absence of a clear and present threat to the civil order. Deprogrammers employed the same coercive tactics they accused cults of using, including isolation, sleep deprivation, and bombarding targets with information until they capitulated. Some conceded the similarity and insisted on the need to fight fire with fire. Others denied the equivalency, invoking the categories of coercion and freedom to characterize cult actions as entrapment and deprogramming as liberation. All agreed that the ends justified the means: deprogramming enabled a deceived and coerced member to use "freedom of choice, and freedom of association in order that he may make an *informed* and *voluntary* decision regarding his cult affiliation."[41] The subject of deprogramming demonstrated his free choice by leaving the religious organization.

Deprogramming remained a complicated and problematic strategy that eventually led to the collapse of the anticult movement. Deprogrammers claimed a high rate of success, while opponents argued that failures outnumbered successes. No hard statistics are available, but anecdotal evidence reveals that some never returned to the religious community from which they had been removed, especially if they became convinced that coercion or manipulation played a role in their recruitment or retention. Yet many more resisted and eventually returned to their religious communities. Beginning in the mid-1970s, deprogrammers, who initially avoided conviction (as had Ted Patrick in the case of Kathe Crampton), were increasingly convicted of kidnapping and jailed for their actions. During that time, court rulings and congressional legislation signaled an increasing accommodation of religious free exercise, culminating in the 1993 Religious Freedom Restoration Act. Shortly thereafter, a deprogramming case resulted in CAN's demise. In 1995, the object of an unsuccessful deprogramming won a million-dollar claim against CAN, citing physical and psychological trauma during the attempted deprogramming. The jury went on to challenge the anticult movement's understanding of freedom, claiming that the deprogrammers "were involved in a conspiracy to deprive [the subject] of his civil and religious liberties" and that they had acted in ways "utterly intolerable in a civilized community."[42] The damages bankrupted CAN, which had to sell its limited assets at auction. Although other anticult groups continued, none rose to the influence of CAN or its predecessor organizations. The modern anticult movement had effectively ended.

LEGACIES AND LESSONS OF THE ANTICULT MOVEMENT

In the end, reality never matched the anticult movement's rhetoric. No wide-scale cult crisis emerged. There was no sustained increase in either the number of alternative religious communities or the number of Americans joining them. Nor did the era's alternative religious communities become a threat to the American social order or the safety of its citizens. Many of the religious organizations the anticult movement first identified in the 1970s dwindled or died out completely, not because of the anticult movement but because new religions are simply hard to sustain. These upstart groups suffered the same fate as many before them. The handful of larger religious communities that were the primary targets of anticult efforts all continue to exist, including the Children of God (now called the Family), Scientology, and the Unification Church. None release membership statistics, but recent surveys suggest their membership levels range from a few thousand in the Family to the mid-tens of thousands for Scientology and the Unification Church. Most persist without controversy, although they remain nontraditional religions on the American religious landscape, generate occasional curiosity, and carry a lingering stigma for having been labeled "cults." (The exception is Scientology, a long-time anticult target and CAN's primary adversary in the 1990s, which has remained an object of media fascination and, more recently, become the subject of critical inquiry by reporters and scholars.) While opposition to these religions continues, mostly made up of disaffected former members, opponents are greatly outnumbered by contented members, who testify to the meaningful beliefs, practices, and community they have found through their religious affiliation.

The anticult movement did have some early successes, particularly in defending specific acts like deprogramming as a necessary action to remove adult children from religions the movement considered coercive and dangerous (the legality of removing minors who joined against their parents' wishes was never in question). In addition, the movement established itself as the primary source of information for the media and community leaders. Though they often failed to understand the nature of their children's choices and changes, the parents who founded and sustained the movement were not always mistaken in their belief that their adult children were being psychologically or economically manipulated, or even abused. But, as recent incidents in large and historic Christian denominations make clear, these failings are not limited to the alternative religious communities the anticult movement targeted. When parents sought to act in their own children's best interest, their actions were understandable and often defensible. However, when they expanded that concern into a national effort to restrict a whole class of alternative religious communities, it became intolerance.

Religious innovation has long been a source of tension in American society. The friction is especially acute when the beliefs and practices of new religious movements appear to challenge the social structures and liberal democratic values that make the existence of alternative religious communities possible. American history is replete with conflict between nonliberal religions and the individuals and groups composing the surrounding liberal society. Not surprisingly, it is minority and nonconformist religions that pose the most challenging tests to the preservation of free exercise. From Catholics and Mormons in the nineteenth century to Christian Scientists and Scientologists in the twentieth century, and now Muslims in the twenty-first, that conflict has inspired efforts to limit constitutional protections for religions whose values appear to diverge from liberal democratic values. The conflict in values can be real and not always easily adjudicated. Yet one hallmark of a liberal society is the freedom it affords individuals, short of a demonstrable public threat or violation of rights, to exercise values other than unambiguously liberal ones. During the last quarter of the twentieth century, the anticult movement was enlisted in this long-standing debate about the character and limits of freedom in a liberal society. In its history and in its legacy, the modern anticult movement ensured the American experiment in religious toleration remained a lively (and contested) one.

NOTES

1. This project was supported in part by a Hackworth Grant from the Markkula Center for Applied Ethics at Santa Clara University.

2. Flo Conway and Jay Siegelman, *Snapping: America's Epidemic of Sudden Personality Change*, 2nd ed. (New York: Stillpoint Press, 1995), 74–78; "Cult Awareness Network Cofounder's Claims Fraudulent," typescript in Institute of Church-State Studies Vertical File Collection, Baylor University, http://contentdm.baylor.edu/cdm/ref/collection/cs-vert/id/9866; "Parents Join to Combat Radical Youth Sect," *New York Times*, 21 February 1972; Larry Eskridge, *God's Forever Family: The Jesus People Movement in America* (New York: Oxford University Press, 2013), 191.

3. Henrietta Crampton, "History of CAN," 16 February 1988, in "CAN History," box 97, Cult Awareness Network Collection, Department of Special Collections, Davidson Library, University of California Santa Barbara (hereafter cited as CAN Collection); "Kathe Crampton's Story," *CFF News* 3 (April 1975): unless otherwise noted, issues of *CFF News* are in "Citizens Freedom Foundation (1 of 2)," American Religions Collection MSS 1, Department of

Special Collections, Davidson Library, University of California Santa Barbara (hereafter cited as ARC MSS 1); Henrietta Crampton, "Killing Her Softly with His Love," undated typescript in "Citizens Freedom Foundation-Corr. [4/5]," ARC MSS 1; Henri Crampton to *New York Times*, 9 January 1983, typescript in "Crampton, Henrietta," box 87, CAN Collection.

4. Nearly every study of new religious movements includes a section on the anticult movement. See, for example, David G. Bromley and Anson Shupe, "The Future of the Anticult Movement," in *The Future of New Religious Movements*, ed. David G. Bromley and Phillip E. Hammond (Macon, GA: Mercer University Press, 1987), 221–34; Eugene Gallagher, *The New Religious Movements Experience in America* (Westport, CT: Greenwood Press, 2004), 3–13; Philip Jenkins, *Mystics and Messiahs: Cults and New Religions in American History* (New York: Oxford University Press, 2000), 187–207; Jeffrey Kaplan, *Radical Religion in America: Millenarian Movements from the Far Right to the Children of Noah* (Syracuse, NY: Syracuse University Press, 1997), 127–63; J. Gordon Melton, *Encyclopedic Handbook of Cults in America*, rev. ed. (New York: Garland, 1992), 344–58. Two book-length studies of the anticult movement have appeared: Anson D. Shupe Jr. and David G. Bromley, *The New Vigilantes: Deprogrammers, Anti-Cultists and the New Religions* (Beverly Hills, CA: Sage, 1980), and Anson Shupe and Susan E. Darnell, *Agents of Discord: Deprogramming, Pseudo-Science and the American Anticult Movement* (New Brunswick, NJ: Transaction, 2006).

5. "Parents Lose Daughter to 'the Family,'" *Reading Eagle*, 17 June 1979.

6. Undated typescript in "Citizens Freedom Foundation [3/5]," ARC MSS 1.

7. William Rambur, CFF fund-raising appeal, February 1975, in "Citizens Freedom Foundation [3/5]," ARC MSS 1; "Deprogrammer Loses," *Canton Report*, 5 May 1976.

8. Thomas Jefferson, "A Bill for Establishing Religious Freedom," 1779, "Founders Online," National Archives, http://founders.archives.gov/documents/Jefferson/01-02-02-0132-0004-0082.

9. *Reynolds v. United States*, 98 U.S. 145 (1879).

10. "CFF Affiliate form," in "CFF Board," box 106, CAN Collection (emphasis in original).

11. Ted Patrick with Tom Dulack, *Let Our Children Go!* (New York: E. P. Dutton, 1976), 37–58.

12. Henri Crampton to *New York Times*, 9 January 1983, in "Crampton, Henrietta," box 87, CAN Collection; National Convention National Council of Jewish Women, "Topical Statement: Cults," March 1979, in "CAN History," box 91, CAN Collection.

13. "What Does CFF Believe?" *CFF News* 2 (January–February 1975).

14. Crampton, "Killing Her Softly with His Love," ARC MSS 1.

15. American Psychological Association memo from Board of Social and Ethical Responsibility for Psychology (BSERP) to members of the Task Force on Deceptive and Indirect Methods of Persuasion and Control (DIMPAC), 11 May 1987, in "Legal—Fishman Case," ARC MSS 1; J. Gordon Melton, "Brainwashing and the Cults: The Rise and Fall of a Theory," introduction to the forthcoming book *The Brainwashing Controversy: An Anthology of Essential Documents*, ed. J. Gordon Melton and Massimo Introvigne, posted on the website of the Center for Studies on New Religions, http://www.cesnur.org/testi/melton.htm.

16. "What CFF Believes!" *CFF News* 1 (November 1974).

17. "How Can You Get at Somebody Who Controls a Kid's Mind?" *CFF News* 2 (January–February 1975).

18. William Rambur, CFF fund-raising appeal, February 1975, in "Citizens Freedom Foundation—Corr," ARC MSS 1.

19. "Remember Guyana," *CFF News* 3 (December 1978).

20. "Legal Aid Aimed at Religious Cults," summary of article from *Dallas Morning News*, 1 January 1978, in *CFF News* 3 (7 January 1978).

21. "Kidnap or Rescue," *CFF News* 2 (March 1975).

22. "Cult Awareness Network Co-founder's Claims Fraudulent," Institute of Church-State Studies Vertical File Collection, Baylor University.

23. "CFF-IS Position Statements," 2, typescript in "CFF Board," box 106, CAN Collection.

24. "How Can You Get at Somebody Who Control's a Kid's Mind?"

25. "How Does One Keep His Family Together?" *CFF News* 1 (December 1974).

26. Memorandum from George Slaughter, 21 July 1976, in "Minn Bill," box 135, CAN Collection.

27. See, for example, *CFF News* 4 (15 September 1979).

28. Mimi Jaffe to Norman Dorsen, 4 March 1977, in "Corr-pre 1980," box 97, CAN Collection.

29. J. Gordon Melton to Henrietta Crampton, 1 May 1978, in "Citizens Freedom Foundation—Corr.,"ARC MSS 1.

30. *CFF News* 2 (January–February 1975); Individual Freedom Foundation Educational Trust newsletter (October–November 1978), in "Citizens Freedom Foundation (1 of 2)," ARC MSS 1.

31. Rita Ashdale, *Bulletin*, Philadelphia, PA, 9 November 1977, reprinted in *CFF News* 2 (11 December 1977).

32. Crampton, "Killing Her Softly with His Love," ARC MSS 1.

33. John Sweeny to Carolyn and Elton Helander, 21 January 1980, in "Citizens Freedom Foundation (1 of 2)," ARC MSS 1.

34. "A Guide for New Chapters," November 1983, "Robert Chalenor," box 87, CAN Collection.

35. Individual Freedom Foundation newsletter, Trenton, MI, July 1979, in "Citizens Freedom Foundation (1 of 2)," ARC MSS 1.

36. Letter from Free Minds and Freedom of Religion, 26 May 1978, in "Minn Bill," box 135, CAN Collection; Doug Stone, "Magistrate: Charity Law Unconstitutional," *Minneapolis Tribune*, 4 May 1979; *Larson v. Valente*, 456 U.S. 228 (1982).

37. "Hawaii Bill" and "Minn Bill" in box 135, CAN Collection.

38. Ann Lindgren to Sen. Dole, "Personal Information," 16 September 1981, folder 1, box 363, Robert J. Dole Senate Papers, Robert J. Dole Archive and Special Collections, Robert J. Dole Institute of Politics, University of Kansas (hereafter cited as Dole Senate Papers); letters in "Pro Cult/Against Hearing," folder 12, box 363, Dole Senate Papers; Anne Lindgren to Mike Petit, 13 September 1983, folder 1, box 363, Dole Senate Papers; "Dole Transcript," folder 19, box 360, Dole Senate Papers; 1976 Dole Hearings, "Dole CEFM DININ 1976," box 106, CAN Collection; "Justice Dept. Ruled Out Inquiries into Cults," *CFF News* 3 (15 December 1978).

39. John Sweeny, "A Letter from CFF President," *CFF News* 4 (18 October 1979), in "Citizens Freedom Foundation [3/5]," ARC MSS 1.

40. Priscilla Coates to Board of Directors, "Resume of Activities Related to CFF," 27 February 1983, in "CFF Board," box 106, CAN Collection; "Proposed—other states," box 135, CAN Collection.

41. CFF-IS position statement, p. 3, typescript, in "CFF Board," box 106, CAN Collection (emphasis in original).

42. Shupe and Darnell, *Agents of Discord*, 183.

Chapter Nineteen

America beyond Civil Religion

The Anabaptist Experience

Kip A. Wedel

When Ron Desimone traveled from his home in Elkhart, Indiana, to nearby Goshen College to watch a women's basketball game in 2008, he was "very surprised" to learn the small Mennonite college did not play the national anthem before athletic events. He e-mailed Goshen's athletic director, Tim Demant, who explained that the policy was derived from Goshen's Anabaptist heritage. Unmollified, Desimone fired off additional e-mails to college officials. When these went unanswered, he contacted several conservative media figures, one of whom, radio host Mike Gallagher of New York City, criticized the school's policy on his show. In the week that followed, Goshen College heard from hundreds of infuriated Americans. Even Desimone was surprised by the magnitude of the response. "I don't want to cause a big stink about it," he told a reporter. "I didn't think it would escalate to this."[1]

Neither Goshen's policy nor Desimone's criticism was entirely new. Since its establishment in 1894, Goshen College had never played the national anthem, and public ire about Anabaptist beliefs in America was at least as old as the Puritans. But Desimone's timing struck a nerve. Since the terrorist attacks of 2001 and the wars in Afghanistan and Iraq that followed, displays of American civil religion had intensified, and public performances of the national anthem were considered vital manifestations of patriotism. In the wake of the unwanted publicity that followed Desimone's complaint, the college president instructed the vice president for student life and dean of students, Bill Born, to form a task force to consider the matter in depth. Had the policy outlived its usefulness? Could Goshen play the anthem while remaining true to its heritage? The task force proposed a compromise: Goshen should play "The Star-Spangled Banner," but only an instrumental version to avoid the song's martial lyrics, thought by some to be incompatible with the values of a historic peace church. In autumn 2009, the President's Council accepted the recommendation.[2]

College officials hoped the matter was settled, but when they announced the new policy on January 21–22, 2010, "a firestorm of opposition" erupted.[3] This time criticism flowed not from right-wing radio hosts, but from Anabaptists. A Mennonite minister in Iowa launched a Facebook page titled "Against Goshen College Playing the National Anthem," and a petition against the new policy on the Jesus Radicals website attracted hundreds of signatures.[4] Another online commentator accused Goshen of "foreplay with our DC-based empire."[5] So distressed was the American Anabaptist community that calls to revisit the decision reached the college's board of directors. On August 19, 2011, President Jim Brenneman announced that he had been directed by the board to find an alternative song. Henceforth, "America the Beautiful" would sound before Goshen's athletic events instead of "The Star-Spangled Banner."[6]

To many of Goshen's Anabaptist critics, the controversy was about more than basketball and patriotism. It also involved the precarious relationship of Anabaptism to American civil religion. American civil religion is a conflation of political and religious rhetoric—some say a separate religion—that infuses the civic life of the nation with a transcendent aura.[7] Politicians who describe the United States as a nation "under God," Memorial Day speakers who imply that America's wars were fought for universal moral principles, and ordinary Americans who revere national symbols or rituals, such as the American flag or national anthem, all participate in civil religion. Yet civil religion tries to make its claims as inoffensively as possible. It avoids topics of sectarian controversy and speaks vaguely of a generic God most religious Americans can recognize. Moreover, civil religion lends itself to multiple uses. Sometimes it comfortingly posits a benevolent God who superintends earthly affairs; sometimes it rouses Americans to action in war, humanitarianism, or progressive state building by describing the United States as embodying universal aspirations; and sometimes it speaks words of judgment, reminding Americans that even the United States must answer to a higher power. Some scholars have labeled these its "pastoral," "priestly," and "prophetic" strains, respectively.[8]

In each case, because of civil religion's protean nature and its appropriation of religious symbols and language, adherents tend to downplay or deny the potential for conflict between their religion and public expressions of allegiance to the nation. Many of Goshen's conservative critics articulated this perspective, viewing religious conscience and ritual expressions of national allegiance as compatible, if not mutually reinforcing. Goshen's Anabaptist critics, however, disagreed, objecting to such expressions of civil religion as an idolatrous conflation of religious and political loyalties. The kerfuffle over Goshen's anthem revealed a paradox that Anabaptism long had presented to American civil religion: What is a civil religion meant to be inoffensive and devoted to religious liberty to make of a church that finds civil religion offensive and seeks the liberty to live without it?

CIVIL RELIGION AND ANABAPTIST THEOLOGY

Anabaptists in the United States include Mennonites, the Church of the Brethren, Mennonite Brethren, Brethren in Christ, Hutterites, and various Amish and smaller groups. Though ethnically diverse, they all hail theologically from the so-called left wing or radical branch of the sixteenth-century Protestant Reformation. Historians of Anabaptism describe the movement as arising simultaneously in multiple parts of Europe in the 1520s, but the most contentious doctrines separating them from other reformers centered on the nature of baptism and the appropriate relationship between church and state. In addition, although Anabaptists agreed with the Protestant Reformers that salvation was a gift of God available outside the Catholic Church, they refused to interpret the doctrine of *sola fide* (faith alone) as strictly as many Protestant contemporaries. In a 1541 book, Dutch theologian and Mennonite namesake Menno Simons attacked the Lutheran assertion that "faith alone saves, without any assistance by works," even going so far as to say the Lutheran formulation did more to justify Protestants in their wickedness than to transform them into disciples.[9] Discipleship, in the Anabaptist view, involved more than the receipt of grace. It entailed following Christ's ethical example without qualification. As they saw it, Christians were transformed both as individuals and as social creatures because they participated in a radically new kind of community committed to the ethics of nonviolence and love that Christ preached. In effect, Anabaptists accepted *sola fide* in the sense that they agreed that genuine grace (and thereby salvation) came from God without interference by formal institutions, but they resisted the notion that works were somehow distinct from faith. Unlike secular pacifists of a later age, they did not propose that human action alone could create a loving, universal community, but they did call upon Christians to turn from this fallen world and participate instead in the alternative community Christ had offered to the world.[10]

Such an uncompromising interpretation of discipleship led to a separatist notion of the church. The alternative community Anabaptists envisioned comported neither with the church of medieval Catholicism nor with the state churches of most Protestant Reformers. Both seemed hopelessly compromised by their close association with monarchical power. Seeking to identify the common core of their faith, Michael Sattler and an assembly of other German and Swiss Anabaptists met in a German border town in 1527 to draw up the Schleitheim Confession of Faith. "We have agreed that a separation should take place from the evil which the devil has planted in the world," they insisted, adding that "we simply will not have fellowship with evil people, nor associate with them, nor participate with them in their abominations."[11] Ideally, the state and its churches would respect the consciences of individual believers, but since that was unlikely, the state was not to be obeyed on matters touching upon conscience. Anabaptists understood that their separation might require emigration or provoke persecution, and they accepted the grievous consequences. In short, these early Anabaptists developed a doctrine of two kingdoms in which the kingdom of the world, representing human defiance of God, stood against the kingdom of God, representing the Creator's plan for creation. The former implicated all of the world's states and state churches in sinful rebellion, while the latter persisted as a remnant, persecuted church operating apart from these fallen institutions. As the Schleitheim Confession put it, "There has never been anything in the world and among all creatures except good and evil, believing and unbelieving, darkness and light . . . and neither may have anything to do with the other."[12]

Anabaptists clarified their doctrine of the two kingdoms with biblical exegeses that emphasized two covenants in God's relationship with human beings. The first was the eternal moral law of the kingdom of God. It had been announced in the Ten Commandments, but was revealed fully only in the ministry of Christ, who showed humans what their society would look like if they were obedient. The second covenant, made necessary by human sinfulness, was a "concession to sin" that did not redeem humanity but gave it orderly government while in a fallen state. In the Anabaptist view, Christians lived in the first covenant, meaning their community strove to resemble the kingdom of God even though it physically existed in the world. But governments, including their police and military apparatuses, were part of the second covenant. In a sense, they also were instituted by God, but their work was not the work God allotted to Christians.[13]

Both the doctrine of two kingdoms and the two-covenant theology would figure prominently in Anabaptist critiques of American civil religion. The doctrine of two kingdoms required that churches be shielded from state meddling, and the two-covenant theology indicated that churches and states were designed for different ends, and potentially at odds with one another. Unlike Martin Luther, who argued that God established churches and states to carry out separate but complementary tasks, or John Calvin, who thought churches and states should work together to make society more godly, Anabaptists saw inherent conflict between the transcendent kingdom of God and the earth's temporal, historical kingdoms. They likened church-state alliances to what one twenty-first-century evangelist called "mixing ice cream with horse manure."[14] One may hope it will improve the horse manure (that is, import the church's witness into the state), but it really ruins the ice cream (or transfers the state's corruption into the church).

CIVIL RELIGION AND AMERICAN ANABAPTISTS

Martyrdom and migration dogged Anabaptists during much of their European sojourn, but those who moved to the United States in the eighteenth and nineteenth centuries found something else: a government that recognized religious liberty. Instead of a state church, the United States developed a free church tradition that allowed even Anabaptists to form their own church polities and to worship as they wished. However, the free church model was too fractious to provide the young nation with symbols of national unity, so a civil religion developed alongside it, indicating that America was the recipient of providential favor, that it played a divinely sanctioned role in history, and that its symbols deserved reverence as reflections of its exceptional nature. Clergyman Samuel Langdon set the tone early on when he preached in 1788 that divine provision of a victory over Great Britain, a leader of the caliber of George Washington, and a vast continent for expansion fell "little short of real miracles and an heavenly charter of liberty for these United States."[15] American civil religion was theologically fuzzy enough to unite Episcopalians, Presbyterians, some Baptists, Methodists, other Protestants, and eventually Mormons, Catholics, and Jews in a shared understanding of civic endeavors. In doing so, it linked notions of transcendence (however vaguely defined) to the historical life of the United States.[16] While certainly not a European-style state church, American civil religion looked to Anabaptists like a softer version of the same error, a confusion of the two kingdoms.

World War I illustrated the point. American Mennonites overwhelmingly denounced the war and U.S. participation in it, along with the wartime use of civil religion. When the federal Committee on Public Information dispatched "four-minute men" to argue for the war in local theaters, labor halls, civic clubs, and churches, some Americans interpreted their prowar pleas in religious terms. Methodist minister Isaac J. Lansing was so convinced "our pure motives and purposes have received upon them the divine sanction [that] God could not express himself in antagonism to what we are doing." He spoke for millions when he dismissed pacifists as "bloodless tools" of the enemy, and public expressions of civil religion soon became a litmus test for loyalty, or, in a phrase of the time, "One Hundred Percent Americanism."[17] "The clergyman who does not put the flag above the church had better close his church," Theodore Roosevelt pronounced without a hint of irony.[18] American Mennonites felt pressured into buying war bonds against their principles or suffered persecution when their resistance to civil religion was interpreted as disloyalty. Ora Troyer of West Liberty, Ohio, was fined for removing his daughter from a public school that required her to salute the American flag. The judge who sentenced him said refusing to salute the flag was "not conscionable" and "the forerunner of disloyalty and treason."[19] Other Mennonites endured violence or were imprisoned. The Mennonite preacher Charles Diener was tarred and feathered at his home in McPherson County, Kansas, because his church flew no American flag, and his father received the same treatment for not giving to the Red Cross, though he gladly gave to other charitable organizations. Similarly, John Schrag was beaten and nearly lynched in Burrton, Kansas, when he refused both to buy war bonds and to hold a flag in a victory parade.[20] At the same time, thousands of Mennonite draftees felt betrayed by the government when they reported to camp having been promised "noncombatant service" but were instead trained as regular soldiers. Some were even beaten and tortured by fellow soldiers when they resisted being taught to kill.[21] Incarcerated Mennonites frequently suffered abuse at the hands of other prisoners.

What these young men and other Mennonites hoped to demonstrate was that following the centuries-old teachings of their faith did not amount to disloyalty. They thought they could be Anabaptists and Americans at the same time; even the trauma of World War I could not disabuse them of that assumption. If anything, it led to redoubled efforts by American Anabaptists to prove they were loyal and productive citizens. Charles Diener's father may have found the Red Cross too close to the belligerents for his liking, but Mennonites collectively opened their purses en masse. From 1917 to 1919, giving to the Mennonite Board of Missions more than quadrupled, while giving to other Mennonite institutions rose as well. Some of this money went to domestic Mennonite institutions that primarily served Mennonites, but some also went to Mennonite institutions that helped others in American society, such as poor communities served by domestic missions. The most notable initiative was international; the Mennonite Central Committee coordinated with Herbert Hoover's American Relief Association to end the Russian famine.[22] At the same time, World War I reinforced American Anabaptists' commitment to two-kingdom theology. For those whose fathers were brutalized or for families whose houses were streaked with yellow paint in the name of "One Hundred Percent Americanism," the outside world indeed looked like what the drafters of the Schleitheim Confession had called "the evil which the devil has planted in the world."

This tension between their civic duty to be good citizens and their theological obligation to be separate led to revealing struggles over civil religion in the interwar years. At the center of one controversy was George R. Brunk, a Virginia Mennonite bishop. In 1930, a twelve-year-old Mennonite boy in Newport News, Virginia, defied a law requiring him to salute the American flag while at school. Before the U.S. Supreme Court's 1943 decision in *West Virginia State Board of Education v. Barnette*, such laws were common in the United States. When the local school board decided to respect the boy's decision, a bevy of veterans' groups and other patriotic organizations vehemently objected. They sought to rebut the boy's religious objection to the flag salute on the grounds that it was a political and not a religious act and accused the boy of undermining national unity. Virginia Mennonites, including Brunk, countered that the flag salute smacked of militarism offensive to a Mennonite conscience and argued that a religious exemption from it was consistent with established exemptions from military service or oath taking. At the same time, they insisted they were decent and responsible citizens. Virginia Mennonites found themselves in an uncomfortable position. On the one hand, they wanted to be recognized as loyal, law-abiding, and productive Americans; on the other hand, their faith prevented them from participating in a civic ritual most Americans considered a fundamental expression of loyalty.[23]

Nowhere was the tension more obvious than in Brunk's explanations of his position. The bishop defended the Mennonites' biblical and constitutional arguments against the flag salute, while also acknowledging the need for national unity. Brunk shared his critics' political conservatism and tried to strike a moderate tone. A short time before, a group of Amish in Delaware rejected both the flag salute and the Pledge of Allegiance so strongly that they pulled their children from the public schools. In contrast, Brunk distinguished between the flag salute, which he said spoke words "to" the flag, and the Pledge of Allegiance, which spoke words "of" the flag.[24] It was a subtle distinction designed to navigate through a difficult situation, but even Anabaptists were unconvinced.[25]

Though similar tensions flared between American Anabaptists and the wider American community during World War II, the Cold War, and Vietnam period, they rarely reached the intensity of the confrontations of the World War I era. President Franklin Roosevelt's Selective Service director, Lewis B. Hershey, thought preserving minority and individual rights during wartime helped make the United States exceptional, so he adopted a more lenient policy toward conscientious objectors than had the Wilson administration.[26] When conflict did occur, it often centered on a civil religion symbol or ritual, such as the recitation of the Pledge of Allegiance or controversies over the absence of flags in Mennonite church sanctuaries.

Part of the difficulty through the first half of the twentieth century resulted from the lack of a clear understanding of civil religion as a concept and practice. Without such reflection, parties to the conflicts over civil religion typically characterized them as pitting "patriotism" against "pacifism." However, that began to change in the 1960s. Sociologist Robert N. Bellah's 1967 article "The American Civil Religion" inspired a cottage industry of explanations, elaborations, and refutations.[27] Anabaptist writers found criticism of civil religion a handy way to articulate long-held grievances regarding American foreign policy or other social concerns and, more important, to explain why those grievances were derived from deeper theological sources than a mere "belief" in nonviolence.

Interest in civil religion peaked in the mid-1970s. Preparing for the American bicentennial in 1975, the Peace Section of the Mennonite Central Committee (MCC) distributed a "Civil Religion Packet" for use in churches.[28] Meanwhile, popular Mennonite publications such as the *Gospel Herald* and the *Mennonite* published dozens of articles about civil religion, often identifying it by name, and Anabaptist publishing houses such as the Mennonite-affiliated Herald Press produced books on the subject. Predictably, the writers of these materials were generally skeptical about American civil religion. Some rejected civil religion as a false faith, complaining that it compromised the prophetic witness of the church or accusing it of restricting the universality of the gospel. Others countered that certain types of civil religion could enhance the work of the church, even if it could not be perfectly reconciled with Anabaptist theology. Both those who completely rejected it and those who acknowledged that it possessed some utility emphasized that civil religion was distinct from the gospel announced in the New Testament. In his 1976 book *Our Star-Spangled Faith*, Donald B. Kraybill spoke for many bicentennial-era writers when he said that the United States' penchant for likening itself to ancient Israel made it susceptible to ancient Israel's mistakes—including the treatment of God as an ethnocentric tribal possession. By leaving Americans with the impression that national interests were coterminous with God's will, civil religion redefined God's will in terms of American national interests, Kraybill wrote. That rendered him "an antique god—not the one who more recently revealed Himself through Jesus Christ."[29]

A related charge was that civil religion undermined the church's capacity to speak prophetically to the nation, including to the U.S. government. David Augsburger maintained that because civil religion stamped the United States with God's approval in a manner meant to offend no one, it preached the "lowest common denominator of American religious faith."[30] It therefore did more to reinforce milquetoast moral and religious values than to elevate them. Mennonite minister James C. Longacre added that by giving the work of the church to the state, civil religion hollowed out the American church's witness. American Christians' constant talk about individual morality, while laudable, was a way of avoiding engagement with social evils the gospel also called to the Christian's concern. "The American church in the main has in no way significantly confronted the persistent sins of racism, exploitation, violence, and war," Longacre wrote. "On major moral issues in the society the church has been consistently and amazingly ineffective."[31] Attracted by the nonviolent New Left's opposition to segregation, economic injustice, the Vietnam War, and rising military spending, some Mennonites reinterpreted two-kingdoms theology in a manner that added nuance to the Schleitheim Confession's strict separationism. Perhaps, they reasoned, Christians could support state activities (like desegregation or antipoverty initiatives) that seemed to embody the social values of the kingdom of God if they were careful to eschew other state activities (like the observance of civil religion) that seemed to blur the two kingdoms.

Anabaptists also objected to civil religion on the grounds that it undermined the universality of the gospel. In *A Dream for America* (1976), John A. Lapp contrasted the civil religionist's love of country to God's love of all creation. The proper religious framing of history, including American history, is one of love and redemption, he wrote, but the redemption of which the Bible speaks reconciles creation to Creator—it is a much bigger story than the fate of the United States. "The global nature of Christ's lordship will provide a universal basis for evaluating events," Lapp continued. "The Christian will be as concerned about Peking as about Washington; Mao will be as much an object of his prayers as is Gerald Ford."[32]

Two-kingdom theology thus inclined Anabaptists to hear pronouncements about a "Christian nation" as Caesarian attempts to claim commitment that ought to be directed to God, and two-covenant theology led them to resist claims that the United States embodied divine purposes. No nation was sanctified where it stood—even ancient Israel sinned grievously. As Longacre noted, the war in Vietnam, sufferings of the poor, and public corruption epitomized by Watergate only underlined the fact that Americans would do well to feel less good about themselves.[33]

Some Anabaptists took a more moderate stance. They agreed that civil religion was not the faith of the Bible, but refused to condemn its symbols and assumptions wholesale. Not all civil religion was created equal, this line of thought suggested. Much was harmless and some could even be useful to the church. When the Rev. Peter B. Wiebe spoke at a flag dedication ceremony in Hesston, Kansas, on February 23, 1970, he declared that religious minorities have a particular reason to admire what the flag stands for: "I became a citizen of the country eight years ago, and I did not have to swear the oath (I could affirm), and I did not have to promise to take up arms," he noted with approval.[34] But Wiebe also did not believe that adoration of the flag precluded one's obligation to speak critically of the nation or its actions. In the first part of his speech, he associated the flag with "the best for which the American people stand," but in the second part, he invoked familiar Anabaptist criticisms of U.S. policy.[35]

Wiebe's assertion that American civil religion need not contradict the church's witness was developed at greater length by James C. Juhnke, a Mennonite who ran for Congress on the Democratic ticket in 1970. In a subsequent essay, Juhnke developed a three-pronged defense of the selected use of civil religion during his campaign. First, he wrote, it was so ubiquitous as to constitute the lingua franca of a diverse American nation. Even American Anabaptists internalized it. As a youth, he wrote, he "learned the 'Star-Spangled Banner' at about the same age as I learned 'Gott ist die Liebe.'"[36] Second, he noted that American civil religion had a prophetic strain that could be used to oppose military adventurism, racism, economic exploitation, and other social maladies as powerfully as its other strains could promote them. In the speech with which he began his campaign on June 10, 1970, Juhnke appealed to America's religious sense of identity to oppose the Vietnam War. "Our national covenant contained no clause obligating us to spend billions of dollars piling overkill upon overkill," he said. We must "find the fulfillment of America's promise in those humane, Judeo-Christian, democratic ideals which are the heart of our common creed."[37] And finally, Juhnke challenged his fellow Mennonites to reflect on the relationship of two time-honored Anabaptist values—separatism and discipleship. Might the former be carried so far as to thwart the latter by disengaging from a culture sorely in need of the Anabaptist witness?

Juhnke's campaign was emblematic of a shift in Anabaptist political thinking that ran deeper than attitudes about civil religion. An earlier generation of American Mennonites embraced "nonresistance," or the total refusal of political coercion, including nonviolent coercion. The position was famously articulated in Guy F. Hershberger's *War, Peace, and Nonresistance*, wherein the author found even Mohandas Gandhi's nonviolent campaign against British imperialism unacceptable, since it sought to "bring about the submission of the opposition through compulsion."[38] When Hershberger's book was published in 1944, American Mennonites still smarted from their experiences during World War I and, like other immigrant groups, worried about losing their cultural distinctiveness. They found nonresistance compatible with both their reading of the Bible and their desire for cultural separation. After World War II, however, a younger generation wondered if such separatism did not constitute hiding one's lamp under a bushel. A group of church leaders who convened at Winona Lake, Indiana, in 1950 explored what came to be known as the "Lordship of Christ" position, which held that society "must be constantly brought under the judgement [*sic*] of Christ."[39] During the 1960s, an emphasis on the Lordship of Christ informed Anabaptist political activism in the civil rights and antiwar movements and was given theological justification by John Howard Yoder, among others.[40]

Juhnke drew particular attention to the old formulation's inadequacy in addressing U.S. foreign policy. He suggested that after World War I, when Mennonites realized that some of their fellow Americans considered them unwelcome or disloyal, a "great compromise" was reached in which the government allowed them nonmilitary service alternatives and they concentrated on being useful and politically quiescent citizens. Of course, even apoliticism constituted a political choice, and "the tragedy was that the trade-off came at the price of Mennonite silence in the face of American militarism and imperialism at midcentury and beyond."[41] If separatism made Mennonites politically irrelevant, Juhnke reasoned, the judicious use of civil religion could actually enhance their prophetic witness. "We need to be more self conscious about finding symbols which speak powerfully to powerful men with stopped ears," he wrote. "In accepting this challenge we should not eschew the rhetoric of civil religion at its prophetic best."[42]

TESTING THE LIMITS OF AMERICAN CIVIL RELIGION

Goshen College's national anthem controversy provoked a response from critics who decried conscientious objections to public expressions of national loyalty, as if religious conscience and civil religion were always compatible. Either unaware of or unsympathetic to the Anabaptist critique of civil religion, blogger Paul Ibbetson criticized Goshen's position by asserting that "Americanism, patriotism and Christianity are not negative forces opposing one another in this country; they are the intermingled essence of what has made, and continues to make us unique." He also suggested that those who chose not to play the anthem were "ideological foes that wish to destroy all we hold dear."[43]

For their part, those Anabaptists who feared that civil religion had begun to corrode a venerable Mennonite institution were uncomfortable with Goshen's short-lived choice to play an instrumental version of the anthem. Some of the comments on the Young Anabaptist Radicals website suggested that institutional preservation had trumped the school's religious mission. One reader suggested that Goshen sought to "attract more students whose parents are conservative" on the theory that political conservatives tended to be wealthier; another surmised that the college feared for its federal funding.[44] At the same time, division among Anabaptists over civil religion's potential prophetic value continued. In a chapel sermon delivered a day before the college's decision to play the anthem was announced, Goshen College president Jim Brenneman echoed Juhnke's argument that opposition to civil religion was counterproductive if it simply marginalized the Christian voice. "We need to create a culture of assent alongside our historic culture of dissent," he explained.[45] But another Internet commenter thought not playing the anthem was a superior witness. He argued that the "media attention from Fox News and others over the school's refusal to play the national anthem was a golden invitation for Goshen to teach students and community members about peaceful alternatives to military and economic domination."[46]

If the Goshen controversy reopened long-standing disagreements between Anabaptists and others about public expressions of national feeling, and among Anabaptists about the degree to which civil religion could be of value to the church, the controversy also shed light on that part of American society that lies beyond its civil religion. Taken as a whole, the American Anabaptist experience suggests that while civil religion is an important instrument through which diverse Americans negotiate their national identity, not all Americans accept it. It can unify *and* divide; yet it is certainly less coercive than the conventional alternatives. In a recent comparative study, historian Emilio Gentile distinguished between civil religion and political religion. The former, he argued, complements democracy and religious pluralism because it allows the final arbiter of each individual's faith to be the individual. Instead of demanding its citizens' highest loyalties, it simply tries to convince them that their existing religious commitments are compatible with loyalty to the nation, if not with every national policy. Political religion (a "sacralization of politics" that Gentile associates with the European dictatorships of the 1930s), by contrast, is undemocratic and intolerant because it demands to be exalted above other faiths.[47]

Throughout much of modern American history, Anabaptism has tested civil religion's capacity to accommodate peaceful dissent. In particular, it has forced Americans to confront the question: Can civil religion serve as a cultural and political adhesive while simultaneously allowing some Americans to eschew its familiar manifestations and even launch penetrating theological criticisms of it? The answer seems to be "potentially." During World War I, civil religion stood at the center of sharp conflicts between Anabaptists and the wider culture, sometimes resulting in imprisonment and violence. But for the most part, Anabaptists have flourished in the United States, and they have enjoyed a level of legal protection in their faith that never existed in Europe. One historian has written that the story of American Mennonites in the twentieth century was "one of moving from the margins of society to more participation in society's institution, its culture, and its values" while simultaneously retaining "their own discernible community."[48] Though often loath to admit it, Anabaptists may stand in relation to the civil religion in much the same way as nonbelieving Americans. Both remain on the margins, and both are grudgingly tolerated.

The central tension lies between American civil religion's commitment to pluralism and religious freedom, on the one hand, and its role as a national unifier and marker of loyalty, on the other. It is a tension that demands constant refinement and attention. A skeptic might say that America's tolerance of civil religion's dissenters simply reflects their small numbers. If outsider groups such as the Mennonites constituted a substantial minority, the logic goes, they would be harder to tolerate. However, American civil religion has shown that it is flexible enough to complement religious pluralism and constitutional guarantees of religious freedom even to the point of tolerating those who step beyond it. Were the United States to develop a more overbearing national political faith, it might force Goshen College to make its basketball games more conventional, but in doing so, it would make American religious life much less vibrant.

NOTES

1. Mike Gallagher interview with Bill Born, Townhall.com, 10 November 2008, accessed 26 January 2012, http://townhall.com/talkradio/mikegallagher/311604; "Timeline for National Anthem Discussion/Decision at Goshen College," Goshen College, updated 21 August 2011, accessed 26 January 2012, http://www.goshen.edu/news/pressarchive/01-22-10-national-anthem395/timeline.html; quotes in Jesse Davis, "Conservative Radio Host Upset with No-Anthem Policy at GC," *Goshen News*, 12 November 2008, accessed 19 January 2012, http://goshennews.com/local/x395823263/Conservative-radio-host-upset-with-no-anthem-policy-at-GC.

2. "Timeline," Goshen College; Joseph Liechty, "The National Anthem Debate at Goshen College," *Journal of Religion, Conflict, and Peace* 3 (Fall 2009), accessed 26 January 2012, http://www.religionconflictpeace.org/node/38; "Goshen College Announces Plans for National Anthem's Implementation," Goshen College press release, 10 March 2010, accessed 31 March 2012, http://www.goshen.edu/news/pressarchive/03-10-10-anthem-protocol430.html; "National Anthem Dialogue and Implementation to Continue at Goshen College," Goshen College press release, 17 February 2010, accessed 31 March 2012, http://www.goshen.edu/news/pressarchive/02-17-10-national-anthem2-419.html.

3. Liechty, "The National Anthem Debate at Goshen College."

4. "Resistance to the National Anthem at Goshen College," Jesus Radicals, accessed 26 January 2012, http://www.jesusradicals.com/theology/resistance-to-the-national-anthem-at-goshen-college-2/.

5. Comment by "victor" at 10:18 p.m., 7 February 2010, in Timn, "James Brenneman, J. Lawrence Burkholder and a New Mennonite Theology of 'Loyal Opposition' for Goshen College," Young Anabaptist Radicals, 25 January 2010, accessed 31 January 2012, http://young.anabaptistradicals.org/2010/01/25/james-brenneman-j-lawrence-burkholder-and-a-new-mennonite-theology-of-loyal-opposition-for-goshen-colleg/.

6. James E. Brenneman, "Decision Regarding an Alternative to Playing the National Anthem at Goshen College," Goshen College press release, 19 August 2011, accessed 27 January 2012, http://www.goshen.edu/anthem/docs/anthem-alternative.pdf.

7. Sociologist Robert N. Bellah famously described it as existing "alongside of and rather clearly differentiated from the churches," though in the same paragraph he alternatively called it a "religion" and a "religious dimension." Robert N. Bellah, "Civil Religion in America," *Daedalus* 96 (Winter 1967): 1.

8. Richard V. Pierard and Robert D. Linder, "President and Civil Religion," in *Encyclopedia of the American Presidency*, ed. Leonard W. Levy and Louis Fisher, vol. 1 (New York: Simon & Schuster, 1994), 203–6.

9. Menno Simons, "The True Christian Faith," in *The Complete Writings of Menno Simons, c. 1496–1561*, ed. John Christian Wenger, trans. Leonard Verduin (Scottsdale, PA: Herald Press, 1956), 333–34, quote on 333.

10. The fullest overview of sixteenth-century Anabaptism remains George H. Williams, *The Radical Reformation*, 3rd ed. (Kirksville, MO: Truman State University Press, 2000). For a briefer treatment, see C. Arnold Snyder, *Anabaptist History and Theology: An Introduction* (Kitchener, ON: Pandora Press, 1995).

11. Michael Sattler, "The Schleitheim Articles," in *The Radical Reformation*, ed. Michael G. Baylor (Cambridge: Cambridge University Press, 1991), 175.

12. Sattler, "The Schleitheim Articles," 175. Snyder has argued that Schleitheim should not be regarded as speaking for all Anabaptists, for many did not share Sattler's biblical literalism or fiery tone. Nevertheless, two-kingdom theology did become a hallmark of the movement. See Snyder, *Anabaptist History and Theology*, 185–91.

13. Guy F. Hershberger, *War, Peace, and Nonresistance* (Scottsdale, PA: Herald Press, 1944), 14–22.

14. Quoted in John Oliver Mason, "Meet Evangelist Tony Campolo," *The Progressive*, August 2005, accessed 1 February 2012, http://www.progressive.org/?q=mag_camp0805.

15. Samuel Langdon, "The Republic of the Israelites an Example to the United States," in *God's New Israel: Religious Interpretations of American Destiny*, ed. Conrad Cherry, rev. ed. (Chapel Hill: University of North Carolina Press, 1998), 98.

16. On the historical development of American civil religion, see Robert N. Bellah, *The Broken Covenant: American Civil Religion in Time of Trial* (New York: Seabury Press, 1975), chaps. 1–2, and Robert T. Handy, *A Christian America: Protestant Hopes and Historical Realities* (New York: Oxford University Press, 1971).

17. Quoted in Ray H. Abrams, *Preachers Present Arms: The Role of the American Churches and Clergy in World Wars I and II, with Some Observations on the War in Vietnam* (Scottsdale, PA: Herald Press, 1969), 58, 131.

18. Ibid., 194.

19. Grant M. Stoltzfus, *Mennonites of the Ohio and Eastern Conference from the Colonial Period in Pennsylvania to 1968* (Scottsdale, PA: Herald Press, 1969), 182.

20. On World War I, see James C. Juhnke, "Mennonites and Ambivalent Civil Religion," *Mennonite Quarterly Review* 65 (April 1991): 162; Juhnke, "Mob Violence and Kansas Mennonites in 1918," *Kansas Historical Quarterly* 43 (Autumn 1977), 344–50; and Juhnke, *Vision, Doctrine, War: Mennonite Identity and Organization in America, 1890–1930* (Scottsdale, PA: Herald Press, 1989), 212–15, 224–25.

21. Allan Teichroew, "Mennonites and the Conscription Trap," *Mennonite Life*, September 1975, 11–12.

22. James C. Juhnke, "Mennonite Benevolence and Revitalization in the Wake of World War I," *Mennonite Quarterly Review* 60 (January 1986): 20–21, 23.

23. David A. Zercher, "Between Two Kingdoms: Virginia Mennonites and the American Flag," *Mennonite Quarterly Review* 70 (April 1996): 168–77.

24. Ibid., 179–80.

25. Ibid., 189–90.

26. Perry Bush, *Two Kingdoms, Two Loyalties: Mennonite Pacifism in Modern America* (Baltimore: Johns Hopkins University Press, 1998), 72–73, 96–97; Nicholas A. Krehbiel, *General Lewis B. Hershey and Conscientious Objection during World War II* (Columbia: University of Missouri Press, 2012), 17–19.

27. Robert N. Bellah, "Civil Religion in America."

28. "Civil Religion Packet," MCC Vertical File, VII, box 1 a6061, Mennonite Library and Archives, Bethel College, North Newton, KS (hereafter MLA).

29. Donald B. Kraybill, *Our Star-Spangled Faith* (Scottsdale, PA: Herald Press, 1976), 174–77, quote on 177.

30. David Augsburger, "In 'Civil Religion' We Trust?" in "Civil Religion Packet," MLA, 2.

31. James C. Longacre, "Religion and the State: The Contemporary American Scene," in *Citizens and Disciples: Christian Essays on Nationalism*, ed. David Schroeder (Akron, PA: MCC Peace Section, [1974?]), 14, MLA.

32. John A. Lapp, *A Dream for America* (Scottsdale, PA: Herald Press, 1976), 105.

33. Longacre, "Religion and the State," 14.

34. Peter B. Wiebe, *The Symbol of Our Country* (Hesston, KS: Hesston College Office of Public Relations, 1970), 3, MLA. Wiebe was pastor of Hesston Mennonite Church.

35. Ibid.

36. James C. Juhnke, "Mennonites and a Christian America," in *Citizens and Disciples*, 18.

37. Quoted in ibid., 18.

38. Hershberger, *War, Peace, and Nonresistance*, 1, 202–3, 295–96, quote on 1.

39. Bush, *Two Kingdoms, Two Loyalties* 178–85, quote on 181.

40. John Howard Yoder, *The Politics of Jesus*, 2nd. ed. (Grand Rapids, MI: Eerdmans, 1994). See also Leo Driedger and Donald B. Kraybill, *Mennonite Peacemaking: From Quietism to Activism* (Scottdale, PA: Herald Press, 1994), and Ervin R. Stutzman, *From Nonresis-*

tance to Justice: The Transformation of Mennonite Church Peace Rhetoric, 1908–2008 (Scottsdale, PA: Herald Press, 2011).

41. Juhnke, "Mennonites and a Christian America," 20.

42. Ibid.

43. Paul A. Ibbetson, "Goshen College Declares War on National Anthem," RenewAmerica, 16 June 2011, accessed 28 March 2012, http://www.renewamerica.com/columns/ibbetson/ 110616.

44. Comment by "ST" at 6:26 p.m., 26 January 2010, and comment by "victor" at 10:18 p.m., 7 February 2010, in Timn.

45. James E. Brenneman, "Getting to Yes and Amen! The New GC 'School of Thought,'" chapel sermon, 15 January 2010, Goshen College, accessed 31 January 2012, http://www. goshen.edu/news/ pressarchive/01-20-10-brenneman-chapel394/sermon.html.

46. Comment by "Ted Houser" at 11:57 a.m., 26 January 2010, in Timn.

47. Emilio Gentile, *Politics as Religion*, trans. George Staunton (Princeton, NJ: Princeton University Press, 2001), xiv–xv, quote on xiv.

48. Paul Toews, *Mennonites in American Society, 1930–1970* (Scottsdale, PA: Herald Press, 1996), 342.

Index

Abbott, Lyman, 197, 203
ACLU. *See* American Civil Liberties Union
Act of Toleration (1689), 61n8; acceptance of, 59; backlash after, 57–59; Catholics and, 59–60, 63n29; confusion about, 55; dissent over, 57–58; lapse of, 60; limits of, 54–55; Methodist missionaries and, 112; passage of, 56–57; purpose of, 57; riots against, 58, 62n22; Test Act and, 58–59; Whigs and, 55–56, 57, 58
Act of Uniformity (1662), 23, 27
Adams, John, 166
administrative state, 280n3
Affordable Care Act, xii–xiii
AFL-CIO, 273, 274
Africans, 7–8, 107–109. *See also* slaves
Alden, Mrs. G. K. *See* Pansy
Allred, Rulon C., 265n26
alternative religious communities, 292–293, 301
America: for Anabaptists, 309; Protestantism of, 142
American Civil Liberties Union (ACLU), 245, 247
"The American Civil Religion" (Bellah), 311
American Council of Christian Churches, 270
American Daily Advertiser, 137

Americanists, 199, 200
American Jewish Congress, 293–294
American Magazine, 118–119
American Magazine and Historical Chronicle, 119–120
American Party (Know-Nothing Party), 166–167
American Protective Association, 196
American Psychological Association, 292
American Relief Association, 310
American Revolution, 158n7, 309; Catholics and, 126; Catholics' religious freedom and, 135–136, 138; eighteenth-century American periodicals and, 126, 127; religion in, 127
"America the Beautiful," 306
Amish, 311
Anabaptists, 309; Goshen College for, 14–15, 305–307, 315; origins of, 307; *sola fide* for, 307. *See also* civil religion and American Anabaptists; Mennonites
Anabaptist theology: civil religion and, 307–309, 311; concession to sin in, 308–309; discipleship in, 307; kingdom of God in, 308–309; Schleitheim Confession of Faith in, 307–308, 310, 317n12; separatism of, 307–309
Anderson, Isaac, 108
Anglicans: missionaries to slaves by, 103; in Pennsylvania, 44; Quakers and, 60; sacraments for, 58–59; for South

321

About the Contributors

Chris Beneke is associate professor of history at Bentley University. He is the author of *Beyond Toleration: The Religious Origins of American Pluralism* (2006) and coeditor (with Christopher S. Grenda) of *The First Prejudice: Religious Tolerance and Intolerance in Early America* (2011) and (with Christopher S. Grenda and David Nash) of *Profane: Sacrilegious Expression in a Multicultural Age* (2014).

James B. Bennett is associate professor of religious studies at Santa Clara University. He earned his PhD in American religious history at Yale University. He is the author of *Religion and the Rise of Jim Crow in New Orleans* (2005) as well as articles on American Christianity and the intersection of religion and race in the United States.

Teresa M. Bejan is an assistant professor of political science at the University of Toronto. She received her PhD with distinction from Yale University and was a fellow in the Society of Fellows in the Humanities at Columbia University in 2013–2014. Bejan has published articles on toleration and civic education in *History of European Ideas*, the *Oxford Review of Education*, and several edited volumes. Her current book project is titled "Mere Civility: Tolerating Disagreement in Early Modern England and America." In it, she examines calls for civility today in light of seventeenth-century debates about religious toleration and so-called persecution of the tongue.

Jacob Betz is a PhD candidate in history at the University of Chicago. He's held a prize lectureship in the University of Chicago's Human Rights Program and has published on Native American religious freedom. Betz's dissertation is titled "Catholicism, Religious Liberty, and Group Identity in

America, 1870–1920." It explores the efforts of American Catholics to create institutional, political, legal, and religious pluralism at the turn of the twentieth century.

Jon Butler is adjunct research professor of history at the University of Minnesota, Twin Cities, and Howard R. Lamar Professor Emeritus of American Studies, History, and Religious Studies at Yale University. His books include *Power, Authority, and the Origins of American Denominational Order*; *The Huguenots in America: A Refugee People in New World Society*; *Awash in a Sea of Faith: Christianizing the American People*; *Becoming America: The Revolution Before 1776*; and (with Grant Wacker and Randall Balmer) *Religion in American Life: A Short History*. His articles and essays have appeared in publications such as the *Journal of American History*, *American Historical Review*, *William and Mary Quarterly*, and *Church History*. He is writing a book about religion in Manhattan from the Gilded Age to the 1960 Kennedy election titled *God in Gotham* and is president-elect of the Organization of American Historians.

Steven K. Green is the Fred H. Paulus Professor of Law and adjunct professor of history at Willamette University in Salem, Oregon. He also serves as the director of the interdisciplinary Willamette Center for Religion, Law, and Democracy. Before joining the Willamette faculty in 2001, Green served as legal director and special counsel for Americans United for Separation of Church and State in Washington, DC. Green has participated in many of the leading church-state cases before the U.S. Supreme Court, including as co-counsel in *Zelman v. Simmons-Harris* (the Cleveland voucher case). Green is the author of *Inventing a Christian America* (2015); *The Bible, the School, and the Constitution: The Clash that Shaped Modern Church-State Doctrine* (2012); and *The Second Disestablishment: Church and State in the Nineteenth Century* (2010), as well as more than thirty scholarly articles on religion, history, and the law. He is also the coauthor of *Religious Freedom and the Supreme Court* (2008), a casebook in church-state law.

Christopher S. Grenda is professor of history at Bronx Community College of the City University of New York. He is coeditor (with Chris Beneke and David Nash) of *Profane: Sacrilegious Expression in a Multicultural Age* (2014) and (with Chris Beneke) of *The First Prejudice: Religious Tolerance and Intolerance in Early America* (2011). His work has also appeared in the *Journal of Church and State*, *Journal of Law and Religion*, and *Politics and Religion*.

Evan Haefeli is an associate professor of Atlantic history at Texas A&M University, having previously taught at Columbia, Tufts, and Princeton Universities. His most recent book is *New Netherland and the Dutch Origins of American Religious Liberty*. Haefeli has also written about captivity narratives, the New England frontier, witchcraft, colonial revolts, and book publishing in New England. Recently a fellow at the Cullman Center for Scholars and Writers, New York Public Library, his next book (under contract) is a study of religious toleration and English overseas expansion from 1497 to 1707.

Cristine Hutchison-Jones earned her BA in American studies and religion from Florida State University, and her PhD in religious and theological studies from Boston University. Her dissertation, "Reviling and Revering the Mormons: Defining American Values, 1890–2008," explores images of the Mormons in American news, fiction and nonfiction writing, and television and film. She is the author of "Center and Periphery: Mormons and American Culture in Tony Kushner's 'Angels in America'" (in *Peculiar Portrayals: Mormons on the Page, Stage, and Screen*, 2010). Dr. Hutchison-Jones currently works in administration at Harvard Law School.

Christopher C. Jones is a PhD candidate in history at the College of William and Mary. His dissertation, "Religion and Revolution in the Atlantic World: Methodism in North America and the Caribbean, 1760–1815," examines the expansion of Methodism amid ongoing political revolution, mass migration, and emergent antislavery activism throughout the Atlantic World. Jones has published articles in the *Journal of Mormon History* and *BYU Studies Quarterly* (2012), as well as (with Stephen J. Fleming) a chapter in Miranda Wilcox and John Young's edited collection *Standing Apart: Mormon Historical Consciousness and the Concept of Apostasy* (2014).

Susanna Linsley completed her graduate work in early American history at the University of Michigan. Her dissertation, "The American Reformation: The Politics of Religious Liberty, Charleston and New York, 1770–1830," argues that churches were sites where early Americans invented and participated in politics. Dr. Linsley has held postdoctoral positions at the University of Michigan and Texas A&M University and taught at both the college and high school level. She currently teaches history and literature at the Webb Schools in Claremont, California.

Paul Matzko is a Milton B. Dolinger Graduate Fellow in the Department of History at Pennsylvania State University. His chapter draws from his dissertation, "The Rise of the New Christian Right: Religious Broadcasting, the State, and the Origins of a Conservative Christian Grassroots, 1941–1976," which explores the role of religious broadcasting as both a tool for social movement organization and as a site of political contention for conservative

Catholics and evangelicals. Matzko has also worked on an interactive time-line of American religious history for the Association of Religion Data Archives in partnership with the Lilly Endowment.

David Mislin is assistant professor in the intellectual heritage program at Temple University. He received his PhD from Boston University. His first book, soon to be published by Cornell University Press, explores the liberal Protestant embrace of American religious pluralism during the late nineteenth and early twentieth centuries. His essays have appeared in the *Journal of the Historical Society* and *Religion and American Culture*.

Andrew R. Murphy is associate professor of political science at Rutgers University, New Brunswick. He is the author of *Conscience and Community: Revisiting Toleration and Religious Dissent in Early Modern England and America* (2001) and *Prodigal Nation: Moral Decline and Divine Punishment from New England to 9/11* (2009) and the editor of *The Political Writings of William Penn* (2002) and *The Blackwell Companion to Religion and Violence* (2011). He has coauthored (with David Gutterman of Willamette University) a forthcoming study of religious and political identities in the contemporary United States (2015) and is currently working on a biography of William Penn (1644–1718).

Keith Pacholl is associate professor of history at the University of West Georgia. His research examines the interaction of religion, education, and periodical literature in eighteenth-century America, and he has published several articles and book chapters on the subject, including "Education, Religion, and the State in Postrevolutionary America" (*Religion and the State*, 2012); "American Access to Periodical Literature in the Eighteenth Century" (*The International Journal of the Book*, 2007); and "'Let Both Sexes Be Carefully Instructed': Educating Youth in Colonial Philadelphia" (*Children in Colonial America*, 2006).

Nicholas Pellegrino is a PhD candidate in the history department at the University of Nevada, Las Vegas. His dissertation examines Catholic experiences with religious freedom in early America. He has published articles in the *Journal of History and Cultures* and the *Journal of Military Experience*. He has also written review essays for a number of publications, including *American Catholic Studies, Nova Religio, Pacific Northwest Quarterly*, and *New England Quarterly*.

Shawn Francis Peters is an internationally recognized expert on religious liberty issues. He has been featured by CNN, PBS, Court TV, *Time* magazine, and the *New York Times*, and he is the author of four books, including

The Catonsville Nine: An American Story. Peters holds an undergraduate degree from Rutgers University and graduate degrees from the University of New Hampshire, the University of Iowa, and UW-Madison, where he now teaches in the Integrated Liberal Studies Program.

Scott Sowerby is associate professor in history at Northwestern University. He is the author of *Making Toleration: The Repealers and the Glorious Revolution* (2013), which was awarded the Royal Historical Society's Whitfield Prize for the best first book on British history. His other publications include articles in *Past & Present, Journal of British Studies, English Historical Review*, and *Parliamentary History*.

Denise Spellberg is professor of history and Middle Eastern studies at the University of Texas at Austin. She is author of *Thomas Jefferson's Qur'an: Islam and the Founders* (2013) and *Politics, Gender, and the Islamic Past: The Legacy of 'A'isha Bint Abi Bakr* (1994). An alumna of the International Seminar on the History of the Atlantic World, her research on Islam in early modern Europe and the United States won the Carnegie Corporation of New York's Carnegie Scholars Award (2009–2011).

Ronit Y. Stahl is a postdoctoral fellow at the John C. Danforth Center on Religion and Politics at Washington University in St. Louis. She completed her PhD in history at the University of Michigan in 2014 and is a recipient of a Charlotte W. Newcombe Dissertation Fellowship, as well as the Arthur Fondiler Award for the best dissertation in the Michigan University history department. Stahl is working on a book titled *God, War, and Politics: How the American Military Chaplaincy Built a Multi-Religious Nation*.

Evelyn Savidge Sterne is associate professor and director of graduate studies in history at the University of Rhode Island. She is the author of *Ballots and Bibles: Ethnic Politics and the Catholic Church in Providence* (2004). Sterne has written articles on machine politics and working-class religion. Her current research focuses on evangelical Protestants in twentieth-century New England. A former Young Scholar in American Religion at the Institute for the Study of Religion and American Culture, she has received support for her work from foundations that include the Pew Program in Religion and American History, the Institute for the Advanced Study of Religion at Yale, and the American Philosophical Society.

Kip A. Wedel is assistant professor of history at Bethel College in North Newton, Kansas. His work focuses on American civil religion in popular culture, the history of radio, and Anabaptist history. Wedel's recent publications include "Permission to Dissent: Civil Religion and the Radio Western,

1933–1960," in *Religion and American Culture*, and *The Obligation: A History of the Order of the Engineer*. Prior to teaching, he owned and published a weekly newspaper in Iowa. He holds a PhD in American history from Kansas State University.